D1474895

The publisher gratefully acknowledges the generous contribution to this book provided by the Ahmanson Foundation Humanities Endowment Fund of the University of California Press Foundation.

Brecht at the Opera

CALIFORNIA STUDIES IN 20TH-CENTURY MUSIC

Richard Taruskin, General Editor

Brecht at the Opera

JOY H. CALICO

University of California Press

BERKELEY   LOS ANGELES   LONDON

University of California Press, one of the most distinguished university presses in the United States, enriches lives around the world by advancing scholarship in the humanities, social sciences, and natural sciences. Its activities are supported by the UC Press Foundation and by philanthropic contributions from individuals and institutions. For more information, visit www.ucpress.edu.

University of California Press
Berkeley and Los Angeles, California

University of California Press, Ltd.
London, England

© 2008 by The Regents of the University of California

Library of Congress Cataloging-in-Publication Data

Calico, Joy Haslam, 1965–
  Brecht at the opera / Joy H. Calico.
      p.   cm. — (California studies in 20th-century music ; 9)
  "An Ahmanson Foundation book in the humanities"
  Includes bibliographical references (p.   ) and index.
  ISBN 978-0-520-25482-4 (cloth : alk. paper)
    1. Brecht, Bertolt, 1898–1956—Criticism and interpretation.
  2. Brecht, Bertolt, 1898–1956—Knowledge—Music.   3. Opera.
  I. Title.
    ML423.B7C35   2008
    782.1092—dc22   2007044714

Manufactured in the United States of America

17   16   15   14   13   12   11   10   09   08
10. 9   8   7   6   5   4   3   2   1

This book is printed on Cascades Enviro 100, a 100% post consumer waste, recycled, de-inked fiber. FSC recycled certified and processed chlorine free. It is acid free, Ecologo certified, and manufactured by BioGas energy.

For Chris

Contents

Illustrations

TABLES

Acknowledgments

No author writes alone. Many institutions and people made it possible for me to research and write this book, and it is a great pleasure for me to acknowledge their contributions to my work. My first debt of gratitude is to Howard Pollack, who invited me to teach a graduate seminar on Brecht and his musical collaborators at the University of Houston in 1999. The seeds for this project took root in that course, as the students and I detected an operatic undercurrent running throughout Brecht's oeuvre. I am very grateful to Illinois Wesleyan University for Artistic and Scholarly Development Grants that funded archive research in New York, Washington, D.C., and Berlin in the summers of 2000 and 2001, and for a leave in the fall semester of 2002. IWU also provided funding to hire excellent student assistants Sara Hoffee and Sarah Nicholas Price. I must thank Carolyn Abbate for accepting me as a participant in her National Endowment for the Humanities summer seminar on opera stagings at Princeton University in 2002. I was fortunate to be there with an extraordinary group of colleagues who also became friends, particularly Kevin Amidon, Nancy Goldsmith, Derek Katz, and Hilary Poriss, from whose expertise this book benefited considerably. That experience led me to reconfigure my project in its current form.

Vanderbilt University covered the cost of indexing with a Research Scholars Grant book subvention in 2005. Mark Wait, dean of the Vanderbilt University Blair School of Music, has been extraordinarily supportive. His office defrayed costs associated with using Konrad Ressler's photographs of Brecht, typesetting musical examples, and German-language copyediting and translation consultation; many thanks to Gary Shields and Claudia Schlee, respectively, for their excellent work in those areas. Dean Wait also granted me a leave in fall 2005, during which I had the good fortune to be the Anna-Maria Kellen fellow in residence at the American Academy in

Berlin. I can hardly thank Gary Smith and the staff of the academy enough for that opportunity. They provided me with an idyllic environment in which to think and write and a cohort of brilliant fellows who gave generously of their time and knowledge. Lydia Moland, Anson Rabinbach, Fred and Lea Wakeman, Steffi Kandzia, Ralf Michaels, Norman and Cella Manea, Avis Bohlen, David Calleo, Jim Mann, and Caroline Dexter will find their voices scattered throughout these pages. I would also be remiss if I neglected to thank Yolande Korb for her superhuman efforts as the academy's library runner. I am grateful to the Vanderbilt committee that selected my proposal for an NEH summer stipend for suggesting I consult Carolyn Dever, professor of English. Carolyn offered valuable advice on numerous drafts, and the fact that I received an NEH summer stipend to complete the archive work for this project in 2005 is due in no small part to her counsel. Fortunately for me she also became a dear friend in the process. I thank the National Endowment for the Humanities for that award, because it allowed me to complete the archival research for chapter 3. Any views, findings, conclusions, or recommendations expressed therein do not necessarily represent those of the National Endowment for the Humanities.

Werner Grünzweig, director of the Music Division of the archives of the Akademie der Künste in Berlin, has facilitated my research with generosity, good humor, and great efficiency for a decade. Daniela Reinhold, archivist of the Paul-Dessau-Archiv of the Akademie, has responded quickly to many queries and requests, sharing her vast knowledge of Dessau's music and of that collection to expedite this work. I am grateful to Maxim Dessau, Paul Dessau's son, for granting access to his father's papers. Thanks are also due to Helgard Rienäcker and Anouk Jeschke, former and current archivists of the Hanns-Eisler-Archiv of the Akademie, for their help when I used that collection. Rolf Harder and Dorothee Aders of the Bertolt-Brecht-Archiv of the Akademie der Künste provided gracious assistance and guidance on the numerous occasions I worked there or wrote with questions. I am very grateful to Dave Stein, archivist of the Weill-Lenya Research Center in New York, whose intimate knowledge of Weill's papers proved to be an invaluable resource. He has answered countless questions with enthusiasm and patience. Several other archivists and librarians also provided assistance: Harry Miller, reference archivist at the Wisconsin Historical Society; Michael Schwarz of the Walter-Benjamin-Archiv of the Akademie; Therese Hörnigk, director of the Literaturforum im Brecht-Haus; Suzanne Lovejoy and Jessica Lang of the Yale Music Library; Marty Jacobs, Theater Curator, Museum of the City of New York; Joellen ElBashir, curator of the Manuscript Division, Moorland-Spingarn Research Center at Howard

University; Marje Schuetze-Coburn, Feuchtwanger librarian, and Rachelle Balinas Smith, supervising library specialist, Specialized Libraries and Archival Collections, both of the University of Southern California; Richard Dickerson, university archivist, and Julie Grob, librarian, both of the University of Houston, M. D. Anderson Library Special Collections; Valerie Yaros, Screen Actors Guild historian; Avery Clayton of the Western States Black Research and Educational Center; Therese Muxeneder, archivist of the Arnold Schoenberg Center in Vienna; Lorenz Erren of the Deutsches Historisches Institut Moskau; and Pelle Leenards of IDC Publishers. Special thanks are due to the former and current library staff of the Anne Potter Wilson Music Library of the Blair School of Music at Vanderbilt University, who specialize in making the impossible look easy: Sara Beutter, Dennis Clark, Catherine Gick, Michael Jones, Steven Nordstrom, Robert Rich, and Holling Smith-Borne.

I thank Cambridge University Press for permission to publish material in chapter 4, which is a substantially revised and expanded version of my article "The Trial, the Condemnation, the Cover-up: Behind the Scenes of Brecht and Dessau's *Lucullus* Opera(s)," published in the *Cambridge Opera Journal* 14, no. 3 (2002): 313–342. © 2002 Cambridge University Press. Reprinted with permission.

I am grateful to Werner Grünzweig for permission to publish here those materials from the Paul-Dessau-Archiv of the Akademie der Künste that first appeared in that article, as well. Support for that research was provided by the Deutscher Akademischer Austausch Dienst and the Berlin Program for Advanced German and European Studies, and the opinions expressed therein are not necessarily those of the granting institutions.

I thank Suhrkamp Verlag for permission to publish an English translation of Brecht's text fragment from *The Voyages of the God of Happiness*; original German in Brecht, *Werke. Große kommentierte Berliner und Frankfurter Ausgabe,* ed. Werner Hecht, Jan Knopf, Werner Mittenzwei, and Klaus-Detlef Müller (Berlin and Weimar: Aufbau Verlag; Frankfurt am Main: Suhrkamp Verlag, 1988–2003), 10: 933–937. That translation, and some material from chapter 3, will appear in Joy H. Calico, "Brecht on Opera and/in the Americas," *Opera Quarterly* 22, no. 3 (forthcoming). Thanks also to the Fotomuseum Division of the Münchner Stadtmuseum for permission to use Konrad Ressler's classic photographs of Brecht for the cover art.

I am grateful to Beth Levy, Laurie Silverberg, Joel Haney, Kevin Bartig, Edgardo Salinas, Feng-Shu Lee, and Hannah Chan for their enthusiastic, meticulous research assistance in Los Angeles, Berlin, New Haven, Moscow, and New York, Chicago, and Urbana, respectively. Vanderbilt students

Catherine Nelson, Anna Viviano, and Daniel Jansen provided exceptional research assistance closer to home. I am most thankful to Beatrix Brockman for her German-language copyediting. I am humbled by the generosity of the many people who responded to my letters and emails as I tried to unearth information about various aspects of Brecht's work and their contexts. These kind souls did not know me but offered assistance nonetheless: Bernth Lindfors, Gertraud Steiner-Daviau, Anna Bean, Mona Z. Smith, Glenda Gill, Haun Saussy, Sister Francesca Thompson, Thomas Phleps, Paisley Livingston, Tom Kuhn, Jonathan Skolnik, G. D. Hamann, Kevin Hagopian, Christian Rogowski, Harry Elam, Daphne Muse, and Lorraine Brown.

The truly collaborative nature of research was revealed to me as my interdisciplinary work took me into various circles of scholars in North America and Europe, each of which welcomed and taught me. Musicologists Stephen Hinton, Kim Kowalke, Sally Bick, Albrecht Dümling, Jürgen Schebera, Johannes Gall, Peter Schweinhardt, and Maren Köster generously shared their research on Weill, Eisler, and Dessau and their collaborations with Brecht. James Grier patiently answered many questions about the principles of music editing, and Jennifer Shaw expounded upon her work about the nature of intertextuality and fragments. Leslie Sprout and Danielle Fosler-Lussier helped me make sense of various issues related to the Popular Front and socialist realism, respectively. Rose Subotnik and Jürgen Lodemann responded generously to my queries about Albert Lortzing, and Esbjörn Nyström was quick to answer the call when I needed help tracking a particular piece of Brecht correspondence. Richard Nangle of the International Hanns Eisler Gesellschaft is a veritable font of information, and David Steinau and James Parsons provided valuable insights into Eisler's *Hollywood Songbook*. I must also thank Steinau and David Imhoof for inviting me to participate in a symposium dedicated to that work at Susquehanna University in 2003, where I met the irrepressible Jim Miller of the North American Hanns Eisler Forum. Jonathan Neufeld kindly guided me through the thicket of philosophical literature on the musical work and its performance, and Paisley Livingston responded cheerfully to all queries about the nature of art and intention. Germanists Marc Silberman, Julia Hell, and Vera Stegmann engaged me in substantive debate on various topics concerning Brecht, theater, and politics; and Karl-Heinz Schoeps offered his illuminating analyses of Brecht's poems. James K. Lyon shared his correspondence with Clarence Muse and answered numerous questions about Brecht's life in the United States. Eric Bentley was a lively correspondent, quick to proffer expertise and access to his extensive network. Durk Talsma and Joe Lappin were remarkably patient guides in matters of psychology and cognition. Alexander Meier-Dörzenbach, dramaturge for Stefan Herheim's 2005 production of *La forza del destino* at the Berlin Staatsoper, proved to be an extraordinary resource, engaging in lengthy correspondence and facilitating contact with Jörn Weisbrodt, head of Artistic Production Special Projects at the Staatsoper. Correspondence about Bieito's productions with Maggie Bell proved enormously illuminating. Theater scholar Roger Bechtel was kind enough to direct me to Marvin Carlson, who knew precisely how to answer questions about the tradition of production books in German theater. The music theater working group of the International Federation for Theatre Research, under the guidance of Clemens Risi, was influential in shaping my ideas about gestus and estrangement. The chapter on estrangement in particular is indebted to the work of Risi and David Levin, two scholars whose intellectual acumen is surpassed only by their generosity. Stegmann provided feedback on most of the manuscript, as did two anonymous readers, and Risi and Levin read the manuscript in its entirety. It is immeasurably better for their input.

I can imagine no better editor than Mary Francis at the University of California Press, who has been a tireless supporter of the project for many years. She deftly guided this neophyte author and her manuscript through the labyrinth of revision and production and recommended its inclusion in this series California Studies in Twentieth-Century Music. I am very grateful to series editor Richard Taruskin for his attention to my prose and to my arguments. Many thanks are also due to the copyeditor, Jimmée A. Greco, production editor Jacqueline Volin, and assistant acquisitions editor Kalicia Pivirotto for their unflagging attention to detail, patience, and good humor. Given the extraordinary assistance acknowledged in these pages, any remaining errors in fact or judgment are clearly mine alone.

I must thank the members of my department, particularly Cynthia Cyrus, who was my vigilant chair while I finished this book. Thanks are due to colleagues Greg Barz, Dale Cockrell, Jen Gunderman, Michael Hime, Douglas Lee, Jim Lovensheimer, and Melanie Lowe for fostering an environment hospitable to creative intellectual activity.

The role of friends in such an undertaking can scarcely be overestimated. Since 1998 Britta Duvigneau has offered an oasis of hospitality in Berlin, and many ideas presented here first saw the light of day in her beautiful flat. Robin Murphy and Susan Boynton proved to be equally good hosts while I conducted research in New York, as did Frank and Leslie Holland in Washington, D.C. In addition to those already mentioned, I have been the beneficiary of a remarkable support system of good friends and mentors both within and without my home discipline of musicology: Kent Cook, Sheri Czapla, Anne Demo, Danielle Fosler-Lussier, Bryan Gilliam, Malachi Hacohen, Jeongwon Joe, Alyson Knop, Neil Lerner, Cary Nathenson, Valerie Orlando, Pamela Potter, Roger Roe, Michael Velting, Katrin Völkner, Paul D. Young, and Laurel Zeiss.

Finally, I owe an enormous debt of gratitude to my family. My parents, Larry and Malissa, are sources of great comfort and strength. My sister, Hope, has followed this process very closely, acting as sage and ally through the countless small victories and setbacks that inevitably shape a long-term project such as this. I thank them for their unconditional love and support. My greatest thanks are reserved for my husband, Chris. Archival research has frequently required us to spend periods of time apart, and he has borne this with resilience, grace, and good humor. My semester in residence at the American Academy in Berlin was extraordinary in no small part because it was also the first time Chris was able to accompany me on an extended research trip. As a young naval aviator he could not possibly have known that "for better or for worse" would include so many evenings spent at the Berliner Ensemble and at the opera, looking for connections between the two. I am eternally grateful for his enthusiasm, his insights, and his companionship in this enterprise. This book is dedicated to him.

Introduction

Bertolt Brecht was ambivalent about opera. He was not alone; the state and fate of opera dominated German theater discourse in the 1920s, and as a man of the theater Brecht would have had a keen interest in those debates. His oft-quoted vociferous criticisms of the genre's shortcomings have generally been taken at face value, and scholars have confined their study of opera in his oeuvre to the three pieces he designated as completed operas: *The Threepenny Opera, The Rise and Fall of the City of Mahagonny,* and *The Judgment of Lucullus.* Despite the substantial body of literature devoted to his collaborations with composers and the significance of music in his oeuvre,[1] no study systematically interrogates or theorizes about Brecht's lifelong engagement with opera as distinct from other musical genres. Even those studies that connect his music theater texts and theories to opera do not trace the significance of that genre in its various manifestations throughout his career,[2] yet, remarkably, its continual presence is one of the few constants in a life marked primarily by upheaval and flux. In the thirty years between 1926, when he began working with Kurt Weill, and his death, in 1956, Brecht undertook roughly two dozen opera projects.

"Opera projects" include both those that came to fruition and those that remained unfinished. The vast majority of Brecht's operas obviously fall into the second category, but the fact remains that he actively pursued plans for many different operas over the course of three decades, nursing projects and frequently returning to them over time even as he completed other pieces. This engagement took many forms: the completed texts Brecht identified as operas; the use of operatic models in his theoretical writings and plays; his preoccupation with Richard Wagner, which waxed and waned but never disappeared; an unacknowledged, perhaps inadvertent, debt to pre-Wagner opera and the theory of other opera reformers; and, most consistently, the incomplete fragments that formed the backdrop for his creative activity. Taken in the aggregate, this engagement suggests that Brecht retained an abiding, albeit equivocal, interest in the genre's potential, even as he made public statements to the contrary. His inflammatory rhetoric, the relatively few operas he completed, and his reputation as a pioneer of political avant-garde theater have diverted attention from the centrality of opera to his life's work. Opera, or what he understood opera to be as an artistic genre and as a social institution, informed his texts for the stage, the use of music in those pieces, and their modes of performance practice. Opera is perhaps the least likely and yet one of the most formative influences on Brecht's entire oeuvre.

The specter of Wagner looms large in any study of Brecht and opera. The trajectory of Brecht's Wagner reception began with youthful obsession, moved to a rejection of Wagner on aesthetic, social, and political grounds, and culminated in repudiation of the composer as a forerunner of fascism.[3] Flirtation with and ultimate rejection of Wagner was a hallmark of modernism, but it certainly had ample precedent. Since the 1870s, recovering Wagnerians have been almost as numerous as practicing disciples. Each new generation of disillusioned devotees reads Nietzsche's *The Case of Wagner* and *Nietzsche contra Wagner* as the first step in recovery, taking some cold comfort in the knowledge that even Nietzsche was bamboozled by endlessly unresolved chromatic harmony, perpetual melody, and the confluence of the arts into the mishmash of the *Gesamtkunstwerk*.[4] In the years surrounding World War I, artists chose sides, either consciously cleaving to the Wagnerian tradition or actively seeking alternatives.[5] Brecht undertook opera projects as a reaction against Wagner and his dominance of the European stage.[6]

Wagner and Brecht were frequently arranged as polar opposites in the debate on the fate of German opera in the 1920s, and that perception has become conventional wisdom.[7] Yet Brecht's mature relationship to Wagner is not just one of opposition; as in any polarity, the poles are also bound together by the current flowing between them.[8] Beginning with the superficial, one can compile an extraordinary list of biographical parallels between the two men: Each enjoyed enormous financial success with a theater piece at age thirty, was driven into exile, was a revolutionary, showed an interest in using as models *Measure for Measure* and Sophocles' *Antigone*, and persuaded the state to give him his own theater and to support it. Cicora sees in Wagner's self-styled reputation as a man of the theater, rather than an opera composer, a maneuver designed to validate and legitimize his music drama project.[9] Wagner was a composer who became a librettist; Brecht was a poet and playwright who became a librettist (although this was a title to which he objected strenuously, insisting on his full rights as an author).[10] Politics and aesthetics were closely linked for both men, who saw theater as a potential instrument of social revolution. Some scholars have interpreted aspects of the music drama as epic, such as the prevalence of narrative and monologue and even the work of the leitmotif (Nieder, Schumacher, Kesting, and Brown).[11] Adorno recognized this in his 1963 essay "Wagner's Relevance for Today," in which he wrote that "the fundamental conception of the *Ring* is not actually dramatic. . . . If one wanted to draw out the paradox, one might speak, in regard to the entire *Ring* and other works of the mature Wagner, of epic theater—although the rabid anti-Wagnerian Brecht would not have wanted to hear this and would be at my throat."[12] Others note the indebtedness of Brecht's anti–music drama innovations to pre-Wagnerian opera (Kowalke, Hinton, Nieder, Schneider, and Vieira de Carvalho), and Stegmann sees Ferruccio Busoni's 1916 proposals for operatic reform as a blueprint for epic theater in general.[13]

In fact, the magnetic field that binds the polarity of Wagner and Brecht to each other may contain far more than opera. Matthew W. Smith traces Brecht's attempts to develop a comprehensive theater experience to Wagner's Gesamtkunstwerk. By using "discontinuity and contradiction . . . as a means to the creation of the 'unified whole' rather than [as] a subversion of it," he created "a kind of unity through juxtaposition,"[14] thus perpetuating an aesthetic of totality. Martin Puchner argues that the entire modernist theater project was a reaction against the Wagnerian theatricality that had come to dominate the stage.[15] Evidently he does not consider it significant that Wagner was not just a man of the theater but an *opera composer*, and therefore does not pursue this argument to what I see as its tantalizing, fantastical conclusion: What he posits amounts to an assertion that modernist theater is directly descended from the modernist struggle with Wagner, and no one engaged more fully in that battle than Brecht. To put it bluntly, modernist theater, of which epic theater has long been the standard-bearer,[16] may be the illegitimate child of opera. It should come as no surprise, then, that Heiner Müller identified Robert Wilson, a theater director who has enjoyed extraordinary success with opera, as Brecht's legitimate heir.[17] If my extrapolation is viable, then there are broad ramifications for examining the force field that links Brecht to Wagner, the latter standing in for opera more generally as discussed below.

The aforementioned qualifier "opera, or what he understood opera to be," is deliberate. In this study, Brecht's use of the term "opera" is understood in three ways, two negative and one positive, or at least benign. First, when Brecht criticized opera in his theoretical writings, he argued against it on two fronts: as a genre and as a social institution. When disparaging opera as a genre, his language was characterized by the modernist tendency to take a rather simplistic interpretation of Richard Wagner's music drama as representative of all opera.[18] As Lawrence Kramer has written, "Wagner became both central and radically extrinsic to the institution of Opera, both its primary model and its primary antagonist, its authentic self, beyond emulation, and its monstrous Other."[19] Brecht's complaints about the narcotic effects of continuous music refer to Wagner and his followers, and not to Mozart, whose operas he admired. The rhetorical inversion whereby music drama is transformed from a subgenre of opera to its definitive, negative, generic essence is symptomatic of the anti-Wagnerism that underpins modernist theater. It is worth noting that Wagner criticized the operatic tradition against which he rebelled in much the same terms that Brecht would later excoriate Wagner. Where Wagner dismissed Rossini with talk of "the intoxication of an opera-night's narcotic fumes,"[20] Brecht subsequently railed against the intoxicating effects of the music drama.

Second, all species of opera traditionally shared the status associated with the opera house as venue, and Brecht opposed the ways in which that institution participated in the reproduction of social hierarchies. He used "music drama" as a stand-in for "opera" in his critique of that institution on sociopolitical grounds because it represented the most extreme example of everything he despised about the bourgeoisie. It is hyperbole for argument's sake. Third, Brecht applied the generic designation "opera" to many texts he wrote himself. Clearly, that term is not meant to connote music drama, as in the usage above. References to his own pieces as operas may constitute parody, self-conscious satire, critique of the associated social institution, or an effort to refunction the genre.[21] This was frequently bound up with theories of audience perception designed to combat the narcotic effect of Wagner's continuous music. Given that the refunctioning of the genre was part of his agenda, ascertaining genre by generally accepted characteristics is ineffectual. Therefore I define as operas those texts in Brecht's oeuvre that he designated as such.[22] Recent scholarship in aesthetics concedes a certain kind and degree of actual intentionalism or sanction when identifying genre, fragments, and features of a particular piece.[23] My decision to define as operas and, later, as fragments those texts that Brecht had designated as such follows from this: Quite simply, Brecht applied the generic title "opera" to particular music theater pieces in his oeuvre and not to others. Nomenclature represents an appropriation of the genre in an effort to refunction it as an alternative to the opera he criticized in his theoretical writings (music drama).

Opera is also relevant to those projects Brecht did not identify as such because he developed other genres as antidotes to opera in terms of artistic content and social function, so that they are essentially defined by what they are not. Broadly construed, these can be seen as comprising a category of "anti-opera," texts whose generic qualities were deliberately and aggressively calculated in opposition to it.[24] The negative model established the parameters for the anti-operas so that they in turn remain tied to those roots. The notion that Brecht used opera *only* as a negative example against which he could devise oppositional theories is too simplistic, however, and ignores a pattern of productivity. Opera projects, both completed and abandoned, gave rise to new or revised theories of performance and audience perception, facilitating the reconception of nonoperatic theater. His experiences with opera proved to be creative and formative, shaping the subsequent course of his entire oeuvre. And, despite public posturing to the contrary, he apparently did not consider opera beyond all hope as an art form or as a social institution, returning to it as he did again and again.

It is not merely a matter of considering opera as an influence on Brecht. The word "engagement" more accurately encompasses the multifarious ways in which he encountered, wrote, criticized, theorized, and attended opera. Eric Bentley cautions against three fallacies to which studies of influence are prone: The assumption that influence is inherently a good thing; the opaque meaning of the word, which in many applications does not allow for "accidental coincidence, natural affinity, and confluence"; and the assumption that just because an artist draws on a source, that source is exerting influence.[25] While Bentley's polemical essay takes the tone of the gatekeeper charged with protecting Brecht's legacy from marauding hordes of the uninitiated, his point is well taken. This study is unconcerned with determining whether his engagement with opera may have been good or bad. Nor does it aim to prove one-to-one correlations between specific operas and particular plays, opting instead for greater contextualization to allow instances of affinity and confluence to emerge. It is not always possible to know which way the current flowed.

This engagement in all its many forms is significant because opera was omnipresent for Brecht, not only in his theoretical texts and stage pieces but also on his worktable, in his conversations, and in his diaries. Such projects were not necessarily thrust upon him by particular composers, producers, or situations; he initiated many of them himself, with a variety of collaborators. He undertook them in the Berlin of the Weimar Republic, in exile both in Europe and the United States, and in communist East Germany. The paradox of his public disavowal of the genre and what now appears to be a kind of surreptitious flirtation is a delicious one, especially in a man who prized contradiction so highly.

This book argues that opera played a decisive role in several aspects of Brecht's work and examines this role in five chapters. Two chapters treat the significance of opera for the development of Brecht's theoretical concepts of performance practice and audience perception (epic theater as a new contract between the theater and its audience; gestus), and two examine his engagement with opera in particular cultural historical circumstances (fragments from his work as an American exile, opera in the work of East German national identity). The last chapter proposes that Brecht's legacy for opera is the aesthetic of estrangement that defines nonliteral productions of canonical pieces. A chronological survey of roughly two dozen projects will establish the well-nigh continuous presence of opera in Brecht's oeuvre and contextualize the specific texts and problems addressed in each chapter. The three primary stages of Brecht's career are demarcated musically by particular genres and composers and more generally by political regimes and geographical locations: the Weimar Republic (1918–33); the Nazi regime and exile from it (1933–41 in Europe, 1941–47 in the United States); and East Germany (1948–56).

In 1924 Brecht moved to Berlin and by 1926 had begun working with Weill, who had already made a name for himself as a promising young opera composer. At the height of anti-Wagnerism the pair produced both alternative kinds of opera and anti-operatic *Lehrstücke*, Brecht's greatest critique of opera. Most projects in this period are written with Weill, although he also worked on Lehrstücke with Paul Hindemith and Hanns Eisler. Aside from the early *Mahagonny Songspiel* (another generic mutation and a study for the subsequent larger piece), all the music theater texts from the frenetically productive and experimental period 1926–30 represent one extreme or the other, either operas or Lehrstücke: the prototype *Threepenny Opera, Lindberghflug, Lehrstück*, the epic opera *Rise and Fall of the City of Mahagonny*,[26] the school opera *He Who Said Yes*, and *The Decision*.[27] Furthermore, Brecht's most comprehensive writings about epic theater are contained in his famous remarks to *Mahagonny*, an opera by any standard, which suggests that opera provided substantial impetus for his theory.[28]

This polarity is investigated in chapter 1, "Lehrstück, Opera, and the New Audience Contract of the Epic Theater," which argues that the primary goal of epic theater was the renegotiation of the audience's contract with the theater-going experience, and that this was the result of Brecht's simultaneous engagement with both opera and anti-opera in the late Weimar Republic. The new contract of epic theater redistributed the balance of power between the spectating audience and the stage, and the significance of Brecht's proactive spectating audience member for political theater can hardly be overestimated. It was instrumental in the development of Louis Althusser's theory of spectatorship as an act of living critique that produces a new consciousness in the audience member,[29] and in Augusto Boal's Theatre of the Oppressed project working in tandem with Paolo Freire's Pedagogy of the Oppressed in Brazil. These transform the spectator into a spect-actor, à subject with agency that extends well beyond the theater.[30] The epic theater audience contract also informs recent theories of performance and audience perception in *non*political theater. Susan Bennett's landmark book *Theatre Audiences: A Theory of Production and Reception* takes Brecht's theories of audience experience as a primary point of departure in her study of the contribution of the audience to performance.[31] Neil Blackadder challenges Bennett's normative audience model, noting that it assumes "a basically passive, well-disposed audience" and neglects "the complication posed by spectators who actively resist performances," surely a position Brecht would have invited.[32] Willmar Sauter invokes the work of Hans-Georg Gadamer when he writes about the communication that occurs between stage and house during performance: "The 'message' is not something which is neatly packed and distributed to an anonymous consumer; instead, the meaning of a performance is created by the performers and the spectators together, in a joint act of understanding."[33] Erika Fischer-Lichte and Jens Roselt have argued that the audience be understood "as participants, or teammates, whose participation—meaning their physical presence, perception, reception, and reaction to the performance—brings forth the performance."[34] Christel Weiler sees in the participatory Lehrstück audience the progenitor to such contemporary performance theory,[35] which now assumes a type of audience participation that would be virtually unthinkable without the precondition of Brecht's epic theater. This chapter posits that both opera and Lehrstück are fundamentally musical genres and argues that this renegotiated audience contract was essentially an attempt to liberate the listening spectator from musical manipulation so that she could formulate an independent response to the performance.

Brecht completed no operas in the late Weimar or European exile period, yet he continued to make plans for operas, even as he claimed that the genre should neither be perpetuated in its current state nor survive rehabilitation.

In the summer of 1930, the *Wiesbadener Tagblatt* reported that he was adapting Jaroslav Hašek's 1923 novel *The Good Soldier Schweyk* for an opera, and at about the same time he completed an opera libretto for Weill's *The Bread Shop (Der Brotladen)*.[36] Apparently Hindemith was expecting a libretto from Brecht that year as well, although it never materialized.[37] In 1932 Brecht and Eisler worked on the *Schweyk* opera until it had to be abandoned in accordance with the wishes of Hašek's heirs. That summer *Welt am Abend* reported that Eisler had begun a new opera, *Aufbau des neuen Menschen*, with Sergei Tretyakov and Brecht for the Leningrad Opera,[38] although this project did not come to fruition either. The most unlikely prospect may have been the purported operetta *The Joys and Sorrows of the Smaller Pirates (Freuden und Leiden der kleineren Seeräuber)*, to be written with Eisler as a vehicle for Mae West.[39] In 1937 they undertook a marginally more plausible enterprise, developing the entire plot and some music for the first act of a grand opera entitled *Goliath*.[40] Brecht's ambivalence was almost certainly a factor in his inability to complete these projects, as were a host of inhospitable circumstances introduced by the Nazis' rise to power and Brecht's ensuing exile.[41]

Chapter 2, "The Operatic Roots of Gestus in *The Mother* and *Round Heads and Pointed Heads*," argues that the ways in which Brecht developed gestus in the period of European exile are indebted to opera. "Gests" are stylized behaviors designed to reveal the socially constructed nature of human interaction. During the mid-1930s Brecht was forced to develop a highly pragmatic performance theory because his pieces were now performed without the benefit of his direct supervision. Whereas gestus had been situated almost exclusively in the performer's visible body in motion and stasis, new circumstances prompted him to locate the gestus in the fixed, notated score, which was then realized via the performer's temporal, sounding body.[42] The direct link Brecht identified between music and gesture in the mid-1930s is reminiscent of the standard operatic stage practice known as mimesis.[43] This analysis of the operatic heritage of gestus is not intended as a validation of Brecht's theories, however.[44] On the contrary; when Brecht relocated the gestus to the notated musical score, its realization in the temporal, sounding body of the performer produced the voice-object. As Carolyn Abbate has argued, the voice-object is primarily associated with opera but is present in any sung genre and becomes "the sole center for the listener's attention."[45] I maintain that Brecht did not anticipate the emergence of the voice-object when he shifted the emphasis from the showing body to the sounding body. This chapter problematizes the standard models of gestus by Pavis and Suvin by inserting music into the equation and theorizing about the disruptive role of the voice object in their schemes.[46] This was also the time in which Brecht encountered the brilliant Mei Lanfang in Moscow, a Chinese opera singer whose performance made an enormous impression on him.[47]

While exile in Europe seemed to galvanize the playwright, the six years he spent in the United States were comparatively lean in terms of completed pieces. His habit of nursing along opera projects, however, continued.[48] He attempted a rapprochement with Weill and pitched no fewer than three opera projects to him: He returned to *Schweyk in the Second World War*, proposed a new *Good Person of Szechwan* as a "half-opera," and pushed an African American adaptation of *Threepenny Opera*. In 1943 Brecht took up the *Goliath* opera again, and in 1945 he returned to a subject that had been in the back of his mind since *Baal*, shaping the *Voyages of the God of Happiness* into an opera. Roger Sessions set a translation of the radio play *Lucullus* as an opera in 1947, but Brecht was not involved in the project. His last operatic proposal in the United States was a film of Offenbach's *The Tales of Hoffmann* in a new version, which he pitched unsuccessfully to director Lewis Milestone in May 1947.[49]

Chapter 3, "Fragments of Opera in American Exile," is a study of three unfinished pieces scarcely mentioned in the literature.[50] It has two overarching purposes: to argue the value of unfinished texts for Brecht studies on at least three fronts; and to posit these particular fragments as manifestations of a link between the United States and opera that Brecht had conceived long before he lived there. I will develop the second premise in the chapter and frame the larger discussion of fragment studies here. Brecht saved and organized vast quantities of drafts and notes, not only for the posthumous reconstruction of his oeuvre but for his own use, as his generative process frequently involved a return to previously abandoned material. Despite the quantity of evidence and its relevance to Brecht's creative process, however, the great majority of unfinished pieces remain unstudied. (The conspicuous exception is *Fatzer*, which constitutes over five hundred pages and was staged in a version by Heiner Müller in Hamburg in 1978.)[51] Neither Günter Glaeser's edition of forty-eight fragments, which appeared as volume ten of the thirty-volume *Große kommentierte Berliner und Frankfurter Ausgabe* in 1997,[52] nor subsequent calls for further study have elicited a substantial body of scholarship pertaining to the newly available fragments, operatic or otherwise.[53] My argument in favor of the study of fragments begins with the standard rationale, which is the potential for gaining insight into an artist's creative process. Tracing the fragmentary tributaries to a completed text is akin to identifying birth parents: Various traits may take on new, additional meaning once the family lineage is known. When particular fragments engender multiple texts (some of which may bear little outward resemblance to each other or to the progenitor), a facile conception of Brecht's texts as a sequence of discrete, completed pieces in distinct genres is brought into question. Study of the unfinished texts gives rise to a model of his oeuvre as a complex, intertextual web instead, and that reconfiguration presents numerous areas of new inquiry.[54] Among those new areas is the significance of genre designation for incomplete texts. When Brecht designated a project as an opera, that nomenclature was deliberate and carried specific connotations;[55] therefore, when material from an incomplete opera is explored in another, nonoperatic text, the generic residue informs the new project.

Brecht's unfinished texts are also valuable in understanding his creative process because they are exploratory.[56] This flexible adjective leaves open the possibility that the ultimate goal is not predetermined but might change in the process of writing, planning, and brainstorming. Completed pieces are never an entirely accurate measure of the time and energy Brecht invested in his work (nor of the genres that occupied him at any given time) because unrealized plans, incomplete projects, drafts, and fragments outnumber those he deemed sufficiently complete to publish by a ratio of approximately three to one.[57] A surfeit of incomplete texts tended to coincide with periods of intense creative activity in general, as in the years 1919–22, which yielded forty-nine unfinished pieces of various kinds, and 1926–30, which generated forty-eight.[58] This is typical of the rather arbitrary nature of creative energy in which numerous ideas are developed, revised, recycled, or set aside, depending on a host of concerns, both aesthetic and practical. Chapter 3 proposes to examine such texts within their historical contexts, tracking possible filial relationships to other projects and treating the fragments as valuable explorations rather than artistic dead-ends.[59]

In fact, the concept of text as inherently open-ended and in a perpetual state of flux is such a definitive characteristic of Brecht's aesthetic that any concept of his oeuvre that omits the fragments is itself incomplete. Symptomatic of the modernist crisis in which artists rejected the bourgeois illusion of the fixed, timeless, autonomous artwork as an expression of an artist's self,[60] manifestations of this open-endedness range from the use of estrangement devices in performance practice and stage production to collective rather than individual creative process.[61] The attitude that even a published text is still a work in progress is evident in the title under which Brecht wanted Malik to publish his collected texts: *Versuche* (Attempts), instead of the more common *Werke*.[62] Brecht habitually revised complete, published pieces and republished them in new versions, often based on what he had learned from performances of those texts in the interim. In other words, the conventional criteria for completion—the creator's consent to publication or performance and recognizable adherence to generic, formal, and stylistic norms—do not apply; nor does the common presumption that such a text, particularly in the fixed medium of traditional print (as opposed to the mutability of the internet), represents its "best" incarnation.[63] Therefore scholars cannot necessarily presume that the incomplete state of the aforementioned notes, unfinished projects, drafts, and fragments is indicative of a negative value judgment on Brecht's part.

Brecht published texts in order to try them out on performers and audiences and reserved the right to revise such texts as he saw fit because he was most concerned with their completion in performance. He wrote that he could not complete a dramatic text without the stage, a clear indication that his performance experience dictated revisions.[64] Each performance constitutes a unique, ephemeral experience shared between those onstage and those in the audience, for which bodily actions and responses are essential. A discussion of text and performance requires a clear delineation between "text" and "work."[65] In much musicological scholarship the score or recording constitutes the text, and the term "work" is reserved for its "realization and depends equally on the text plus the performance. The work thus exists in a potentially infinite number of states, whether in writing (score) or sound."[66] Therefore live performance of a text is the means whereby a text is rendered a work, and within Brecht's aesthetic of open-endedness, that performance can be said to constitute *a* completion (if not *the* completion) of a text as a work.[67] This argument has had various incarnations, perhaps most literally in Susanne K. Langer's scholarship,[68] although traces of it appear elsewhere in musical phenomenology and in Vladimir Jankélévitch's insistence that "real music is music that exists in time, the material acoustic phenomenon."[69] These models are relevant because so many of Brecht's dramatic texts were musical, although their relevance to nonmusicalized theater texts is also evident. (They too are performative, require human engagement, and are experienced temporally.)

Therefore it is possible to situate Brecht's entire oeuvre within a general aesthetic framework of incompletion, in which exploratory conventional fragments occupy one extreme of the spectrum and published pieces occupy the other, but even they remain asymptotical. Given this range, the question of why certain texts remain fragments in the conventional sense misses the mark. When all Brecht's texts can be considered open-ended, the distinction between those that achieved sufficient aesthetic and genetic completion to warrant publication and those that did not can be distilled to a matter of degree.

The frequency with which Brecht returned to opera even while living in exile, without viable performance prospects, confirms that the medium served multiple purposes. Each case study represents a different type of engagement: revision of an extant piece; return to an abandoned opera; and initiation of a new project. The first was his 1942 proposal that he and Weill revise *Threepenny Opera* for an all–African American production based on actor Clarence Muse's adaptation. The project did not reach fruition for a variety of mostly logistical and legal reasons,[70] but it marked Brecht's first examination of race relations in the United States. When it failed to materialize, he explored that subject in other productions via black actors in whiteface in otherwise all-white casts. The second project was a continuation of work on the *Goliath* project he and Eisler had begun six years earlier in Skovsbostrand. This collaboration represents an attempt to reconcile political differences over the viability of the Popular Front and its attendant aesthetic, as Eisler's surviving sketches reveal that his score was to have been a twelve-tone one. The third opera fragment is *Voyages of the God of Happiness*, which occupied Brecht and Dessau in California in the spring of 1945. This was an exploration of the traditional operatic device of anthropomorphized allegory, and Dessau completed three songs for the first scene in particell, or compressed short score, before they abandoned it. These three projects are examined as manifestations of the particular circumstances of American exile and as part of a network that includes completed, nonoperatic texts of the period (*The Visions of Simone Machard*, *Hangmen Also Die*, an adaptation of *The Duchess of Malfi*, the English version of *Life of Galileo*, and the English adaptation of *Fear and Misery* as *The Private Life of the Master Race*).

Brecht testified before the House Committee on Un-American Activities on 30 October 1947 and fled to Europe the next day. In the midst of this transitional turmoil and until the end of his life, he continued to field operatic prospects. The composer Gottfried von Einem secured from him a commitment to participate in the Salzburg Festival, and together they planned an opera in 1948–49 entitled *Of the Joys and Sorrows of the Larger and Smaller Pirates* (*Von den Freuden und Leiden der größeren und kleineren Seeräuber*), evidently a resuscitation of the reputed Mae West project of 1935.[71] In February 1950 the American publisher Edward B. Marks notified Brecht that Aaron Copland was interested in a libretto and asked him to contact the composer (there is no evidence that he ever did so); two months later Brecht helped Caspar Neher and composer Rudolf Wagner-Régeny iron out problems in their comic opera *Persische Episode* (also known as *Der Darmwäscher*) in anticipation of a production at the Komische Oper.[72] In 1950–53 Brecht was involved in two major opera projects, each of which resulted in high-profile cultural political debates in the fledgling German Democratic Republic (East Germany).[73] *The Trial of Lucullus*, the radio play turned libretto with music by Dessau, was a test case for early GDR cultural politics in 1951,[74] and Eisler's libretto for the opera *Johann Faustus* ignited a firestorm of controversy over the appropriate treatment of the German cultural heritage.[75] Apparently undeterred, Brecht considered several more operas in the final years of his life. These included a collaboration with Eisler entitled *King Frederick, the Miracle of the House of Brandenburg, or the Seven Year War (Fridericus Rex, das Mirakel des Hauses Brandenburg oder Der Siebenjährige Krieg)*, and another opera with Dessau tentatively known as *From the Baker's Wife (Des Bäckers Weib)*, and in the final year of his life they discussed prospects for an opera about Albert Einstein.[76]

Chapter 4, "*Lucullus*: Opera and National Identity," argues for the significance of *Lucullus* in the nation-building project undertaken by both the ruling SED (Socialist Unity Party) and prominent intellectuals in the Soviet-Occupied Zone, subsequently the German Democratic Republic. Because the GDR was a socialist state founded on the ruins of fascism and created and sustained by Soviet power, it had a unique national identity problem in that "it lacked indigenous legitimacy—whether national or political—from the outset."[77] Artists and party functionaries alike recognized opera's capacity to contribute to the GDR's foundation myth, as all parties believed that culture played a pivotal role in the construction of national identity but could not agree on precisely what form it should take. The political machinations that surrounded the premiere, ostensible revision, and repremiere of *Lucullus* are examined to demonstrate the ways in which Brecht negotiated his tumultuous relationship with the SED; how Dessau's music fared in the process; and the ways in which the party balanced its delicate relationships with Moscow and the Western press.

Chapter 5, "Brecht's Legacy for Opera: Estrangement and the Canon," argues for Brecht's relevance to opera today, an argument situated within the larger debate about his contemporary utility in general. There is widespread disagreement on the subject. Kalb finds Brecht's brand of didacticism ineffectual in the information age;[78] Jameson acknowledges a certain "Brecht fatigue" in overexposure;[79] Wright observes that Brecht's efficacy is neutralized by apolitical deployment of superficial elements of the style in mediated experience;[80] Oesmann argues that Brecht's relevance can be best sustained in a postcommunist world by minimizing his debt to Marxism;[81]

while Kruger opposes his ahistorical depoliticization because of his current prominence in societies outside North America and Europe.[82] In 2005 the *Chronicle of Higher Education* took the tenth anniversary of the publication of John Fuegi's incendiary *Brecht and Company: Sex, Politics, and the Making of the Modern Drama* as an occasion to survey the state of Brecht scholarship in North America. Reporter Peter Monaghan determined that Brecht had survived the posthumous sex scandal only to be brought low by something far more pedestrian: his induction to the twentieth-century literary canon.[83] Witness such high-profile New York productions as the Public Theater's *Mother Courage* starring Meryl Streep, and *Threepenny Opera* featuring Alan Cumming and Cyndi Lauper at Studio 54.

There is little point in arguing with the assessment that Brecht's *literal* political relevance in North America and Europe may be at an all-time nadir, except perhaps as a spectacular negative example (a type of usefulness he actually may have appreciated in a perverse sense, given the frequency with which he taught his own lessons this way).[84] Heiner Müller's edict that "to use Brecht without criticizing him is to betray him" was made manifest in Müller's own work,[85] and that tradition continued with Soeren Voima's 2000 treatment of *The Decision* as *The Contingent*, in which the role of the Communist Party is taken by the United Nations, whose blind adherence to abstract rules of neutral engagement frustrate a young American, and he is executed by the UN for noncompliance.[86] Despite the state of current international affairs, seeking evidence of Brecht's relevance *only* in manifestations of major pedagogy,[87] which is to say in participatory pieces of explicit political engagement, will inevitably disappoint; as Kalb noted, it is a method little used in Europe and North America today.

I argue that Brecht's principle of minor pedagogy, however, is thriving, in the form of estrangement that defines nonliteral productions of canonical opera. Minor pedagogy, which empowers the spectating audience member to engage with traditional bourgeois theater in a new way, is custom-made for this repertoire. Kruger's two-stage definition of estrangement—disillusion followed by understanding[88]—is precisely the sensation many directors seek to create in such a staging, and it is the reason many spectating audience members attend. This does not include productions that deploy shock value for its own sake, akin to those texts Andrzej Wirth decried as "Brecht reception without Brecht."[89] But director's opera does not *have* to be all style and no substance (Brecht without Brecht); there are directors who exploit the friction between what an opera *sounds* like (say, nineteenth-century Italian music) and what it *looks* like (anachronistic settings and costumes, for example) with great success. I examine this in the final chapter by recounting the means and moments of estrangement experienced in a nonliteral production of Verdi's *La forza del destino* directed by Stefan Herheim (Berlin Staatsoper, 2005). The frisson of estrangement in an encounter with a nonliteral staging of an opera one thinks one knows can be a source of great pleasure. Ever prescient, Brecht anticipated that spectating audiences would eventually become inured to the effects of estrangement: "You know, human nature knows how to adapt itself just as well as the rest of organic matter. Man is even capable of regarding atomic war as something normal, so why should he not be capable of dealing with an affair as small as the alienation [sic] effect so that he does not need to open his eyes. I can imagine that one day they will only be able to feel their old pleasure when the alienation [sic] effect is offered."[90] Perhaps this will be true, eventually. In the meantime, my experience of estrangement with such performances continues to be marked by memorable moments of disillusion and understanding that enrich my engagement with a particular opera and with opera-going as social practice. In that sense, the book comes full circle. It was Brecht's resistance to the musical manipulation of spectating audience members at the opera that prompted his renegotiation of the audience contract in the first place. In the twenty-first century, in Europe and North America, it may be the opera house rather than the spoken theater that offers a spectating audience member the best opportunity to assess Brecht's performance practice theory.

The title of the book is meant to capture this topsy-turvy state of affairs. It alludes to cultural touchstones that simultaneously honor and deflate operatic conventions, such as the Marx Brothers' film *A Night at the Opera* and the classic Queen album of the same name, but it also exploits a certain ambiguity inherent in the preposition. Like many common prepositions, *at* is polysemous. "Brecht *at* the opera" might mean simply that the playwright is in attendance, but it also conjures George Crabbe's ominous text, sung repeatedly in Benjamin Britten's operatic masterpiece *Peter Grimes:* "Grimes is *at* his exercise." In that case, *at* is decidedly less benign. The preposition that links Brecht to the opera in the title of this book embodies the ambivalent nature of that relationship. That ambivalence is the subject of this study.

1   Lehrstück, Opera, and the New Audience Contract of the Epic Theater

Lehrstücke (learning plays) and opera occupy opposite ends of the continuum for audience experience in musical theater.[1] Brecht observed that the social contract in effect for opera audiences stipulated not only that participants empathize with characters, suspend disbelief, and submit to emotional manipulation, but that they do so under the influence of the powerful narcotic of continuous music. Similar conditions were imposed in nonoperatic theater, but opera was the most extreme example because of its perpetual, manipulative musical presence. Brecht countered this in two ways: from within the system, in his two operas (*Threepenny Opera* and *The Rise and Fall of the City of Mahagonny*), and from outside the system, in his four Lehrstücke (*Lindbergh Flight, Lehrstück, He Who Said Yes*, and *The Decision*), which did not require an audience at all. Lehrstücke could effectively render attendees a nonaudience by transforming them into participants or, at the very least, prospective participants. Brecht's simultaneous work in both genres in the late 1920s generated the theory of epic theater and determined its primary goal: renegotiation of the audience's pact with the theater and, by extension, the citizen's contract with society.[2] The fact that epic theater's provenance is also musical, as it emerged from his simultaneous engagement with two diametrically opposed musical theater genres, Lehrstück and opera,[3] warrants further inquiry.

DEFINING THE LEHRSTÜCK (1928–1930)

Brecht ran the Lehrstück experiment concurrently with the opera experiment, thereby attacking the problem of the audience contract from both sides at once.[4] In this period he wrote the interactive radio play *Lindbergh Flight (The Flight over the Ocean)*, usually identified as a Lehrstück; *Lehr-*

stück (The Baden-Baden Lesson on Consent); He Who Said Yes/He Who Said No; The Decision; and *The Exception and the Rule*.[5] These texts are interleaved chronologically with work on *Threepenny Opera* and *The Rise and Fall of the City of Mahagonny,* and their simultaneous gestations provided ample opportunity for cross-pollination and confluence. Lehrstücke were written for a specific time and place, namely, that of the late Weimar Republic and a society thought to be in transition to socialism; when conditions were no longer hospitable, Brecht stopped writing them. Only *The Horatians and the Curiatians* (1934) and the fragment *Demise of the Egotist Johann Fatzer* (1927) fall outside the chronological frame.

My purpose in this analysis is to reclaim the Lehrstück as a musical genre and establish its status as the anti-opera musical theater tributary to the new audience contract; therefore a brief overview of the Lehrstück is in order.[6] The following features are generally agreed upon as definitive of the genre: the Lehrstücke are intended more for the performers than for an audience; the roles are to be rotated among amateur performers; and they serve a didactic purpose. (Note the conspicuous absence of an essential musical component; I will return to this in a moment.) The Lehrstücke unify the production and consumption of art in a single reciprocal process that challenged the concept of audiences as mere consumers of cultural products.[7] Of course, as Roswitha Mueller observes, "Audience reception, the insistence that the audience develop an altogether different attitude, is at the core of Brechtian theory,"[8] but it has a particular manifestation in the Lehrstücke that undermined the implicit passivity of the word "reception." The principle that theater *required* performers and an audience, and that those participants had to be discrete entities, had been the premise of all previous audience contracts in the theater. The Lehrstücke represented a radical affront to that basic tenet.

Over time, however, the perception of the role of the audience has become distorted. Brecht had written, "[The Lehrstücke] do not *need* an audience" (emphasis added),[9] but Jameson writes of the necessary *"exclusion of the public"* (emphasis added),[10] demonstrating the ease with which the absence of necessity becomes the necessity of absence. The slippage in this conventional wisdom is to blame for much confusion about the genre, for even under Brecht's supervision the Lehrstücke were staged for nonperforming audiences more often than performing ones. *Lindbergh Flight, Lehrstück,* and *The Decision* all debuted before spectating audiences. Eisler described the premiere of *The Decision* as an event, and it is the text most often cited as paradigmatic of the Lehrstück. But the advertising campaign, the prominent venue selected for the premiere (the Berlin Philharmonic, albeit at 11:30 P.M.), and the post-performance questionnaire distributed to audience members all call into question the exclusion of a spectating audience as an essential feature of the genre.[11] Apparently these plays could be useful for nonperforming audiences even at the time of their premieres. It is more accurate to say that a Lehrstück *may* have a spectating audience but that its primary function is not to play to those members.[12]

THE LEHRSTÜCK AS A MUSICAL GENRE

Based on the genesis and content of *Lindbergh Flight, Lehrstück, He Who Said Yes,* and *The Decision,* I would add two defining features to the list of characteristics cited above, and both pertain to music: A composer was involved as bona fide collaborator from the piece's inception, and music is essential to its realization because it imposes order on an otherwise loosely structured genre and facilitates the collective experience of the participants. If these criteria are accepted as definitive of the genre, then they also problematize the conventional wisdom outlined above, as we will see. In this context the music is not primarily intended to persuade or entertain an audience but rather to instruct its performers, so it is a fundamentally musical genre, anti-operatic in both conception and purpose. The music is traditionally underestimated in Brechtian literature, thanks in no small part to the playwright's own efforts to "demusicalize" the genre in later theoretical texts.[13] Krabiel's reassertion of the primacy of music in the Lehrstück, in which he posited that it is related "to the musical genre in origin, form, and purpose,"[14] was a landmark moment in its reception, and the historic Berliner Ensemble production of *The Decision* in 1997 prompted further reconsideration along musical lines.[15]

I would go beyond describing it as being *related to* a musical genre, however; the Lehrstück *is* a musical genre. *The Horatians and the Curiatians* (1934) and the *Fatzer* fragment (1927), both of which fall chronologically outside the main body of the repertoire, and *The Exception,*[16] originally planned as a Schaustück (traditional play with spectating audience), are the only Brechtian Lehrstücke not conceived with a musical collaborator from the start. Others were initially written for music festivals, namely the Baden-Baden Festival in 1929 (*Lindbergh Flight* and *Lehrstück*) and its successor, Neue Musik Berlin in 1930 (*He Who Said Yes* and *The Decision*). They were promoted by the musical press across the ideological spectrum, from *Zeitschrift für Musik* and *Melos* to the left-leaning *Musik und Gesellschaft.* By 1931 these journals could report a good-sized repertoire of Lehrstücke and related pieces, much of it written by people outside Brecht's immediate circle.[17]

The articles lumped together Lehrstücke, school operas, cantatas, and various plays, a gesture that can be interpreted in multiple ways: Musicians viewed the Lehrstück as a close relative of the school opera and therefore as some sort of operatic subset; the boundaries of a new generic category are inevitably fluid and permeable so that a text a playwright might call a Lehrstück could be designated as a school opera by a composer; all musical pieces intended for amateur performance were of a single genus. The collaborators themselves did not always agree on nomenclature, and sometimes they were inconsistent even unto themselves. Weill called *He Who Said Yes* a school opera, the designation which appears on the score published by Universal Edition, while Brecht usually referred to it as a Lehrstück, which is how it is identified in the nonmusical literature, although he too deemed it a school opera on occasion.[18]

Regardless of what they called the genre, Weill and Brecht had similar aims, and variants can be attributed in part to their differing perspectives as composer and playwright. The didactic function of the Lehrstücke is apparent in both text and music. Thematically, consent (*Einverständnis*) in the form of self-sacrifice for the greater good is prominent in three of the texts as a parable for teaching the method (*Lehrstück, He Who Said Yes,* and *The Decision*).[19] Weill emphasized the musical lessons to be learned from the school opera *He Who Said Yes* and balanced this with the importance of music as a tool for learning nonmusical lessons:

> The music of a didactic opera must absolutely be calculated for careful, even lengthy study. For *the practical value of didactic opera consists precisely in the study,* and as far as the performers are concerned, the performance of such a work is far less important than the training that is linked to it. At first this training is purely musical, but it should be at least as much intellectual. . . . *It is absolutely worth every effort, therefore, to see that a didactic piece offers the students the opportunity of learning something in addition to the joy of making music.* (Emphasis in original)[20]

Musicologists treat this repertoire differently than scholars of literature, theater, and German, primarily because Brecht's penchant for revision frequently renders obsolete those texts for which music had been composed.[21] Three of the core Lehrstücke exist in multiple published versions. Their initial texts were conceived with a composer who wrote the music as Brecht wrote the text, but, with the notable exception of *The Decision*, the playwright revised the literary texts alone, and subsequent versions did not receive new musical settings.[22] *The Flight over the Ocean,* for example, was originally entitled *Lindbergh Flight* and remains known as such among many musicians, despite the fact that Brecht revised and retitled it twice. The original performance at the Baden-Baden Festival in 1929 was billed as a radio play, included music by both Weill and Hindemith, and was a demonstration of the interactive potential of the radio medium.[23] Audiences gathered around radios in various rooms for the first hearing and then attended a "live" performance of *Lindbergh Flight* in which they were in the same space with the performers.[24] Shortly thereafter Weill recomposed Hindemith's sections (the pieces that represented nature and the final chorus) and published the score as a cantata under the original title. In 1930 Brecht published an expanded text as *The Flight of Lindbergh*, "a radio Lehrstück for boys and girls"; in 1950 he added a prologue, suppressed the name of the pilot, and changed the title to *The Flight over the Ocean* to sever the connection with Lindbergh, whose Nazi sympathies had since been revealed. Yet Weill's score, essential to any realization of the text, was never reworked to accommodate Brecht's revised texts, and the original collaborative version between Weill and Hindemith had been withdrawn.

A similar fate befell another piece from the 1929 Baden-Baden Festival, *Lehrstück*, with music by Hindemith. The composer published the piano-vocal score with the original text in the same year. Brecht, who took issue with Hindemith's preface to the score because it described the work's sole purpose as "engaging all those present in the work's execution," published a revised and expanded text in 1930 as *The Baden-Baden Lesson on Consent*.[25] Mueller may have taken her cue from the playwright when she referred to Hindemith's score as "the piano excerpt for the *Lehrstück*," a description that represents a gross trivialization of the composer's contribution to a work that features nearly continuous music. She summarizes Hindemith's preface as follows: "Since the purpose of the learning plays was simply to let everyone present participate and not primarily to create specific acts, the form of the piano music should be adjusted to whatever purpose was at hand."[26] Surely it is not the musical form but the sequence of discrete movements to which Hindemith referred when he wrote, "The order given in the score is more a suggestion than a set of instructions. Cuts, additions, and re-orderings are possible."[27] There is no "plot" contingent upon a particular sequence of events and therefore no reason to adhere strictly to the published sequence of movements. (With the pragmatism typical of *Gebrauchsmusik*, Hindemith also noted that the instrumentation was subject to change, depending on availability.)

In yet another communication breakdown between musicologists and scholars of other disciplines, Brecht's revised text, known in German as

Das Badener Lehrstück vom Einverständnis, is typically translated into English as either *The Baden-Baden Cantata of Acquiescence* or *The Baden-Baden Lesson on Consent,* presumably to avoid confusion with the original *Lehrstück.* The *Cantata* title confuses the issue, however, because "cantata" is a musical genre, but this version of the text does not have a musical setting. Brecht's latter version is most widely known among nonmusic scholars today while musicians continue to work with the text featured in Hindemith's published *Lehrstück* score, and this perpetuates miscommunication. Mueller writes, "*The Baden-Baden Cantata of Acquiescence* was an immediate critical success at the Baden-Baden Music Festival of 1929."[28] Obviously this cannot be true; the revised text is not identical to the Lehrstück which was performed there, and it has no music, so it would have had no place at a music festival. This statement is typical of the way in which various text versions tend to get conflated, as if they were all identical to the final version, and without regard for the musical setting that was essential to the initial inception but subsequently shed.

This is problematic for Weill's musical setting of *He Who Said Yes* as well, which treats the first version of Brecht's play. Brecht was disturbed by its initial popular reception as a "model of religious traditionalism and suicidal self-sacrifice, a relic from feudal times."[29] When the children who performed the work at a Berlin school suggested improvements, he revised the text and added a companion piece called *He Who Said No,* but Weill's music for the revised version has never been published, and he did not compose music for the new text. Brecht left a note saying, "The two little plays should if possible never be performed separately," yet how one should realize such a performance, if it is to include music, is unclear.[30] Musicians focus on the Lehrstück texts for which a musical setting exists, which in these cases are necessarily the earliest performed versions, while literature-oriented scholars are apt to take subsequent versions as definitive. The crucial role of the composer in the initial collaborations is most often lost in revision, however, and the absence of revised settings appropriate to revised texts renders later versions of little use in reconstructing the musicality of the genre.

The plurality of valid generic designations and versions of each piece that coexisted in 1931 has been effectively winnowed to a narrow, litero-centric field that treats Lehrstücke almost exclusively as Brechtian plays, privileges his final versions of the texts, and takes little account of their musical origins. Jameson writes, "We have every interest in disentangling the evolution of the Lehrstück from the related yet independent destiny of music in the Brechtian theatre."[31] Certainly it is legitimate to discuss Brecht's oeuvre without considering its music, but the literocentric argument is now the dominant discourse. It assumes that the Lehrstück text could and *did* evolve independently from its music and, by extension, the contribution of those collaborators. It omits the music, as if it had played no role in achieving the primary objectives of these pieces. Further, to declare that the genre's evolution needs to be "disentangled" from its essential musical identity, as if the music somehow encumbers it and obfuscates its meaning, bespeaks a fundamental misunderstanding of the genre. Jameson goes so far as to refer to the "integration" of music into *Lindbergh Flight*— scarcely an accurate assessment of the role of music in that text, presupposing as it does the primacy and autonomy of the literary text and its author. Nor does Heiner Müller acknowledge a significant role for music in his own Lehrstück project, which "presumes/criticizes Brecht's Lehrstück theory and praxis."[32]

To be sure, musicologists bear some of the blame for the predominantly amusical treatment of these texts. The Lehrstücke have not always been considered worthy of musical study, even though Weill himself identified *He Who Said Yes* as his most important composition to date in 1935.[33] Musicological legitimization of Weill in the wake of his commercial success in the United States focused on pieces considered traditionally substantial, such as large-scale operas and concert pieces. Furthermore, the entire category of Gebrauchsmusik, while historically significant, has no canonical repertoire because it lacks the institutional apparatus necessary to sustain such a tradition. When it is performed at all, Gebrauchsmusik tends to surface in theaters and university theater departments, institutions with largely nonmusical priorities and agendas.

The tendency to read the Lehrstücke as plays without music or as plays with optional music has obscured understanding of the genre's inception and performance and, it may be extrapolated, the significance of music for the epic theater. Andrzej Wirth notes, "The critical discourse in German studies has overlooked that the Lehrstücke are libretti and can be interpreted only in relation to the vocal, musical, and choreographic performance."[34] Wirth's choice of the word "libretti" connotes an essential rather than optional relationship with music. It stands to reason that any genre fundamentally predicated upon participation would require performance to be understood, and that that performance must include music. These are not plays to be read and studied like *Schaustücke;* they must be sung, played, danced, and staged.[35]

The genre's flexibility, while applicable to acting, reciting lines, and blocking, is countered by the prevalence of music and its inherently structured nature, since it must take place in defined time and pitch. Writing from his experience as the director of many Lehrstück productions, Wirth observes, "The music locks out the freedom of improvisation and is not only a distancing but also a disciplining medium."[36] "Disciplining" can refer to a couple of aspects of music. First, the temporal specificity of music necessarily imposes a pace and a sequence on an event. Second, performing music as part of an ensemble requires a uniformity of execution that can only be acquired by learning one's part and rehearsing it with others, and that requires discipline. Amateur instrumentalists, for whom such plays were intended, could hardly be expected to sight-read their parts or follow a singer; nor could an amateur singer keep up with an instrumental arrangement that does not always feature her melody without rehearsal. Rehearsal provides the familiarity necessary for professionals to improvise, but amateurs do not possess the requisite skill and will perform the music as learned (barring memory slips). Even the skilled amateurs to whom Brecht had access in Weimar-era Berlin, such as the workers' choirs, rehearsed extensively, learning their parts by reading notation or by rote memorization.[37] The music thus performs two crucial functions in dialectic with the rest of the Lehrstück agenda: It imposes a degree of order on an otherwise flexible text, and it facilitates communal participation.

THE MUSICAL EVIDENCE IN FOUR LEHRSTÜCKE

To substantiate the claim that the Lehrstück is essentially a musical genre, and more specifically an anti-opera musical genre, two questions must be answered: How pervasive is music in these pieces, and how integral is its role to the realization of a Lehrstück? Simply put, the answer to each question is "very." The state of Lehrstück research is precisely the inverse to that of opera studies, which is to say that the primary body of scholarship devoted to the former concerns the genre as literature, theater, and theory, whereas the vast majority of work on opera treats the music. The relatively recent expansion of that scholarship to include focus on opera libretti, productions, and performance studies has been highly productive, and I submit that an expansion of Lehrstück research to include a focus on music could be similarly illuminating. Therefore my admittedly music-centered analysis is meant to challenge the conventional wisdom as outlined in the previous section by privileging an aspect of the genre that has been neglected, thereby reconfiguring the possibilities inherent in all aspects of the genre. For example, the wholesale rotation of roles among participants as a defining generic feature of the Lehrstück is less convincing when one takes the music into account, since some roles require musical training and a particular vocal range. How would one ensure that all participants have the requisite skill and voice type to execute all solos? Likewise, the assignment of all roles to amateurs is not practical from a musical perspective, since many roles demand a degree of technical proficiency that cannot be reasonably assumed among amateurs. Finally, the notion that these didactic plays are meant to teach the participants rather than the audience, or that the participants and the audience are the same, is undermined by the fact that only one of these texts includes a part specifically written for the audience, yet all were premiered before spectating audiences.

Because the Lehrstücke are little known musically compared to their operatic counterparts, this analysis focuses on their scores to a degree not required in discussions of *Threepenny Opera* and *Rise and Fall of the City of Mahagonny*. Four scores and their respective libretti are relevant: Hindemith and Weill's collaborative score for *Lindbergh Flight*, Hindemith's *Lehrstück*, Weill's setting of *He Who Said Yes*, and Eisler's music for *The Decision*.[38] The prevalence and prominence of music is determined most fundamentally by considering the quantity of musical numbers, the significance of purely instrumental pieces without text, and the amount of text set to music. How the music is deployed reveals its function in the realization of a work. To that end, the music in these four Lehrstücke is examined in three broad categories: instrumentation and discrete instrumental pieces in each piece; the distribution and type of sung pieces for solo, choir, and audience; and the use of melodrama (accompanied speech).

The sheer quantity of music in the original versions of these pieces is the greatest argument in favor of the genesis of the Lehrstück as a musical genre. The collaborative setting of *Lindbergh Flight* by Weill and Hindemith originally consisted of fifteen segments, and all but three were sung and set to music.[39] It is written for mixed, four-part choir and seven solo parts: Lindbergh (tenor); Sleep (alto); Fog, First Fisherman, and Reporter (baritones); Snowstorm and Second Fisherman (basses). *Lindbergh Flight* differs from the others in that only one participant is an amateur: The character of Lindbergh is sung by the listener at home, who follows a score as he listens to the other parts broadcast over the radio.[40] The text chronicles Lindbergh's flight across the Atlantic through newspaper reports and personification of the obstacles he encounters in the forms of fog, snow, fatigue, and fear of mechanical failure. *Lehrstück* is written for two male singers, speaker, chorus, dancer (originally filmed dance episode), three clowns, and orchestra. A pilot is injured in a plane crash and appeals for help but is made to see that he does not deserve it; instead, he is told to reconcile himself to death and acknowledge his own insignificance. Scene 6, which features a spoken scene for the clowns in which they cut off the limbs of a giant one by one, generated a scandal at the Baden-Baden Festival. The piece has seven sections, and each is set almost entirely to music.[41]

He Who Said Yes is based upon the fifteenth-century Japanese Noh play *Taniko*, which Brecht knew through Elisabeth Hauptmann's German translation of the English adaptation by Arthur Waley. Brecht's libretto uses most of Hauptmann's text and incorporates the idea of active consent *(Einverständnis)*, which is reiterated in the chorus at the beginning of each of the two acts.[42] A boy makes a school trip across the mountains to obtain medicine for his sick mother, but the route becomes too difficult for him and he is unable to continue. Tradition dictates that he must choose whether the rest of the group turns back on his account or throws him into the valley below so that the others may continue, but the choice is illusory. Custom requires that he agree to the self-sacrifice, which he does, after ensuring that his companions will acquire the medicine for his mother. The entire libretto is set to music; there is no unaccompanied dialogue.[43]

The Decision took shape almost simultaneously with *He Who Said Yes* and formed a counterplay or "un-identical twin" to it.[44] To the basic premise of the Noh play Eisler added a new mission and location inspired by his brother Gerhart Eisler's Comintern work in China. Three comrades report that they had to execute a fourth because he repeatedly compromised their communist mission, and they ask the party in the form of the Control Chorus to pass judgment on their decision. The fourth comrade's sympathy for individual suffering led him to disobey orders and jeopardize the organization of the workers' movement, and he tells his comrades that they must kill him to preserve the integrity of the mission. They do so, and the Control Chorus affirms their decision because he was a threat to the well-being of the collective. Sublimation of the individual to the group and the cause struck many as unnecessarily harsh, and protests arose from both the Right and the Left.[45] *The Decision* contains a prologue and eight scenes.[46] It is longer than previous Lehrstücke and features a greater variety of musical forms and textures. It includes frequent passages of unaccompanied spoken dialogue, typically at the beginnings and ends of scenes, but also interspersed within and between musical numbers. Although the percentage of text set to music in this piece is smaller than that of the others, it is nevertheless an overwhelmingly musical experience because it takes longer to deliver text via song than speech and the audience hears music for a much larger percentage of the performance than it hears unaccompanied dialogue.

Instrumentation and Instrumental Passages

Weill and Hindemith's *Lindbergh Flight* was composed for a larger ensemble than subsequent Lehrstücke because it was intended for radio broadcast, and the orchestra would have been a professional group performing live in a studio. At the Baden-Baden premiere, the Frankfurt Radio Orchestra played for *Lindbergh Flight*. On the other hand, Hindemith composed the *Lehrstück* orchestra parts for low-, medium-, and high-range instruments to facilitate doubling and substitution, and amateurs performed these parts on string instruments at the premiere. The offstage brass ensemble could also be augmented or substituted and was originally composed of members from the Lichtental Music Society. *He Who Said Yes* specified a complement of woodwind, keyboard, percussion, and plucked instruments, while *The Decision* was composed for brass, piano, and percussion. The preponderance of brass may be attributed to the prevalence of community bands in Germany during the Weimar Republic era.

These pieces are only nominally staged, so there is little need for instrumental music to accompany action without text. *Lindbergh Flight* has two segments with sizeable introductions, one with a substantial postlude, one with a lengthy saxophone solo, and another with two eight-measure interludes. Hindemith's *Lehrstück* contains only a few segments of instrumental music to accompany action, most extensively in the clown dismemberment scene. The first and last pieces in Weill's score for *He Who Said Yes* are identical; each chorus is framed with a substantive instrumental introduction and postlude. In the interim there are scarcely four consecutive measures of music without singing and no discrete instrumental pieces. Eisler's score for *The Decision* is also framed by a chorus with a lengthy prelude, and most other instances of purely instrumental music are similarly situated. The distribution and donning of masks in number 3a features an instrumental accompaniment, and number 8b, "Supply and Demand," has a memorable fourteen-measure interlude after verses one and two.

Choir, Solo, and Audience Singing

Music is well-nigh omnipresent, then, and vocal music outweighs any strictly instrumental component. These two features align the Lehrstück more closely with opera than with any other theatrical genre, so the deployment of these musical components must undermine that association if the Lehrstück is to succeed as anti-opera. This subversion is accomplished primarily with the chorus, which, according to Brecht's music-drama orientation, played a minimal role in opera and undermines the diva-driven emphasis on the individual singer. The Lehrstück always includes a chorus and is generally thought to privilege the choir over the soloists, as befits a text for amateur performance with a didactic focus on groups or causes larger than the individual. There is great variety in these four pieces, however, with regard to the distribution of weight between soloists and chorus in the number of pieces, the length of those pieces, the type of vocal writing, and the level of virtuosity required. The difficulty of some of the music and the use of some professional and semiprofessional performers at the premieres undermine the notion that such texts are meant only for amateurs. Certainly the genre was calculated to capitalize upon the burgeoning workers' choir movement in the Weimar Republic, but only *The Decision* is truly chorus dominated. In fact, several reports of performances of *The Decision* in 1930 and 1931 describe it as a choral work of one variety or another,[47] and Reinhard Krüger interprets its "scenic choral work as the new form of the Lehrstück."[48] It is one of the many curiosities of the genre's history that the least-performed text, and the one whose prominent use of the chorus actually distinguishes it from the other three, came to be representative of the entire repertoire.

The Hugo Holles Madrigal Society, apparently a semiprofessional choir, was the chorus for the premiere of Weill and Hindemith's *Lindbergh Flight*. The prevalence of the chorus in *Lindbergh Flight* may give the appearance of community—the chorus sings in half of the twelve musical sections—but it does not function in the same way in which the live, participatory choruses of the other Lehrstücke do because it is mediated by the radio, as is every element of this piece except the part of Lindbergh. Some of the soloists were established, operatically trained singers, such as the Hungarian bass Oskar Kálmán, who had created the title role in Bartók's *Bluebeard's Castle* in 1918 and here sang Snow; and Josef Witt, a tenor with a notable career at the Vienna Staatsoper, who premiered the role of Lindbergh as a demonstration.[49] The Hugo Holles Madrigal Society also sang the premiere of Hindemith's *Lehrstück*, and this choral writing is considerably more difficult than that of *Lindbergh Flight*. It ranges from imitative polyphony to homophonic chorale style to parallel octaves and unison. The chorus figures prominently in five of its seven sections, but despite this substantial choral presence, the solos in *Lehrstück* are conspicuous because they are even more virtuosic, particularly those for the tenor who plays the downed pilot. This role was also premiered by Witt, and the second soloist was Kálmán.[50] The vocal writing is less deliberately diatonic and melodic throughout, and the orchestral parts do not always double the vocal lines. The text that bears as its title the name of the genre is perhaps the least appropriate for amateur performance where the singers are concerned.

He Who Said Yes strikes a balance between soloists and chorus. Four of the six numbers in the first act are for soloists only, and one of them features a trio for the soloists, a rare ensemble piece in the Lehrstück repertoire for individuals whose parts are delineated as such rather than as a collective singing homophonically. By contrast, the second act has six numbers, only one of which omits the chorus. It may impress as being even more pervasively choral because the three students who want to hurl the boy into the valley tend to sing as a single unit. In the choral frame that begins each act and provides the finale, the choir explains the moral of the story; elsewhere it narrates, describing events but not participating in them. Weill's choral writing tends to be homophonic, with instances of paired imitation between upper and lower voices. For both soloists and chorus, the vocal lines are either doubled in the instruments or clearly supported harmonically through chord progressions. Unlike Hindemith's solo parts in *Lehrstück,* Weill's solos in *He Who Said Yes* are not particularly virtuosic and could be performed by amateurs with adequate rehearsal.

The identity of the choir in *The Decision* changes depending on the situation.[51] The choir interacts with the comrades as a collective character (the committee), and as that committee, it provides the raison d'être for the entire play, because it requires the comrades to reenact the events that led them to kill their colleague. (At the premiere the choir was an overwhelming physical presence as well, as it included hundreds of singers from three workers' choirs.)[52] The choir sings in almost every number: It assumes the roles of others involved in various scenarios, and, most famously, it declaims party doctrine in Eisler's inimitable *Kampflieder* style. Eisler was widely recognized as the leading art-music composer committed to the workers' chorus movement, and the militant choral presence associated with *The Decision* reflects this orientation.[53] The revolutionary songs he was composing for the movement in general and for the agitprop troupe Das rote Sprachrohr (The Red Megaphone) had the greatest influence on his choral writing for the Lehrstück.[54] He had also experimented with choral writing in a larger nondramatic genre in the cantata *Tempo der Zeit,* a piece for amateurs on a text by David Weber about the double-edged sword of "progress" that had also been performed at the Baden-Baden Festival in 1929.[55] H. H. Stuckenschmidt noted the significance of Eisler's involvement with the workers' choruses:

Eisler . . . plays a unique role in musical life today. Without figuring prominently on the programs of bourgeois concerts, he is one of the most performed composers and moreover a thoroughly popular man among the working class. He came out of Schoenberg's school and is able to turn his hand to strong composition, and he has a simplicity of melody and harmony that has secured him the broadest publicity among the workers. . . . Only those who ignore the difficulty of writing a deliberately comprehensible choral setting for workers can reproach him for monotony.[56]

Hindemith and Weill had already established themselves as opera composers, but Eisler had not completed an opera (nor would he, despite many attempts) and was not operating from that reputation or orientation.

Paradoxically, and in stark contrast to the choral presence, *The Decision* also features what may be the most operatic material in all the Lehrstücke in scene 5 ("What Is a Man, Anyway?").[57] The extensive recitative between the fourth comrade and the merchant (88 measures) is immediately followed by a long strophic solo for the merchant, replete with three verses and instrumental interludes (184 measures); this solo is one of the most popular and enduring of Eisler's songs. Together they constitute a set piece of some 272 measures of continuous music. Recitative is perhaps the quintessential operatic feature, as it facilitates continuous music where all other musical theater genres resort to spoken dialogue. It is traditionally speechlike in melody and rhythm, sparingly accompanied, and sung by one person at a time. It is bound by no musical form save that of the text, and it is subject to considerable manipulation of tempo and word stress by the performer.

The most anti-operatic moments are those in which the audience members become performers. This happens in only one case, when the audience is designated as The Crowd in *Lehrstück*. At the premiere the lyrics and notated music written explicitly for the spectating audience were projected onto a screen; participants were thereby activated and transformed into performing audience members. At several points the audience sings in unison in the form of a liturgical response, yet another allusion to the religious or catechistic roots of the genre. A few audience members (shills) sing accompanied only by sustained chords in the orchestra, and the entire audience responds verbatim. There are also sections in which a group of audience members repeatedly interjects a chantlike phrase as if it were an antiphon. The deliberate incorporation of the audience problematizes the generalization that spectating audiences were prohibited from attending Lehrstücke, and, at the same time, it challenges the other favorite notion that audience

Example 1.   Hindemith, *Lehrstück* section 1: rehearsal I, audience response

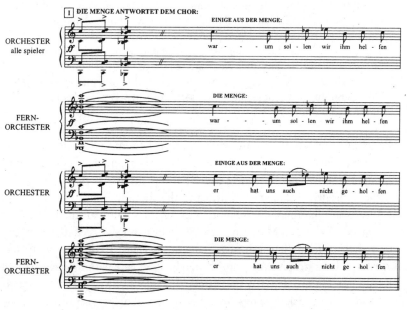

Example 2.   Hindemith, *Lehrstück* section 7: rehearsal B, a few members of the audience respond

participation is an essential feature of the genre since it occurs only in one of these four pieces. See sung audiences responses in examples 1 and 2.

Melodrama (Accompanied Speech)

Melodrama, the musicological term for spoken text with musical accompaniment, is another distinctive feature of the Lehrstück that supports a claim to musical, anti-opera status. Accompanied speech had in fact been a popular feature of the Singspiel and of German Romantic opera, but it did not survive the nineteenth-century transition to music drama. Composers incorporated melodrama into some unstaged pieces at the turn of the century, such as Schoenberg's *Gurrelieder*. The phenomenon of accompanied speech, and even rhythmic and pitched speech, was also familiar to audiences from the popular melodramas cultivated as middle-brow culture near the turn of the century.[58] After *Pierrot Lunaire* (1912), melodrama was revived for the stage in modernist pieces such as Berg's *Wozzeck* (1923) and *Lulu* (begun in 1927) and Stravinsky's neoclassical *Histoire du soldat* (1918). Accompanied speech became part of the anti-opera stance because it so clearly undermined the melodic and singerly excess of opera.

Both *Lindbergh Flight* and *Lehrstück* contain brief instances of the simplest type of melodrama, in which occasional spoken lines are delivered over music. *He Who Says Yes* has no accompanied speech, and *The Decision* contains several prominent sections of melodrama that run the gamut of pre-*Pierrot* accompanied speech possibilities. These works include largely unaccompanied spoken dialogue punctuated by chords at the ends of lines or at specific points in the text. For example, Number 2a of *The Decision* is called "recitative," but in fact no singing occurs; instead, three comrades converse as a unit with the fourth, each line punctuated by a three-chord motive in the orchestra. Another type of melodrama is rhythmic speech, in which the rhythms are precisely indicated, the text is aligned as in sung music, but there is no assigned pitch. This is typically accompanied, and the speaker synchronizes her speech with the rhythms the orchestra plays.

Perhaps the most distinctive aspect of *The Decision* is its several pieces of rhythmic speech for the chorus. These range from the brief unaccompanied phrases that affirm the comrades' decision at the ends of scenarios, to the speech choruses accompanied by steady, eighth-note drumming, to rhythmic spoken interjections in otherwise sung choral movements. The effect of the chorus speaking together rhythmically as a collective, accompanied only by drums, is particularly powerful. The speaking choruses became strongly associated with the Lehrstücke and with agitprop performances, and would also become a topic of debate under the Third Reich, when they were incor-

Example 3.   Eisler, *The Decision* Number 3b: mm. 1–10

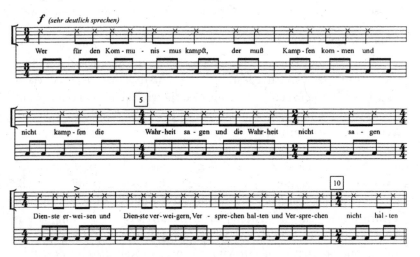

porated into the *Thingspiel* ("a form of mass outdoor performance, a historical story framed by a trial, planned in the early years of the Third Reich as the Nazis' distinctive, monumental theater form"). National Socialist Propaganda Minister Joseph Goebbels recognized the choruses' persuasive power and, "fearful that audiences would find the religious and socialist associations in the speaking choruses too appealing, ordered a nationwide ban on them."[59] See the rhythmic speech chorus in example 3.

Allusions to Religious Genres and Rituals

The uncanny resemblance the Lehrstück bears to the oratorio is another way in which the genre can be construed as anti-opera. The role of the chorus, reliance upon narrative, near-static staging, and tendency to promote ideology are all standard features of the oratorio. In fact, many early reviewers described *The Decision* as an oratorio long before Eisler revealed that he and Brecht had used Bach's *St. John Passion* as a model,[60] and at least one critic anticipated the elevation of the party to atheistic religion when he wrote that communism was to Brecht as Catholicism had been to the Romantics.[61] The oratorio has historically been the sacred, unstaged counterpart to opera, and now the Lehrstück appropriated the oratorio's most distinctive features (chorus, narrative text, and static staging) to mark it as the opera's participatory, and therefore populist, activist alternative.

The oratorio genre raises the specter of religion and its significance for

Brecht. An avowed atheist who subjected religion to scathing critique in many instances, he nevertheless retained an intellectual curiosity about organized religions and a literary interest in the Bible.[62] His religious education had been extensive, and familiarity with the catechism manifested itself in the theater in references to the rituals of liturgy. The Lehrstück's roots in function and form are ritualistic, running to catechistic instruction and the Christian oratorio respectively in the blasphemous manner he had already established with his *Hauspostille*.[63] Hinton has noted that the generic designation "Lehrstück" carries deliberate and provocative religious connotations, acting as "a didactically motivated supplement to the *Hauptstücke* (main elements) of the Catechism."[64] He also finds that within the texts "the diction and the structure of *Lehrstück* are redolent of catechistic teachings, not just in the interrogative style but also in the inductive method of investigation. . . . Sacred means (underscored by Hindemith's sparse polyphonic choral style) serve highly profane ends."[65] Needless to say, the significance of music in those rituals would not have been lost on Brecht.

The primary functions of the music in the Lehrstück—to order its structure and facilitate communal participation—become apparent in the demands the music makes on the chorus. Not only is this true in the dramatic sense, meaning that the chorus articulates structure through narration and through its recurring presence as a frame to delineate acts and sections; it is also true in the symbolic sense. Choral music literally organizes a crowd into a collective, transforming a motley assortment of individuals singing different parts into either a sophisticated organism capable of performing as many as four polyphonic tasks simultaneously or a strong unison in which the individuals speak as one. The first is the symbolic musical manifestation of a complex machine with all parts working in harmony, and the second gives sonic form to ideological uniformity and agreement. Even when the chorus does not play a character per se, it represents the collective wisdom, the larger ideological force that counters and corrects the whims of individuals. The chorus provides structure for the individual singers just as musical form orders the genre as a whole. More so than in earlier Lehrstücke, the choir in *The Decision* is a descendant of the *turba* in Bach's Passions because its identity changes depending on the situation.[66]

Critics for whom the right to self-determinacy is sacrosanct recoil in horror at the choir's penchant for assimilation through annihilation of the individual, and it would be difficult to deny that that is a crucial aspect of all ·but *Lindbergh Flight*. It is a point effectively made by the choruses, and raised a problem that Brecht and Eisler recognized but were unable to solve:

These choruses not only facilitated mass participation but also tended to have a quasireligious effect that was highly emotional and difficult to manage, and this effect could easily lead to an unthinking mob mentality.[67] In short, choruses could generate both the desired result and its opposite. A chorus teaches dialectical thought because it enacts and facilitates the conflict between the short-sighted, emotional self-interest of the individual and the greater good of society (or the party), but in reality, there is no guarantee that the will of the mob necessarily reflects the greater good of society when it is singing. Regardless, the music imposes order on an otherwise loosely structured genre because it is the means whereby the collective takes the form of a chorus. This cannot be approximated or re-created simply through reading the plays or staging them any more than an opera is realized by reading the libretto or blocking the action. The Lehrstück requires the music, particularly the chorus, to concretize the lesson.

OPERA, THE ANTI-LEHRSTÜCK

Conditions in the volatile Weimar Republic were ripe for the innovative Lehrstück as an alternative to opera and its audience contract, but even so, Brecht continued trying to rehabilitate the corrupted opera genre from within. The two operas he wrote with Kurt Weill, *Threepenny Opera* and *The Rise and Fall of the City of Mahagonny*, are so much more familiar than their Lehrstück counterparts that brief synopses are sufficient for our purposes. Elisabeth Hauptmann translated John Gay's *The Beggar's Opera* in the winter of 1927–28, and Brecht pitched an adaptation of it to the impresario Ernst Josef Aufricht for production at the Theater am Schiffbauerdamm. Weill retained only one song from Johann Christoph Pepusch's original score (number 3) and composed entirely new music for the rest of the text. The libretto was also considerably different from Gay's and, as with the Lehrstücke libretti, continued to be revised long after the 1928 premiere. The revision Brecht published in his collected works in January 1932 was prepared without Weill and includes substantial changes.[68] His essay "Notes to the *Threepenny Opera*" was written at the same time and is therefore more accurately understood as a commentary on the most recent edition of the libretto and his emerging ideas about epic theater than as a commentary on the collaborative piece he had written with Weill three years earlier.

Despite its official subtitle as "a play with music," Brecht and Weill both described *Threepenny Opera* as the opera prototype.[69] It consists mostly of solo songs connected with spoken dialogue, and each act culminates in an ensemble finale. The tone of "Notes" reflects a backlash against the tremendous popularity of Weill's *Threepenny* music and the precipitous decline in the collaborators' personal relationship. (The final straw would come during Berlin *Mahagonny* rehearsals in December 1931; their last piece, *The Seven Deadly Sins*, was completed long distance in 1933 and with minimal interaction.) In "Notes" Brecht downplayed the significance of the music, but their opera prototype nonetheless provided the pretext for a discussion of epic theater performance practice and the audience contract.

Brecht and Weill's second opera collaboration was *The Rise and Fall of the City of Mahagonny* (1930), which grew out of their 1927 Songspiel *Mahagonny*. This piece is considerably less song-oriented than either *Threepenny* or its hybrid Songspiel progenitor, as it features continuous music and recitative, albeit in closed forms interrupted by placards and other production devices, but no speech. Thanks to the changing sociopolitical situation in Germany and increasing tensions between the playwright and the composer, the opera was problematic from the start. Despite having committed to premiere the work, Otto Klemperer of the Kroll Oper rejected it, citing the depravity of the libretto, and this became a recurring theme in the text's early reception. Virtually every production demanded cuts, beginning with the scandalous premiere in the Neues Theater in Leipzig, and a much-truncated version was finally staged in Berlin in 1931 at the Theater am Kurfürstendamm, once again under the auspices of Aufricht. The text Brecht published in *Versuch* in 1930 is not identical to the libretto for which Weill composed the score, and the accompanying "Notes," written with Peter Suhrkamp, are appended to this text rather than to the composed version.[70] Therefore I begin with "Notes on the Opera *Mahagonny*," as its publication preceded "Notes to the *Threepenny Opera*."

Epic Theater in "Notes on the Opera 'Mahagonny'"

Brecht's and Weill's views diverged on many aspects of this opera, and the composer had recently published several essays about *Mahagonny* to which Brecht now apparently felt compelled to respond.[71] "Notes on the Opera *Mahagonny*" began as a screed against the institution and art form of opera and became the blueprint for epic theater and its audience contract. The description of epic theater is couched in both operatic and anti-operatic terms, a reflection of Brecht's simultaneous immersion in both opera and Lehrstück. His wide-ranging critique of opera in this essay can be distilled to a renunciation of the way in which the opera treats its spectating audience, particularly where the music is concerned. The operatic apparatus, or culture industry, serves its own needs by reproducing the society that facilitates its survival and gains the complicity of that society by drugging its citizens.[72] That sedation comes courtesy of the music, which aids and abets the apparatus in insidious ways:

> The opera *Mahagonny* pays conscious tribute to the senselessness of the operatic form. The irrationality of opera lies in the fact that rational elements are employed, solid reality is aimed at, but at the same time it is all washed out by the music. A dying man is real. If at the same time he sings we are translated to the sphere of the irrational. (If the audience sang at the sight of him the case would be different.) The more unreal and unclear the music can make the reality . . . the more pleasurable the whole process becomes: the pleasure grows in proportion to the degree of unreality.[73]

This paragraph warrants scrutiny because it makes several claims for music's culpability that subsequently determine its use in epic theater. First, music is the agent of irrationality in opera. Weill had written something similar in 1929: "In *Die Dreigroschenoper*, which we designated from the beginning as the prototype of opera, the music again assumes its irrational role: it interrupts the plot when the action has arrived at a situation that permits music and song to appear."[74] The implication is that the genre otherwise might be rational and realistic, but the power of music negates that simply by its presence. Brecht's concept of epic theater differs from Walter Benjamin's in significant ways, but this position is related to Benjamin's statement about the orchestra pit in his essay on epic theater: "What is at stake today in the theater can be articulated better in relation to the stage than to the drama. It is a matter of covering up the orchestra pit."[75] The pit is the physical space that separates the audience from the stage, demarcating the real space from the theatrical one. Covering the pit bridges the gap that is the hallmark of the theater tradition Brecht inherited and rejected, but Benjamin's remark also contains the seeds of distrust in music as well. The orchestra pit needs to be covered and muted as a means of defense, because the siren song of music originates therein. (For Wagner the orchestra was part of the apparatus that ruined the illusion and needed to be hidden beneath the stage.)

Second, Brecht reasons that music transforms reality into unreality, and the amount of pleasure experienced by an audience member is determined by the degree of unreality; the more music, the more irrational the situation becomes, and the more pleasurable. The word he uses for pleasure is *Genuß*, with its connotations of hedonism and excessive indulgence, rather than *Freude* or *Vergnügen*.[76] It is a particular *kind* of pleasure, then, one akin to narcosis. If that argument is carried to its next logical step, Brecht is implying that the music is the source of this kind of pleasure. He invokes the quintessential operatic moment of a character dying onstage yet continuing to sing in full voice to the bitter end, and the accompanying parenthetical remark hints at the role he is theorizing for music in the epic theater. Because the audience does not, in fact, spontaneously burst into song at the sight of a dying man onstage, the fact that the dying man continues to sing *should* make that moment strange. In the opera it doesn't, presumably because the wash of continuous music, the excess of narcotic, has dulled the audience's senses. But in a music theater work in which the music is mostly limited to song-sized doses in the context of speech, music *could* have the effect of making strange. For the critical audience, music should become a marker of the unreal.

Third, Brecht argues elsewhere in the essay for the separation of the elements because the *Gesamtkunstwerk*, Wagner's total work of art, was also guilty of bewitching the audience,[77] and he assigns music a particular role in this process: "The process of fusion extends to the spectator, who gets thrown into the melting pot too and becomes a passive (suffering) part of the total work of art. Witchcraft of this sort must of course be fought against. Whatever is intended to produce hypnosis, is likely to induce sordid intoxication, or creates fog, has got to be given up."[78] If music is the irrational force that corrupts an otherwise realistic art form because it renders the whole genre unreal, it stands to reason that music is also the active ingredient in the alchemy that produces the (con)fusion of Gesamtkunstwerk. Separation is necessary to guard against music's tendency to dominate the rest of the text as well as the audience (this by intoxication or anesthetization), but Brecht does not take the draconian measure of banishing it from the epic theater. The act of quarantine acknowledges the danger, but controlled retention of the musical element admits its efficacy. As in *Threepenny Opera* (and with the exception only of the *Mahagonny* opera, which was an attempt to take "opera" as the subject of an opera and exploit its culinary nature), epic theater then confined music almost exclusively to the song: small doses, attached to Brecht's own lyrics, as opposed to the continuous, beguiling euphony of the music drama.

The concentration of music in individual songs may have appealed to Brecht as anti-operatic because he equated all opera with the continuous music of the music drama, but Weill welcomed the number format as a return to pre-Wagnerian opera. He recognized its advantages for a composer since it freed him from "the ungrateful duty of supplying the background for the incidents of the stage, of sustaining the plot."[79] Stephen Hinton, Kim Kowalke, Christoph Nieder, and Mário Vieira de Carvalho have each noted that many of Brecht's anti–music drama innovations bear a striking resemblance to pre-Wagnerian opera, particularly baroque opera seria (three-act structure, six principal characters, ensembles confined to act finales).[80] The most significant similarity is the central role assigned to the song, which is equivalent in prominence to that of the aria in opera seria. The song format, independent of the connective tissue of recitative, allowed the order of musical numbers to be changed, and their narrative character permitted substitutions and reassignment of numbers to different characters.

The song has a formal function in the epic work that is similar to that of the aria in opera seria, but it is employed toward a different dramatic end. Vieira de Carvalho describes the baroque opera seria aria as a highly stylized formula that exhibited detachment and self-control via the socially acceptable manner in which characters presented a single stereotyped emotion, or affect. This began to change during the Enlightenment, when opera was liberated from strict forms by flexible music that gave the impression of being natural and facilitated what was supposed to be a more spontaneous and genuine expression. However, the effort to render onstage the perfect illusion, artifice as nature, resulted in opera productions that were ever more complex, as seen in Wagner's operas. "Thus, what was at stake in the middle-class alternative was not taking off or discarding the mask, but rather making it cling more closely and imperceptibly to the face."[81] The exhibition of emotion in song was not Brecht's goal, but he did employ the number-opera form to call attention to the social masks to which people had grown so accustomed that they were no longer aware of their presence, either on themselves or on others. Song is a prime vehicle for estrangement because the music does double duty in this context: It renders that moment in the play strange, because it is irrational for a character who has otherwise been speaking to burst into song; and that moment in the play renders the music strange, because it reveals the ways in which the audience is constantly manipulated in a regular opera-going experience.

Given Brecht's distrust of music's maleficence, the new responsibilities with which it was now entrusted for epic theater ("the music communicates," "sets forth the text," "takes the text for granted," "takes up a position," "gives the attitude") were intended to limit its efficacy by forbidding its traditional work of intoxication, but Weill did not experience this as restrictive.[82] He understood this mode of composition to be the means by which music was reinstated as the primary element of the opera and to which the text was subservient.[83] The age-old duel between librettist and composer ended in a draw: Each believed that epic theater ensured the primacy of his own medium.

"Notes to 'Threepenny Opera'"

Published a year later, "Notes to *Threepenny Opera*" focused on performance practice and audience attitude in the epic theater audience contract, some aspects of which are likewise indebted to pre-Wagnerian opera, particularly baroque opera seria. Aspects of Brecht's performance practice mark a return to that aesthetic of staging and acting, as Kowalke notes: "The singer was expected to bow to the spectators in the loges, smile at the orchestra and the other players, walk about the stage, complain to his friends that he was not in voice, and usually exit after the completion of the aria. The aria . . . was directed not to his colleagues on stage but to the audience."[84] Similarly, Brecht wrote that a performer getting ready to deliver a song is helped "if he is allowed to make visual preparation for it (by straightening a chair perhaps or making himself up, etc.)."[85] This should prevent undue emoting in song: "In no case therefore should singing take place where words are prevented by an excess of feeling."[86]

Likewise, the behavior of the opera seria audience can be seen as a forerunner of Brecht's epic theater audience. Members ate, drank, talked, and played cards throughout, turning their attention to the stage only when favorite singers delivered arias. Such detachment, if not outright disinterest, would render didactic messages moot, but it does suggest an audience in control of its faculties. Their behavior reminds one of Brecht's famous edict that a spectating audience member should adopt an attitude of "smoking-and-watching. Such an attitude on his part at once compels a better and clearer performance as it is hopeless to try to 'carry away' any man who is smoking and accordingly pretty well occupied with himself."[87] This is a far cry from the manipulated, anesthetized audience Brecht associated with opera and moves the audience closer to that which he imagined for the Lehrstück.

Brecht's performance practice theory for singing, however, could hardly be less indebted to opera. Whether intended to protect the spectating audience member from the seduction of the singing voice as a vehicle for music[88] or to minimize Weill's contribution to the wildly successful *Threepenny Opera*, these comments have resulted in the substantial demusicalization of Brecht's stage texts in performance.[89] He made two remarks in particular that have engendered a tradition whereby actor-singers feel obligated or liberated to completely disregard the musical setting in favor of speech or to recompose melodies as desired: "[The performer] must not follow [the melody] blindly"; and "there is a kind of speaking-against-the-music which can have strong effects, the results of a stubborn, incorruptible sobriety which is independent of music and rhythm." These comments are often invoked to justify practices that disregard the fact that the actors who created these roles were also trained as singers. It could almost be balanced with Brecht's next line—"If he drops into the melody it must be an event; the actor can emphasize it by plainly showing the pleasure which the melody gives him"—if "if" were not such a strong qualifier.[90]

CONCLUSIONS

It has been argued that Brecht's simultaneous work on both Lehrstücke and opera generated the structure, performance practice, and audience experience of epic theater for the fundamental purpose of a new audience contract, and music was essential to that project. Reinstating the role of music in the inception of epic theater, arguably Brecht's most influential bequest, raises several questions. The purpose of the new audience contract was to break with the opera tradition Brecht had inherited, and yet these components remain tethered to both pre-Wagnerian opera and to music drama. Furthermore, Brecht assumed a one-to-one correlation between spoken theater and opera, as if the presence of music were the only difference between the two, but he failed to recognize that "non-Aristotelian dramaturgy, a sign of modernity in plays, appears in opera . . . as a piece of tradition."[91] In other words, Brecht's bold anti-Aristotelianism has limited power on the opera stage because that space was never Aristotelian in the first place. Historically, opera plots do not observe the unities of time, place, and action; they routinely feature illogical stories and nonlinear development, partly as a function of musical time. Singing takes longer than speech, even without excessive ornamentation and melismas, and additional instrumental music expands performance duration exponentially, so that time constraints prohibit the inclusion of all the requisite Aristotelian connections. It also means that audiences of operas that predate the music drama are accustomed to the lurches in dramatic tempo that are the inevitable by-product of alternating recitative and aria. Opera audiences are essentially inured to such formal devices from long overexposure and are well accustomed to compensating for missing dramatic links.

Given its long tradition of epic properties, then, opera was a logical place for Brecht to find effects for epic theater. According to Vera Stegmann, "The theory of epic theater inevitably becomes a theory of epic music theater," and Ernst Schumacher noted, "Epic theater in the Brechtian sense was only conceivable as musical theater," but one can venture even further.[92] While Brecht advocated the "epic-ization" of opera by bringing that genre up to the level of theater, in many respects pre-Wagner opera was already at that level. Because music drama was a reaction against the then-prevailing style of opera, Brecht's response to music drama resulted in a return to its predecessor and even shared some elements with music drama indirectly. One might ultimately observe the opposite, which is to say that epic theater represents the "opera-ticization" of the theater.

Epic theater emerged from the negotiation between innovation (writing Lehrstücke, pieces that required no audience whatsoever) and renovation (rehabilitating the opera), during which two different roles for music emerged, both pertaining to the audience: structural and communal for the Lehrstück because it was participatory, and as means of gestus and estrangement in the epic opera for its spectating audience. The new contract meant that the apparatus—the impresario, the librettist, the composer, or the actor-singer—no longer dictated audience response because participants were emancipated to behave as self-actualizing entities. It permits and facilitates an independent, conscious, critical response from audiences unaccustomed to being in that position.

The contract is predicated upon several unspoken conditions, however, that, once examined, call the whole deal into question. Among them is the assumption that a critical attitude will necessarily yield the "appropriate reaction," that is, one that is consistent with Brecht's social and political message. The implication is that audiences will agree with the Brechtian perspective once they are sufficiently educated and skilled in the ways of critical detachment, but then they are in fact only "free" to the extent that they would have agreed with him anyway, had they known enough or otherwise been able to do so. Other preconditions suggest a certain naïveté about human nature, such as the assumption that critical detachment will result in reassessment and a change of attitude, when it may only reaffirm the benefits of the status quo. Finally, it assumes that people need to, want to, and *will* change, if given sufficient motive and opportunity.

Is the audience free to reject such epic machinations, just as the new contract freed them to resist operatic manipulation?[93] The contract gives spectating audience members permission to use their social X-ray vision, but does it permit them to train those sights on Brecht? Presumably the answer would be yes, that in fact it is even unnecessary because the plays are transparent, all the means of production are visible, and there is no hidden agenda. And yet there most certainly *is* an agenda, as Nicola Chiaromonte has noted: "Brecht's dice are loaded and are meant to be."[94] Do such texts in fact open up possibilities for subjectivity, or do they coerce the audience with a roll of the loaded dialectical dice? If audiences *choose* to resist or to "misunderstand," refuse to abide by the snake eyes they invariably roll, or decline to roll the dice at all, indulging instead in the hedonistic pleasure *(Genuß)* of music or humor, has the contract been fulfilled? What happens when the audience genuinely reclaims its right to self-determination in all situations, including the experience of epic theater? Perhaps such an event would signal the arrival of utopia and the irrelevance of Brecht's theater project, but in the meantime, his plays can feel every bit as manipulative as the Wagnerian theatricality he rejected. The liberation of the audience to formulate a critical response suggests that the contract was actually intended for engagement with opera or other bourgeois theater rather than for performances of Brecht's own epic pieces.[95]

2 The Operatic Roots of Gestus in 'The Mother' and 'Round Heads and Pointed Heads'

The tectonic plates of Brecht's life underwent a fundamental shift in the 1930s, as the familiarity of Weimar-era Berlin declined into the uncertainty of exile. This shift precipitated change in every area of his work: in primary musical collaborator, from Kurt Weill to Hanns Eisler; in generic concentration, from Lehrstück and opera to plays designed for audiences; in audience, from like-minded thinkers to uninformed, passive spectators; and in performers, from the politically astute amateur to the traditionally trained professional. Because Brecht's theory and his implementation of it changed with and responded to his circumstances, his writings in this period, as in any other, belong to a particular historical moment and constitute his response to it.[1] This historical moment was singularly significant for the development of the notion of gestus. Brecht had been accustomed to exercising considerable control over his productions, but from here on he would no longer be assured of personal involvement or of performers and audiences who understood the method, the message, its realization, or its critical reception. These changing conditions resulted in the playwright's granting of a privileged status to music when theorizing gestus for the plays of this period.

Nascent notions of gestus coalesced in theoretical writings attached to the stage projects dating from the twilight of the Weimar Republic and the early years of exile, during which time his circumstances necessitated a certain pragmatism.[2] *The Mother* (1932) and *Round Heads and Pointed Heads* (1936), both written with Hanns Eisler, are examined here for three primary reasons: One or both collaborators explicitly identified the music in these pieces as gestic; one or both encouraged performers to seek appropriate gests in the music of those plays; and the shows were written for different audiences and thus feature different musical styles, offering a wide variety of musical manifestations of gests. Particularly after the ill-fated New York pro-

43

duction of *The Mother* by the Theatre Union in 1935, Brecht lauded Eisler's music as a corrective to inaccurate performance practice.[3] The rhythm, melody, and style of a character's music are fixed in the notated score in a way that pacing, inflection, and characterization cannot be fixed in the libretto. Pointing prospective directors and performers toward the music as the bearer of gestus was intended to ensure more appropriate interpretations of his work. Gestus remained a function of the body, but the emphasis shifted away from the visual body in space (moving and stationary) and toward the sounding body in time. Facilitating productions in absentia occasioned a reorientation away from the showing body and toward the auditory one because the score can exercise a kind of authority over temporal performance practice that the written word cannot, but the ease with which Brecht apparently ceded so much to music at a particularly unstable time merits a closer look.

My analysis of *The Mother, Round Heads and Pointed Heads*, and their attendant theoretical writings will not merely demonstrate that one branch of the gestus family tree is musical; I will argue that the whole genus can be traced to operatic ancestors.[4] To that end, I propose a reconceptualization that theorizes its operatic heritage and privileges its temporal, musical dimension in the sounding body.[5] I will show that the by-product of situating the gestus in the musical score, therefore requiring a sounding body for realization, is that the body produces the voice-object in the process, a phenomenon that dominates all else on stage and resists containment via the gestus.

First, however, there is the thorny matter of the definition and genesis of gestus, perhaps the slipperiest term associated with Brecht's epic theory.[6] Gests are stylized behaviors designed to reveal the socially constructed nature of human interaction, and the theory emanates from Brecht's rejection of the bourgeois notion of split subjectivity.[7] Externalizing everything once understood as internal in order to reveal its social construction requires a body, and at its most fundamental, both gestus and its relative *Haltung*, or "attitude" (Brecht himself did not consistently distinguish between the two), emanate from the body.[8] Brecht chose the term "gestus," which was first introduced by the philosopher, critic, and dramatist Gotthold Ephraim Lessing (1729–1781) in a 1767 critique of actors in Hamburg. Lessing castigated those whose hand motions were excessive, as if pantomiming, and too generalized to be meaningful. As a remedy he prescribed the "individualizing gestus," specific, distinct, and meaningful, apart from *"Geste"* or *"Gebärde,"* both established German terms for gesture.[9] Lessing's original use of the "semi-technical term gestus" clearly refers to a specific, deliberate motion.[10] Furthermore, unlike the word *"Gebärde,"* "gestus" evokes and even invites associations with the explicitly physical *"Geste."* The description of gests as "stylized behaviors" obviously has its origins in the definition of gesture, "a movement of the head or body to convey an idea or meaning"; the additional criteria imposed upon it, meaning the social significance of that meaning or its precise stylization, constitute its gestic quality. Peter Ferran's summation of the term is instructive: "However abstract, the meaning of gestus contains these essentials: social behavior; attitudinal perspective; demonstrative enactment."[11]

STYLIZED GESTURE IN THE NINETEENTH CENTURY

Of course the emphasis on stylized gesture did not originate with Brecht. Like other aspects of modernism that rebelled against naturalism, it had been standard stage practice in the first half of the nineteenth century. One strand of its development appears to have been highly musicalized from the start. The system of codified stage movements developed by François Delsarte (1811–71), uncle of Georges Bizet and a singer with the Paris Opéra-Comique, was immensely influential. Delsarte believed that the proper motion generated the desired emotion in an actor, rather than vice versa, and to that end he developed an extensive gestural repertoire appropriate for all emotional situations.[12] Émile Jaques-Dalcroze (1865–1950), the father of the eurhythmic approach to music education, had studied Delsarte's method and in 1906 published his own set of rhythmic gymnastic·exercises.[13] He too was first trained as a musician, in this case as a composer. He studied with Gabriel Fauré, Léo Delibes, Anton Bruckner, and Johann Nepomuk Fuchs, served as professor of harmony at the Geneva Conservatory, and produced over two dozen musical theater pieces in various genres (pageants, operas, operettas, and *saynètes*—the French translation of a Spanish term generally applied to short, farcical productions). His work with the Swiss theatrical designer Adolphe Appia at Hellerau led to a Russian tour in 1912, which included demonstrations and lectures at the state theater in Saint Petersburg.[14] There, Vsevolod Meyerhold incorporated eurhythmics into his actor training program, and Brecht's debt to that Russian director, particularly with regard to the notion of gestus, is well documented.[15] Prompted by the fact that the Ballets Russes trained at the Dalcroze Institute at Hellerau before it premiered *The Rite of Spring* in 1913, Daniel Albright has persuasively argued for Dalcroze as a founding father of modernism because he represents "the modernist urge to restore corporeality to art."[16] That is to say, Dalcroze's work represents the recuperation of a corporeality that had characterized prenaturalist art, as in Delsarte's method, with which Dalcroze was quite familiar.

Brecht's concept of gestus, fundamentally grounded in the body and essential to his epic theater project, is another manifestation of this modernist agenda. The prenaturalist gestural style does not reappear on the epic stage unfiltered; now gests must socially signify, and they are designed at least in part to achieve estrangement. They mediate the spectator's experience so that events onstage cannot be viewed as real, or the performer conflated with the character. Nevertheless, the appearance of stylized if not outright choreographed gestures was characteristic of earlier nineteenth-century performance practices against which naturalism had rebelled and to which modernism subsequently returned.

The moving body is closely associated with music and rhythm in the theories of gesture put forth by Delsarte and Dalcroze, both professionally trained musicians working at the more musical end of the theater spectrum. Delsarte's training technique focused on the synchronization of body and voice. Dalcroze described his movement technique as "living plastic" and thought that it could, "in the absence of sound, manifest every attribute of music: he dreamed of 'a scale of gestures' exactly comparable to the diatonic scale, and thought the lines traced in space by the twirling or running body could be described as legato or staccato."[17] He proposed multiple functions for the ideal music: It would be determined by an intimate knowledge of physiology and muscle contraction; it should not only accompany but should be capable of eliciting and sustaining gestures; and it should be able to act as counterpoint to the bodies.[18] Elsewhere the primacy of rhythm to Dalcroze's project is consistently highlighted. Weill's own description of musical gestus recalls some of this rhythmic emphasis, and while no direct link can be established, one wonders if the training Lotte Lenya received in the Dalcroze method in Zurich in 1914 was a contributing factor to Weill's own formulation. Even though Brecht's understanding of gestus eventually extended beyond the actors' bodies to include other elements of production, it never lost the primacy of the corporeal.[19]

As discussed in the introduction and chapter 1, there are numerous points of contact between Brecht and Wagner; ambivalence about the triangulation of music, gesture, and the body is another. Parsing their theories is complicated because both artists succeeded in imposing closed systems of theory and art, perpetuated by scholarly obeisance, in which the explication of each man's art is based upon his theoretical writings and, conversely, the legitimization of his theory upon his art, despite notoriously unruly and contradictory evidence. Rather than ignoring these inconsistencies, however, or attempting to force congruence where none exists, one can mine them for clarification. Mary Ann Smart demonstrates this with regard to Wagner's ambivalence about the relationship between music, gesture, and the body: "While Wagner's writings famously contradict and obscure his musical practice, those contradictions themselves are rich sources of meaning, pointing to a continuous engagement with gestural music, even as Wagner remained undecided about whether physical gesture was properly the premise or the result of musical expression."[20] Brecht's gestus and Wagner's gestural music are both indebted to the nineteenth-century operatic stage practice of mimesis, and the essence of the playwright's dilemma in the 1930s can be described in the same terms Smart uses for Wagner's ambivalence, that is, whether gestus was "properly the premise or the result of musical expression." This is because both artists proceed from the assumption that music carries meaning that can be communicated to an audience.[21] As a basic tenet of nineteenth-century German Romanticism, Wagner's adherence to it is unremarkable, but Brecht's is less expected. This assumption is inherent in Weill's discussion of gestus and then in Brecht's when he emphasized music for its realization in the mid-1930s, yet the scholarly literature proceeds from this premise without interrogation.[22] Given this quintessentially Romantic presupposition underlying Brecht's modernist theater, then, it should not surprise that his theorizing of music and the body should bear some familial resemblance to Wagner's.

BRECHT, WEILL, AND GESTUS

The playwright's first reference to gestus by name appears in a footnote to the oft-quoted "Notes" appended to the final version of the libretto for *The Rise and Fall of the City of Mahagonny* in 1930, which postdated Weill's musical setting.[23] The note is attached to this text: "The intention was that a certain unreality, irrationality, and lack of seriousness should be introduced at the right moment, and so strike with a double meaning." The rather obtuse footnote attached to it reads in part: "This limited aim did not stop us from introducing the element of instruction, and from basing everything on the gest."[24] The note does not elucidate much, but the fact that it is attached to the line "so strike with a double meaning" hints at the significance of the nontautological aspect of gestus. The exegesis of that somewhat opaque footnote put forth by eminent Brecht scholar John Willett has become the standard: "Gestus, of which gestisch is the adjective, means both gist and gesture; an attitude or a single aspect of an attitude, expressible in words or actions."[25] Willett chose "gest," an obsolete English word meaning "bearing, carriage, mien," to which might be added "deportment."[26]

Willett then invoked Weill's description of the term in his interpretation of Brecht's reference: "Weill introduces the term thus: "Music, he says, is particularly important for the theatre because 'it can reproduce the gestus that illustrates the incident on the stage; it can even create a kind of basic gestus (Grundgestus), forcing the action into a particular attitude that excludes all doubt and misunderstanding about the incident in question.' "[27] In subsequent references by other scholars, this summary is further augmented to incorporate the social aspect noted above but is otherwise virtually universal as a point of departure.[28] If the word "gesture" implies motion, then Willett's choice of the word "gest" connotes stasis: Bearing, mien, deportment, and carriage refer to attitudes or ways of being as well as ways of moving. This may be interpreted as an elision of the concept of gestus with that of Haltung, a mutational definition consistent with Brecht's own inconsistent use of the terms, and one that reinforces their shared genealogy. It also emphasizes the attitude which produces a word or action in addition to the word or action that is the manifestation of that attitude. It is helpful to understand the reference to "gist" not in the generalized, colloquial sense but in the legal sense, which is "the point on which an action rests," as in the grounds for action in a suit. In that context, gist is the "essential ground or object . . . without which there is no cause of action."[29] Gestus thus encompasses gist and gest—both stasis and motion.

WEILL, BUSONI, AND GESTUS

When revisiting the genesis of gestus with an eye toward its operatic antecedents, several noteworthy points emerge. Brecht's first published reference to gestus, meaning not only the concept but also a direct reference to it by that name, appears in conjunction with *The Rise and Fall of the City of Mahagonny*, a piece that is unequivocally an opera. Second, in the absence of explicit evidence from the playwright, Willett allowed Weill's exegesis of gestic music to stand in for Brecht's definition of gestus in general. While the likelihood that Weill's definition was one Brecht would have invoked publicly or verbatim cannot be ascertained, the fact that gestus appears to have emerged from their immensely fruitful collaboration facilitates this slippage, and the symbiotic nature of their collaboration precludes a parsing of each participant's precise contribution. In the final analysis, mounting evidence of an operatic tributary confirms Willett's inclination to substitute Weill's explanation in the absence of one from Brecht.[30]

Kim Kowalke's assessment, that gestus was the concept that mediated the relationship between Brecht and Weill, could also be emended to read that Busoni mediated that relationship. Busoni, Weill, and Wagner constituted the operatic foundation of the epic theater project.[31] This is true regarding notions of both physical and musical gesture and the function of music in relationship to action on the stage. In his 1916 expanded edition of *Sketch of a New Aesthetic in Music* (*Entwurf einer neuen Ästhetik der Tonkunst*), Busoni had written, "The greater part of modern theatre music suffers from the mistake of seeking to repeat the scenes passing on the stage. . . . which is not only a needless and feebler repetition, but likewise a failure to perform [the composer's] true function."[32] The notion that music should be able to provide commentary and its own perspective on text is a familiar Brecht mantra, and he is known to have owned Busoni's *Sketch*.[33]

Fritz Hennenberg argues that Weill was receptive to Brecht's epic theater because it resonated so completely with Busoni's operatic perspective.[34] In a 1926 essay about the renewal of operatic form in Busoni's *Faust*, Weill engaged in a polemical endorsement of Busoni's view that music should furnish a commentary for the events on the stage rather than simply reiterate them.[35] Given the high esteem in which Weill held his teacher, whose "love belonged entirely to opera,"[36] it is no surprise that establishing a reputation in opera was a priority for the student. Weill wrote extensively about the state and fate of contemporary opera and pointed in 1928 with optimism to his epic theater work with Brecht, noting, "The gestic character of music is the most important result of my work thus far."[37]

Hennenberg has also written that Busoni's theory of *Schlagwort* anticipated Brecht's gestus.[38] In his 1921 article "Sketch of a Foreword to the Score of *Doctor Faust*, Including a Few Thoughts on the Possibilities of Opera," Busoni advocated on behalf of the *Schlagwort*, or "catchphrase," for opera; it is also translated as "abridgment." As opposed to the verbose libretto of the music drama, Busoni preferred a succinct text that allows the music to expand and does not seek to explain everything verbally. It is essential in nature, with nothing superfluous, and "can sum up the inner part of the text of an opera." Furthermore, "it can be transferred in a changed form to the action in general." He cites as an example of a visual abridgment the entrance of a rival suitor, whose costume, bearing, and actions identify him as a nobleman and whose advantages in the competition for a lady's hand will be deduced immediately by the audience without any verbal explanation.[39] The abridgment is a form of communication in lieu of text. That Busoni's example draws on the symbols of class status makes the affinity with Brecht's gestus all the more apparent. The composer promoted abridgment as a means of minimizing the libretto to gain more space for music in the opera production, which would not have been the playwright's motivation, but the device is the same.

The Weill explanation Willett cited in his commentary comes from the

most thorough published airing of the subject by anyone in the Brecht circle during Brecht's lifetime, including the playwright himself. Weill published "Concerning the Gestic Character of Music" in *Die Musik* in March
1929. Despite numerous ambiguities and apparent contradictions in the practical realization of gestus, this essay remains a Janus-faced landmark in the
theoretical literature. Its essential ideas are found in the work of both Busoni
and Brecht: Gestus reveals the essential social relationship of one character
to another rather than internalized, psychological states; it is rooted in
rhythm;[40] and musical gestus communicates a meaning other than or in
addition to that of the literary text, often via the Song (with a capital S).[41]
Weill and Brecht had each used the English word "Song" to denote a genre
quite distinct from the lied, one with popular, cabaret, even crass stylistic
allusions. Weill cited "Alabama Song" as the model for gestic music in this
article, suggesting that the Song genre had a particular capacity for gests. The
penultimate sentence of the essay is noteworthy for its bold assertion of the
indispensability of music for the epic project, which was, at its core, about the
human condition as socially constructed: "But for the theatrical form that
aims at saying something about mankind music is indispensable because of
its capacity for fixing the gestus and elucidating the action."[42]

Willett's conflation is perceptive, even if it is superficially problematized
by Brecht's statements about gestus near the end of his collaboration with
Weill. Brecht wrote and published "Notes to the *Threepenny Opera*" after
the play and published it in 1931, three years after the opera's premiere and
one year after the notes for *Mahagonny*. A crucial distinction between the
composer's notion of gestus and that of the playwright emerged in the
Threepenny notes. For Weill, the gestus resided in the musical text, and for
Brecht, it resided in the performer who realizes the work onstage. Weill
understood gestus as situated in the music and fixed in the setting of the
lyrics, first in rhythm ("music has the capacity to notate the accents of language, the distribution of short and long syllables, and above all, pauses"),
and then in the creative deployment of "the essential means of musical
expression—the formal, melodic and harmonic construction."[43] As the composer, Weill determined the gestus of a scene and character and thus dictated
performance ("Music has the potential to define the basic tone and fundamental gestus of an event to the extent that at least an incorrect interpretation will be avoided, while it still allows the actor abundant opportunity for
deployment of his own individuality of style"). Not surprisingly, he interpreted gestus as a means of ensuring the primacy of music in musical theater by asserting its independence from the text (*"Naturally gestic music is
in no way bound to a text,"* emphasis in the original).[44]

By contrast, Brecht situated gestic realization in the performer's body in performance practices that minimized the musical setting and took the literary text as a point of departure for actors' choices in the rendering of words, music, and movement. His directions in "Notes to the *Threepenny Opera*" are among the most quoted performance instructions in all the literature: "The actor must not only sing, but show a man singing. . . . His aim is . . . to show gestures that are so to speak the habits and usage of the body." His remarks about the actors' treatment of the songs may have exerted the most authority over the realization and ultimate reification of the so-called Brechtian performance practice: "As for the melody, it must not be followed blindly: there is a kind of speaking-against-the-music which can have strong effects, the results of a stubborn, incorruptible sobriety which is independent of music and rhythm. If he drops into the melody it must be an event."[45]

"If" one deigns to sing the melody appears calibrated to counter the composer's assertion that gestus resided in his songs.[46] Regardless of motivation, Brecht entrusted the performer with considerable responsibility in the creation and communication of gests on the stage. This was an investment he could afford to make in Berlin in 1931 because conditions were still conducive to his project; he had access to the performers and audiences for which his plays were written. These instructions have become synonymous with Brechtian performance practice in part because they are attached to his most popular piece, but ahistorical interpretation and uncritical application to his entire oeuvre has given rise to a performance practice in which actors freely ignore all aspects of the music, barking lines over the orchestra without regard for melody and frequently disregarding rhythm, tempo, dynamics, and phrasing as well. Contentious relationship aside, the evidence that Brecht was singularly concerned with the music for his plays renders the normalization of such an extreme performance practice specious at best. His understanding of gestus naturally reflected his own training and current priorities, as did Weill's, but these differences did not preclude their successful collaboration. The major discrepancy—the situating of gestus in the text or in the performer—gained renewed significance and urgency in the mid-1930s, at which point Brecht was apparently more inclined to accept the composer's locus of gestus in the text, and even more specifically in the music.

WAGNER AND MIMESIS

At first glance Wagner appears a far less likely source of gestic impulse, except as the negative example against which Brecht rebelled. The course of Wagner's operatic career is typically described as a progression from outer to inner drama, with a turning point at about 1870. This move away from the primacy of the visual, the physical gesture, and the body toward the interior and the metaphysical is lauded as one of his greatest achievements.[47] However, in her work on mimetic music in nineteenth-century opera, Mary Ann Smart reminds readers of the enduring significance of gesture and the body for Wagner:

> The word "gesture" (Gebärde) meant much to Wagner; it echoes through his theoretical writings, employed as an amulet against the excesses of contemporary French and Italian opera, with their "undramatic" indulgence in vocal ornament and melodic pleasure for its own sake. For Wagner the reformer, gesture was the generative kernel from which both melody and speech rhythm should grow, as well as the crucial link to ancient Greek drama, in which (as some nineteenth-century thinkers imagined) music, word, and gesture had been perfectly fused. Wagner was less willing to acknowledge the importance of gesture in the musical conception of his own operas. For the most part musicological commentators have obediently followed suit, allowing physical movement an important role only in the early operas, after which the visible is understood to be sublimated into quasi-linguistic leitmotivic systems and mythical allegory.[48]

At the heart of her argument lies an unduly neglected line of criticism in Nietzsche's famous *Nietzsche contra Wagner* of 1888, the recuperation of which refocuses her perception of Wagner's music. By the time Nietzsche wrote that Wagner was "essentially a man of the theater and an actor, the most enthusiastic mimomaniac, perhaps, who ever existed,"[49] eighteen years had passed since the inception of the music drama, an operatic genre ostensibly interiorized and unconcerned with the physical exterior—that is, with gestures and the body. Yet even in the music dramas Nietzsche detected and mistrusted "Wagner's continuing attachment to an earlier model of gesture and stage movement, [his] affection for extended pantomime scenes and . . . frequent reliance on small-scale coordination between music and gesture."[50] In the face of claims to a new, superior operatic genre that transcended the physical plane, Nietzsche faulted the music drama for its retention of the literal, choreographic relationship between music and gesture that had animated opera in the first half of the nineteenth century.

Nietzsche's complaints also provide a link to Brecht: "If it was Wagner's theory that 'the drama is the end, the music is always a mere means,' his *practice* was always, from beginning to end, 'the pose is the end; the drama, also the music, is always merely its means.' . . . the Wagnerian drama, a mere occasion for many interesting poses!"[51] Smart notes that the word translated as "pose" is *"Attitüde"* in the original German, an elevated term meaning "posture," and clarifies that it refers not to sustained held positions but to "all stagings that emphasized external appearances at the expense of true (Dionysian) spontaneity."[52] First, Brecht's preferred term "Haltung" is frequently given as a synonym for *"Attitüde."* Second, Nietzsche's dismissal of Wagnerian drama as nothing more than an excuse for "many interesting poses" connotes a series of discrete, atomized, stylized gestures or actions, which, except for the criterion of social significance, may be understood as analogous to gests. Finally, the absence of heat-of-the-moment spontaneity in favor of deliberate stylization is an essential component of Brechtian theatrical performance. The fatal, anachronistic flaw Nietzsche identified in music dramas, then, is among the pre-Wagnerian operatic virtues recovered for the epic theater: the primacy of the body in stylized positions and movements. If Wagner considered gesture to be the "generative kernel from which both melody and speech rhythm should grow," then the moving, posing bodies onstage can be understood to evince or even create the music, to conjure it forth from the orchestra. Smart notes that the music in the first scene of *Die Walküre* (1856–70) "can be heard as generated by the gestures it accompanies."[53]

According to Brecht in the mid-1930s, the music generated the gestus, but the primacy given to the performers' visual bodies in motion and stasis remains relevant. His improvisatory rehearsals constituted a lab in which gests were tried on, revised, discarded, perfected; ideally, performances consisted of isolated, socially signifying, stylized physical events that were intended to be read as such. When precomposed music is present (as opposed to improvisatory music), such calculated if not outright choreographed movements are apt to be perceived as mimesis. It may even have had something of the effect of the early synchronized film score to it, as film was a medium that fascinated Brecht and Weill in this period. This is precisely the context in which "Nietzsche worried that Wagner's emphasis on movement and on music yoked to movement was manipulative" because it exerted an irresistible pull on the unsuspecting audience.[54] As part of the modernist agenda to recover the body, any linking of movement to music in the epic theater would have had the opposite effect: The overt self-consciousness of such synchronicity was a means of estrangement. A mimetic relationship between music and the performing body would thus tie Brecht to earlier nineteenth-century, pre-Wagnerian opera as an anti-Wagner gesture. Paradoxically, however, if Nietzsche's instincts were correct, it also tied Brecht, almost certainly unwittingly, directly to the contradictions inherent in the music drama.

GESTUS AND EISLER'S MUSIC

If Brecht's initial conception of gestus was one of corporeality in the form of the showing body, his reconsideration of that concept in the mid-1930s entailed a shift emphasizing the sounding body. The revision was dictated by contemporaneous production needs pertaining to *The Mother* (1932) and *Round Heads and Pointed Heads* (1936) and facilitated by the operatic origins outlined above. The relocation of primary residence from the moving body in live performance to the fixed, notated musical score did not eliminate the body; the gestus is inherent in the music but requires the performer's realization via her sounding body. Unlike the writings examined above, which privileged the contradictory musical setting to generate multiple meanings, Brecht's pragmatic writings of the mid-1930s explicitly admit different types of gestic music. These two plays demonstrate very different means of fulfilling the requirements of epic theater, determined by the interrelated demands of their respective genres, performers, and audiences. One style, exemplified by the score for *The Mother*, features a rather more traditional relationship between text and music in which the music reinforces or conveys the same meaning as the text. The other is the more famous contradictory text-music relationship described in Brecht's and Weill's earlier writings and clearly evident in the Songs of *Round Heads and Pointed Heads*.

A musical setting augments the literary text, either by reinforcing it or by contradicting it, and thus defines the gestus for the actor and for the audience. It contains information about a character's attitude that the actor uses to develop that role beyond what is presented in the written text, while the style of music the actor performs reveals the character's attitude to the audience. An actor can glean much about a character from the libretto, but its delivery and therefore its interpretation necessarily leave much to the performer's discretion: pacing, emphasis, rhythm, volume, general tone, and mood, not to mention movement and posture. An effective musical setting is definitive because many elements that reveal the attitude are set by the notation. Music as performed by an ensemble is a temporal art and must move in a uniform fashion, if it is to make aural sense. Because those fixed elements are not as susceptible to (mis)interpretation, the gestus becomes transparent in the songs.

At the local level, attitude is established via rhythm, meter, and melody because those elements determine the pacing, word stress, and declamation of text delivery. Volume also contributes to emphasis. The composer thus determines which words are brought to the fore and which recede through the means of metric placement, note duration, pitch, relative dynamic level, and repetition or lack thereof. General tone and mood are established via the more abstract "musical style," which is bound up with matters of instrumentation, references to familiar genres and traditions, quotations, tempo, and mode (major, minor, or modal). It has been noted that Brecht ascribed to musical style socially signifying meaning, as did Eisler. If exegesis is to serve any useful function, one cannot simply refuse to engage because proof that music is in fact capable of carrying extramusical meaning remains elusive. From a purely pragmatic perspective, and Brecht was nothing if not pragmatic, actors need to glean utilitarian information from the score and the libretto for the work of character construction.

The meaning for contemporary actors and audiences is almost certainly not what it was when Brecht and Eisler wrote these pieces. Furthermore it is plausible, if not likely, that no performer has ever performed nor any audience ever perceived the meanings of these texts quite the way Brecht and Eisler envisioned them; nevertheless relevance demands interpretation.[55] It is possible and even imperative to address historical context, however, and to use intertextual readings to determine effective performance practice. Therefore these interpretations are not put forth as definitive but as suggestions for a historically informed performance practice. A skilled composer can deploy musical style as symbolic shorthand, an efficient route to character delineation and audience comprehension that trades on stereotypes, assumptions, and the conventions of a particular time and place, just as opera composers have always done. Eisler had certain compositional proclivities that he parlayed into gests for both parallel musical settings and contradictory ones: metric irregularity, the use of stylistic allusions and quotations (his own music and others'), and inconclusive song endings. Because the evolution of theory was a pragmatic response to performance in each case, I begin with the plays and their musical settings before examining theory and critiques in the secondary literature.

'The Mother'

Eisler initially composed nine songs for Brecht's adaptation of Gorki's novel *The Mother* in the fall of 1931, and these were performed when the show premiered at the Komödienhaus am Schiffbauerdamm in Berlin on 17 January 1932; it subsequently underwent numerous revisions.[56] The title character, Pelegea Vlassova, a poor woman who is initially afraid for her son because of his involvement in revolutionary politics but is won over to the cause and becomes one of its staunchest and most effective advocates, even after her son is put to death for his activism. *The Mother* was written for a

Example 4.   Eisler, the "Mother" motif in "The Torn Jacket," from *The Mother:* m. 3

mixed group of performers comprising both professional actors and amateur agitprop performers and was specifically aimed at the working class. Eisler's task was to create music appropriate for this ensemble and meaningful to a proletarian audience.

The show is unified musically by a recurring melodic motif, variants of which figure prominently in five of the nine songs. Fred Fischbach has dubbed it the "mother motif" and traces it beyond this piece to opus 33, "Four Cradle Songs for Working Mothers" (1932), in which it is especially prominent in numbers 2 and 4.[57] The two pieces are linked by time, place, subject matter, and motive, a constellation of connections lending credence to Fischbach's argument that the motive somehow became associated with the figure of the proletarian mother for Eisler. In the staged piece it appears even in songs not sung by or about her, however, so it is not merely a reminiscence motif associated with the title character. Its appeal is primarily musical: It is simple, memorable, singable, easily transposed, susceptible to sequential treatment, metrically mutable, and amenable to different harmonizations. In other words, it is a catchy tune. The arch-shaped melodic contour is also conducive to Eisler's pronounced preference for minor and Phrygian modes. See the "mother motif" in example 4.

The presence of some professionals in the ensemble may account for the numerous substantive solos for singing voice. The first is "In Praise of Communism," performed by the title character when she encounters some workers who say they have been told that communism is a crime.[58] The title and lyrics suggest a rousing paean in Eisler's patented *Kampflieder* style, but in a rare contradictory musical reading in this piece, Eisler's setting is instead lyrical and understated. The song is in the key of F minor, the dynamics are soft, and the accompaniment is initially quite sparse. The piano repeats chords throughout, the trumpet and trombone alternately double the vocal line, and the drum appears only in the contrasting middle section. In the concluding segment, the trumpet doubles the melody while the trombone imitates them at the rhythmic interval of two beats and the pitch interval of a fourth below. The mother motif is the primary building block of the melody.

In this instance, Eisler's use of metric irregularity accommodates the rhythm of Brecht's unmeasured text. Portions are set almost as recitative,

Example 5. Eisler, "In Praise of Communism," from *The Mother:* mm. 1–8

with great attention to word stress, particularly in the B section. The distinctive rhythmic feature of the melody is its anacrusis setting, in which phrases begin on upbeats, most often on the "and" of one. If he had set it in the more obvious *Kampflied* style, support for the communist cause would be asserted with confident downbeat strokes in a march style, probably sung by a chorus. Here, the song is performed by a soloist; it is predominantly triple time; and it is rhythmically less insistent than settings of comparable texts. The text in the excerpt in example 5 is "It stands to reason, anyone can grasp it. It's not hard./If you're no exploiter then you must understand it./ It is good for you, find out what it really means."[59]

At least two dimensions of gestus can be discerned in a musical setting: that which the audience understands on first contact, usually in terms of musical style; and that which is discrete, which actors use for their studied performances. The musical style, meaning the total effect of the elements listed above, effectively conveys a message, and in this case the style is understated, perhaps unexpectedly so. The performer can pinpoint specific musical gests to clarify the appropriate attitude, which is that understanding communism is *"leicht,"* or easy, as well as vitally important. An actor conveys this not only by singing the song without undue fanfare but also by preserving its austerity, which is to say adhering closely to the notation to foreground its many repetitions of basic rhythmic and melodic patterns without slipping into pedantry or condescension. The contrapuntal accompaniment in the final section of the song evokes the learned mien of the baroque, lending a certain weight to the plain, repetitive vocal part and communicating that the simple message is also serious.

The lengthy instrumental prelude and postlude to another song, "In Praise of the Vlassovas," would later provide the basis for the play's overture. It is in the style of a Bach invention, drawing once again on the baroque stylistic allusion to connote learnedness; that Eisler studied Bach as inspiration for *The Mother* is both evident and well documented.[60] The trumpet and trombone are in imitation while the piano moves in perpetual eighth notes, a pattern evocative of the frenetic bicycle music he composed for the film *Kuhle Wampe*. The most distinctive feature of this piece is its combination of counterpoint with speech; the chorus speaks rhythmically in unison throughout. This may be a concession to the limits of the original chorus members and possibly a Lehrstück remnant from *The Decision*, but it is also a fascinating juxtaposition of contradictory styles. The baroque instrumental filigree, at once both complex and delicate, is interwoven with forceful, unison speech. The song commands two symbols of power: education (the musical style) and class unity (unison speech). The recourse to melodrama is more than just a simplification of musical means for untrained performers; it constitutes sonic proof that the workers are capable of appropriating that erudite framework for purposes of the revolution while retaining their working-class identity. Unison speech—the absence of singing—is the most important social gestus for the performer, while the audience is likely to be struck by its combination with the anachronistic baroque texture. The text of the excerpt from "In Praise of the Vlassovas" in example 6 reads, "All those Vlassovas of all countries, in their mole-burrows/Unknown soldiers who serve the Revolution/We can't do without them!"[61]

Perhaps the best evidence that epic theater does not preclude emotion is "Eulogy," the song in which workers report to Pelagea Vlassova that her son, Pavel, has been killed. The choir sings in unison throughout. The melody leaves no question that the workers and the mother are grief stricken, but the poignant music chafes against the lyrics. Brecht's text

Example 6. Eisler, "In Praise of the Vlassovas," from *The Mother:* mm. 40–46

recounts the connection between the victim and the workers who had produced the instruments of his destruction (those who built the wall against which he stood before the firing squad, the throngs who worked at the factories to make the chains, rifles, and bullets used against him) but says very little about Pavel; in that regard it does not read like a eulogy.

The tension between this abstract, impersonal text and Eisler's musical setting is palpable. Eisler cautions against wallowing in the musical pathos with the admonition "moving, don't drag," and he effectively thwarts the temptation with an unexpected conclusion to the musical tension generated in the harmonic progression at measures 11–19. Again he alludes to the baroque in the imitative counterpoint between trumpet and trombone, inverting and modifying the main melodic motif introduced by the choir in its initial a cappella entrance. The markers of a funeral march are invoked: steady march beat, trombone and drum, the minor mode. The recurring musical refrain comprises three iterations of the mother motif in long, steady note values. The irregular meter nevertheless retains its steady half-note beat throughout so that the pulse never varies. The text of "Eulogy" excerpted in example 7 reads, "But he saw them crowded full / with that huge throng, whose numbers had always grown / and still grew."[62]

The lessons learned from performances of *The Mother* are evident in "On the Use of Music in an Epic Theatre," which Brecht wrote after his visit to the United States in 1935. The now mythically disastrous production of *The Mother* mounted by Theatre Union that year was a valuable learning experience. According to Brecht, the American workers' dream of class mobility was incongruent with the aims of the German workers' movement; the American working class had no real tradition of radical political theater; and the Theatre Union was run by middle-class intellectuals who gave workers what they thought they needed rather than what they might have wanted.[63] In other words, the situation lacked nearly all the preconditions necessary for a successful production of *The Mother*. Given the many ways in which Brecht believed even a well-intentioned company had missed the mark, he sought to minimize future misunderstandings by instructing potential directors and performers to seek gests in the music. He also clarified that more than one type of music can be gestic, describing Eisler's score for *The Mother* as both non-Song *and* supremely gestic. He deliberately referred to "In Praise of Learning" as a "piece" *(Stück)*, and "In Praise of the Dialectic" as a "final chorus" *(Schlußchor)*, noting that the former "is infected by the music with a heroic yet naturally cheerful gest." The score for *The Mother* could not contradict its text in a satirical manner because of the nature of its original audience and performers. Brecht wrote, "If you imagine that the severe, yet delicate and rational gest conveyed by this music is unsuitable for a mass movement which has to face uninhibited force, oppression and exploitation, then you have misunderstood an important aspect of this fight."[64]

Brecht's discussion of *The Mother* specified that gests were found in the music but acknowledged that their realization is dependent upon the actors: "It is, however, clear that the effectiveness of this kind of music largely

Example 7.   Eisler, "Eulogy," from *The Mother:* mm. 66–73

depends on the way in which it is performed. If the actors do not start by getting hold of the right gest then there is little hope that they will be able to carry out their task of stimulating a particular approach in the spectator."[65] This suggests two things: If the gestus is located in the score and the actors recognize it, then the music animates the actors by generating appropriate physical motions and poses, which is a corollary to Nietzsche's Wagnerian mimesis. However, "the way in which it is performed" also implicates the sounding body in the form of singing, and this is the noteworthy shift in emphasis. Locating the gest in the notated score still requires realization via the performer's body, but now it is particularly via the *sounding* body.

Eisler's writings about *The Mother* are limited to his critique of the New York production, in which his concept of gestus is consistent with Brecht's. His notes complement those Brecht wrote for the communist journal *New Masses* in 1935 but presumably never published,[66] and, predictably, he is explicitly concerned with the musical shortcomings of the production. Eisler's essay was intended for publication in the *Daily Worker,* but there is no evidence that it ever appeared in print, either. (This is hardly surprising, since it would have been poor publicity indeed for the American Left to acknowledge that its efforts to promote the work of two of its most admired German artists had been deemed ineffective and misguided.) He noted that his music was not appropriate for the conventional uses of musical theater (singing and dancing, as in musical comedy, and emphasizing and illustrating the drama), implying that it had been interpreted as such. Eisler's first concern was not for the sanctity of his score but rather that "an artistically wrong presentation of the music leads, strangely enough, to serious political errors," and he cited two instances in which the Theatre Union's inappropriate staging interfered with the political message of the songs. He asserted that "music of the type written for *Mother* . . . is meant to force the interpreters into a certain attitude, a certain gesture."[67]

A list of performance practice problems that obfuscated the message suggests that the performers had not hewn closely enough to the performance instructions or to the notation: "Singing without sentimentality or pathos, coldness of recitation without dryness, exact understanding of the tempo, the avoiding of accelerandos and ritenutos where they are not marked. The differences between various ways of playing such as portamento and non legato, light staccato, etc."[68] Inadequate musical performance resulted in the transmission of misinformation to the audience, who in turn misunderstood the political message, and that produced a situation with potentially dire consequences. The list of performance transgressions also confirms that Eisler meant for the music to be sung. The manner in which the performers sang was problematic, but he did not propose to resolve that with speech instead.

'Round Heads and Pointed Heads'

Round Heads and Pointed Heads was written under quite different circumstances than those which gave rise to *The Mother*. Brecht began working with Weill, who referred to the project as an operetta,[69] and then continued with Eisler, who later exaggerated its musical component when he referred to it as an opera.[70] The first version of the text, which began as an adaptation of Shakespeare's *Measure for Measure*,[71] was completed in 1932 and did not indicate that Brecht planned to incorporate music, at least not on the scale to which it was eventually scored. Eisler assisted Brecht and Margarete Steffin on the piece while on the Danish isle of Fyn in 1934, and he wrote songs for it there and in Paris that year. Erwin Ratz completed a piano reduction by September, and they hoped to publish the play with the score but had to abandon that plan for financial reasons. Brecht continued to revise the play, and Eisler wrote two additional songs before it finally premiered in Copenhagen in November 1936; the final version of the play was published in 1938 in the second volume of Brecht's *Gesammelte Werke*.

By this time the concurrent rise of the Nazi Party had persuaded Brecht to transform the text into an avowedly, and explicitly, antifascist piece.[72] Its themes of fascist demagogy and racist politics were clearly topical, as was his interpretation of the Nazis' rise to power: The theory that big business was behind Hitler's success and exploited racial tension as a smokescreen to conceal a corporate economic agenda enjoyed considerable currency in the early to mid-1930s, although history has since proven it woefully inaccurate. The play does not refer to the Nazis by name, either as a party or as individuals, but the analogy is so transparent that it discourages performance now. Despite the fact that Brecht frequently revised his own texts years after the fact, he never reworked this play according to the historical evidence, relegating the play and its songs to relative obscurity.[73]

Eisler's skill for establishing gestus through metric irregularity is evident in "Lied der Nanna" from scene 2, which takes place in a brothel. In this, her entrance aria, Nanna recounts her initiation into prostitution. The prostitute was a favorite character for Brecht because her commodification was a literal manifestation of capitalist exploitation. Brecht's text is strophic with its refrain in three verses, and Eisler's setting conforms to that structure. The text for verse 1 is as follows:

> There was I, with sixteen summers
> Prenticed in the trade of love
> Ready to take on all comers.
> Nasty things occurred
> Frequently I'd heard
> Even so I found it rather rough.
> (After all, I'm not an animal, you know.)[74]

Brecht's verses are presented in groupings of three lines in verses 1 and 2, and four lines in verse 3, followed by a full stop (period or colon), and in each case Eisler's meter thwarts the full stop through enjambment. The ten-measure verse is metered as follows: 4/4, 2/4, 4/4, 2/4, 4/4, 2/4, 3/4, 3/4, 4/4, and 4/4. In each verse the full stop in the text occurs without repose in a bar of 2/4 or 3/4. The text alone leaves open the possibility that an actor may interpret these lines as self-pity, but if the performers adhere strictly to the meter, that reading is precluded by the propulsion of shortened, irregular measures. The temptation is to round off each bar to four beats for a square, leisurely reading, but as written, the meter permits no dead space in which to wallow in sentimentality. Eisler employs rhythm and meter to help the performer recognize the character's situation and convey it accurately to the audience.

Gestic musical citation is masterfully exemplified in Madame Cornamontis's song "Kuppellied" ("Panderer's Song") from scene 9. She has been trying to teach the aristocrat Isabella the skills of prostitution so that she may sleep with a man who holds her brother's fate in his hands and thus save his life. Isabella is hopelessly inexperienced, and it is decided that the prostitute Nanna will take her place, if Isabella will pay her for the service.

Isabella asks, "She'd be willing to do that for money?" To which the madame replies, "More than willing. Cash is an aphrodisiac." Each of the two verses consists of two sections, four lines followed by a group of nine.

"PANDERER'S SONG" (VERSE 1 AND REFRAIN)

Oh, they say to see the red moon shining
On the waters causes girls to fall
And they'll talk about a woman pining
For some lovely man. But not at all!
    If you want to know what makes them swoon.
    It's his chequebook, not the moon.
    Try to look at it in this light:
    Decent girls won't take to bed
    Any gent whose wad is tight
    But they can be very loving
    If a fellow sees them right.
    It's a fact: cash makes you randy
    As I've learnt night after night.[75]

The first three and a half lines suggest a romantic sentimentality about the euphoria of infatuation, but the end of the fourth line abruptly veers off course: In modern times, nothing produces that sensation except cold, hard cash. Eisler uses stylistic allusion followed by outright citation, contradicting the text throughout.[76] For the romantic section he conjures a vulgar honky-tonk via instrumentation (clarinets, saxophone, trumpets, trombone, percussion, banjo, piano, and bass) and accompaniment pattern (oom-pah, stride-style bass movement underneath a syncopated, chromatic melody).[77] The stylistic allusion is shown in example 8.

But when the punch line is revealed in the lyrics, it is also revealed in the accompaniment: The famous love-death motif from *Tristan und Isolde* makes its appearance. Eisler reverses the juxtaposition of incompatible references found in the text, invoking the Wagnerian symbol of true love just as the text reveals that humanity's only true love is lucre. He cites the famous chord and rising half-step figure three times, in successively higher octaves, in the enharmonic equivalent of the first statement of Wagner's original (instead of $F-B-D\sharp-G\sharp$, it is spelled $F-C\flat-E\flat-A\flat$). Wagner's orchestration of this progression is confined to woodwinds, but Eisler's jazzy stage band ensemble begins with saxophone and trombone, adds wa-wa trumpet and clarinet, and culminates in the full wind complement. See the love-death quotation in example 9.

In a letter to Brecht, Eisler wrote of this song, "It owes its effect above all to the fact that the music is frightfully common and vulgar. It must be sung

Example 8. Eisler, "Panderer's Song," from *Round Heads:* mm. 1–9

Example 9. Eisler, "Panderer's Song," from *Round Heads:* mm. 14–19

by a fat, drunken old hag with remains of a Titianesque beauty. It is musically easy to sing, but difficult to interpret, and very free in tempo. . . . The only thing left to mention is that . . . I have used the main motif from Richard Wagner's *Tristan und Isolde* as an accompaniment, since one must always honor the masters where honor is due."[78] The Wagner quotation effectively defines the song. Certainly it reminds listeners that the idealized love of Tristan and Isolde also required a facilitator, albeit a potion rather than money. The elixir of sensuous harmonization cannot hide the fact that modern love is reserved for sex, power, and money.

Inconclusive songs may be open-ended in terms of rhythm, melody, and harmony. Of the sixteen songs in *Round Heads and Pointed Heads,* fully half can be said to exhibit this trait to a notable degree, as in scene 7, when a judge sings "Lied von der belebenden Wirkung des Geldes" ("Song of the Invigorating Effects of Money").[79] In the previous scene the judge and his courtroom had been quite shabby, but now, thanks to a change of regime, the judge is well dressed and his courtroom is being redecorated. He steps to the front of the stage and sings directly to the audience as the scene unfolds behind him. The text for each verse is divided into two sections, and Eisler sets the first as a quasi-recitative and the second in a perpetual mobile patter style. Example 10 shows the end of the song, which abruptly interrupts a sequential pattern and provides no rhythmic preparation for the fact that the relentless eighth notes will simply stop with a dotted half note on the downbeat.[80]

Similarly, in "Die Ballade vom Wasserrad" ("Ballad of the Waterwheel"), Nanna describes the wheel of fortune: Sometimes leaders are on top and sometimes on the bottom, but it is the little people like herself who do the work of the water, perpetually turning the wheel from underneath, and they always remain in that position. Brecht divided each verse into two sections; Eisler sets the first as a quasi-recitative, and the second is characterized by driving rhythmic propulsion. This time, however, the eighth notes simply stop—there is no downbeat, no ritard, and no preparation, as shown in example 11. The text of the excerpt reads, "If finally, with liberating strength, the water drives its own concerns."[81]

"Nanna's Song" is harmonically open-ended. The text of the refrain consists of four lines of ten syllables each, in which lines two and four rhyme. The musical setting observes this regularity in meter and rhythm, and the regular 4/4 of the refrain anticipates conclusion on a downbeat, but it ends instead on beat 4. This effect is tempered by the *poco pesante* marking, one of the few instances in which Eisler specifies any kind of resistance at the end of a song, and the real open-endedness is due to the harmonic progression in the refrain. The eight-bar refrain begins in the area of A♭, and after considerable harmonic wandering the last measure lands on C – E♮ – G – B♭ in first inversion, a major supertonic seventh in the key of B♭, which should resolve to the V (F). This chord also obscures the mediant/submediant relationship between the initial key area of the refrain, which is A♭ (I) and its dominant E♭ (V). The ambiguity is resolved when the refrain is followed by a return to the verse and its initial hint of F minor (in which the final chord of the refrain acts like a V7 chord), but its appearance at the end of the final refrain feels unfinished. The text reads, "Thank the Lord the whole thing's quickly over / All the loving and the sorrow, my dear. / Where are the teardrops you wept last evening? / Where are the snowfalls of yesteryear?"[82] The open-ended harmony is also appropriate for a text that ends in a question, as illustrated in example 12.

Example 10. Eisler, "Song of the Invigorating Effects of Money," from *Round Heads:* mm. 125–131

Example 11. Eisler, "Ballad of the Waterwheel," from *Round Heads:* mm. 90–95

Example 12. Eisler, "Nanna's Song," from *Round Heads:* mm. 17–21

The gest of open-endedness can signal indecision, ambivalence, or possibility for individual characters. Songs disrupt the experience of time because spoken dialogue and action are necessarily experienced as taking place in real time, while musical time, manipulated by tempo, meter, and rhythm, is experienced differently.[83] The performer must also *show* that she is in fact singing and that she is aware this has happened, thereby separating the performer from the character. All of this is possible, and effective, in epic theater in part because songs are typically finite; they have clear beginnings and endings that cut them off and distinguish them from what is happening around them in time (typically, spoken dialogue). But inconclusive songs impinge upon the play, and their open-endedness lingers into the next scene, perhaps as a residual question.

"On the Use of Music in an Epic Theater" also includes commentary on Eisler's songs for the final *Round Heads and Pointed Heads* score. He identified some excerpts as gestic Songs, noting that that play was addressed to a wider, more general public and thus "takes more account of purely entertainment considerations." The stylistic allusions to cabaret and operetta found in Songs would not have been meaningful for the audience of *The Mother* and were therefore reserved for pieces intended for a different demographic. In 1935 Brecht defined gestic music in conjunction with his retrospective discussion of Weill's Songs: "Gestic music is that music which allows *[ermöglicht]* the actor to exhibit certain basic gests on the stage. So-called 'cheap' music, particularly that of the cabaret and the operetta, has for some time been a sort of gestic music."[84] In this translation the verb *ermöglichen* is rendered as "to allow" but is perhaps more forcefully rendered as "to enable" or "to make something possible."

If appropriate music makes it possible for an actor to exhibit certain gests and that is one of the essential components of the epic theater, then it must be of far greater significance than it appeared to be in 1931, when Brecht advised performers that the melody was optional. Peter Ferran interprets the cabaret influence as primarily one of performance practice rather than musical style, but the cabaret also implies a particular type of music, what Brecht called "cheap" music, with its attendant instrumentation, rhythms, and catchy tunes.[85] Furthermore, some have interpreted these remarks to mean that only Songs are gestic,[86] but it is clear from his assessment of the non-Song music of *The Mother* that this is not necessarily true, although the Song genre did have a specific type of gestic quality. "Nanna's Song" and "Panderer's Song" from *Round Heads* are among Eisler's most popular pieces and were also the last two he composed for the play. When he sent them to Brecht, who was in rehearsal for the premiere in Copenhagen, the accompanying letter stated: "N.B.: don't let the actors speak too much in the songs. The singing brings the gestures with it and *makes it easier* for them" (emphasis in the original).[87]

Brecht's essay "On Gestic Music" dates from 1937, two years after the Theatre Union's production of *The Mother* and one year after the premiere of *Round Heads and Pointed Heads* in Copenhagen. That his lengthiest general discussion of gestus appears under such a heading lends further support to the argument that it has musical antecedents, but it is also rife with the type of contradictions Smart noted in Wagner. Furthermore, it is uncharacteristically abstract, as he provides no concrete examples from his own texts or anyone else's. (The hypothetical ode to Lenin may have referred to Eisler's cantata, but regardless he cited no specific excerpts from it.) The essay asserts that the social gest is one that allows conclusions to be drawn about the social circumstances and that the gest must be very specific to the person and situation in question; otherwise, freed from the restraints of imminent practical application, it is more theoretical, even fanciful, offering numerous memorable images (communists mourning, fascists striding over corpses) but no appropriate gests. And despite its title, it is not particularly focused on music. Brecht locates the gest in the music when he writes that a composer must set a social gest to adopt a political attitude in music, but the final paragraph places the responsibility once again on the performer: "A good way of judging a piece of music with a text is to try out the different attitudes or gests with which the performer ought to deliver the individual sections. . . . For this the most suitable gests are as common, vulgar, and banal as possible. In this way one can judge the political value of the musical score."[88] As in his critique of the Theatre Union's 1935 production of *The Mother*, this suggests that music generates the appropriate gests of motion and pose in the actor as a kind of mimesis, and while Brecht does not mention singing explicitly, no discussion of the performance of song can eliminate the act of vocal production entirely. This ambiguity—Is the gest situated in the score or in the performer?—can be summarized by paraphrasing the tension Smart identified in Wagner's writings: Is gestus more properly the premise (the notated score) or the result (the sounding body) of musical expression?

MUSIC IN CRITICAL MODELS OF GESTUS

Relocating gestus from the gesturing body to the score required a sounding body to make it audible. The modernist fixation on reinstating the corporeal was retained, but now the body was at least as much a sounding one as a showing one. This sounding body is the element most conspicuously absent from critical models of gestus. The gestus guides performance, thus ensuring appropriate interpretation. Once the gestus was situated in the musical score, however, even one as anti-Wagnerian as Eisler's, an additional consequence became possible: Its realization in the sounding body might produce the voice-object, a phenomenon that trumps all else—music, lyrics, drama, staging—and resists control via the gestus or any other means. Carolyn Abbate describes the voice-object as follows: "An attraction to opera means an attraction to singers' voices—this goes without saying. But there is also a radical autonomization of the human voice that occurs, in varying degrees, in all vocal music. The sound of the singing voice becomes, as it were, a 'voice-object' and the sole center for the listener's attention. That attention is thus drawn away from words, plot, character, and even the music as it resides in the orchestra, or music as formal gestures, or abstract shape."[89] Brecht attempted to suppress the voice-object through various performance instructions so that audience members would not succumb to its siren song, since opera's narcosis included not only the composer's music but also its manifestation via singers' performances. Efforts to neutralize the voice-object separated the music theater experience from that of the opera house, in which prima donnas continued to peddle the sonic dope Brecht so mistrusted, but, as Abbate points out, the source of the voice-object is not confined to the sounding body of the opera diva; it is present in all vocal music. The voice-object is as conspicuously absent from theorizing about music and gestus as it is overwhelmingly present in its praxis. In this section, I problematize common critical models of gestus by including music and extrapolating the role of the voice-object.

Variants of two general theories have exhibited staying power among scholars and performers. Rainer Nägele, Darko Suvin, and others who take the work of Walter Benjamin as their point of departure understand gestus as a manifestation of Haltung and the quintessential dialectic of motion and stasis, simultaneously both frame and interruption. Others, such as French theorist Patrice Pavis, understand gestus primarily as a means of estrangement, as that which divides the actor into character and performer for the audience. Silberman describes the resulting space between the two as the "emotional and intellectual space in which alternatives and possibilities develop."[90] Interjecting music into these models enriches their potential for multivalent interpretation.[91]

Suvin writes that Haltung involves "the two main elements of bodily involvement and use of dynamics," encompassing both action and position, or, as Nägele describes it, motion and stasis. It is "the union of a subject's body-orientation in spacetime and of that body's insertion into major societal 'flow of things.'"[92] Benjamin interpreted the interplay of motion and stasis slightly differently when he ascribed to gestus the property of being simultaneously both closed frame and interruption.[93] The interruption isolates, or frames, individual gests, and because these isolated gests are not smoothed out in the epic theater, they dispel the illusion of naturalness in everyday social life. Suvin's conflation of "spacetime" reminds readers that motion, action, position, and stasis are experienced not only in space but in time.

Given the association of gestus with corporeality and temporality, it is surprising that music has not figured more prominently in these analyses. After all, the singing body is clearly engaged in a demanding physical activity. Singers breathe visibly and audibly, and the spectator can see and hear that the fruit of her body's labors is the voice-object. To listen to music is to experience a particularly manipulated passage of time. Likewise, the physical body occupies space while the sounding body occupies time, thus the convergence of spacetime. It is not as simple as stating that the song functions as an interruption to the dramatic action of the play because, as Ferran has so rightly noted, during the song, the song *is* the action.[94] However, within the context of a predominantly spoken show, the appearance of song and of singing does disrupt the temporal experience. Song interrupts the passage of nonmusicalized time, with its unaccompanied, unmetered speech, and manipulates another, musicalized experience of time through the imposition of meter, rhythm, and tempo. Eisler's penchant for varieties of strophic settings also contributes to the sense of a caesura or stoppage. Thus song may be experienced simultaneously as both motion and stasis, as regulated musicalized action and nonmusicalized suspension, as the condensation of "the dialectic of both static rigidity and movement," which was Benjamin's definition of gestus.[95]

For Pavis, gestus generates estrangement. Its work at the juncture of theory and praxis, text and performance, is to split the actor into both character and performer. The audience may then recognize the constructedness of the social interaction onstage and, by extension, the protean nature of any social situation. "The gestus radically cleaves the performance into two blocks: the shown (the said) and the showing (the saying)."[96] The character is responsible for the "shown" (the said), and the performer is responsible for the "showing" (the saying). Gestus divides the "shown" from the "showing" and mediates between them.

In song, Pavis's shown becomes the sung, what I will call "that which is sung," and his showing becomes the singing, or "the act of singing." The text and music, which the composer and the author have dictated and over which they therefore have control, are the sung, or that which is sung; the singing, the act of singing, is entirely in the hands of the performer, and, despite theorizing the realization of this moment, neither poet nor composer have any meaningful control over it in performance. Brecht referred to the gestic split when he wrote, "The actor must not only sing but show a man singing."[97] Operating at the interface of that which is sung and the act of singing and dividing them from one another, gestus is simultaneously concerned with both that which is fixed via text and music—that which is sung—and that which can only be realized by the performer—the act of singing (see table 1). In other words, it is a theory of literary and musical composition in which librettist and composer assert their authority over texts, and it is a theory of live temporal performance over which those texts and their creators can exert no authority whatsoever in the performative moment.

The generic category of song has a function of reflexive estrangement that pertains regardless of the gests particular to any given piece. Estrangement in a song operates in two ways: The music makes strange that moment of the play, while the play makes strange that moment of music. The appearance of song calls attention to the unnaturalness of a person singing in the midst of nonmusical activity, reminiscent of the temporal manipulation discussed above, reminding spectators that this is a play and not reality (the music makes strange the play). At the same time, the sudden presence of song in an unexpected moment or manner (something other than a love song at a point in which audiences have come to expect one, or a love song that conveys unexpected sentiments) and the undeniable pleasure song brings after its absence triggers the recognition that one is easily manipulated by music in a traditional operatic or theatrical experience (the play makes strange the music). In addition to its suitability for reflexive estrangement, song splits the subject into the act of singing, a very different activity than the act of speaking that surrounds it, and that which is being sung, a very different product than the spoken word. The audience is hypersensitive to both, because the reflexive estrangement calls such attention to the song in this context.

The gestic split also has another, perhaps unintended, consequence: It produces the voice-object as that which is sung even more prominently than it produces text or melody as that which is sung. Kowalke interprets Brecht's attention to the details of sung performance as an effort to "reserve space within the song for his own poetic voice/persona and to dictate readings of his texts by both composer and performer."[98] In that case, Brecht

TABLE 1. *Gestic Split*

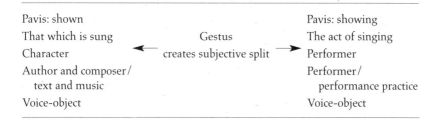

Pavis: shown		Pavis: showing
That which is sung	Gestus	The act of singing
Character	← creates subjective split →	Performer
Author and composer / text and music		Performer / performance practice
Voice-object		Voice-object

reinserted his presence into the act of singing to neutralize the voice-object, the result of the sounding body. Abbate's description of the voice-object as the "radical autonomization of the human voice" refers to its abstraction, a phenomenon separated from the music and the singer. Following Michel Poizat, Abbate distinguishes among a rational, text-oriented mode of vocalism (recitative); that of the voice-object; and a third level "at which either of the first two are breached by consciousness of the real performer, of witnessing a performance."[99]

For Poizat and Abbate, the third level refers primarily to moments of such extreme vocalism (or vocal distress) that the listener is roused from voice-object worship and, as if by the sudden reactivation of gravity, flung to earth in the realization that one is in fact witnessing a human performance. Brecht strove to create a related awareness with the gestus, since its split reminds the audience that the performer is not the character. The crucial difference is that, according to Brecht, the audience should not be brought to this awareness through the extraordinary beauty or athleticism of the voice-object or even the appearance of vocal difficulty; the awareness is to be induced via his literary text. The voice is a vehicle for the libretto. In that way, gestus reflects the literal authorial desire to animate the performer and dictate a performance mode that preserves this hierarchical relationship for the audience.

I would argue that once the voice-object is produced, however, the bargaining power of the literary author and his text are severely diminished. One is aware that an actor is singing because voice quality changes and the voice-object appears. The gestic split is not as simple as Pavis suggests, once the gestus appears in song rather than speech, motion, or stasis. The speaking voice is primarily a vehicle for information, but the fetishization of the singing voice-object in musical theater and opera, as theorized by Abbate, suggests that its ultimate function is quite different. The presence of a beau-

tiful tone could render an audience spellbound and anaesthetized. Furthermore, its presence signifies that the text, action, and music are mere pretense
for the existence of the voice-object. The split is then between the act of
singing and that which is *literally* sung (the voice-object), which the act of
singing produces, rather than between the act of singing and that which is
sung, meaning the text and melody the singer *re*produces. Since Brecht as
author occupies neither side of the split in the former configuration, efforts
to control the act of singing are calculated to insert his presence into that
which is sung.[100] He may have underestimated the voice-object, because it is
capable of simultaneously occupying both sides of the split. That which is
sung can be subsumed by the voice-object because it is literally and immediately "being sung" and is therefore more prominent than the text and
melody; it even serves to mediate the text and melody. The act of singing can
also be subsumed by the voice-object because it is the physical manifestation of that act.

Pavis later adapted his interpretation of gestus to respond to contemporary theories of the social function of corporeality[101] and acknowledged that
Brecht's "gestus runs the risk of suppressing the body,"[102] but his focus
remained on the showing, spatial body at the expense of the sounding, temporal one. In fact, when music is interjected into his model the danger is just
the opposite: The body's voice-object threatens to overwhelm the gestus.
The only way to know someone is singing is to hear the voice-object that
action produces; without its physical presence, there is no discernible act of
singing. In that case, no gestus-induced cleavage can trump the voice-object,
because it is capable of simultaneously dominating both sides of the divide.
The voice-object is able to do what Brecht attempted to do with his theory
of gestus, which is to occupy both halves of the split subjectivity. It can
supersede the text, music, and action of a piece, but, more important, it can
render the gestic split impotent: It may prevent the audience from experiencing estrangement because the separation of the performer from the character is irrelevant when both are subservient to the voice-object. As the literary author, Brecht has the least authority in this relationship. The
voice-object, while discrete from the music, requires music to become fully
realized, but it does not require text. On the other hand, the composer has
the advantage in this collaboration, although it is doubtful that Eisler would
have seen being used as a vehicle for the voice-object as advantageous. The
dominant element, the voice-object, requires the music and thus the composer; the text and its librettist are optional.

Pavis ultimately triangulated the gestus when he wrote that the work of
the actor and director seeking the desired gestus "has always to be comple-

mented by the spectator's own work, the spectator having the last word, i.e., the right to watch/control the playwright's 'view.' "[103] The work of the audience brings us once again to the contract between spectating audience members and the stage discussed in the previous chapter, but Pavis's conception of a strictly visually oriented audience omits music and voice-object, and, by extension, much of the work of the performer. As a result, a whole spectrum of the experiential performance-half of the gestic split remains untheorized. The tendency is to describe the gestus visually, as pertaining solely or primarily to the gest communicated physically and visually onstage via posture, movement, gesture, proximity to others, and location onstage, or literarily, when elements of plot, character, social status, and social relationships apparent or latent in Brecht's text and stage directions are mined for gestus that can then be translated to the physical-visual. But visual cues enacted onstage are multiplied or contradicted by aural cues that problematize the audience's work in perceiving the gestus.[104] The omission of the aural from the equation reflects an orientation in literature and theater for which words and images are paramount, but any theorizing that omits the music and the singing is necessarily incomplete. No matter. The operatic origins of gestus will out whenever the voice-object emerges and asserts its primacy.[105]

3 Fragments of Opera in American Exile

On 13 May 1941, Brecht and his small entourage left Helsinki, embarking upon a harrowing journey by rail and sea that traversed Siberia and the Pacific Ocean and finally deposited them at the port of San Pedro, California, on 21 July. Thus began a six-year stint in the United States during which his work was shaped by the exigencies of wartime, his status as an enemy alien, linguistic barriers, and financial crises. He was without his customary cohort of female intellectuals and coauthors whose contributions to his work and personal life had become indispensable: Margarete Steffin had succumbed to tuberculosis en route; Ruth Berlau moved to New York shortly after they arrived; and he would not cross paths with Elisabeth Hauptmann again for some time. Conditions required Brecht to generate an inordinate amount of correspondence for a man who had previously shown little predilection for letter writing. He wrote for commercial purposes to an extent unknown since the success of *Threepenny Opera* had catapulted him to celebrity status in Europe. His theory-oriented writing stopped almost entirely, presumably because he lacked access to a theater company to explore, test, revise, and prime his ideas.

Even so, his fundamental work habits remained virtually unchanged. He worked collaboratively, had several projects underway at all times, adapted to the structures available to him to some extent, and mined extant texts for material. In six years in the United States he wrote some fine poetry and three original plays (*The Visions of Simone Machard, Schweyk in the Second World War, The Caucasian Chalk Circle*); coauthored an adaptation (*The Duchess of Malfi*); revised *Galileo*; oversaw Eric Bentley's English translation of *Fear and Misery* as *The Private Life of the Master Race*; and contributed to the screenplay for *Hangmen Also Die*.[1] The dramatic projects were mostly conceived for mainstream venues. In addition to *Hangmen*,

Visions was also written with Hollywood in mind; he and Feuchtwanger sold the rights to MGM in February 1944. *Schweyk, Chalk Circle,* and *Duchess* were all written for Broadway, the latter as a showcase for the popular émigré actress and former member of the Brecht circle Elisabeth Bergner. Furthermore, virtually every dramatic piece on the list emanated from pre-existing material: *Visions, Chalk Circle,* and *Schweyk* were all derived from material with which Brecht had been engaged in Europe; *Galileo* and *Master Race* were his own plays; and *Duchess* was an adaptation of a play by another author (John Webster).

Interwoven and overlapping with the completed texts are at least seven unfinished projects he identified as operas at some stage in their development. (Roger Sessions also set an English translation of the radio play *Lucullus* as an opera during this time, but Brecht was not involved in the translation or the production.) All remained incomplete as operas, although *Schweyk* and *Good Person of Szechwan* eventually featured substantial scores by Eisler and Dessau, respectively. The other projects include six pages of notes for an opera based on his 1935 poem "Marie Sanders,"[2] a pitch to director Lewis Milestone for a film version of Offenbach's *The Tales of Hoffmann,* and the fragments examined in this chapter, all based on extant material.

The preponderance of previously existing material is typical of Brecht. It also highlights the importance of abandoned fragments, sketches, drafts, and notes as sources for new projects and suggests a model of his oeuvre as a complex web of interrelated texts irrespective of their state of completion or publication. The presence of seven exploratory opera fragments in this network of American exile texts is significant, because Brecht had already formulated a link between opera and Americana in the 1920s. He was one of several artists to recognize the rich potential for satire inherent in the combination of the opera genre (a marker of the highest, old-European culture) with the sights and sounds of the United States (the youngest, brashest, and, by many standards, least cultured of nations).[3] *The Rise and Fall of the City of Mahagonny* is saturated with the influence of Charlie Chaplin's masterpiece *The Gold Rush* and represents the culmination of that phenomenon. Mythologized themes of big cities, boxing, the Wild West, gangsters, miners, and lumberjacks informed much of Brecht's work in the 1910s and 1920s,[4] and interwoven among these published pieces are additional dramatic fragments designated as operas, such as *Prairie: Opera after Hamsun* and *The Man from Manhattan* (originally known as *Sodom and Gomorrah*).[5]

In this chapter I examine three unfinished operas as components of the network of texts from the American exile period, considering how Brecht viewed the opera-America complex once he was actually living in the United States. These fragments represent three modes of engagement with opera: revision of a completed text with the all–African American adaptation of *Threepenny Opera;* return to an abandoned fragment in the *Goliath* opera; and initiation of a new opera, derived from extant nonoperatic material, in *The Voyages of the God of Happiness.* In each case Brecht was working out more than operatic drafts, however. These opera projects were sites of exploration for issues such as race consciousness in the United States, the political and aesthetic ramifications of the Popular Front, and the viability of parable as a vehicle for antifascist drama.

BRECHT MEETS RACE IN THE UNITED STATES (1935)

The all-black adaptation of *Threepenny Opera* by Clarence Muse is the grail of the Brecht-Weill American period; it appears that no text survives, but the project is well documented in the diaries and correspondence of Brecht, Paul Robeson and his wife Eslanda, the actor Clarence Muse, Brecht's agent George Marton, and Weill.[6] Brecht was heavily invested in the plan, and with good reason. The original version had been Brecht's most successful theatrical project to date, so it made good business sense to bring it to the American market in an adaptation reflective of the most current production trends. The addition of race to the cheeky incongruence of class (low) and genre (high) that had made *Threepenny Opera* and its progenitor, *The Beggar's Opera*, models of parody would surely be a delicate and complex operation.

Any such synthesis would require a far greater knowledge of race relations in the United States than Brecht had ever demonstrated, however. The vaguely construed notion of North American geography put forth in his stage projects was populated almost entirely by white characters: The gangsters, miners, pimps, and prostitutes were all white. (With the exception of Krenek's *Jonny spielt auf,* African Americans are conspicuously absent from this highly stylized landscape in European opera, even as its soundscape freely availed itself of jazz.) For all the jazz in Weill's scores, Brecht himself was not particularly knowledgeable about the music or concerned with it as a manifestation of African American culture. The novel appeal of jazz in the Weimar Republic was due largely to its status as a hip medium for flouting societal norms. That rebelliousness exploited both its alien musical style and the racial Otherness of its origins, but the social conditions that gave rise to its iconoclastic appeal were never a subject of serious inquiry for Brecht.[7]

His interest in African American culture may have been genuinely piqued during his first trip to New York in 1935, at which point African Americans and their sociopolitical agendas were becoming prominent in two intersecting arenas of interest to him: theater and leftist politics. There was reason to be optimistic about the fate of African American theater just then and about the integration of black performers into mainstream venues on Broadway. Beginning in 1930, vehicles ranged from black plays by white playwrights (Marc Connelly's Pulitzer Prize–winning play *The Green Pastures*) to black shows by black writers and composers (*Run, Little Chillun* by Hall Johnson in 1933). Operas included Virgil Thomson's "opera to be sung," *Four Saints in Three Acts*, with a libretto by Gertrude Stein in an all-black production directed by John Houseman, and George Gershwin's *Porgy and Bess* at the Alvin Theatre in 1935–36. African American theater culture received a crucial boost when the Works Progress Administration (WPA) established the Federal Theatre Project (FTP) in 1935; it spawned sixteen Negro Theatre Units in major American cities before it was discontinued in 1939.[8]

This was also a period in which many prominent African American intellectuals saw communism as a viable means of achieving social change through the Popular Front, which promoted an alliance of antifascists regardless of class, party, or national identity. In the United States, this agenda was easily expanded to include opposition to institutionalized racism. The Communist Party (CPUSA) could boast links to radicals such as Richard Wright, Margaret Walker, Frank Marshall Davis, William Attaway, Lloyd Brown, Langston Hughes, Ralph Ellison, and Robeson, all of whom were active in the party directly or through its various cultural clubs and publications.[9] Since so many exiled Germans were leftists, the CPUSA and the Popular Front more generally constituted the point of contact between the two groups of intellectuals.[10]

Thus Brecht's first visit to the United States in October of 1935 coincided with the emergence of a powerful network of prominent African American intellectuals, WPA projects, nonblack members of the CPUSA, fellow travelers, and their émigré German counterparts. V. J. Jerome, chairman of the CPUSA Cultural Commission and editor of *The Communist*, introduced Brecht to Marc Blitzstein and his wife, Eva Goldbeck; Brecht renewed ties with the director Joseph Losey, whom he had met the previous year in Moscow, who in turn introduced Brecht to Houseman, then head of the FTP's Negro Unit in New York.[11] Brecht saw at least one all-black show, Gershwin's *Porgy and Bess*, in which he is said to have admired Rouben Mamoulian's stage direction;[12] he proposed an all-black production of *Round Heads and*

Pointed Heads to Houseman and encouraged him to undertake an all-black production of Shakespeare's *Measure for Measure,* suggesting at least a passing familiarity with Orson Welles's famous voodoo *Macbeth*.[13] Brecht would have been aware of concurrent discussions in New York about the viability of all-black shows from an economic as well as from a social perspective.

Brecht's awareness of the African American experience, such as it was, seems to have begun at this time; how well he understood racism in the United States remains unclear.[14] What he did know was filtered through the theater, which was heavily subsidized by the state in the mid- to late 1930s, and through the network of nascent civil rights activists and leftist intellectuals of that period. On 23 November 1935, Brecht and Eisler sat for an interview with Jerome and discussed ways in which Brecht's approach differed from that of Archibald MacLeish. Brecht stated that, in contrast to MacLeish, he "would give the various classes that diction that historically belongs to them." Jerome tested that assertion, asking Brecht what kind of language he would use for Negroes in a play set in the American South circa 1800. He said he would use standard English instead of dialect, and when Jerome noted that American audiences expected to hear slaves speak dialect, Brecht recognized that expectation as an opportunity to create a classic estrangement experience. Eisler asked what Negroes thought of dialect, and Jerome's answer was that of the black intellectuals he knew from political circles: "The emancipated Negro looks upon the dialect as a hangover of slavery."[15] Apart from identifying the characters as "the Negroes," race is conspicuously absent from their discussion. Brecht's assertion that he would use dialect "only as an expression of class struggle" bespeaks his European Marxist background, in which dialect was strictly a marker of class. He appears to have been unaware of the importance of race signification that was inextricably bound up with dialect in the American context.

Race and the African American 'Threepenny Opera' Project (1941–1942)

When Brecht returned to the United States in 1941 his circumstances were very different. Instead of immersing himself in the New York theater scene, he joined a now-famous community of exiled German leftist intellectuals on the West Coast, many of whom were befriended by American communists.[16] The primary creative medium in California was the Hollywood film industry rather than the theater. The FTP infrastructure that had been in place when Brecht had visited in 1935, and that might have subsidized avant-garde theater, had been dismantled. Furthermore, the African American Left was concentrated in New York, so their voices were less present in intellectual and artistic circles on the West Coast.[17] In short, Brecht's experience with the leftist intellectual network on the West Coast was more monochromatic than it had been in New York six years earlier. Schoenberg student and scholar Leonard Stein observed that, as far as he knew, "neither Eisler nor Brecht . . . ever visited the black part of Los Angeles to see what we then called the Negroes—and I think that they hardly ever visited the workers' quarters in Los Angeles either."[18] Brecht's lack of interaction with working-class African Americans surely shaped his perception of the inter-sections between race and class in the United States.

He was in contact with one prominent African American shortly after he arrived in California, however: Renaissance man Clarence Muse (1889–1979). Muse's long and storied career included a law degree, stints in min-strel shows and vaudeville, and at least 140 film credits. These ranged from roles in mainstream Hollywood movies to those in the parallel if vastly underfunded universe of black cinema, an enterprise that produced films for black movie theaters during the Jim Crow era.[19] For most of his Hollywood career he played stereotypes favored by whites, such as faithful servants and childlike characters, but in the black-cast films, he broke new ground. Muse cowrote and starred in *Broken Strings* (1939), in which he played a violin virtuoso who suffers a career-ending injury and rechannels his musical ambitions through his son. He had also directed shows in the FTP Negro Units on both coasts in the late 1930s, one of only a handful of African Americans to do so. Unlike Robeson, whose multifaceted career Muse's oth-erwise resembles, he appears to have eschewed overt political activism.

Just how Muse and Brecht found one another is unclear, as is the precise nature of their work together.[20] The first mention of the project in Brecht's journal is in an entry dated 22 November 1941, when he indicated that he had learned of Muse's adaptation of *Threepenny Opera* for an all-black cast. Brecht was sufficiently aware of theatrical trends to know that African American productions were popular, and an adaptation for a black cast was a viable means of updating or revising a show for contemporary audiences. Certainly Muse and possibly Brecht would have known of Cheryl Crawford's wildly successful touring revival of *Porgy and Bess* crisscrossing the country in 1941–42.[21] A contract was drawn up for a production of Muse's treatment "on the legitimate speaking stage by colored performers" that bears the date 24 February 1942—two weeks before Weill would hear of the project for the first time in a telegram from Brecht's agent, George Marton.[22] The ensuing correspondence and the fate of the production have been recounted elsewhere and will be rehearsed here only briefly.[23]

Brecht hoped to persuade Weill to approve the project by invoking the names of the prominent African Americans said to be involved (Muse, Katherine Dunham, and Robeson) and downplaying changes to the text ("hardly changed anything, except the location [now Washington] and that it is the inauguration of the President instead of the Queen's coronation").[24] Weill attributed the disastrous first staging of *Threepenny Opera* in the United States in April 1933 to its poor translation, however, and was not inclined to endorse another American production without close supervision. In a letter dated 9 March 1942 he informed Brecht that he had collaborated with an American writer on a black adaptation for several years, but the problems that emerged when revising an eighteenth-century English ballad opera for African Americans seemed as yet intractable. This had been evident in Weill's recent efforts with Charles MacArthur and presumably also in attempts dating from as early as 1939 with Louis Simon and Harold Smith.[25]

Weill asked to see the translation nonetheless and quickly arranged a meeting with Robeson so that he could discuss it with prospective producers in New York.[26] A flurry of correspondence ensued from Brecht, Marton, and Muse, and Eslanda Robeson sent a letter attesting to Muse's integrity and talent, but no copy of Muse's treatment was forthcoming. In his third letter on the subject Brecht described the text as follows: "What Muse has shown me is simultaneously sympathetic [to the German version] and original, all of a careless grandeur and yet quick and vigorous." Elsewhere he wrote that Muse had shown him one of his songs and it appeared to be "original and strong," but Muse himself was not completely happy with it yet.[27] (Robeson also reported having seen some of the text, so its existence was not fabricated simply to further Brecht's cause.) Marton believed that the copyright did not apply in the United States at all, so they would need only "a prudent contract." Since this would not have to be *the* definitive performance of *Threepenny Opera* in the United States, they should "leave these people to work with a free conscience." Brecht wrote that experience had led African American artists to assume "the craziest double-crossing and racist machinations," which is why they wanted to establish a permanent black theater, and why he hoped Weill would send them assurances of his good faith to proceed.[28]

Only Weill's side of the correspondence with Muse survives, but he appears to have been genuinely moved by Muse's sincerity and willing to facilitate a performance as long as its musical integrity could be preserved. He proposed various compromises to protect his and Brecht's interests should a Broadway production become feasible at a later date. In the meantime Brecht enlisted Theodor Adorno to act as intercessor. In an argument that may surprise some familiar with Adorno's essays on jazz from the 1930s, he urged Weill to surrender his rights to the music on grounds of authenticity. Black musicians could then compose or improvise "actual" jazz adaptations rather than playing the "jazz-arrangement style" Weill had used in his original score.[29] Weill's response was angry, not only because Adorno expected him to give up his intellectual property rights but also because the argument had revealed Adorno's complete ignorance of Weill's original score.[30]

Even so, the project might have gone forward had the contract been remotely viable. Weill response to it is documented in a furious telegram to Marton: "It is the most shameful proposition that ever has been made to me. My agent and my publisher did not find one paragraph in this document that would even serve as a basis for discussion."[31] Weill had been prepared to relinquish his earnings to Brecht, who was in dire financial straits, but when he realized that Brecht had agreed to a deal that would pay him only $10 a week on a show that, "in a proper setup, could have assured [Brecht] a comfortable living for a long time," Weill withdrew from the negotiations.[32] No further negotiations were forthcoming from either side, and the all–African American production of *Threepenny Opera* assumed its official status as an unfinished project of the exile period. Had it come to fruition, this rendition of Brecht's American-opera topos would have been the first to feature African Americans. As it stands, the unrealized *Threepenny Opera* project constituted Brecht's most sustained collaboration with an African American. Despite the fact that the adaptation was never realized, Muse himself considered their collaboration a milestone: "To have recognized the genius of Bertolt Brecht's American years thru the eyes of a Black American is, in my opinion, a golden asset."[33]

Whiteface and Passing(?)

In a prime example of the importance of unfinished projects in Brecht's textual network, the failed all-black *Threepenny Opera* catalyzed an investigation of black-white race relations in two other theater projects, *The Private Life* (1945) and *The Duchess of Malfi* (1945–46).[34] These productions were extraordinary in at least two ways: Each show featured a single black actor in an otherwise all-white cast at a time when mixed casts were rare; and in each case that actor performed in whiteface, which was unheard of.[35] Brecht had a hand in casting, and as the most subversive element on otherwise traditional production teams, he was almost certainly involved in the decision to have the African American actors wear whiteface. Unlike its inverse, the portrayal of African Americans by white actors in blackface, this constitutes a conspicuously rare occurrence that has garnered surprisingly little attention.[36] In 1933 the costume designer for *Four Saints in Three Acts* had lobbied to have the black performers' bodies painted white or silver on the grounds that the variety of skin tones onstage would interfere with her color scheme. The plan for full-body paint was gradually reduced to white face paint and eventually to just white gloves, and actors' faces retained their natural skin color.[37] That any production a full decade later would feature a black actor in whiteface, let alone two different actors in two different shows in which Brecht's participation is the common denominator, surely invites interrogation.

Maurice Ellis played the narrator in *The Private Life of the Master Race* at the City College of New York's Theatre of All Nations 11–17 June 1945, and Canada Lee played Daniel de Bosola in *The Duchess of Malfi* at the Ethel Barrymore on Broadway 15 October–16 November 1946.[38] Brecht's most extensive public comments on African Americans are preserved in an interview with Ann Hornemann during rehearsals for *The Private Life*. They appeared on 16 June 1945 in *The People's Voice*, a left-wing black newspaper published by Adam Clayton Powell Jr. in Harlem.[39] Hornemann described a scene in which she found Brecht "enthusiastically but patiently working with a deep baritone voiced Negro actor who was portraying the role of a Nazi soldier from Bavaria."[40] When she asked Brecht why he had cast an African American as a Bavarian soldier, "His answer seemed to tell the whole story of his approach to the theatre: 'Because he is good. The color is not important, it is the talent that counts.'" He declared Broadway to be unoriginal compared to what he had seen under the auspices of the WPA project and lamented its demise. When Hornemann asked what kind of roles Negroes should play, he responded at some length: "That is a silly question. It's so childish, so idiotic to talk about: 'Negro parts.' They should play everything. I mean everything—Shakespeare, Ibsen, O'Neill, and I don't mean Negro versions of Shakespeare—like Macbeth, I don't like that idea. If he plays Hamlet, let him be a Danish prince, if it is Ibsen, let it be an interpretation of the Norwegians, and if it is O'Neill, let him be an American." His swipe at Welles's 1936 *Macbeth*, a WPA project, is noteworthy, particularly when what is known of Muse's *Threepenny Opera* adaptation suggests that it might have resulted in a similar product. Brecht's assertions that the classics should not be adapted in any way to accommodate the race of the actors, and that audiences should judge only the quality of the performance when a black actor portrayed a white character, bespeak a utopian colorblind meritocracy. Brecht surely knew this was not the reality of the situation, but how well he understood the nuances of that context is unknown. Near the end of the article Hornemann wrote, "I asked the Negro actor Maurice Ellis what he thought of the play. He was very happy about it, only bothered a little about putting 'all that paint on my face.'"

Ellis's reference to whiteface is telling within the context of Brecht's color-blind remarks.[41] While no expert in race relations, Brecht could appreciate the concept of racechange well enough in the performative sense to exploit its estrangement potential. In her classic study, Susan Gubar sees racechange as liberating and defines it as "the traversing of race boundaries, racial imitation or impersonation, cross-racial mimicry or mutability and white passing as black or black passing as white, pan-racial mutuality."[42] Helen Gilbert applies Gubar's work specifically to whiteface performance, albeit in indigenous Australian and Canadian cultures, in ways that are relevant to this discussion. In contemporary whiteface performance, the failure to pass constitutes a more complex—even if more conscious—political project, in part because perceptions of this highly theatricalized racechange are likely to be refracted through the historical mirror of blackface impersonation, with all its ambiguous, indeed scandalous, associations.[43]

With the crucial distinction that the black actors involved in Brecht's productions almost certainly did not instigate the use of whiteface themselves, Gilbert's theory is clearly related to the estrangement effect Brecht pursued in *The Private Life* and *The Duchess of Malfi*. This is confirmed in Burton Rascoe's review of *The Private Life*, which includes a valuable account of the use of makeup: "Just why Dwight Marfield (a good actor) should have to wear two burnt-cork smudges on his cheeks to indicate that he is a worker, or that Clarence Derwent should have to wear putty eyebrows to indicate he is a judge, or that Maurice Ellis, the narrator (a Negro) should have to wear white calcium on his brow and cheeks (leaving the natural dark of his skin otherwise exposed) to indicate that he is an Aryan, Nordic, nasty Nazi— these are things I can't quite figure out."[44] Ellis was made up sparingly and deliberately, so that his natural skin color was equally apparent, and he wore that makeup alongside other (white) actors who were similarly conspicuously made up. In other words, Ellis's narrator was decidedly *not* passing, and the white actors' caricature makeup foregrounded that tension. Whiteface calls even more attention to the presence of the original color underneath—particularly when applied in this manner—and to the racism that necessitated its concealment in the first place. White audiences would be unable to view the character without recognizing that he was actually a black man pretending to masquerade as a white person, and, ideally, they would consider why a black man should attempt to pass at all.[45]

Canada Lee's performance as Daniel de Bosola in the adaptation of

Webster's *Duchess of Malfi* caused an even greater sensation.[46] The *New York Times* anticipated the opening on 15 October as follows: "In what is believed to be the first instance of its kind, Mr. Lee will be donning white make-up to portray the part of the villainous Daniel de Bosola. Mr. Lee is reported to be using a white paste, heretofore applied medically to cover burns and other disfiguring marks, to help create the illusion."[47] The same day the *New York Herald Tribune* declared, "Tonight's production marks a stunt new to the annals of the theater," and noted that it had not been without its problems: "The casting of a Negro actor in an important role created certain difficulties during the tryout tour, as the Wilmington booking was canceled by the management of the Playhouse with the evasive explanation that 'we just didn't care to play the attraction on those days.' "[48] The following morning the *Tribune* panned the production: "The Negro actor, Canada Lee, puts on white-face to play the role of evil's henchmen [sic]. The latter stunt, incidentally, is little more successful than the exhibit itself."[49] The *New York Times* was more generous, praising Lee's performance and noting, "Here he is playing in white face; and, as a matter of fact, inside his make-up he counterfeits a white man about as successfully as a white man in burnt cork counterfeits a Negro—which is hardly at all. But that is only an amusing detail by comparison with the intelligence, ease and scope of Mr. Lee's acting as Bosola."[50]

The white critics cited above were unable to recognize whiteface as a device of estrangement in these productions of *The Private Life* and *Duchess of Malfi*.[51] They found it confusing, annoying, and distracting, and the *New York Times* critic tried to ignore it altogether. That is not to say that it was any easier for African Americans to interpret. Lee repeatedly stated his hope that this characterization would "open up vast new fields to the Negro actor whose parts previously have been limited by color" and believed the role would constitute "a long step toward becoming 'actor Canada Lee,' not 'Canada Lee, Negro actor.' "[52] Bill Chase of the flagship black newspaper *New York Amsterdam News* hailed the historical significance of "the presentation of an actor solely on his ability and without thought of his color." Lee and Chase carefully sidestep the fact that Lee's presentation onstage was actually quite race conscious. Their reasons for doing so are obvious; and while he may have been cast without regard for skin color, race certainly determined the mode of presentation once he was hired. Lew Sheaffer of the *Brooklyn Eagle* reported that Lee's "turning 'whiteface' in *The Duchess of Malfi* angered many of the sepia intelligentsia." White critics who claimed that Lee was so good that they were able to forget he was "a colored man in makeup" meant that "his principal claim to fame was his ability to successfully impersonate a white man." Many years later Lee's biographer would assert, "He only permitted himself to be painted because in 1946, that was the only way he could play a white man on stage."[53] It was an incident of racechange that might have been designed to provoke cross-race dialogue (Gubar) or to taunt predominantly white audiences (Gilbert), but as a device of estrangement it appears to have overestimated the audience's ability to respond critically.

Given this context, then, it seems unlikely that *Threepenny Opera* could have borne the additional layer of race signification in the United States of the 1940s, particularly as opera was not the medium for social critique that it had been in Weimar-era Berlin. Nevertheless the prospect is intriguing to contemplate in the context of Gilbert's notion of passing—or, more precisely, of *failing* to pass, as evident in these productions of *The Private Lives* and *Duchess of Malfi*. The original *Threepenny Opera* worked as parody precisely because, despite its title, it deliberately *failed to pass* as an opera in conspicuous and important ways, just as its predecessor *The Beggar's Opera* famously had done. The adaptation of an eighteenth-century, white, English opera parody for an all-black cast in the United States of the 1940s, however, would have run the risk of becoming a travesty in which black performers were once again judged by how well they passed as characters widely known to have been white in the original version.[54] Even though the all-black *Threepenny Opera* project remained unrealized because of contract disputes, Brecht redirected its exploration of race consciousness in the United States to two nonoperatic productions.

'GOLIATH'

The *Goliath* project represents Brecht's second mode of engagement with opera while in the United States: the return to a previously abandoned text. He and Eisler had begun work on the opera in 1937 at Skovsbostrand on the Danish isle of Fyn, the playwright's base of operations during his European exile. *Goliath* proved to have remarkable staying power, surviving not only Brecht and Eisler's extended period of geographical separation but also a significant political and philosophical disagreement. Jost Hermand astutely noted that the two had much in common but also recognized a major difference: "Over the course of his life, Eisler tried to appropriate the old bourgeois art tradition as only he could, and he never denied how much he owed to it. Brecht tended to look down upon the cultural tradition of his social class."[55] In the mid-1930s this distinction manifested itself in a conflict about the Popular Front, which Brecht opposed and Eisler supported. This fundamental tension surely contributed to their inability to complete

Goliath, since Eisler saw the opera as an opportunity to explore his particular cultural interpretation of the Popular Front, according to which dodecaphony could be the next weapon of the workers' movement in the fight against fascism.[56]

The Popular Front

The disagreement about the viability of the Popular Front emerged at a crucial juncture in the history of the European Left, in what is known as the fourth phase of the Communist International (1934–39), or the Comintern. This organization was founded to promote communism throughout the world, and it was dominated by the Soviet Union. An ongoing rift between socialists and communists of various stripes had weakened the Left to such an extent that it failed to mount effective opposition to the Nazi Party in Germany. Leadership in Moscow proposed a hasty rapprochement among all leftists in the form of the United Front, but it quickly became clear that a still more radical strategy was required.[57] The transition from the United Front, in which socialists and communists cooperated for the greater good of antifascism, to the all-inclusive Popular Front, known in the United States as the People's Front, in which these parties welcomed antifascists of all sociopolitical stripes, even the bourgeoisie, took just one year (1934–35).[58] The new agenda was announced at the Comintern's Seventh World Congress in the summer of 1935: "In the mobilization of the toiling masses for the struggle against fascism, the formation of a *broad people's antifascist front on the basis of the proletarian united front* is a particularly important task. The success of the entire struggle of the proletariat is closely connected with the establishment of a fighting alliance between the proletariat on the one hand and the toiling peasantry and the basic mass of the urban petty bourgeoisie constituting a majority of the population of even industrially developed countries, on the other."[59] Comintern leader Georgi Dimitrov reviewed conditions in numerous countries, such as Belgium, Denmark, Great Britain, Poland, Spain, France, and the United States, and encouraged leaders in each to implement the new strategy according to its particular circumstances and demographics. In the United States, for example, "so important a country in the capitalist world," the proletariat was encouraged to organize in conjunction with the large bourgeoisie classes, because "the success of fascism in the United States would change the whole international situation quite materially."[60] The *Daily Worker,* the central organ of the Communist Party USA, prefaced its congressional report with an editorial proclaiming, "The heart of the congress decisions is contained in the new tactic of the people's front. This is a new tactic made necessary by a changed world situation, but the policy of winning over the oppressed middle classes of city and countryside for [the] struggle against capitalism is as old as scientific Communism itself."[61] Thus the Popular Front mobilized a broader swath of the global population by including the middle classes and sought to marshal the nationalism of each Comintern section by encouraging leaders to implement the new strategy according to their respective domestic circumstances.

While Dimitrov described the unique opportunities and challenges of various Comintern sections around the world, the German Left was cited only as a negative example of collapse caused by infighting and ineptitude. Those who had escaped were now in exile and came away from the Seventh Congress without the nationalist impetus granted other units, and some, like Eisler, appear to have derived momentum primarily from the new inclusion of the middle classes. In that regard, the Popular Front must have seemed custom-made for him. A student of Arnold Schoenberg, Eisler had broken with his teacher in 1926 and renounced his bourgeois musical training as elitist and irrelevant to his newfound mission in the workers' movement. He then dedicated himself to writing well-crafted, diatonic, functional music, but after visits to the Soviet Union in 1930 and 1931, he also took up dodecaphony again. He combined it with elements of jazz, workers' songs, and neoclassicism in a return to concert music, possibly inspired by the conductor-less orchestra collectives he encountered in the Soviet Union.[62]

In this context Eisler was predisposed to interpret the Popular Front's inclusionary agenda as an endorsement of a synthesis he had already begun to investigate, which was the use of twelve-tone music as a vehicle for leftist politics. He voiced this position most clearly in an essay coauthored with Ernst Bloch in 1937, as a salvo in the so-called expressionism debate carried out in the German-language exile press in the late 1930s. Bloch and Eisler argued against both bourgeois claims for artistic autonomy and workers' claims that artistic traditions must always be easily accessible, building their case for the relevance of the avant-garde to the Popular Front. The essay, titled "Avant-garde Art and the Popular Front," is staged as a debate between a skeptic and an optimist. The skeptic doubts that "art forms like atonal music and abstract painting that are so complicated and foreign to the people" can serve a mass movement and points out the contradiction of such artists sharing political ground with the Popular Front while rejecting "democratic artistic taste." He accuses the optimist of opportunism since the avant-garde finds itself in an exceedingly bad position: "Isolated from the masses, fascism threatens to destroy it." The optimist, however, maintains that the avant-garde and the Popular Front must enter into a mutually beneficial symbiosis. Artists need the Popular Front because it "defends artistic freedom and provides the artists with honest material" and because following the vital social movements of the time keeps art relevant. Similarly, the Popular Front needs the avant-garde because "it is not enough to possess the truth; rather it is necessary to lend it the most current, precise, and colorful expression."[63]

Eisler was elected chairman of the International Music Bureau, the music division of the Comintern, at the Seventh Congress.[64] Perhaps his candidacy was appealing in light of the Popular Front's expanded inclusion policy, since aspects of his biography that may have been previously problematic were now less so (he may or may not have been a member of the party; he was bourgeois born and bred; his association with Schoenberg was widely known).[65] The solidarity of the working class and the bourgeoisie united against fascism paralleled the reconciliation of his training with his political convictions, and for Eisler this meant, among other things, putting consonant twelve-tone music at the service of leftist, politically committed texts.[66] *Goliath* is just such a piece.

Meanwhile, Brecht wholeheartedly supported the consolidation of the Left in the form of the United Front, as witnessed by "Song of the United Front," cowritten with Eisler in 1934, but no such collaboration was forthcoming on the topic of the Popular Front. He made this position quite clear at the Writers for the Defense of Culture conference in late June 1935.[67] Brecht had already issued a scathing critique of the Popular Front in "Five Difficulties of Writing the Truth," and he did not back down from that position at the conference, deriding as obsolete the spiritual humanism and patriotism endorsed by other participants.[68] He demanded that the group discuss Marxism instead of culture, and, exasperated by the passive, elitist agenda of the conference, he sent a bitter report to the artist George Grosz: "We have just saved culture. It took four days, and we decided it was better to sacrifice everything else rather than to let the culture go under. We want to sacrifice 10–20 million people for it."[69] In 1935, then, Brecht's opposition to the Popular Front placed him at odds with the Comintern, with Moscow, and with Eisler.[70] The playwright was as much at odds with dodecaphony as he was with socialist realism, but shared opposition to the latter and commitment to antifascism were sufficient to preserve the friendship and collaboration between Brecht and Eisler.[71] They found common political ground where they could (Brecht provided the text for Eisler's antifascist cantata *Against War [Gegen den Krieg]*), and, when necessary, they worked separately; Eisler set texts by Ludwig Renn, José Petere, and Erich Weinert for the Eleventh International Brigade in Spain in January 1937.

'Goliath' in Europe

From February to September of 1937 Eisler spent most of his time in Skovsbostrand, near Brecht, during which time they began work on *Goliath*. Drafts dated by Margarete Steffin, her correspondence with Walter Benjamin, and a letter from Brecht to Bernhard Reich indicate that the opera was underway no later than 8 March. Initial progress was swift, and they drafted the text of the entire first act in a few weeks. Work was suspended in April so that Brecht could concentrate on *Señora Carrar's Rifles (Die Gewehre der Frau Carrar)*. During that hiatus Eisler worked on several other projects, some of which featured texts by Brecht but did not involve his direct collaboration, such as the nine political cantatas to be performed in Prague. They took up *Goliath* together again in September, but Eisler left for Prague in October and then immigrated to the United States in January 1938. The opera was incomplete at his departure and would remain so.[72]

Opera was an unlikely choice for both parties. In 1937 Eisler committed little time and energy to pieces without immediate viable performance prospects, and few projects could have been as untenable as an opera production at that time. Because Brecht rejected the Popular Front agenda for its collusion with the bourgeoisie at this particular point, opera was also an unlikely choice for him; not only was it the definitive cultural institution of the bourgeoisie, but this opera was to be twelve tone, the most elitist and least accessible music of the avant-garde in the 1930s. Nevertheless, he undertook the project with zeal, either for the sake of friendship or out of recognition that every possible antifascist strategy deserved exploration. It bears remembering that Brecht had two of his three complete operas under his belt by this time, while Eisler famously would never finish one; like Brecht's, his own oeuvre is rife with abandoned opera projects. The composer with whom Brecht is said to be most compatible is also the one with whom he did not complete an opera.

Goliath was to have been a tour de force, resonating with layers of biblical and political allusions and put forth in opera on a grand scale: Drafts reveal plans for four substantial acts (The Election of Goliath; David and Goliath; Goliath's Rule; and Goliath's Decline); a large orchestra (three flutes, three oboes, three clarinets, three bassoons, contrabassoon, four horns, four trumpets, three trombones, bass tuba, contrabass tuba, percussion, violins, violas, cellos, and basses); arias and recitatives; soloists and chorus.[73] The libretto had its origins in Brecht's fragment *David* (1920–21). That early text, which stayed true to the plot of its biblical model, provided the scaffolding for *Goliath;* the opera plan retained the biblical names, a few plot elements, and the central friendship between David and Jonathan. And just as Brecht had used "Ga" to stand for Germany in *The Horatians,* so the biblical city of "Gad" represents Germany in *Goliath.*[74] Otherwise, the opera is more closely related to the antifascist parable *Round Heads and Pointed Heads* and to another fragment about the nature of dictatorship, the unfinished novel *The Business Affairs of Mr. Julius Caesar* (October 1937). The Old Testament conflict with a foreign army is transformed into a domestic class struggle in which the Philistines represent capitalists; the rigged election that ushers Goliath into power alludes to the Nazis' 1936 victory; and the giant's insatiable appetite for food and war represents capitalist greed and Germany's annexations.[75] The libretto refers to Strength through Joy (Kraft durch Freude), a group sponsored by the Third Reich's German Labor Front intended to monitor citizens' free time through organized leisure activities (*BFA* 10:755). An allusion to the rift that necessitated the United Front is found in act 2, where tension between two groups who should be allies (here embodied in tradesmen and farmers) is shown to enable the dictatorship. Only nominal sketches survive for acts 3 and 4: Jonathan visits David in exile and they read the forbidden text that explains solidarity; the Philistines question Goliath's selection of David's sister Miriam as his bride; "the poor people of Gad," as they are always identified in the libretto, fortify David on the night before his battle with the giant, thus demonstrating the strength of solidarity. The relevance to European politics in 1937 is obvious.

The myriad strands of biblical and political commentary in the libretto are interwoven with significant musical references as well. Titles for a song and an aria are found in the libretto without corresponding lyrics ("Lied von Goliaths schwacher Stelle" and "Man kann nie wissen" [*BFA* 10:758, 760]); the word "Intermezzo" is inserted into one scene in Eisler's hand (*BFA* 10:772); a ballet is planned (*BFA* 10:754); and Brecht published lyrics for two songs whose position in the remaining libretto is unclear. ("Jonathan und David" and "Lied des Speichelleckers" were never set to music.) The collaborators deliberately situated their texts in dialogue with the German operatic tradition with at least four specific allusions, expanding the dense network of references and meanings. The leaders' response to election results, "O schöner Augenblick! O tiefe Rührung," is probably an allusion to Pizarro's revenge aria from Beethoven's *Fidelio,* "Ha! Welch ein Augenblick—Die Rache werd' ich kühlen."[76] The context, in which a character is thought to be dead but is actually alive, certainly suggests *Fidelio* as the source. It might also refer to Albert Lortzing's parody of that aria in *Ali, Pascha von Janina:* "Ha schrecklich—Will ich meine Rache kühlen" cleverly mimicked not only the music of Pizarro's vengeful aria but also its language. The first line of

"O schöner Augenblick" is also identical to that of an aria in Lortzing's 1848 opera *Regina*, which is a story of workers' resistance and revolution.[77]

The second possible operatic allusion is the name assigned to the group "the poor people of Gad" (die armen Leute von Gad). In Alban Berg's *Wozzeck* the text "We poor people" (Wir armen Leut')" bears one of the primary leitmotifs associated with the title character on three occasions (act 1, scene 1: Wozzeck to Hauptmann; act 1, scene 3: Marie to Wozzeck; and act 2, scene 1: Wozzeck to Marie). Berg had written his own libretto based on Georg Büchner's incomplete play *Woyzeck* (1836). Brecht's admiration for Büchner is well known, and Berg's masterpiece, while not dodecaphonic, was the most successful opera associated with the Second Viennese School. "Die armen Leute" may invoke a dramatic fragment by a playwright that was influential for Brecht, and it certainly pays homage to a modernist operatic landmark.[78] The third and most conspicuous way in which *Goliath* engages the operatic canon is seen in the preliminary outline, which identifies the first scene of act 2 as "Die Meistersinger von Gad" (*BFA* 10:753). This reference to Wagner may also represent another link to Lortzing, whose *Hans Sachs* (1840) is said to have influenced Wagner's *Meistersinger* (1868).

The most interesting musical reference speaks directly to Brecht and Eisler's collaboration and to Eisler's interpretation of a Popular Front aesthetic: "Goliath falls asleep to 'good' music. Exploited by 12-tone musicians who sing theirs quickly (they have nothing else with them)" (Goliath schläft ein bei "guter" Musik. Ausgenutzt von Zwölftonlern, die schnell ihr's singen [sie haben nichts anderes mit], *BFA* 10:755). Given their close collaboration at the initiation of the project, such a reference almost certainly means that Brecht knew Eisler was planning a dodecaphonic setting. Evidence of the composer's musical plans survives in three different sources: one undated typed page of libretto text bearing a musical motif; four pages of tone rows and fragments of text settings in a sketchbook dated 1935–37; and thirty-three pages of tone rows, particell, and partitur excerpts from act 1.[79] The typed libretto excerpt corresponds closely to *BFA* 778–779, although capitalization has been standardized in that edition (the original had no capital letters, as was Brecht's habit). The heading indicates that this is the opening of act 2. The libretto features a substantial choral lament for "the poor people of Gad" and a solo for the "rebel" Tulok, who agitates for the uprising. Tulok can be said to represent the ultra-left wing of the German Communist Party in the mid-1930s, which maintained that a revolution from below was the only way to affect change.[80] This fragment includes the barest sketch of a melodic motif, without text, time signature, or clef, although it may be deduced that it is in the bass clef, given its range above the staff. The melody is strongly diatonic, establishing the key of G as the dominant and resolving to C as tonic, and bears no resemblance to tone rows in the other two sources. Its rhythm does not correspond conspicuously to any particular passage of text on this page, although it can be made to fit Tulok's first line: "And thus you build him the spoon so that he can guzzle better" (und so baut ihr ihm den Löffel, daß er besser fressen kann; HEA 3.1.1833, similar to *BFA* 10:778).

The *Goliath* material is situated between the *Lenin Cantata* and sketches marked "Prague, October" in the sketchbook from 1935–37. The tone rows on folio 9v are identical to the prime and retrograde inversion of the first row found on folio 2r of the third source (HEA 457). Text fragments are set to the retrograde inversion on 9v and then continue on 10r, where F♯, the last note of RI-0, is used as G♭, the first note of P-0, and doubles as a pivot into a statement of the row in its original form. This is a favored method for Eisler. I designate this row P-0 because it appears to be the first one he composed, and the drafts to follow are based on it and its permutations. The small intervals, diatonic orientation (note especially the C major triad at the end), and symmetrical intervallic construction are characteristic of the tone rows he employs most.[81]

$$G♭ - F - D♭ - C♭ - E♭ - A - A♭ - D - B♭ - C - E - G$$
$$\text{m2} \quad \text{M3} \quad \text{M2} \quad \text{M3} \quad \text{tr} \quad \text{m2} \quad \text{tr} \quad \text{M3} \quad \text{M2} \quad \text{M3} \quad \text{m3}$$

Only P-0 and its standard permutations (R-0, I-0, and RI-0) provide the basis for the music Eisler drafted. The texts in these drafts correspond most closely to *BFA* 10:768–777, from the first act. The first two Philistine choruses of act 1 survive, each in particell and partitur: "Die armen Leute von Gad" (also known as "Ihr Leute von Gad") and "Lament of the Philistines" ("Klage der Philister"). In the first chorus Eisler used R-0 in the instrumental introduction and P-0 in the vocal line (folios 5r particell, 15r partitur). The partitur for the lament (23v and following) delineates solo lines for "Go[liath]," "Li," "A," and "Th." According to the musical setting, then, Goliath would have been a tenor, not a bass, as the libretto fragment states in *BFA* 10:757.[82] This designation is consistent with Brecht's general disdain for the operatically trained tenor voice and also anticipates the vocal characterization of the title role in *Lucullus*.

The vocal line of the lament begins with the end of I-0, pivots on F into RI-0, and then shares the F♯ at the end of that row as the G♭ that begins the next statement of P-0 (folio 9r particell, 23v partitur). Its melody constitutes a flexible presentation of the row in which notes may be repeated either individually or in pairs. Segmentation that reinforces distinctive rhythmic and melodic motifs, the deliberate construction of rows conducive to triadic or diatonic orientation, and melodic lines that favor small intervals are all features of his particular deployment of dodecaphony that lend themselves particularly well to comprehension of the musical argument in conjunction with a political text.[83] These strategies are also evident in *Deutsche Sinfonie* and in the nine chamber cantatas of 1937.

'Goliath' in the United States

Goliath surfaced intermittently in the United States, beginning with an announcement of Eisler's arrival in the *New York Times* on 30 January 1938: "Hanns Eisler, who is at work on an opera entitled *Goliath*, will lecture on 'The Future of Music' and conduct a workshop in vocal composition during the spring term at the New School for Social Research." Inasmuch as Eisler had a reputation in New York at this time it was as a musician–political activist, so the opera reference was meant to establish his credentials to lead a workshop in art-music composition. *Goliath* may have had greater significance for Brecht, however. He wrote to the Eislers from Helsingfors in early 1941, thanking them for their efforts to secure a visa for Steffin and noting that he planned to bring *Goliath* with him on the journey: "When the ocean is still enough, I will prepare the second act."[84] The fragments identified as *BFA* 10:778–782 consist of dialogue from act 2, suggesting that Brecht did precisely that; an additional copy with notes in Steffin's hand indicates that they had worked on the material before he began the seafaring leg of his journey.[85] It is also the only project Brecht mentioned in his first letter to Eisler once he reached California in July: "I have *Goliath* with me, I wait for your signal as to how to proceed."[86] In a short, taut letter reporting the grave logistics of exile survival (catching the last ship out, Steffin's death, asking for employment), this unfinished collaborative project may have represented reconnection and some semblance of normalcy.

Eisler moved to California in the spring of 1942,[87] at which time he renewed ties with Schoenberg, completed the film music project funded by the Rockefeller Foundation, began to gain a foothold in Hollywood, and resumed work with Brecht. He was a stabilizing presence for the playwright, who wrote, "When I see Eisler it is a bit as if I had been stumbling confusedly around in some crowd of people and suddenly heard myself called by my old name."[88] The composer began writing the forty-seven songs that would become *The Hollywood Songbook* and for which Brecht's poems formed the heart of selected texts on the theme of exile; other poets represented include Anacreon, Mörike, Rimbaud, Eichendorff, Pascal, Goethe, Viertel, and Hölderlin.

This project intersected with *Goliath* in the form of "An die Hoffnung," the first of six Hölderlin fragments Eisler set for the collection. The manuscript is dated Pacific Palisades, 20 May 1943, and includes a note in his hand: "Possibly include in 'Goliath' (in the 'singers' competition scene')—(then set it for strings!)"[89] Evidently the opera was still on Eisler's mind, but since nothing else survives of that scene it is not clear how the song would have fit into it. It is not dodecaphonic, and its musical content is not derived from the *Goliath* tone rows; instead, it is a model of motivic saturation. Allusions to the B–A–C–H motto abound in developing variation. Dümling, Phleps, and others have traced Eisler's use of the B–A–C–H motif as an antifascist symbol in a whole network of exile pieces, both twelve tone and non–twelve tone.[90] It can be rendered in small intervals (minor second–minor third–minor second), which would be consistent with Eisler's preference and could suggest a relationship to the prime *Goliath* rows, but here it most often omits the A, and the interval from B♭ to C is rendered as a descending m7 instead. Thus the distinctive intervals are the minor seventh and minor second, melodic markers of atonality, if not necessarily of dodecaphony.[91]

This is the only indication that texts by anyone other than Brecht might appear in the libretto. The relevance of this particular poem cannot be deduced from the surviving opera fragments, but the choice of poet is indicative of Hölderlin's hallowed status among the Left in exile.[92] Eisler set eleven texts by this classical poet, more than by any other, and he discussed his settings of Hölderlin's fragments with Brecht frequently. In June 1943 Brecht wrote, "Eisler has written two magnificent cycles for *The Hollywood Songbook*, poems by Anacreon and Hölderlin. This opens up a possibility of achieving dramatic choruses, since the compositions are now totally gestic."[93] The puzzling reference to dramatic choruses in connection with the apparently unstaged song cycle genre may indicate that Brecht knew Eisler was considering "An die Hoffnung" for *Goliath*.

It is also difficult to resist reading significance into the link between the eternal fragmentary condition of the *Goliath* project (a fate which must have become increasingly clear to the collaborators as time went on) and the Romantic fragment as genre, exemplified by the Hölderlin text Eisler thought to imbed in that opera's singing contest. The accretion of nineteenth-century German symbols is conspicuous: *The Hollywood Songbook* was an extension of the lied tradition, the song contest parodied Wagner, and the Hölderlin fragments were emblematic of a Romantic literary genre. Friedrich Schlegel's famous definition of the Romantic fragment ("a fragment, like a small work of art, has to be entirely isolated from the surrounding world and be complete in itself like a hedgehog") argued that "the detachment or isolation of fragmentation is understood to correspond exactly to completion and totality."[94] Eisler's plan to insert Hölderlin's Romantic fragment, by definition self-contained and isolated, into a contemporary fragment as part of an allusion to Wagner seems calculated to challenge Wagner's all-encompassing Gesamt-kunstwerk model.

By late 1944, however, Brecht and Eisler appear to have reached an impasse. Brecht wrote that he was having "frequent conversations about music (connected with the *Goliath* opera) with Eisler and Dessau," and complained that "modern music converts text into prose . . . and then poeticizes that prose . . . and at the same time makes it psychological."[95] It has been shown that Eisler's *Goliath* would indeed have been "modern," and Brecht had praised similar settings for songs in *The Hollywood Songbook*, but ultimately he remained unconvinced that such music could be effectively translated to the stage. Nevertheless he continued to discuss the *Goliath* project, exploring yet another solution for working through the most problematic genre of the German theatrical tradition within Eisler's interpretation of Popular Front aesthetics.[96]

Goliath also survived into the postexile period, after a fashion. The libretto Eisler published for *Johann Faustus* in 1952 (he never completed the score) was indebted to several versions of the popular *Faust* legend and adopted stylistic aspects of those texts, such as the interpolation of biblical and mythological characters. He incorporated several Old Testament stories into the magic scene (act 2, scene 3), including the fight between David and Goliath, and used the story to serve his Marxist interpretation of the Faust legend.[97] While Eisler's *Faustus* does not cite the *Goliath* fragments, the selection of this story is noteworthy, given the myriad possibilities for the scene and the long history Brecht and Eisler already had with that theme in an operatic form. The final link in the *Goliath* network of texts is the return of Hölderlin's "An die Hoffnung," which Eisler included in his orchestral cycle *Serious Songs* (*Ernste Gesänge*, 1962). The music for its incarnation in *Serious Songs* is identical to that of its 1943 progenitor except that it is orchestrated for strings—the instrumentation Eisler had indicated he would use were he to interpolate the song into the *Goliath* singing contest.

'VOYAGES OF THE GOD OF HAPPINESS'

Voyages of the God of Happiness exemplifies Brecht's third and, given his circumstances, perhaps most unexpected mode of engagement with opera in American exile: the initiation of a new project.[98] The subject matter had been on his mind for some time, and he considered several genres as potential vehicles (poem, play, film script, song cycle) before settling on opera with Paul Dessau in 1945. In this section I will argue that opera was uniquely conducive to a particular exploration of parable and allegory in exile. The literature on parable in Brecht's oeuvre has only recently revisited the dogmatic rejection of the exile texts as depoliticized parables, a move which began in the 1960s and culminated in Heiner Müller's influential rejection of those pieces as representative of an "emigration into classicism."[99] Silberman acknowledges that argument when he writes, "The formal reductionism of the parable plays from this period seems to function as a kind of protective shield against the impossible contradictions of reality." But then he posits a reassessment of these texts when he credits Brecht with adapting his dramatic work to the crisis of that historical moment, countering, "Representation, aesthetics, and the work of imagination become political acts with a use value comparable to labor."[100] If parable as a subset of allegory can be a means of engagement, as Silberman suggests, then opera is well positioned to facilitate that mission. It has deployed allegory to great effect since the seventeenth century,[101] and such abstractions reappeared on opera stages in the twentieth: the Composer, the Prima Donna, and the Tenor in Richard Strauss's *Ariadne auf Naxos* (1916); the debate about the true nature of opera carried out between a poet, a composer, a director, and an actress representing their respective arts in Strauss's *Capriccio* (1942); and the personifications of good and evil in Stravinsky's *The Rake's Progress* (Anne Trulove and Nick Shadow, respectively, 1951), to name a few. Brecht's use of the genre as an exploration of allegory, then, places *Voyages* firmly within the operatic tradition. I will situate his fragment within the opera's textual networks, including attempts by two other playwrights, Müller and Peter Hacks, to complete the libretto after Brecht's death.

According to Brecht, the germ for *Voyages* was present in *Baal* some twenty years earlier.[102] It lay mostly dormant until 1939, when he was working on *Good Person of Szechwan*, another parable in which gods descend to earth. That Christmas he dedicated a poem entitled "Song of the God of Happiness" to Steffin; it was later expanded and retitled "Seventh Song of the God of Happiness" (*BFA* 10:927–929). He recorded in his journal on 16 November 1941 that he bought a Chinese amulet for forty cents in Chinatown, and at some point the following year he gave the figurine, or one like it, to Fritz Lang with the epigram, "I am the God of Happiness." An entry for 30 October 1942 states that *Voyages* was among the projects he was discussing with Feuchtwanger, and nine months later he decided the material should take the form of a song cycle instead (*Journals* July 1943).

He reworked the poem he had given Steffin, wrote new texts, and gave them to Dessau to set. Dessau had recently moved from New York to California, where he worked as a gardener and picked up some assignments as orchestrator and arranger for Universal and Warner Brothers' studios.[103] Brecht also discussed *Voyages* with Lang as one of several potential screenplays in October.

Meanwhile Dessau set the poems Brecht had given him as "Four Songs of the God of Happiness" (*BFA* 10:927–930). Autographs housed at the Paul-Dessau-Archiv (PDA 1.74.255.1–3) are dated "Hollywood, 1944– 9 February 1945," and additional score manuscripts in the Bertolt-Brecht-Archiv are dated as late as 16 October 1945 (BBA 204/1–45). The BBA manuscript includes a setting of "The Eleventh Song of the God of Happiness" (*BFA* 10:930) that is inscribed "For Brecht's Birthday," presumably 10 February 1945. Dessau described these songs as his contribution to a new kind of domestic music making, and they are exceedingly simple. For example, the first song in the set, known as "The Seventh Song of the God of Happiness" and by its first line, "Friend, if you devote yourself to me," is a strophic setting of an eight-verse poem. It is essentially diatonic (G major– D major) and features Dessau's trademark undulating duple-triple meter. The accompaniment is for guitar, a domestic music-making instrument that reflected the pragmatism of émigré wartime life since it was portable and more affordable than a piano.[104]

The decision to use the *Voyages* material for an opera instead was reached in January 1945. Brecht and Dessau worked on this project most intensively in the first half of that year, drafting the scene disposition (*BFA* 10:922–924), the prologue (*BFA* 10:933–934), and this first scene (*BFA* 10:935–937). Brecht then wrote texts for additional songs that were to appear elsewhere in the opera (*BFA* 10:931; probably also 10:932–933). Dessau made substantial headway on the first scene, drafting particells of two versions of the opening dialogue between the God and the Farmer and one aria for each (PDA 1.74.257.1–4). Recitative variant b is dated "Hollywood, end of March, 1945," and the Farmer's aria is dated "Los Angeles, May 1945"; the other two are undated.

The plot of the surviving texts is as follows: After a messenger informs the God that his temples are desecrated and neglected on earth, the God descends to investigate this sacrilege for himself. His ignorance of the human condition is evident from his first earthly encounter, with the Farmer. That naïveté also makes him vulnerable to the treachery of the mob, as his newly recruited followers later betray him and hand him over to be executed (*BFA* 10:921, 925–927). The God is immortal, however, and returns to life after each "execution." The most conspicuously American element of the libretto can be found in scene 1, in which the God undertakes a mission rather like that of John Chapman, better known by his alias, Johnny Appleseed.[105] The God gives the Farmer an apple and advises him not to swallow the seeds so that he can plant them and improve his lot in life, but the Farmer replies that having seeds is no help if a man owns no land. The God advises him to exercise squatter's rights in the overseer's absence and then sets out for the West. No English translation of the text is available in print, so the prologue and first scene on which Dessau and Brecht collaborated are provided below (*BFA* 10:933–937).[106]

PROLOGUE: The God of Happiness receives a report from earth and formulates a plan

High above the clouds the God of Happiness receives a messenger

GOD: You messenger, with the scorched wings
Welcome to the hills of clouds
What are you so excited about?
Before you hurry to the greater gods
Let the lowest ones know too, why don't you!
Who will know if you linger here?
Say, how do my affairs stand on earth?
Are my disciples still the same?
Is the God of Happiness sufficiently revered?
And are my temples well maintained?

MESSENGER: Your temples look like dens of iniquity.
The sound of the organ long ago gave way to money
    scraping
Whores come and go, drunks bawl,
And the opium victim lies paralyzed.
Your boys are the card players
Stock jobbers, horse race gamblers
Of the many who seek happiness
Few become happily fatter.

GOD: But that has nothing to do with me!

MESSENGER: It is maintained by some clerics
Who sell at an enormous price
Tickets for admission to five paradises:
One has only to wait for one's death.
To the many who dwell in the cellars
You live in the highest regions.
To them, the smile on the faces of their dead
As the muscle sets itself in a cramp

Means that the dead finally have sighted you,
And are satiated by your spiritual bread.

GOD: But up here one needs no bread!

MESSENGER: And there below one has rocks.

GOD: Yes, it appears so to me, seeing the earth
Futilely rotating as it attempts in the fiery glow
Of eternal wars
To shake off its burden of ticks and lackeys
And I believe
The time has come, after so many years of leisure, to go
down there.

SCENE 1: The God of Happiness gives away an apple

Dawn. A ragged Farmer stands in front of a ramshackle hut riddled with bullet holes as the God of Happiness passes by.

GOD: Day is breaking.

FARMER: So?

GOD: So nothing. If it suits you this way.

FARMER: What are you looking for here?

GOD: I seek nothing.

FARMER: That, for example, can I also be.

GOD: Don't you know who I am? Look at me!

FARMER: I see only that you have two coats.

GOD: Friend, it is cold.

FARMER: I am aware of that; I'm cold.

GOD: So get a couple of planks to make a fire. There's a forest.

FARMER: Quite right: It is not here. And a coat would come in
handy for the trip.

GOD: The best way to warm up is with a little jug of warm
beer.

FARMER: Nowadays the rats live longest.

GOD: So it is said: Learn from them, friend.

FARMER: Of course. Only one needs rat teeth for the bite.

GOD: If you refuse mine, you still have none. The joy would
not be so great.

FARMER: Yet it would be a little joy.
We stupid farmer folk
See too little joy.

> War or peace
> For us there is no difference.
> What their cannons forget
> Is gobbled up by the interest rates.
> The crop goes in their warehouse
> We wipe out our stomachs with beets.
> Past the tavern
> We lead our oxen to the cistern.
> We say to the oxen "piss!"
> "Piss!" the oxen say to us.
> We will not have the earth
> Until we are lying under it.

GOD: Brother, you make my eyes wet,
       I see your life is no fun.
       Here is an apple. See, I have three
       So I can give you one.
       I see nothing excessive about it:
       We can both live.
       Only promise me, that you in your greed
       Will not swallow the seeds
       Rather that you, before I depart,
       Will spit the seeds on the ground.
       And should it become an apple tree
       In the middle of your field
       Then come and pick the apples
       From the tree that you have planted.

He offers him an apple, which he has polished on his coat sleeve.

FARMER: Man that is the problem!
       How shall I have a tree?
       That could I have in my wildest of dreams.
       I have no earth.

GOD: Earth is right here.

FARMER: Don't talk nonsense. This land belongs to the overseer.

GOD: And where is he?

FARMER: Fled.

GOD: So he is gone? Well, you are here. Friend, not another
       word!

He gives him the apple and begins to eat one himself.

FARMER: I think I understand you. Give me the apple. *Chooses.*
       Can I have this one?

GOD: If it pleases you.

FARMER: *Eating.* Are you going west?

GOD: Something like that.

FARMER: Traveling all at night?

GOD: Yes.

FARMER: *Looks up.* Dawn is breaking.

The unfinished *Voyages* accompanied Brecht and Dessau back to Europe in 1947, and there Dessau provided a cryptic clue as to the allegorical nature of the God. Shortly after Brecht's death, he published a collection of settings of Brecht's poems that included "Four Songs" as well as "Aria of the God of Happiness." In his preface Dessau explained that they had completed the prologue and the first scene, but the ending had remained unfinished. "A few years later (1950), on the occasion of a guest performance of *Mother Courage* in Weimar, he said to me one morning in the hotel: 'I think I have found the ending for our *God of Happiness* now: Happiness is not to be put to death [in the last scene the God was supposed to be executed]. Happiness is: communism.' Brecht worked on the material again; the complete plan for the opera exists. But working on it without him is unthinkable."[107] The assertion that "happiness is communism" is certainly open to interpretation. At the time Brecht allegedly made this remark, he and Dessau were engaged in a tussle with the East German cultural authorities about the *Lucullus* opera (see next chapter). Perhaps it was ironic from the start; perhaps it became so only after the *Lucullus* affair rendered the operatic equation of happiness with communism utterly implausible.

The Music of 'Voyages'

The arias for the God and the Farmer illustrate the musical language and style Brecht and Dessau had chosen for the opera. The aria for the *God of Happiness* published in the 1957 piano-vocal score is quite similar to the version described above (PDA 1.74.257.4). Autograph particells indicate that the Farmer is a baritone and that his aria begins with the text, "We stupid farmer folk." It has no key signature, but accidentals place him on the flat side, in contrast to the God's sharp side described below. The meter undulates between 2/4 and 3/4, and his vocal line is far more melismatic throughout than that of the God in his aria. The Farmer has extensive expressive melismas on several key words: joy, peace, the second syllable of *verschieden* (different), the second syllable of *gefressen* (gobbled), piss, and the first syllable of the last word in the aria, *liegen* (lie). This style of writing is a marker of Italian operatic genres, particularly the baroque opera seria and the bel canto tradition of the nineteenth century; certainly it is the antithesis of stereotypical Wagnerian vocal writing. In his setting of Brecht's libretto for *Lucullus* in 1951, Dessau would use such writing to mark the upper-class characters (the imperialist exploiters) and distinguish them from the working-class characters (the exploited), but he did make notable exceptions to that characterization. For example, when a queen who has been raped bemoans her fate, a prostitute shares a similar story, and they sing a duet about their common experience in which the prostitute assumes the florid vocal style of the queen. In this way the tragedy of the common streetwalker is dignified and validated as equivalent to that of the queen (see chapter 4).

In the scene between the Farmer and the God, however, it is the Farmer whose aria features virtuosic melismas. Perhaps it is a means of endowing the character with human pathos, since the God is impervious to the frailties that afflict mere mortals. Dessau set the three verses in strophic variation (A, A1, A2), and the first two verses are anchored in a chromatically inflected B♭ major/minor. The vocal line in the third verse begins a whole step lower, but by the third line of text ("We say to the oxen 'piss!'") the melody returns to a familiar pattern on the original pitch of B♭. At the end of each verse the harmony features a C major-minor seventh chord in third inversion so that the B♭ on the bottom continues to sustain the B♭ orientation ("For us there is no difference. . . . We wipe out our stomachs with beets," and the last two lines of the elongated third verse, "We will not have the earth/Until we are lying under it"). The first two verses end with a sustained F in the vocal line; the ear anticipates that it will resolve to B♭, but the line descends a minor seventh to G instead. The last two lines of the aria are once again set to a melody with a strong B♭ major-minor orientation, but this time the seventh-chord harmony dwells on E♭ as well (F-minor seventh chord in third inversion), as if the aria has modulated to the dominant. It ends with a sustained B♭ in the vocal line, but instead of resolving to E♭, it drops the minor seventh to C.

The God of Happiness is undoubtedly a tenor, and his aria includes an indication that it should be accompanied by a muted trumpet onstage. It begins with seventeen measures of arioso singing, in which measures of rolled piano chords alternate with unaccompanied virtuosic singing marked "strictly in time." This section features alternating measures of duple and triple meter. There is one sharp in the key signature, and the accidentals situate the piece on the sharp side, but the harmony is actually defined by the sequences of parallel simultaneities that also characterize the aria proper. These simultaneities are perhaps best described as polychords comprised of two seventh chords, variously half or fully diminished, stacked with root position chords in the left hand and second inversion chords in the right, with the common tone voiced at the top. The result is tonally unstable, but the prevalence of this particular polychord structure establishes a distinctive, consistent sonority throughout.

The aria is in duple 6/8 and continues with the same chord structure, alternating half-diminished D♯- and F♯-seventh chords in the left hand with a persistent recurring C♯ in the right (the seventh of that chord and the common tone of the polychord). This sonority is intermittently ornamented with other nonchord-tone eighth notes in the right hand. At measure 27 ("So I can give you one") the left-hand chord drops to a C♯ half-diminished seventh chord, and the recurring C♯ at the top is ornamented with B, D, and B♭ but still circles around C♯. Interspersed are measures of arpeggios in contrary motion that are rich in cross-relations and rhythmic accents, maintaining Dessau's trademark tension via dissonance and rhythmic disruption. Measure 43 ("Only promise me") recalls the beginning of the aria and then gives way to a section dominated by the G♯ half-diminished seventh chord. Fifteen measures later this modulates a full step higher so that the climax of the aria is rooted in an A♯ half-diminished seventh with the highest reiterated top note yet, a high G♯ ("spit the seeds on the ground"). The harmony returns to D♯ at measure 65 ("Then come and pick the apples / From the tree that you have planted"), and the aria postlude reiterates the figuration of the opening. The aria moves through all the black-note keys in a dominant progression after the modulation to F♯ (D♯ = I; F♯ = III; C♯ = V/F♯; G♯ = V/C♯; A♯ = V/V in G♯ en route back to D♯ = I). The vocal setting features a few sustained high notes, mostly at the beginnings of phrases, but no excessive melismas or ornamentation.

Posthumous 'Voyages'

Despite Dessau's 1957 statement that he could not imagine completing *Voyages* without Brecht, he approached Heiner Müller a year later and asked him to develop a libretto based on the fragment. Müller and his wife, Inge, worked on the project but made little headway. Müller published his own fragment, entitled "God of Happiness," for the first time in 1975, and it bears little resemblance to Brecht's.[108] In his prefatory remarks to the fragment, Müller said that he was unable to complete the project based on Brecht's remnants because the parable genre was no longer appropriate for East Germany by 1958.[109] He could conceive of the God only as a football that was tossed about the playing field. There are a few points of contact between Brecht's original text and the version Müller published in 1975. The God descends from heaven and first appears to the Farmer; when the

Farmer complains that he and his family are starving, the God gives him a basket that will never be empty once something is placed in it. Unfortunately the Farmer has nothing to put in the basket in the first place. This is reminiscent of the first scene in Brecht's fragment, in which the God gives the Farmer an apple and tells him to spit the seeds on the ground so that a tree will grow and he can sustain himself, but the Farmer owns no land.

The connection between Brecht's libretto fragment and Müller's appears tenuous at best,[110] but an earlier version of Müller's text, entitled *G. G.* (an abbreviation for "Glücksgott"), bears a closer resemblance to it.[111] It begins with a prologue in heaven, in which the G. G. receives a report from earth. In the first scene the G. G. drives through a former war zone in a beat-up old car and ends up with youthful recruits, as in Brecht's fragment (*BFA* 10:921). The G. G. is betrayed by them and sentenced to execution but cannot be killed (see the parallel in *BFA* 10:925–927). Revolution breaks out, and the G. G. returns to heaven. He receives a second report from earth and descends once again to find that his disciples have built a false god whom they proceed to execute. Eventually the workers miss the true G. G.; he returns to the land of revolution and is caught up in a folk festival celebrating the arrival of communism. He then disappears, as his presence is no longer required. The epilogue is set in heaven, where some interplanetary tourists arrive to find it deserted and all the gods gone.

When Müller did not finish the project, Dessau sought out yet another collaborator to complete Brecht's libretto. Playwright Peter Hacks took up the *G. G.* text in 1963 and reconceived it as a piece of Americana.[112] He referred to it as a "fable sketch" and *The God of Happiness* as a working title; he also referred to it as *Die Zaubertrommel* (*The Magic Drum*), although the reasons for that are not evident in the surviving sketches. The action takes place in the Rocky Mountains, El Paso, the Rio Grande, San Francisco, and Sacramento; when the G. G. is persecuted for his communist beliefs, he flees to Guatemala, Costa Rica, Colombia, and Chile. Hacks and his coauthor and wife, Anna Elisabeth Wiede, indicated that the scene was set in the United States and Cuba in 1958, "during the time of imperial crisis." Their version of the heavenly prologue features several gods and an invisible choir. A sketch survives of lyrics for a song from act 1, in which "Rosabelle turns the colored floodlights on the dance floor. Enter four older businessmen with elk antlers on their heads" who then sing: "All the bars in the city are already closed, all the women have already been kissed, all the whiskey glasses poured, but the pleasure never ends." The elk-men have drunk more whiskey "than Niagara has water in April." The character Silver Jones invites them to "find a spot at my place, for a little cash" (PDA

1.74.831.1–2). Several American details seem to pay homage to Brecht: his experience as an émigré on the West Coast; his testimony before the House Committee on Un-American Activities; and allusions to *Mahagonny* in the song for the four elk-men and Silver Jones.

For the American reader, the spectacle of "elks" carousing at a conference out of town inevitably conjures images of the Benevolent and Protective Order of Elks of the United States. Founded in 1868 as a New York social club, the Elks became a large, national fraternal and charitable organization, but whether Brecht, Dessau, or Hacks had any knowledge of the American Elks is unknown. Hacks had an interest in eighteenth-century history and may have been aware of the Elks as a distant American descendant of the Freemason tradition. Hacks was also an imaginative, playful writer, and his children's stories are filled with animal characters. The "elks" may also be allegorical figures, but the fragments provide insufficient contextual evidence to determine their precise significance. Nevertheless the prospect of the Benevolent and Protective Order of Elks appearing in a libretto fragment by an East German playwright, which is in turn based on a fragment from Brecht's American exile period, adds one more delightful and wholly unexpected node to the expansive *Voyages* network.[113] The handful of particell drafts that survive reveals that Dessau's setting of Hacks's text would have been far simpler than the arias he set for Brecht's fragment discussed above. This prologue chorus is simple, syllabic, and diatonic, with a small vocal range. The draft of the call-and-response "Elks' Song" is similar, although the harmony is polychordal and the setting features greater rhythmic variety.

Hacks's fantastical Americanization of the *Voyages* libretto fragment brings us full circle to Brecht's early concept of the opera-America complex. These unfinished American opera projects are also interwoven with other texts in extensive, unexpected ways. The unrealized African American adaptation of *Threepenny Opera* appears to have been the impetus for a study of American race relations in two other nonoperatic works; the *Goliath* fragment represents an exploration of the aesthetic possibilities of Eisler's interpretation of the Popular Front for the stage, and themes from *Goliath* also resurface in other fragments of the period, such as *Julius Caesar*; and Brecht seized on the operatic tradition of allegory as a vehicle for parable in *Voyages*. The *Goliath* and *Voyages* fragments also outlived the playwright, playing significant roles in the oeuvres of surviving collaborating composers, where they became imbedded in other networks of texts.

On the one hand, Brecht's three modes of engagement with opera during his American exile confirm that he continued to derive new texts for operas and for other projects from extant material, be it published, fragmentary, or someone else's, just as he always had. On the other, opera and/in the United States did not wield nearly the cultural capital it had on the Continent. While opera continued to symbolize a European ideal of high culture, it was neither prevalent nor important enough to be appropriated by the cultural industry apparatus, particularly on the West Coast. Perhaps Brecht worked on opera without prospects for production in part because, in the inverted reality of American exile, opera appeared curiously impervious to capitalist exploitation. By virtue of being operas in the cultural economy of the United States, *Goliath* and *Voyages* in particular may have been destined "for the drawer" from the start and thus ideally suited for exploratory purposes. In fact, because Brecht was an author who perpetually revised his published, performed texts, his entire oeuvre might be described as unfinished and exploratory; that these projects remained incomplete in the conventional sense need not be construed as indicative of failure. On the contrary, recontextualized within a larger network of texts, they represent significant nodes in Brecht's creative process, further evidence of the integral role of opera in his work.

4 'Lucullus'

Opera and National Identity

Brecht left the United States on 31 October 1947, immediately after he testified before the House Committee on Un-American Activities. He spent several months working in Switzerland and then proceeded to East Berlin, where he would spend the rest of his life; Dessau and Eisler followed shortly thereafter. In 1949 Brecht founded the Berliner Ensemble and resumed his collaboration with Dessau on a new opera project, one they would see through to completion. *The Trial of Lucullus (Das Verhör des Lukullus)* and its attendant dispute marked a watershed moment in the development of cultural policy in the German Democratic Republic (GDR). The March 1951 premiere was closed to the public, revisions were required by the SED (Socialist Unity Party—the ruling party in the GDR), and, amidst much hue and cry from the West German press, a new version entitled *Die Verurteilung des Lukullus (The Judgment of Lucullus)* was performed publicly that October. The literature has tended to treat this episode as an act of totalitarian censorship in the Soviet bloc. Naturally the GDR was subject to Moscow's authority, but it was not a simple case of bending to monolithic Soviet will without question. Reexamination of these events brings three important points to the fore: Opera reprised one of its traditional roles in the German socialist state as a symbol of national identity and an instrument of state power;[1] Brecht's delicate symbiotic relationships with the party apparatus and with the West were in a perpetual state of flux; and the SED engaged in negotiations designed to appease two very attentive yet diametrically opposed audiences in the external (Western) press and the internal (Soviet) apparatchiks.

Brecht and the SED leadership found themselves in a precarious position. The GDR was the only communist state situated in such close proximity to the West, as West Berlin was literally in its own backyard. Brecht was the most famous of the leftist intellectuals to move from a career of "anti-capitalist dissidence to writing within a society officially described as both anti-fascist and beyond capitalism." His role in the new state has been described as that of the mascot of actually existing socialism,[2] even as he continued to nurture an international reputation as a rebel within that system. Ultimately and unexpectedly, given master narratives of this period, scrutiny from the external (Western) audience proved more influential than the considerable pressure exerted by Moscow. Despite protracted internal negotiations and public assertions by the SED that it had the artists firmly under control, Brecht's text was only nominally emended, and Dessau's "formalist" music for the revised *Lucullus* remained stylistically unchanged. The playwright emerged relatively unscathed, while the composer bore the brunt of public criticism, but ultimately neither was required to make extreme artistic concessions. In the process, Brecht honed the diplomatic skills that enabled him to prosper in the GDR,[3] and the SED exhibited far greater acumen and autonomy from Soviet control in its management of early cultural politics than heretofore acknowledged.

CULTURAL CONTEXT

That two committed Marxists such as Brecht and Dessau inaugurated their careers in the fledgling German socialist state with an opera, and that the opera then ignited a firestorm of official reaction, speaks to the status of the genre in a state struggling to define and establish itself. Richard Dellamora and Daniel Fischlin have noted, "Opera . . . gives shape to a symbolic landscape by producing and contributing to myths of national authenticity and legitimacy."[4] For functionaries and intellectuals alike, opera was a crucial piece of German cultural history that could be used as a building block for the new state. They wanted to see GDR culture, defined by self-conscious connections to a pre-Nazi legacy, as proof that the antifascist socialist democratic project could produce a legitimate German state. The SED sought to "appropriate and identify itself with the 'proper' cultural heritage . . . to verify its claim to be the bona fide successor to all 'progressive' and 'humanistic' traditions in the German past."[5] By 1952 the significance of opera for this project was articulated directly in the call for "a new German national opera."[6] All sides were drawn to the traditional symbolism of the genre for nation building and saw its production as crucial to the national legitimacy project.

There may have been agreement that opera had a role to play, but its form, its message, and its sound were major points of contention between SED leadership and intellectuals returning from exile in the West. SED leaders were former members of the KPD (German Communist Party), most of whom had spent the war years exiled in Moscow, being groomed to lead socialist Germany. In cultural matters they adhered to the Soviet party line of socialist realism, the aesthetic mandated by Stalin as the "creation of cultures national in form and socialist in content." In theory, art should reflect not current reality but the potential utopia latent in the present that will emerge eventually under socialism. In practice, socialist realist music was diatonic and accessible and has often been derided as regressive when compared to simultaneous modernist developments in the West.[7]

The antithesis of socialist realism was formalism, which the Soviets viewed as the last gasp of bourgeois capitalist decadence: atonality, experimentalism, modernism. There are two scholarly interpretations of socialist realism: The traditional account views it as a doctrine with such stringent requirements that artists could never hope to meet them; other research has shown that its requirements were effective because they were actually quite amorphous and mutable and kept artists guessing while endowing politicians with maximum powers of destabilization.[8] Strands of both are evident in the treatment of new operas that provided test cases for musical socialist realism in the Soviet Union. The notorious castigation of Shostakovich's *Lady Macbeth* in the newspaper *Pravda* in 1936 provided the template for Andrei Zhdanov's resolution "On the Opera (*The Great Friendship*) by V. Muradeli" in 1948. Zhdanov asserted that listeners could not be expected to tolerate formalist music, "music that is crude, vulgar, based on atonality, on dissonance from beginning to end, music in which consonance is made the exception and false notes and their combinations the rule."[9] Soviet composers got the message. Opera was particularly susceptible to scrutiny because it had a text, it was a publicly performed genre with an established and approved canonical heritage, and it played a central role in the establishment of national identity: "The most important task of Soviet music is to create a Soviet classical opera that has as its contents the ideas and forms of the Stalinist epoch. All the strengths of the entire collective of Soviet composers must be enlisted toward the achievement of this task."[10]

The Resolution of 1948 coincided with the return to eastern Germany of several leftist intellectuals who had been in exile in the United States, including Brecht and Dessau, and a clash of Marxist cultural theories ensued. Brecht and Dessau believed that culture in the socialist state could not take classical bourgeois masterpieces as models. However timeless or universal such models may appear, their value is socially constructed, and they should not be adopted uncritically because they represent and reproduce a social order incompatible with the aims of socialism. A socialist state needed new art forms or, at the very least, refunctioned genres, in Brecht's parlance. With *Lucullus*, Brecht and Dessau attempted to recast opera as an art that would be relevant in this new, antifascist, socialist German context.

Brecht was also actively involved in establishing the apparatus of GDR cultural politics. He was a founding member of the German Academy of the Arts (Deutsche Akademie der Künste, since 1973 known as the Academy of the Arts), the opening ceremonies for which took place in the thick of the *Lucullus* controversy, and was very influential in its workings. The fact that the SED did not have a majority among the academy's working committees enabled Brecht and his allies, including Arnold Zweig, the academy president Brecht had helped place, to manipulate matters by appealing to higher authorities within the party with whom they enjoyed good relations. For example, contrary to Marxist-Leninist norms of governance, "Brecht was instrumental in securing confirmation of the Academy's status as the GDR's highest authority in the arts, over which the Cultural Commission had no say."[11] By maneuvering the academy outside the purview of the commission he assured the institution a degree of autonomy, supervised only at the highest level. Of course, that autonomy was predicated upon Brecht and his faction remaining in good graces with the authorities. This is just one of many ways in which he selectively cooperated and negotiated with the SED to improve the status of the arts and of his own position.

INTERNATIONAL POLITICAL CONTEXT

His relationship with SED leadership was complicated for reasons that extended far beyond aesthetics and cultural policy, however. The party was eager to welcome internationally acclaimed artists to the SBZ (Soviet Occupied Zone) because their endorsement lent legitimacy to the German socialist project. These intellectuals were committed Marxists, and, initially, they were also optimistic about the prospect of realizing the socialist utopia on German soil. But friction developed almost immediately between the leaders who had been exiled in Moscow or had survived the war in camps and those intellectuals returning from the West, particularly the relative peace and prosperity of Hollywood. The special treatment afforded those returning from the West also bred resentment, as the SED promulgated a star system in which prominent German intellectuals living in exile were enticed to come to the SBZ and then to the GDR with promises of privilege and celebrity.[12] Brecht used this to his advantage, as he knew that his voluntary residence in East Berlin was a coup for the SED in both domestic and international public relations.

Perhaps just as important in these early years, Brecht had never been a member of the KPD. Former members were closely scrutinized by the SED, which compiled biographies of their activities during the Nazi period to search for evidence of wrongdoing. The investigations into Nazi-era KPD behavior escalated, and those who had been in exile in the West and those who had been in Western or Yugoslavian camps were declared unfit for leadership positions because they might have been compromised by foreign spies while abroad.[13] This paranoia was exacerbated by the Noel H. Field affair, in which Field, an American communist who had helped the KPD during the war, was now thought to be a double agent working for the United States. Suddenly all Western émigrés were suspected of being operatives recruited by Field, and the ensuing hysteria convulsed leadership throughout the Soviet bloc. After the Field purges, no one returning from the West could reasonably consider him- or herself immune. Despite his position of privilege in 1949, Brecht applied for an Austrian passport on the basis of his marriage to the Austrian Helene Weigel and received notice of his approval a year later. Dessau was not a member of the KPD because he had been rather apolitical before emigration, but he had become an American citizen in 1945 and joined the CPUSA a year later. He retained his American status until 1952 when his German citizenship was reinstated, four years after he had joined the SED. (Brecht never became a member.)[14]

The course of the *Lucullus* controversy was further affected by a wave of anti-Semitism disguised as "anticosmopolitanism" that swept through the Soviet bloc between 1948 and 1956.[15] In a series of articles published in *Einheit* in 1948–49, SED Central Committee member Ernst Hoffmann defined "cosmopolitanism" by listing "a rather complete catalogue of traditional anti-Semitic stereotypes": It radiated from the United States; it came from those who lacked a national homeland and were rootless; and it was capitalist in nature.[16] Jeffrey Herf has noted that "the campaign drew upon mutually reinforcing associations of Jews with the West" to indict both.[17] This conflation was facilitated by Jews' disproportionate representation among KPD members who had emigrated westward. Although Jews constituted only a tiny minority of former KPD members, the party would have made a concerted effort to get them out of Germany in the 1930s. Furthermore their socioeconomic backgrounds tended to be middle class and educated, atypical of the overwhelmingly working-class KPD membership, and these assets would have made it financially possible for them to leave and to survive abroad.[18]

The anticosmopolitan campaign reached a fever pitch in November 1952, when Rudolf Slansky, the second-highest-ranking figure in the Czech

Communist Party, and thirteen accomplices were found guilty of imperialist espionage and Zionism. Slansky and ten others were Jewish. In the GDR the hysteria pitted those who had been in the West, many of whom had vocally supported Jews during World War II,[19] against those returning from Moscow, for whom emphasis on the Jewish Holocaust at the expense of the persecution of the socialist resistance was unacceptable. If one was Jewish, had been in exile in the West, worked with Jews, or had supported the Jewish cause, neither party prominence nor international reputation offered immunity from trumped-up charges and show trials. Brecht was not Jewish, but Dessau and Eisler were. The two composers found themselves entangled in public opera debates that seemed driven in part by their status as undesirable on at least two counts (as Jewish and as Western émigrés—not to mention that Dessau still had his American citizenship in 1951). Gerhard Müller sees in these opera debates, the *Lucullus* controversy of 1951 and the 1953 crisis over Eisler's *Johann Faustus*,[20] the seeds of what could have developed into full-fledged Slansky-style persecution in the GDR.[21] At the very least, these episodes make clear that operas, and the artists who wrote them, were taken very seriously.

THE GENESIS OF 'LUCULLUS'

The opera *Lucullus* had a long gestation period. Brecht began writing an antiwar radio play based on the life of Lucullus while in exile in Sweden in 1939, just after he completed *Mother Courage*. It received its radio premier on Swiss Radio Beromünster in 1940, the same year in which the text was published in Moscow in the German exile magazine *International Literature*. Roger Sessions composed a setting of the translation by Hoffman Reynolds Hays, which Brecht had sent him, for performance at the University of California–Berkeley in 1947.[22] Brecht tried in vain to interest Stravinsky and Gottfried von Einem in setting the text and eventually approached Dessau. The playwright continued revising the radio play in the GDR, adding the crucial final scene in which the court renders a guilty verdict.[23] Dessau began to conceive of their collaboration first as a radio opera and then as a staged opera. He completed four discrete settings of *The Trial* between 1949 and 1951 and produced *The Judgment* in the summer of 1951.[24]

Brecht's title character was based upon the historical figure Lucius Licinius Lucullus (c. 110–56 B.C.E.), who was a Roman general famed for his wealth, his thirst for war, and his lavish culinary tastes. After leading several victorious campaigns, he became commander of the forces in the Third

Mithridatic War (74–64 B.C.E.) and enjoyed eight years of military success despite being unpopular with his soldiers, who resented his harsh discipline and incessant warmongering. Eventually he was deposed by his enemies in Rome and retreated to private life, where the spoils of war enabled him to live luxuriously. The phrase "Lucullan feast," used to describe an extravagant gourmet meal, refers to his opulent hospitality.

Brecht's text begins as Lucullus is carried to his grave in an elaborate funeral procession. As his body passes through the streets, onlookers comment on his reputation and his demise, some remembering his extravagant lifestyle, others his ruthlessness as a general. He is buried alongside the Appian Way with an elaborate funeral frieze depicting his victories in battle. Lucullus then appears in Hades, where he must account before a court for the life he has led. He asks for the frieze from his tombstone and offers to explain the meaning of the scenes to the court, but the judge asks to hear from the people themselves. They appear before the court as ghosts. Two legionnaires testify that Lucullus went to war to acquire wealth for himself, not for Rome; two children slaughtered in the conquest of a city recount their experience; a fisherwoman whose son was killed in battle recalls her grief; and a queen mourns the death of her king. Lucullus's chef describes his good taste, and the peasant who carried the cherry tree from Asia to Rome gives lukewarm testimony in his defense, but it is not enough to save him: Lucullus is condemned to Nothingness. Brecht exposed the dishonorable side of the glorified field general by questioning the value of imperialist war, focusing on the plight of its victims and the culpability of those who wage it.[25]

Dessau's settings share an eclectic, distinctive musical ensemble by operatic standards and a consistently dissonant musical language. In a timbre reminiscent of Stravinsky's orchestration in the 1920s, violins and violas are conspicuous by their absence. The orchestra consists of limited woodwinds (three flutes), brass (three trumpets, three trombones, a tenor horn, and a bass tuba), six or more strings (at least four cellos and at least two basses), three pianos (two prepared, in which foreign objects are attached to the strings to produce percussive sound effects, one normal grand piano), a harp, an accordion, an enormous percussion section (sixteen assorted drums, three gongs, two xylophones, a glockenspiel, temple blocks, a midsized anvil, a large rock with which to beat on a piece of sheet metal), and a trautonium. The trautonium, invented in 1929, consisted of a fingerboard with a resistance wire stretched over a metal rail and coupled to an oscillator. The performer presses the wire to the rail, completing the circuit and manipulating the pitch. Hindemth, Egk, and even Strauss had composed pieces for it, and its distinctive electronic sound had formed part of the technology-obsessed soundtrack of the Weimar Republic. Three marimbas may be substituted for the pianos if necessary. Against this backdrop Dessau employed everything from simple, diatonic, folklike song to operatic parody marked by extreme tessitura and ornamentation. His use of musical styles as sociopolitical symbols for characterization will be analyzed after the relevant events are recounted below.

EVENTS LEADING UP TO THE PREMIERE OF 'LUCULLUS'

The Internal, Soviet Audience

The events that took place between February 1950, when the Deutsche Staatsoper first submitted *Lucullus* for approval as part of its upcoming season, and 17 March 1951, when the SED closed the premiere, played to the internal, Soviet audience.

12 December 1949	Dessau completes version one of *The Trial of Lucullus*
13 February 1950	Ernst Legal, intendant of the Deutsche Staatsoper in East Berlin, submits his season to the Ministry for Education for approval, including *Lucullus*
25 March 1950	Kurt Bork of the Ministry for Education recommends *Lucullus* to the SED Central Committee Department of Culture
18 April 1950	Legal receives permission from the Department of Culture to stage the work
27 June 1950	Dessau completes version two of *The Trial*
19 November 1950	Soviet newspaper *Tägliche Rundschau* attacks the Staatsoper's production of *Ruslan and Ludmilla* by Glinka. It also attacks Legal
28 December 1950	The Ministry of Education asks to see Dessau's score
9 January 1951	The Ministry of Education asks to see Dessau's score again
14 January 1951	Dessau completes version three of *The Trial*

REHEARSALS ARE UNDER WAY

14 February 1951	The SED Central Committee secretariat appoints Egon Rentzsch of the Department of Culture and composer-musicologist Ernst Hermann Meyer to judge the opera and report back to the committee

8 and 9 March 1951	Rentzsch and Meyer attend rehearsals
12 March 1951	Rentzsch and Meyer deliver an overwhelmingly negative report. The SED Central Committee determines that "the opera *The Trial of Lukullus* is not to be publicly premièred and shall be removed from the schedule"
13 March 1951	Selected delegates attend rehearsal and participate in an open forum afterward. It is determined that the performance on 17 March will take place before an invited group only
17 March 1951	Dessau completes version four of *The Trial of Lucullus*. The opera has its closed première at the Deutsche Staatsoper

Subsequent actions taken between 17 March and 12 October 1951, when the revised opera received a public premiere, were ultimately dictated by the external, Western audience, thanks to the West Berlin press, which diligently reported each detail of the piece's suppression. The machinations surrounding *Lucullus* have received considerable attention elsewhere in the literature.[26] They are reviewed here to clarify the publics involved, to highlight the contradictions and compromises in the process, and to map that chain of events onto Brecht's revisions and Dessau's compositional process.

Dessau completed his first draft on 12 December 1949. Ernst Legal, intendant of the Deutsche Staatsoper in East Berlin, submitted the opera for approval with the rest of his proposed season to the Ministry for Education (*Ministerium für Volksbildung*) on 13 February 1950. That ministry, represented by Kurt Bork, recommended the piece to the Department of Culture (*Abteilung Kultur*) of the SED Central Committee, stating Dessau's music "in no way renounces harmony and melody. The comprehensibility of the language and the action is preserved. The attempt to develop a new form of music theater appears to be successful, as far as it is possible to judge from a piano reduction."[27] The Department of Culture expressed initial misgivings, but on 18 April 1950 Legal received permission to stage the opera. He engaged Hermann Scherchen to conduct, and the premiere was set for 17 March of the following year. Dessau completed a second version of the opera on 27 June 1950.

The SED thus appeared to adopt an initial position of support, or at least noninterference, but was soon forced to take action against Legal. The Soviet newspaper *Tägliche Rundschau* published an article attacking a Staatsoper production of Glinka's *Ruslan und Ludmilla* on 19 November 1950, lambasting Legal in particular. This precipitated a decline in relations between the SED and the intendant that resulted in far greater scrutiny of *Lucullus*. The Ministry of Education asked to see Dessau's score repeatedly, although these requests appear to have been ignored. Dessau completed the third version on 14 January but did not submit it for review. It is clear from Brecht's journal entry of the following day that he and Dessau anticipated trouble, particularly with the music:

> Spoke to Dessau this afternoon, the chorus rehearsals have begun for *Lukullus*, but now the Ministry for Education demands to see the parts again, and Dessau would love to postpone the premiere until the fall. I am against it. The subject is so important now that the American threat is so hysterical. Of course Dessau fears an attack on the form, but it will be, should be, less drastic, since the content is so important. Finally both Dessau and I are convinced that the form of the opera is the form of the content.[28]

The "American threat" to which Brecht refers was the amassing of troops under General MacArthur on the Chinese border in September 1950. He was confident that officials would find the antiwar content of his opera so timely that they would be willing to accept the "form"—Dessau's sometimes thorny, dissonant musical language—even as he acknowledged that the music left Brecht and Dessau vulnerable to charges of formalism. Brecht himself found the score compelling and appropriate to the story: "The music has absolutely nothing to do with formalism. It serves the content in an exemplary way, is clear, melodious and fresh. We are imagining things when we start to see formalism everywhere."[29]

Amid the rising tension, the SED gathered informed opinions before passing final judgment. On 14 February the Secretariat of the Central Committee appointed composer-musicologist Ernst Hermann Meyer and Department of Culture representative Egon Rentzsch to judge the opera and report to the committee. They attended rehearsals on 8 and 9 March, and on 12 March delivered an overwhelmingly negative report, based on observations of two and a half scenes. "[The music] contains all the elements of formalism, distinguishing itself by the predominance of destructive, caustic dissonances and mechanical percussive noise; the method of the triad and of tonality, if present at all, is mostly employed for the purpose of parody or of an archaic mysticism."[30] Subsequently, the Central Committee determined, "The opera *The Trial of Lucullus* is not to be publicly premiered and shall be removed from the schedule."[31]

In tandem with this heavy-handed edict, however, the Committee also assembled delegates from various official organizations to attend the rehearsal on 13 March and to participate in a forum afterward. Members of mass organizations, worker and farmer groups, the Free German Youth, the League of Trade Unions, and a handful of intellectuals and musicians took part in a remarkable discussion that is preserved in two transcripts.[32] Not surprisingly, party functionaries reacted to the opera in an almost uniformly negative fashion, and, among the cultural luminaries present, only Scherchen, his pupil Harry Goldschmidt, and Arnold Zweig rose to the opera's defense. Several themes familiar from the Soviet opera debates run through the negative comments. Critics focused on the music separately from text and drama, complained about excessive dissonance and percussive orchestration, insisted that music must be "beautiful," and distrusted satire; modernism was criticized as old-fashioned and irrelevant to the masses, while the bourgeois nineteenth-century model was touted as new and accessible.

Other participants expressed a wide range of opinions, however, many of them positive, and were evidently given free rein to do so. At least one said that the message was too pessimistic and did not provide appropriate heroes, but others stated that the music effectively expressed the text. Some valued the Staatsoper as a venue for experimental new opera, and still others emphasized the importance of music that did not allow the listener to lapse into complacency. Despite professional critics' claims that the opera would not be accessible to the *Volk*, lay participants appeared to weigh the merit of the opera as it pertained to the reality of existing socialism in 1951. Many referred to recent lessons of history concerning censorship, resistance, and the desire for peace. Such comments confirm that the opera was timely, as Brecht had hoped.

Assembling handpicked party members to debate a controversial topic was a standard Soviet tactic, although discussants in the Soviet Union were hardly free to speak their minds. The haphazard course of the *Lucullus* discussion, however, suggests that citizens could indeed voice divergent ideas in the GDR. The outcome does not appear to have been preordained and leaves open the possibility that the participants' opinions played a role in resolving the situation. The discussion continued later in a small, presumably invited group. It was determined that the opera would be performed one time in its current form before a select audience, consisting primarily of organizational representatives from the Free German Youth, the police, and official ministries. The Berliner Ensemble also received a handful of tickets. The fourth version of the opera bears a completion date of 17 March, implying that Dessau was still tinkering with the score even as the curtain went up.

The opera was well received, and a tape of that closed performance confirms that applause drowned out the derogatory whistles. Some eyewitnesses attributed this response to the fact that uninterested members of the Free German Youth, ordered to attend and disrupt the performance by Chairman Erich Honecker, gave away their tickets and West German media snapped them up. Others claim that the party claque was too intimidated and surprised by the genuinely enthusiastic response to resist.[33] If the SED leadership had been attempting to engineer an audience that would reject the piece and validate their increasingly negative position, they failed.

Earlier on the same day, Hans Lauter had delivered a speech to the Fifth Congress of the SED Central Committee entitled "The Struggle against Formalism," in which he identified *Lucullus* as a negative example. The opera caused "direct pain to the ears: a lot of percussion, inharmonious tones, one doesn't know if one should look for a melody. . . . One certainly cannot take such an artwork as an example that will help us to build our democratic culture."[34] Perhaps Soviet pressure or these discussions about the opera's fate had affected Lauter's opinion, because the draft of his speech he had submitted for approval eleven days earlier had made no mention of *Lucullus*. It had singled out Orff's *Antigonae* as an example of musical formalism, taken Legal to task again over the *Ruslan and Ludmilla* episode, and cited Brecht's *The Mother* as a negative example from the theater, but the *Lucullus* opera did not warrant mention on 6 March.[35] In yet a third version of Lauter's speech published on 23 March, his remarks on the opera were included: "The percussion makes the music most inharmonious, and likewise produces distortion of taste. . . . Through such music, which cannot be tied to our classical cultural heritage, one can obviously not develop our new democratic culture, the contents of which are democracy and struggling humanism."[36] On 6 March Brecht had been singled out for criticism by name, and Dessau was not even on the radar; by 17 March Dessau's music was under attack and Brecht's name was mentioned as the librettist, but his text was not publicly criticized.

The External, Western Audience

Before the publication of Lauter's speech, the events described above played only to a small, select, internal Soviet audience. Private meetings of high-ranking officials, opera rehearsals, and invitation-only discussions would have been virtually undetectable to Western observers or the average GDR resident. When the morning edition of *Neues Deutschland* announced on 17 March that the scheduled premiere would not be open to the public, however, that audience was quickly expanded to include the West. In a critical miscalculation, the East German press ignored the private performance for a week while the West German press that had somehow gained access to it filled the information void with accusations of East German censorship, training an unwelcome international spotlight on the young nation's cultural-political birth pangs.

West Berlin papers *Der Kurier, Der Abend, Telegraf, Der Tagesspiegel,* and *Die Neue Zeitung* all reported basic information, and most of what is known of the events in the Staatsoper on 17 March appears to come from accounts in the West German press. Some reviewers noted that subsequent performances announced for Tuesday and Wednesday had been cancelled, and several expressed sympathy for Legal's ongoing problems with the SED. Werner Oehlmann's piece in *Der Tagesspiegel* described Dessau as the successor to Kurt Weill in his mix of musical styles:

> In Paul Dessau, Brecht has found a musician to carry on the work of [Kurt] Weill. But decades of shattered measure and value lie between the *Mahagonny* songs and the artistically organized chaos of the *Lukullus* scenes. Dessau makes music with the fragments of Western music that Stravinsky has left behind. The only aspect continually intact is the incessant pounding rhythm. Out of it rise scraps of melody, concentrated short forms that represent emphasis or suffering, march or signal, call or song. But Dessau is successful in unifying the shards in a mysterious way.[37]

On 21 March, H. H. Stuckenschmidt's account in *Die Neue Zeitung* was prefaced with an editorial statement noting the silence of the GDR press and described the music in great detail: "In its best moments, the music, which ranges from popular to twelve tone, has a character of melancholy and desolation, for which only Mahler is a model." He described the opera as "a new musical form, in some elements related to Claudel-Honegger's *Jeanne d'Arc*" that made a strong impression and would certainly have successors.[38]

East German acknowledgment of the performance finally appeared in *Neues Deutschland* on 22 March. Critic Heinz Lüdecke described the opera as a "failed experiment" and faulted Legal, Brecht, and Dessau. Predictably, his complaints about Legal echoed those of the November 1950 *Tägliche Rundschau* essay. He allowed that Brecht's choice of topic may have been significant when he began the piece in 1939, but he could not see its relevance now that the Soviet Union had the power to bring war criminals to justice. While allowing that "individual songs confirm Dessau's talent . . . a lot of cabaret-like bad habits must be laid aside if he wants to develop from a composer of interesting songs and accompaniments to a creator of musical drama." He compared Dessau to Stravinsky,[39] a rhetorical gesture that would have had a particular resonance in the East German press since Stravinsky was a favorite target of the Soviet campaign against formalism.

"Cosmopolitanism" could apply to Stravinsky, even though he was not Jewish, because he was "rootless," having defected to the West, and he composed modernist music. In the context of the ongoing purge, Lüdecke's association of a Jewish composer with an avowed formalist suggests anti-Semitic motives.

As the only public acknowledgments of the opera in the GDR were negative and were published in the official journal of the ruling party, the SED appeared to have established a firm position of opposition. When Hamburg's *Die Welt* reported on 21 May that a substantially revised opera would be featured in the new Staatsoper season, the journalist Walter Lennig decried "the evil, lurking, furious silence of total propaganda" in the GDR.[40]

Between 17 March and 12 October: Playing to Both Audiences

That silence masked a flurry of activity, however, as officials struggled to anticipate Soviet expectations while monitoring the response of the Western media. In an extraordinary show of governmental interest in the arts, GDR president Wilhelm Pieck invited Brecht, Dessau, and others to his home for a meeting on 24 March, where it was determined that revisions to both libretto and score were required and only a new version could be performed. Under the watchful eye of Paul Wandel, minister of education, Dessau then met on 10 April with a contingent of Soviet composers who were in East Berlin for the ceremony celebrating the founding of the Academy of the Arts. General Secretary of the Soviet Composers' Union Tikhon Khrennikov led a contingent of musicians who listened to a tape of the performance and rendered their verdict: The music was "worse than dissonance"; it was "yesterday's music"! It was "the bestiality of fascism," "noisy and monotonous," and lacking in musical development.[41] See table 2.

These initial meetings pointed toward a hard-line Soviet position on the opera, but further actions taken on 5 May suggest that concerns for the external, Western audience outweighed those for the internal, Soviet audience. Pieck's handwritten notes confirm that a new version would be premiered in the fall, based on text changes Brecht had already made and Dessau's description of forthcoming revisions. The president stipulated that the performance must be open to the public and the press invited to attend. Most significant of all, the new version was not to be subject to official approval. A resolution to that effect was passed by the Politbüro on 15 May and simply stated that revisions must occur before performance: "Pending completion of the planned changes, the production is authorized for the fall."[42] Brecht's assistant Käthe Rülicke confirmed that the fall performance was "not contingent upon Dessau's changes to the music."[43] It is possible that Pieck trusted Dessau to make substantial changes, but the explicit requirements that the premiere be opened to the public and attended by the media suggest that the president had the external, Western audience in mind.

The decisions of 5 May and the corresponding resolution passed on 15 May proved to be binding, and Dessau never submitted a complete score for inspection, despite repeated requests from the Division of Performing Arts in the Commission of Artistic Matters (Kunstangelegenheiten). He ignored them until 29 September—two weeks before the premiere—at which point he submitted only the first scene. Karl Egon Glückselig, Staatsoper chorus master, wrote Legal on 7 August to say that he liked the first half of the score very much and that the manuscript of *The Judgment* bore a completion date of 22 July. In other words, Dessau could have submitted the score if he had felt compelled to do so. Primary manuscript evidence indicates that these extramusical events had very little, if any, influence on Dessau's music for the five versions of *Lucullus* (identified as 1–5, below) and no discernible impact on the musical style of *The Judgment*. Far greater changes occurred before March 1951 than between March and October of that year.[44]

Brecht, on the other hand, *was* required to submit his changes for approval. He sent revisions to Pieck in a letter of 6 April and copies to Ackermann, Bork, Grotewohl, Herrnstadt, and Lauter on 18 April, asking for their approval.[45] The resolution of 15 May, based on the text changes they had already seen and Dessau's promise of revision, signaled their acceptance. The libretto evolved over the course of their collaboration between 1949 and 1951, and text changes accounted for some of the revisions Dessau made to his four settings under the title *The Trial of Lucullus* (versions 1–4).[46] Brecht made the final round of emendations—what amounted to the libretto for *The Judgment of Lucullus*—after the first premiere and, presumably, after the meeting with Pieck, since that occurred only a week after the performance.

Brecht's notes from March 1951 contain four questions that may have been derived from the meeting with Pieck and the playwright's proposed response to each issue. There was some minor concern that the children's role might be misconstrued as opposing heroic honor, but the other questions point to the need to make a sharp distinction between a defensive war, which is permissible because it allows one to defend the homeland, and a war of aggression, which is always deplorable. Brecht needed to clarify that Lucullus was guilty of the latter and suggest ways in which the populace could fight back in such a war. Aside from minor word alterations throughout, Brecht resolved these problems by making substantive changes to

TABLE 2. *'Lucullus' Events, 17 March–12 October 1951*

External, Western Audience and Response	Internal, Soviet Audience and Response
17 March 1951	
Neues Deutschland notes that the premiere will be closed to the public	Dessau completes version no. 4 of *The Trial of Lucullus*
The Trial of Lucullus has private premiere at Staatsoper	Lauter's speech to the Fifth Congress of the SED CC; discussion follows
19 March 1951	
West Berlin papers *Der Kurier* and *Der Abend* publish reports of the premiere	Dessau and Brecht begin letter-writing campaign
20 March 1951	
West Berlin papers *Telegraf* and *Der Tagesspiegel* publish reports of the premiere	Pieck invites Dessau and Brecht to his home
21 March 1951	
West Berlin paper *Die Neue Zeitung* publishes report of the premiere	
22 March 1951	
Negative review by Heinz Lüdecke in *Neues Deutschland*	
23 March 1951	
Excerpt from Lauter's speech published in *Neues Deutschland*	
24 March 1951	
	Pieck, Brecht, Dessau meet with commission. Revisions required to text and music.
28 March 1951	
	Pieck reports to SED CC
7 April 1951	
Nürnberger Nachrichten story	
10 April 1951	
	Dessau meets with Soviet composers

TABLE 2 *(continued)*

External, Western Audience and Response	Internal, Soviet Audience and Response
	5 May 1951
	Pieck, Brecht, Dessau meet with commission. Concerns about media. In light of planned changes, commission recommends new public performance.
	15 May 1951
	SED CC authorizes new production for the fall
	21 May 1951
Hamburg *Die Welt* story	
	22 July 1951
	Dessau completes version no. 5, which is *The Judgment of Lucullus*
	August–September 1951
Revised version of Lauter's speech in *Einheit*	Bork warns Legal that he may not stage the opera without permission and asks to see the score; Bork asks CC for instructions. Rehearsals are under way.
	29 September 1951
	Dessau submits score of first scene only
	8 October 1951
	Rentzsch to Lauter: Brecht's revisions are approved and Dessau promises to overhaul the score. CC withholds judgment until after the performance
	12 October 1951
The Judgment of Lucullus is publicly premiered at the Staatsoper	

scenes 4, 8, and 12. In scene 4 he reassigned the troublesome verses from the children to the Teacher; in scene 8 the King Lucullus had defeated was identified as having fought a defensive war; and in scene 12 Lucullus's Roman legionnaires condemn him amid regrets that they had not helped those whom they defeated in his service.[47] Finally, the title was changed from the process-oriented *Trial* to the more conclusive *Judgment*.

Of course it was standard practice for Brecht to revise a piece after its first performance, based on his own experience and on feedback from other participants and audience members (see chapter 1). For example, discussions with children, young adults, and teachers who had seen or participated in the first version of *He Who Said Yes* revealed that most were dissatisfied with what they perceived to be its undue emphasis on obedience. Brecht wrote a companion piece entitled *He Who Said No* and directed that they be performed as a pair so that audiences could make up their own minds, but when the students remained unsatisfied with this solution Brecht revised *He Who Said Yes* accordingly.[48] The *Lucullus* emendations therefore give the outward appearance of being perfectly consistent with Brecht's established habits of revision—revising a piece based on the way it worked in performance and implementing changes based on the suggestions of others—but machinations behind the scenes suggest that he may have been under extraordinary pressure to comply. He did not dwell on the subject of SED supervision in his journal and did not appear to be overly concerned with the fate of the opera in his summer correspondence. Perhaps he was confident that he would reap the benefit of the relationships he had carefully cultivated with high-ranking party members. Even so, the contents of an anonymous memo found in his papers and dated May 1951 must have given him pause. The unknown author noted that although the press had focused its negative commentary on Dessau's music, "The text is to blame above all." The note castigated Brecht for ideological errors in his libretto, especially his representation of the *Volk* as passive, his failure to distinguish between defensive wars and wars of aggression, and the omission of a political-historical consideration of Lucullus's war. The memo goes so far as to invoke the Stalinist charge of confusing the people *(verwirren)*, previously cited by Lauter. Gerhard Müller asserts that the memo represents notes taken at the 5 May meeting that were then passed to Brecht by an ally as a warning, possibly by Pieck himself.[49] If Müller's assessment is correct, it casts doubt upon the timeline of revisions and who had seen them, as Brecht had already fully addressed the question of just and unjust war well before that date.

Either way, the official activity behind the scenes was in stark contrast to the public front. On 16 May Brecht was asked to speak about the *Lucullus* situation at the first meeting of the Pan-German Culture Conference, and he took that opportunity to engage in some damage control with the West Germans in attendance. He described his excellent working conditions in the GDR (eleven assistants, large rehearsal space, the possibility of engaging guest actors from abroad) and stated unequivocally that "there is no intervention on the side of the authorities. Such reports in the western press are ill-informed."[50] Despite all of this formal activity, both public and private, the opera that was ultimately performed on 12 October 1951 (version 5) featured music that was virtually identical to that which had been performed on 17 March (version 4). Manuscript scores from these two performances and the tape of the first premiere are the smoking guns,[51] proof that appeasement of the external, Western audience was at least as important as meeting Soviet demands for enforcement of the socialist-realist aesthetic, subjection of returning Western émigrés to cosmopolitan purges, and subjugation of the SED to Soviet control. Dealing with Brecht privately and letting Dessau take the fall publicly appears to have been a calculated decision.

THE MUSIC

While comparison of versions 4 and 5 reveals two virtually identical scores and proves the political point, comparing them to earlier versions proves the musical ones. The opera underwent far greater revision before the first premiere than after it—that is, before political pressure was exerted—and the general nature of revision precludes the possibility that changes were made as concessions to that pressure. In versions 3 and 4 (completed between January and March 1951) one can trace Dessau's development of a vocabulary of musical styles and elements as symbols of the characters' sociopolitical positions. Upper-class and royal characters are portrayed with stock operatic gestures, aligning them with the bourgeois tradition and marking them as remnants of the presocialist, fascist era. Working-class characters are marked by a variety of musical styles and elements designed to distance them from that tradition and to establish a new language for opera in the antifascist socialist state. The development of these musical indicators is evident in scene 8, which features testimony from several victims of war and received the most complete overhaul between versions 3 and 4. In addition to setting new text as necessary, Dessau made major musical revisions to two numbers: the duet between two young women, which became a duet for two children; and the section for the Queen and the Courtesan. Analyses of these numbers from versions 3 and 4 illustrate Dessau's demarcation of sociopolitical status in the symbolic deployment of musical language (diatonic, with gradations ranging from triadic harmony to extreme dissonance; or post-tonal), instrumentation, form, voice type, and melody.

The first four versions of *Lucullus* were composed between December 1949 and 17 March 1951, during which time the SED went from supporting the opera in March and April 1950 to having second thoughts in December, investigating the opera in February 1951, and attempting to ban it weeks later. Dessau revised version 1 after it was approved and before the furor began (version 2); he revised further (version 3) as the Ministry for Education repeatedly asked to see the score, although he did not fulfill those requests; and he continued to rewrite (version 4), if the autograph score is to be believed, until the first performance was virtually underway. It would be a mistake, however, to infer from this timeline that Dessau was frantically attempting to meet SED expectations before the March premiere. The music for version 4 is substantially revised from that of version 3, but in only one instance do those changes result in a more consonant, accessible sound. Rather, Dessau's musical revisions appear to have been driven by the continual fine-tuning of his symbolic musical vocabulary, Brecht's evolving text, and practical performance concerns.

Musical drafts indicate that Dessau knew from the onset how he would delineate the title role, and the part remained virtually unchanged from the first version to the last. A signature gesture for the field general provides an example of his musical characterization and a baseline sample to which other musical symbols may be compared. Lucullus is a tenor, often played by a *Heldentenor*.[52] Brecht abhorred the tenor voice as much as he detested the violin, so the fact that the playwright conceived of the title role as a tenor is an indication of his contempt for the character. In his study of Dessau's operas, Gerd Rienäcker distinguishes the lyric tenor from the heroic tenor, who, "saddled with buffa elements, appears in the form of the negative, aristocratic individualist (Lucullus, Bürgermeister), the very ones whom early libretti had celebrated as heroes."[53]

Dessau drew upon stock musical, dramatic, and operatic symbols to represent Lucullus as warmongering, imperial, and elitist. He is often accompanied by the military ensemble of brass and percussion, with the occasional addition of a flute for fanfare. His vocal style is usually loud and high, defiant and bombastic. His opening remark in scene 8 repeats the phrase "I swear" from scene 5 and is typical of his character. Irrelevant text repetition, extreme range, and military ensemble are all symbolic of his social position. Although this character and his attendant musical symbols

Example 13.   Dessau, "I Swear," from *Lucullus* version 5: mm. 6–19. © Maxim
Dessau. Reproduced courtesy of Akademie der Künste, Berlin, Paul-Dessau-Archiv.

would have been considered heroic and noble in traditional opera, in the
new German socialist, democratic antifascist state, Dessau appropriated
these symbols and inverted their meaning. The conquering "hero" is no
longer admirable; rather, the true consequences of waging war and staging
bloody conquest are revealed by other characters in the opera, whose musical styles contrast starkly with Lucullus's. Lucullus's character is evident in
example 13.

For Dessau's symbolic use of musical style to be successful, two preconditions needed to be in place: The audience had to be familiar with the standard operatic repertoire, its characters, forms, and musical styles; and listeners had to recognize the use of these symbols in *Lucullus* as subversive,
questioning the received social hierarchy instead of reinforcing it. This system assumed considerable prior knowledge and defied the socialist realist
mandate to emulate the bourgeois tradition rather than subvert it. The aver-

age operagoer might have assumed a field general to be a heroic figure;
after all, his musical characterization marks him as such, and he is the title
character. Yet if he is the hero, how can all the little people who used to serve
him ultimately condemn him to Nothingness? And why should the anti-
hero get to sing all the music audiences go to the opera house to hear, if
audiences are not supposed to like his character? For those who understood
Brecht's epic theater, these inverse delineations made perfect sense. For
those who did not, such as the party functionaries who had been steeped in
Soviet socialist realism, it was a source of confusion.

Dessau radically reconsidered the use of musical style to delineate other
characters between versions 3 and 4 (and not, as one might have expected,
between versions 4 and 5). This is clearly demonstrated in a comparison of
the scene 8 duet assigned to two young women in version 3, "With Streets
and People and Houses," and then to two children in version 4 as "With
People and Houses." In each case, the two are called upon to testify against
Lucullus by recounting his attack upon their city. In the earlier incarnation,
the duet is dissonant throughout, often aggressively, percussively so; in its
revised and final manifestation, the vocal lines move in parallel thirds and
unisons against unobtrusive diatonic accompaniment.

VERSION 3: "WITH STREETS AND PEOPLE AND HOUSES"

YOUNG WOMEN: With streets and people and houses
                with temples and waterworks
                we stood in the landscape, today
                only our names
                are standing on this blackboard.

SPEAKER: The shade juror who had been a baker bends
            forward ominously and asks:

BAKER: Why?

YOUNG WOMEN: One day at lunchtime pandemonium broke loose
                a river washed through the streets with human waves
                and it carried away everything we had. That
                evening
                only a column of smoke was visible
                on the site that once was a city.

The following is Brecht's text revision for version 4. Changes ranged from
those needing minimal musical attention (excising a word and shifting from
first to third person in the first two verses) to those requiring new music
and perhaps even a new concept (adding a third verse and assigning the
parts to two children).

VERSION 4: "WITH PEOPLE AND HOUSES"

TWO CHILDREN: With people and houses
with temples and waterworks
they stood in the
landscape. Today
only their names stand on this blackboard.

BAKER: Why?

TWO CHILDREN: One day all pandemonium broke loose
A river washed through the streets with human
waves and carried away
everything we had.
That evening only a column of smoke appeared
on the spot that was once a city.

BAKER: Go on.

TWO CHILDREN: And in the cities were
250,000 children
they are now no more.
The great Lucullus
overcame us with his bronze war chariots
and conquered all of us.

In both versions the duet is partitioned by interjections from other characters, and Dessau's settings reflect these natural divisions. In version 3, the first section is marked *piano* and features a static, dissonant accompaniment for two flutes, accordion, and piano. The vocal part is both lyrical and complex, as the second woman imitates the first at the rhythmic interval of one full beat and the melodic interval of a fourth and then a fifth. This section ends a cappella, with the voices in homophonic parallel seconds to emphasize the text "today/only our names are standing on this blackboard." In version 4 this section is greatly simplified. The dynamic is still *piano*, but the diatonic accompaniment features rolled chords in the piano and flutes doubling the vocal lines. The children sing homophonically throughout, first in parallel thirds and then closing in unison at "today/only their names stand on this blackboard." Excerpts from these settings are shown in examples 14 and 15.

The second duet section, which describes Lucullus's destruction of the city, is the site of the greatest stylistic disparity between the two versions. The musical character in the second section of version 3 is drastically different from that of the first section, as the lyrical, imitative vocal writing and amorphous accompaniment are replaced by an aggressively rhythmic, dissonant language. The orchestration features a full contingent of military brass set against a chromatic countermelody in four cellos. Where the vocal

Example 14.   Dessau, "With Streets and People and Houses," from *Lucullus* version 3: mm. 1–9. © Maxim Dessau. Reproduced courtesy of Akademie der Künste, Berlin, Paul-Dessau-Archiv.

Example 15.   Dessau, "With People and Houses," from *Lucullus* version 4: mm. 1–8. © Maxim Dessau. Reproduced courtesy of Akademie der Künste, Berlin, Paul-Dessau-Archiv.

writing in the first duet section was lyrical, here it is entirely declamatory. Both tessitura and range are higher, and the women sing homophonically at the interval of either a major second or a minor second. Its equivalent in version 4, on the other hand, retains the folklike orchestration of the previous section and adds a harp. Flutes double and harmonize the unison vocal line at the interval of a third, while the other instruments provide ostinato quarter notes bouncing between a pedal point on low A and B or D an octave above. These settings are juxtaposed in examples 16 and 17.

Dessau's initial impulse had been to give dissonant, complex music to the

Example 16. Dessau, "With Streets and People and Houses," from *Lucullus* version 3: mm. 18–21. © Maxim Dessau. Reproduced courtesy of Akademie der Künste, Berlin, Paul-Dessau-Archiv.

Example 17. Dessau, "With People and Houses," from *Lucullus* version 4: mm. 12–20. © Maxim Dessau. Reproduced courtesy of Akademie der Künste, Berlin, Paul-Dessau-Archiv.

common people who were victims of war. This language was one way in which Dessau could differentiate the workers from the exploiters, such as Lucullus, whose musical style parodied Wagner's heroic tenors. The duet in version 3 is nonoperatic by comparison, in that it is not a locus of emotional reflection and gratuitous vocal display but a vehicle for text and plot to provoke a critical response from the audience. Rienäcker has noted that Dessau tended to write parts for working-class female characters as altos because women singing in the middle and lower ranges convey "inner human maturity, sorrow and resoluteness that in no way need explaining through lavish noise."[54] The duet parts here are for two characters described only as young women, which suggests lighter, more naïve voices than the altos Rienäcker may have been describing. Even so, the vocal parts are in the middle range, there is no gratuitous vocal display, and the largely homophonic text setting privileges text comprehension.

Why Dessau did not retain this setting or even its style is a matter of speculation. The fact that Brecht changed the characters from young women to children suggests that he was seeking an even greater contrast between the innocence of the characters onstage and the tragic events they witnessed, and Dessau's revisions reflect that reorientation. It is also possible that the singers simply could not learn the difficult dissonant setting in the few rehearsals prior to the March premiere. That Dessau simplified the music as a concession to external political pressure is the least convincing possibility, if only because recasting one number from an entire opera would hardly be sufficient to alleviate official concerns.

While the duet setting in version 4 establishes a clear musical opposition to Lucullus, it is not difficult to see why SED functionaries steeped in socialist realism questioned Dessau's epic use of symbolism. Most would have had expectations of operatic norms but scarce knowledge of epic theater. The audience is meant to side with the children, the Teacher, and other nameless victims of war, but those characters don't get to sing arias, which would have marked them as operatic heroes. Their musical style could be misinterpreted as simplistic, as if common people were incapable of performing anything but folksong. Subsequent operas proved that Dessau did not see this style as the inevitable future of opera in the antifascist socialist state. Rather, the binary opposition of good and evil at work in *Lucullus* required equally polar and inverted musical symbolism, but the cues were susceptible to misreading if one was familiar only with the opera canon and not with Brecht's challenge to it.

If the children's duet exemplifies the stylistic decisions Dessau made regarding music to represent the common people, the segment for the

Queen and the Courtesan reveals the delicate balance he sought between two characters who are both victims of war but represent different social classes. Their duet in scene 8 was drastically revised in each phase of versions 1 through 3 and received its definitive overhaul between 3 and 4. This required a redistribution of dramatic and musical heft that was achieved primarily through reducing the amount and difficulty of the Queen's music while increasing that of the Courtesan. The Queen must be presented as both nobility and as a victim of war while not allowing her royal tragedy to displace the commonplace but no less tragic Courtesan. The text as it appeared in versions 1 and 2 is given here; subsequent changes are noted below as necessary.

VERSION 1 AND 2: "ONCE UPON A TIME"

QUEEN: Once upon a time I went into Taurion
early in the day to bathe
advancing from the olive grove
fifty foreign men
overtook me.
For a weapon I had a sponge
and clear water as a hiding place
to protect myself from their tank
and not for long.
I was quickly conquered.
Filled with terror I looked about
and screamed for my maidservants
and the terrified maids
screaming behind the bushes
all were defeated.

COURTESAN: And why are you here now?

QUEEN: Ah, to show the conquest.

COURTESAN: Which conquest? The one over you?

QUEEN: And over beautiful Taurion.

COURTESAN: And what did he call triumph?

QUEEN: That the king, my husband
with all his armies
could not protect his kingdom
from monstrous Rome.

COURTESAN: Sister our fate is the same
because monstrous Rome
one day could not protect me from itself.

TOGETHER: Sister, our fate is the same.

Dessau initially drew on traditional operatic forms for the Queen. Her aria began as a da capo in which he inserted the second verse in a contrasting style and set the third identically to the first. In version 1 the range and tessitura for the Queen were impossibly high, as virtually every note was above the staff and repeated high Fs were required. Earliest revisions may simply reflect an effort to make the role singable. Using a slightly lower tessitura, though still exploiting the range and agility of the coloratura voice, had the same effect without sacrificing the singer. In version 2 the setting is loosely modeled after the traditional cavatina-cabaletta form. The first part of the final section is sung by the Queen alone, and the second, in which a chorus would traditionally join for the finale, becomes a duet in typical Italianate fashion: The Queen sings her verse alone, the Courtesan repeats it a fifth below, and they conclude by singing together in parallel thirds. A passage from the finale of their duet is shown in example 18.

After version 2, Dessau experimented with various ways of simplifying and balancing this section while retaining essential symbols of nobility in the Queen's part. Many intermediate drafts that are not part of the five main opera versions survive.[55] In version 4 he eliminated all simultaneous singing for the women, reconfiguring the duet as an exchange of dialogue and arias, presumably prompted by Brecht's switch to familiar address (dein, dir) that identifies the Courtesan as the Queen's equal. Her solo begins in the same manner as the Queen's ("als ich"), and she sings her personal history in a discrete aria with its own style rather than simply joining the Queen's song.

VERSION 4: "WHEN I WAS SOLD FOR SEX"

COURTESAN: When I was sold for sex
And I was sixteen years old
I bowed my head to insults and beatings every day.
All for a little oil and bad pasta.
Therefore I know how you suffered
on that terrible day
and I feel for you, woman.

The final incarnation of this segment contains three arias: two short pieces for the Queen ("Once upon a Time" and "That the King, My Husband") and a longer one for the Courtesan ("When I Was Sold for Sex"). The Queen's first aria consists of only one verse, although it still bears the markers of female nobility with coloratura at the ends of phrases, gratuitous text repetition, flute obbligato, and a notated cadenza for the finale. Dessau further equalized the relationship between the two characters by giving the

Example 18.   Dessau, "Sister, Our Fate Is the Same," from *Lucullus* version 2: mm. 88–95. © Maxim Dessau. Reproduced courtesy of Akademie der Künste, Berlin, Paul-Dessau-Archiv.

Courtesan the same instrumentation (plus bass flute) and an aria twice as long as the Queen's second piece. The Courtesan is a mezzo-soprano and her melody is simpler, although she does sing melismas at the ends of two phrases. They are not as long or as elaborate as Queen's, but the similarity is intentional; a note beneath her first melisma reads, "The figuration receives the same value as in the analogous places for the Queen." Finally, a balance of power is achieved within the opera overall because this is the Queen's only scene, and the Courtesan is onstage throughout as a member of the jury.

The musical representation of their social relationship is calculated to simultaneously maintain class differentiation (royalty versus low-class prostitute) while forging solidarity (victims of war and capitalist oppression). It is an ambitious plan, and its interpretation is tricky even for those who have deciphered the opera's stylistic symbolism. The Lucullus baseline has established that characters who sing high, virtuosic music are the class enemy, and the Queen's royal status is consistent with that designation. Yet how does one reconcile that information with her legitimate claim to war crime victimization? She also bears more than a passing musical resemblance to Mozart's Queen of the Night. Can we trust her, or is she, too, lying about the identity of the enemy? The Courtesan is a mezzo-soprano, and, according to Rienäcker's theory, this means that she is an honest, working-class citizen. But if gratuitous vocal display is a marker of the exploiting classes, how are we to understand the melismas in her aria that imitate those of the Queen? Does the apparent effort to bring her up to the Queen's musical level by means of a traditional operatic gesture undermine her credibility as an opponent of exploitation? The simultaneous exploitation and subversion of operatic tradition through musical symbolism is perhaps the greatest attraction of the opera. The primary manuscript evidence confirms that this paradox was a means of addressing musical-dramatic issues and not a concession to political pressure.

CONCLUSIONS

Efforts to appease the two very different but equally attentive audiences resulted in a delicate compromise. The opera was scrutinized after the Soviets publicly attacked Legal; it was castigated in the GDR press; the public premiere was delayed for several months; and the SED announced that it had required the artists to make revisions. This all appears calculated to appease the internal, Soviet audience, which required close monitoring of formerly exiled intellectuals and adherence to socialist realism. As the GDR's most prominent intellectual Brecht was spared the public fray, but the precarious nature of his relationship with the state is apparent in the fact that he alone was required to submit his revisions for approval, albeit privately, while Dessau's musical style was allowed to remain unchanged, despite the sensational negative press the SED had engineered. If Dessau was in fact publicly sacrificed to protect and retain Brecht, it would be consistent with the anti-Semitism of the campaign against cosmopolitanism.

Predictably enough, the external, Western audience lost interest once the scandal of censorship had passed. Critics from both the internal, Soviet and the external, Western audiences who attended the October premiere voiced similar complaints about the opera's modernist tone but, remarkably, no one noted that the score remained virtually unchanged.[56] Granted, the few who had attended the first premiere would have heard it only once, but perhaps more important, all were expecting to hear a thoroughly different opera, given the SED's public demands for revision. And while the SED encouraged the press to cover the October performance, this did not signal complete acceptance of the piece. It was not part of the operatic repertoire in the GDR until the 1960s, and there is evidence that the SED actively interfered to prevent further productions in the 1950s.[57] This is consistent with a practical, long-term commitment to the internal, Soviet audience.

The October performance can be viewed as a public relations coup in which the tiny new socialist government deftly maneuvered between two superpowers. It appears that the SED remained on reasonably good terms with its prominent intellectuals by entering into collusion with them, requiring nominal revisions in exchange for submitting to what was ultimately a meaningless public reprimand that nevertheless satisfied the Soviets. In the process Brecht made sufficient compromises to remain in good standing with the party and banked some political capital on which he would subsequently draw in June 1953. From Moscow, the October performance might have had the sheen of official forgiveness bestowed upon prominent intellectuals, not unlike the redemption that had been orchestrated for Shostakovich at the premiere of his Fifth Symphony. Meanwhile, permitting a second performance, even in an ostensibly revised version, mollified the artists and satisfied the external, Western press by allaying suspicions of censorship, putting an end to the relentless media scrutiny. The opera went on to have its Western premiere when Scherchen conducted version 4 in Frankfurt on 30 January 1952. Radio Frankfurt broadcast the performance on 25 May, and it was rebroadcast on 2 September by the British Broadcasting Corporation in London and Radio Audizioni Italiana in Rome.

Many accounts written since the fall of the GDR that claim to reveal the "truth" about life behind the Iron Curtain actually continue to parrot the party line, claiming that the SED forced Dessau to completely rewrite his score. Portraying the *Lucullus* controversy as an early step in a regime's ineluctable course to repression ignores the genuine, messy processes through which a young nation attempted to establish its identity and the familiar, nation-building role opera played in that agenda. Excluding the opera itself obscures the fluctuating nature of relationships between the state and its star intellectuals, particularly Brecht, and the significance of the arts in the fledgling GDR. The less cynical reader will recall that, in 1951, there was still a sense of hope and optimism for the success of socialism on German soil. The controversy may have begun as a response to the opera and its role in East German nation building, complicated by collateral contextual issues such as Stalinization and its attendant campaigns against cosmopolitanism, Jews, and modernism. But in the end, Brecht, Dessau, and the SED all took actions determined by the realities of playing to two opposing audiences on the international cold war stage.

5 Brecht's Legacy for Opera

Estrangement and the Canon

Having devoted the entire volume thus far to the argument that Brecht's theories and dramatic texts are indebted to opera, I now propose its inverse: Opera is indebted to Brecht. The evidence lies not in librettos and scores but in production, stagecraft, direction, and mise-en-scène and in their effect on the spectating audience member. The experience of attending an opera performance today is frequently shaped by a stage director whose work has in turn been informed by Brecht's audience theory, arguably his most influential bequest.[1] Ever mindful of the danger inherent in sweeping generalizations, I maintain that this is the common denominator among nonliteral productions of canonical operas, regardless of their political or artistic agendas: The staging aims to create the experience of estrangement for the spectating audience member. That experience is a two-step process—"disillusion (*Verfremdung*) constitutes a return from alienation (*Entfremdung*) to understanding"[2]—and it is one of the great pleasures of attending opera as *Regietheater* (director's theater).

The mandate is to take a familiar and, in all likelihood, much-beloved opera and render it unfamiliar.[3] The resulting disorientation, confusion, or outrage is not the endgame of estrangement, however; once expectations have been thwarted, the new perspective triggers cognition, or re-cognition. Defamiliarization reconfigures the relationship of the audience member to that opera and, more ambitiously, even the relationship of the audience member to the act of operagoing. The efficacy of estrangement depends on two things: the spectator's prior knowledge of and experience with the particular opera in question; and the spectator's expectations and prior experience of operagoing in general. This amounts to estrangement from opera (lowercase "o," meaning the individual piece, such as *La forza del destino*) and estrangement from Opera (uppercase "O," as in the concept, institution, and social practice).[4] Estrangement from opera pertains to the work in live performance, what Sauter calls the theatrical event, "in which the meaning of a performance is created by the performers and the spectators together, in a joint act of understanding."[5] Canonical opera is defamiliarized via the unexpected, be it some sort of anachronism, reflexivity, or intertextuality. Estrangement from Opera permits critique of the social infrastructure in which both opera and operagoing participate and is often achieved by implicating the audience in the work of the production. This can be quite literal, as when Hans Neuenfels staged the audience in his 1981 Frankfurt production of *Aida* or Paul Shortt used onstage mirrors to reflect the audience's gaze back upon itself in his 1997 production of *La traviata* for Opera Company of Philadelphia.[6] In the United States, such tactics are likely to be endorsed by marketing departments in hopes of "attracting new audiences by updating old pieces" or "making opera relevant." In Europe, particularly in Germany, these productions provide a director with the opportunity to put her unique stamp on a standard text and to make provocative political, philosophical, and aesthetic statements in the process.[7]

Gundula Kreuzer describes the phenomenon of director's opera as "that much-cited yet little-defined 'radical' mode of production that cares little about original stage directions or 'authentic settings.' Instead, it aims to uncover psychological, political or social threads that tie the work in with topical concerns, thus bestowing the entire operatic enterprise with contemporary relevance."[8] Estrangement via this enterprise is not always or necessarily effective (nor, it should be noted, is the enterprise itself), but it *can* be a very powerful experience for an operagoer. Those with nominal attachment to a particular realization of an opera in performance may find it effective, as may those who know a given opera so well that their engagement with the present radical production is in constant dialogue with normative versions they have stored in their memories.[9] I argue that estrangement has its roots in Brecht's own operagoing experience, and, in that sense, it has come home to roost in opera productions.

In this context estrangement is an instrument of Brecht's minor pedagogy, a means of empowering the audience in its engagement with conventional bourgeois theater repertoire. This is distinct from major pedagogy, the instigation of literal political activism via the theater event to which Louis Althusser's notion of spectatorship is indebted, as is Augusto Boal's Theatre of the Oppressed project working in tandem with Paolo Freire's Pedagogy of the Oppressed in Brazil.[10] Major pedagogy transforms the spectator into a spect-actor, a subject with agency that extends well beyond the theater,[11] and this is the agenda most often associated with Brecht. It is not necessarily applicable in all theater contexts, however, and the comparatively modest mission of minor pedagogy via estrangement is custom-made for canonical opera.

My analysis follows the distinction between live performance and production proposed by Erika Fischer-Lichte. She posits four criteria for a theory of live performance: it is a singular, unique event that arises from the interaction between those onstage and those in the audience; it is ephemeral, as it occurs in the moment and cannot be replicated, and therefore no two are identical; it does not transmit extant meanings but brings forth meanings that emerge from this interaction; and it is characterized by its "eventness," meaning that it facilitates a particular mode of boundary-crossing experience.[12] A production, on the other hand, is the concept that informs the stage half of the relationship in performance.

I feel compelled to issue two caveats before pursuing the argument that an aesthetic of estrangement in nonliteral productions of canonical texts is the Brechtian legacy for opera. First, the experience of estrangement, also known as the V-effect (*Verfremdung*), is not inherently nihilist (and, perhaps it must be said, neither is the phenomenon of director's opera). To minimize the prejudicial effect of the standard grammatical construction (estrangement *from* the opera), and to accommodate the possibility that the engagement might be productive, "estrangement *with* the opera" or "estrangement *and* the opera" may be used to emphasize the second phase of the process as a rapprochement of sorts. Second, despite the negative connotations attached to that term in its various English translations and entrenched conventional wisdom to the contrary,[13] estrangement is not part of a vast Brechtian conspiracy to prohibit pleasure in the theater. Quite the contrary: Its purpose is to facilitate agency in the subjective experience of the spectating audience member,[14] and such moments of defamiliarization and re-cognition can be highly pleasurable. Pleasure in this context is not the hedonistic, intoxicated *Genuß* Brecht derided in his *Mahagonny* notes but the *Vergnügen* to which he refers when he declared that "there is such a thing as pleasurable learning."[15]

In nonliteral stagings of canonical texts the pleasurable experience of estrangement is elicited generally through the disruption of expectation and the subsequent realization thereof, often in the rupture between what is seen and what is heard. In this chapter I theorize the experience of estrangement as both intellectual and physical[16] by interpreting Brecht's ideal "smoking-and-watching" audience through the lens of somatic modes of attention posited by cultural anthropologist Thomas J. Csórdas. Finally, I will reflect on moments and means of estrangement experienced while attending a performance of a nonliteral production by Stefan Herheim (Verdi's *La forza del destino* at the Staatsoper Unter den Linden, 2005).

WHAT IS BRECHTIAN?

First, however, the term "Brechtian" cannot pass unchallenged. The nature, and even the existence, of Brecht's influence on theater as an important, enduring legacy has been variously asserted and refuted by disciples and detractors alike. His plays and theoretical writings are cited often enough, but repertoire and acting style suggest that this amounts to little more than lip service, the canonization of a historical master, rather than the use of a generative, living method that manifests itself in the arts of writing plays and performing them. Michael Patterson sums up the predicament as follows: "Can one claim that Brecht's legacy is anything more than a matter of employing a more or less fashionable label to enhance theatre work ranging from performance art to agitprop?"[17] This is due in no small part to what may be the most enduring and dubious remnant of the entire epic theater project: the term "Brechtian." An indefinite adjective so broadly and casually applied as to be rendered virtually meaningless, it is equally effective as honorific or epithet depending on the speaker and context. Attempts to articulate its meaning frequently devolve into a parody of the definition of obscenity proffered by U.S. Supreme Court justice Potter Stewart in 1964 ("I shall not today attempt further to define the kinds of material I understand to be embraced . . . but I know it when I see it").[18] Both the term "Brechtian" and its mutability are integral to the legacy and invite interrogation.

A host of prominent Brecht scholars have made this observation in one way or another, and I invoke their assessments to establish patterns of usage. Patterson notes that "'Brechtian' can legitimize; it can also limit; it can certainly distort"; and "in a world where all progressive forms of theatre are 'Brechtian,' none is."[19] According to Eric Bentley, "'Brechtian' is often not so much a literary or theatrical term as an exercise in public relations."[20] Marc Silberman describes the indiscriminate application of the term to connote everything from incongruous to naturalistic as the "epistemological decentering" of what is designated as Brechtian in the theater,[21] and Andrzej Wirth has famously decried this as a state of "Brecht reception without Brecht."[22] Similarly, Maarten van Dijk attributes the failure of self-conscious efforts to be Brechtian to "the overwhelming tendency to see Brecht's theory and practice as a style rather than as a method."[23]

"Brechtian," then, appears to be a general term encompassing all manner of anti-Romantic, antibourgeois theatrical characteristics that have "become so much a part of standard stage practice that it is difficult to determine whether they actually result from his influence."[24] The term operates on two levels. At the superficial level of style, "Brechtian" most commonly refers to the requisite sparsely appointed stage, the exposed apparatus, actors who address the audience directly, and various other means of eliminating the fourth wall, all originally designed in opposition to the extravagance of fin de siècle Wagnerian theatricality. Leaving aside the matter of whether these traits originated with Brecht, it is clear that they have come to be associated with him; his "overpowering authority" has long meant that "his work was the central reference point in considering new theatre aesthetics" in the twentieth century.[25] The surface quality of that style is easily appropriated without its attendant method and is now so prevalent as to have virtually become the hegemonic authority against which it once rebelled. Replicating superficial traits without acknowledging that they may no longer generate the desired effect—style without method—is akin to what David Levin describes as a model of reiteration as repetition, rather than reiteration as reinflection.[26]

Silberman's equally valid albeit apparently contradictory observation that "Brechtian" is applied to everything from incongruity to naturalism, however, suggests that the term also operates on a second level related to audience experience. Both meanings may pertain simultaneously or only one may be appropriate in any given instance.[27] Whether invoked to support a positive or negative assessment, the adjective used in this sense consistently implies thwarted expectation—a performance or production that does not comply with one's anticipation of a particular genre, text, or playwright. Over time, canonical texts accrue standard performance practices that affect production design as well as audience experience. (Other expectations come into play where a new text is concerned, but for the purposes of this argument as it pertains to opera, I will concentrate on the canon.) An audience member's perception will be determined by her awareness of this particular text's intertextuality—that is, the ways in which this production engages with others of the same opera, by the same director, or in the same house or of other operas by the same composer; the director's decisions are informed by the same data.[28] When a performance of any canonical opera— by which is meant the generally understood popular, standard repertoire spanning the period from Handel to Puccini—does not fit preconceived notions, the audience member's experience of it is described frequently as Brechtian, regardless of whether the experience was pleasurable or frustrating (or both). This usage does not connote discrete elements of staging or performance practice, as the first one does, but rather their effect. It indicates an audience experience of estrangement, the defamiliarization of an opera the spectating audience member believes she knows and may even love.

TRANSMISSION OF PRODUCTION TRADITION
IN THEATER AND OPERA

It is this second usage of "Brechtian," that which connotes estrangement, which is particularly apt when considering nonliteral productions of canonical opera, those which Levin calls reiteration as reinflection.[29] Opera is distinct from spoken theater in this regard in at least two important ways. The first has to do with tradition, and the second with the work of the audience in a performance. As Levin and others have noted, it has long been standard practice to stage the most canonical of plays, such as those of Shakespeare, in nonliteral ways. Within the context of that performance practice tradition, a literal staging of the play *Macbeth* would be interpreted as conveying some additional meaning: perhaps a deliberate rejection of or gloss upon the phenomenon skeptics describe as "interventionist" production or a self-conscious attempt to reclaim some version of authenticity. The tradition of staging canonical *opera* in nonliteral ways, however, is comparatively recent. Where Wagner's operas are concerned, its roots are in the work of Adolphe Appia and most conspicuously in the Wieland Wagner era at Bayreuth;[30] as applied to opera in general, it is typically traced to the emergence of director's opera in the 1970s. (Adorno complained about the German penchant for updating opera via contemporary costumes and settings in 1969.)[31] In other words, there are considerably fewer production texts with which an opera staging can be intertextualized.

Critics of director's opera frequently note that (some generally agreed upon version of) the musical score and libretto are revered as the sacrosanct, essential material of the text, while stage directions, however copious or reliably attributed to the librettist, composer, or both, are treated as ancillary and optional.[32] Regardless of the origins of this viewpoint or its legitimacy, there is no denying its staying power, not only in the popular imagination but also in the scholarly one. Of course it is possible to follow "the printed stage directions as if they had exactly the same kind of authority as the notes prescribed in the musical score,"[33] but even those meticulously attentive to matters of "authenticity" must concede that such directions do not account for every moment of every operatic performance in the same way a score does.[34] The score is the template for the acoustic in performance, and that sonic component is virtually continual. The lyrics are not omnipresent; there are always instrumental passages that are unsung. Stage directions, however explicit, cannot specify the details of the visual for every second of the performance as it occurs in time to nearly the extent the score determines its simultaneous aural complement. Stage directions are not granted the authority of the score because they are unable to convey a comparable degree of specificity for the duration of the piece. This is not to deny that all manner of interpretive performing decisions must be made with regard to realizing the score as well, but it is a matter of degree.

Acknowledgment of this condition gave rise to the *livre de mise-en-scène*, or production book, first associated with Parisian grand opera in the early nineteenth century. These were typically published in conjunction with the score and sold to opera houses in the provinces, where directors were thought to need guidance realizing the extravagant new expectations of stagecraft and spectacle associated with the emerging grand opera genre. Verdi's experience with the French *livre* is said to have been the impetus for the series of *disposizioni sceniche* (production books) Ricordi published for at least eight of his operas beginning in 1855. Wagner's painstaking attention to stage description and direction in his scores reflects a similar desire to communicate details of appropriate productions as he attempted to impose some element of quality control and interpretive consistency. Unlike the standard procedure in spoken theater, in which *Regiebücher* (director's books, or production notes) were typically kept on file and used in-house in manuscript form, the opera production guides described above were produced for the express purpose of publication and widespread distribution. They were clearly meant to serve as models for productions in far-flung opera houses.[35]

Brecht's contribution to the genre of the production book more closely resembled the tradition of the opera than that of the spoken theater. He was at least obliquely familiar with the operatic version because Weill and Neher had compiled one for *Mahagonny*, although Brecht did not contribute to it. After he returned to Europe from American exile he embarked upon a project of creating so-called model books for publication and widespread distribution rather than just in-house use. The Swiss *Antigone* was the subject of the first one, distinguished by its extraordinary detail and extensive visual documentation in photographs by Ruth Berlau. Despite cautionary disclaimers that the model books should be used as "provisional texts available for fresh inscription in a changed set of circumstances,"[36] the decades following Brecht's death saw the utter ossification of his models, perhaps nowhere more egregiously than in his own theater, the Berliner Ensemble.[37] In other words, the model books were received and followed as if they were opera production books. Verdi's *disposizioni sceniche* were not intended as suggestions or as stimuli to prime the creative pump; rather, they were "binding instructions." According to these original documents, "The task of the stage director is to insure—by instructing and bullying the performers and technical staff—that the work be staged precisely as described therein."[38] Brecht's disciples treated his model books with the same deference for authority, even though he—the authority—had forbidden it.

Regardless of the degree to which Verdi's production books are followed literally today, it is apparent that they were so explicit in the first place because the most likely point of intervention in the network of texts that are handed down and said to comprise the opera is at the level of the visual— costumes, *mise-en-scène*, and action. For those who would experiment with canonical opera, radical treatment of the visual component is not perceived as endangering the opera's essential identity as *that opera*. Technological advances in generating the visual (stage machinery, lighting, filmic techniques, and special effects) have far outpaced those pertaining to the fundamental means of generating the music (the human voice and standard orchestral instruments) and rendered the possibilities all the more enticing. This is one of the myriad issues pertaining to authority, competing authorities in a collaborative text for performance, and a work concept that has tended to privilege the score (and, to a lesser extent, the libretto) as the essential locus of the opera's identity. Roger Parker takes aim at this most sacred of musical cows when he argues that musical revisions may be in order if the beloved opera canon is to offer new pleasures to contemporary audiences. However, the furor that surrounded two of his case studies in particular (Cecilia Bartoli's use of two arias Mozart wrote for a 1789 revival of *Le nozze di Figaro* rather than the "original" arias and Luciano Berio's re-completion of Puccini's *Turandot*) indicates that opera lovers remain far more resistant to radical treatment of the *sound* of opera than to the reenvisioning of its appearance.[39]

THE WORK OF THE SPECTATING AUDIENCE

The second crucial distinction between opera and spoken theater for my purposes concerns the activities in which the spectating audience member is engaged at each event. Consider the etymology of the word "audience." The Middle French and Middle English versions are derived from the Latin *"audientia,"* meaning "a hearing or listening," which is in turn derived from *"audiens,"* the present participle of *"audire"* (to hear). The root of the word is "hearing," and the first definition given in the *Merriam-Webster English Dictionary* is "the act or state of hearing." Yet studies of theater audience perception and reception traditionally privilege the act of *seeing,* and theorizing about audience experience in live theater is overwhelmingly predicated upon the gaze.[40] The term "spectator" is frequently used interchangeably with "audience," as if the two were synonymous.

Because the experience of opera is so significantly auditory, Carolyn Abbate and others advocate recuperating the sonic component, particularly the voice, in the materiality of performance.[41] Of course this is not to say that attending spoken theater does not involve listening. One listens to dialogue, sound effects, and some music and judges an actor's delivery, pacing, word stress, volume, accent, and voice timbre. Sauter has shown that an audience member's "evaluation of the performance as such always correlates with the appreciation of the acting, even if other aspects of the show (the drama, the directing, the set, the costumes, etc.) were estimated lower,"[42] and the voice is an integral part of an actor's performance. But the way one judges the voice as part of an actor's performance is not identical to the way in which one judges and attends to the singing voice at the opera, not to mention the other fundamental acoustic material of opera (melody, harmony, rhythm, instrumentation).[43]

That one listens differently to a live performance of an opera than one listens to a live performance of a play is particularly pertinent for canonical operas, as these are the texts treated in nonliteral stagings. Generally speaking, the music in these operas is diatonic. Even nonmusicians and novice operagoers come equipped with a basic framework for diatonic functions based on exposure to popular music and song forms, if nothing else: the expectation of harmonic progression and chromatic resolution and a sense of repetition and contrast in aria forms. In other words, even if one does not know the opera in question, one nonetheless has general, reasonable expectations of how its music will behave, even if those assumptions remain largely unarticulated. Because spectating and hearing are experienced simultaneously at a live opera performance, the expectation of consistency one brings to the aural experience is easily transferred to expectations for the spectating experience.

The transfer of expectation from one mode of sensory perception to another can extend to an expectation, likely unarticulated, that the visual and the aural should be consistent not only unto themselves but also to one another in a kind of synchronized synesthesia: If it *sounds* eighteenth century, it will *look* eighteenth century. When diatonic operatic music, which is predictable within certain broad parameters, is synchronized with a nonliteral staging, which is almost by definition conceived as a counterpoint to that soundscape, tension is created between the simultaneous stimuli. Human electrophysiology indicates that "information stemming from multiple senses is not likely to be processed in isolation but will tend to be integrated into a multisensory percept under various circumstances."[44] Furthermore, studies by cognitive psychologists suggest that the integration of auditory and visual stimulus "is a process that occurs largely without conscious effort," while behavioral studies hypothesize that "integrating visual and auditory stimuli serves the purpose of enhancing perceptual clarity."[45] The brain's inclination is to integrate simultaneous visual and auditory stimuli, but if those stimuli seem incongruous, the rupture between what one *sees* and what one *hears* can produce estrangement. Because both the music and the mise-en-scène provide well-nigh continuous stimuli, nonliteral productions of canonical opera create ideal conditions for a Brechtian experience.

While that particular incongruence between what is seen and what is heard in nonliteral productions of canonical opera today does not precisely replicate Brecht's operagoing experience, it can reproduce the distancing he describes. The mechanism by which the distance is created is different, but the result is similar. From the distanced perspective the opera looks *and sounds* different; the opera is defamiliarized, and Opera's apparently natural position in the social hierarchy is demystified. Therefore Brecht was able to reconceptualize opera as a theatrical genre and challenge conventional wisdom about its function. He remained in close physical proximity to the performance, which allowed him to experience and participate in the event to the extent he so desired, but the psychological distance enabled a more deliberate response to the auditory and visual stimuli. He experienced this disillusion not as disappointment but as a moment of clarity and agency, which is quite the opposite of falling prey to the spell of operatic music and theatricality. The state of being estranged allows individual spectating audience members to exercise agency over their subjective experiences. Although Brecht's documented moments of estrangement in operagoing frequently resulted in negative assessments of opera and of Opera, it does not necessarily follow that the experience of estrangement is negative. Estrangement is an instrument of minor pedagogy, a means of empowering spectating audience members to engage with opera without unconditional surrender to the siren song of its theatricality.

SOMATIC MODES OF ATTENTION: SMOKING-AND-WATCHING

Brecht emphasized critical thought and objectivity in his discussions of estrangement because he proposed it as an alternative mode of experience to

the normative expectation that audiences be overwhelmed in live performance—be victimized by it, in a sense.[46] His rhetoric served a particular
purpose at the time but has since been decontextualized to legitimize a
notion of estrangement that locates the experience entirely in the intellect.
No doubt this has contributed to its reception as an edict against pleasure. It
is significant, then, that his "Notes to *Threepenny Opera*" describes the
preconditions that would produce the ideal spectating audience experience
in terms of two physical activities: smoking and watching. This is generally
and, I believe, too narrowly construed as endorsing simple skeptical non-
chalance. It is more than that. The two strategies for enabling the audience
member to experience operagoing differently originate in her body: She
should smoke while engaged in "an exercise in complex seeing."[47]

Brecht was fascinated by the smoking-and-watching spectators at sport-
ing events. His rallying cry for smoking in the theater (and in the opera
house) was a symbolic act of resistance against coerced modes of behavior
and response. "In a Shakespearean production one man in the stalls with a
cigar could bring about the downfall of Western art. He might as well light
a bomb as light his cigar."[48] Likewise he invoked smoking in his "Notes" to
Mahagonny when he calls for a new spectating audience attitude in the
opera house: "Can we persuade them to get out their cigars?"[49] Brecht also
endorsed the benefits for actors who play before a house of spectating audience members who smoke, as "it is quite impossible for the actor to play
unnatural, cramped and old-fashioned theater to a man smoking in the
stalls."[50] The smoker will not surrender mindlessly to events onstage
because he is "pretty well occupied with himself."[51]

The model of the smoking person is routinely cited as evidence that a
spectating audience member should maintain an intellectualized distance.
The flaw in this conventional wisdom, however, is that it removes the smoking person's body from the equation, as if the audience experience were
somehow that of a disembodied smoker. The argument that Brecht invoked
the smoking person as the ideal audience member only because she is self-
engaged and detached is not consistent with his other expectations of audience engagement. The act of smoking might be described more usefully as
an aid to *attending* rather than as an aid to detachment.[52] Smoking requires
some level of consciousness of physical sensation and response; one must
attend to it to a certain degree, particularly in a confined, indoor space (tilt
my head so I don't get smoke in my eyes, squint if I do, flick the ash so it
doesn't fall on my clothes, put out the cigarette before it burns my fingers,
remove the shred of tobacco from my tongue, take care not to burn the
patron next to me). This is all quite apart from the chemical pleasure of

ingesting nicotine and the psychological pleasure of partaking of a familiar ritual.

Propagation of the purely cerebral model of the estrangement experience has certainly contributed to a sense among his detractors that Brecht was a theorist whose abstract ideas were not meant for practical application, if not an out-and-out killjoy. Because his supporters would counter with much evidence that he was actually very much a man of the living, breathing theater, it stands to reason that something has gotten skewed in transmission. Really, who among us attends live opera performances to have a strictly intellectual experience? Who would want to? It is easy to imagine circumstances under which *some* audience members want to experience *some* performances that way, but for the vast majority of operagoers, the vast majority of the time, this is not the case. And it is not just because this type of continuous intellectual engagement requires a great deal of concentration and energy. The model of estrangement as an exclusively cerebral experience neglects the fact that one does not pay attention only with one's mind. The body beyond the eye and ear is involved, and necessarily so.

Some confusion surely stems from the contradictory nature of Brecht's writings on the importance of the corporeal audience in live performance. Kruger attributes the inconsistency to Brecht's dual role as director on the one hand, who "appears to embrace the appetite and physicality of theatre," and as the theorizer of audience on the other, who shared with Hegel a preference for the "discerning audience with the desireless eye of judgment."[53] Even so, beginning in 1926 Brecht returned intermittently to the smoking-and-watching audience model, and I interpret this as acknowledgment of what cultural anthropologist Thomas J. Csórdas calls "somatic modes of attention."[54] Csórdas's theory invokes the work of phenomenological social scientist Alfred Schutz. "If, as Schutz says, attention is a conscious turning toward an object, this 'turning toward' would seem to imply more bodily and multisensory engagement than we usually allow for in psychological definitions of attention." He defines somatic modes of attention as "culturally elaborated ways of attending to and with one's body in surroundings that include the embodied presence of others." In sum, "one is paying attention *with* one's body."[55]

Then it is not just a matter of paying attention with one's mind and experiencing the body only as a conduit for sensations of sight and sound; it is a matter of attending with one's body, as well.[56] Most operagoers, if pressed, would probably concede this point, although physical experiences are often described in emotional terms. Spectating audience members are more likely to recount sadness, outrage, relief, pleasure, surprise, or boredom than to specify their physical manifestations (changes in heart rate, posture, position, breathing, facial expression, and muscle tension or relaxation). Those physical experiences are part of the satisfaction of attending, and attending *to*, live opera, and any model that privileges the cerebral at their expense will find little resonance among audiences. Brecht's idea of the smoking person suggests that tapping into a somatic mode of attentiveness via a minor physical act can make one receptive to the state of estrangement, facilitating attention and deliberate perception. Cognitive psychologists have shown that attention affects multisensory integration processes. "When attention is directed to both modalities simultaneously, auditory and visual stimuli are integrated very early in the sensory flow of processing. Attention appears to play a crucial role in initiating such an early integration of auditory and visual processes."[57]

SMOKING AND WATCHING—AND READING

Not surprisingly, given Brecht's preoccupation with the spectator and the art of spectating, the second physical action in which the audience member should be involved concerns visual perception. The use of titles and screens for the "literarization" of the theater engaged the spectating audience member in what Brecht described as an "exercise in complex seeing," meaning watching (perceiving action on the stage and the mise-en-scène) and reading (comprehending the literal text written on placards, for example, or projected on a screen) in quick alternation or simultaneously. According to Csórdas, "We less often conceptualize visual attention as a 'turning toward' than as a disembodied beam-like 'gaze.'"[58] Brecht's distinction between watching and reading rejects the laser-beam gaze in favor of something more akin to "turning toward." Both watching and reading transmit information to the brain via the optic nerve, but they constitute two different modes of processing visual stimuli.

While opera houses still prohibit smoking in the theater, most offer audiences the opportunity to engage in an "exercise of complex seeing" via projected supertitles. In 1982 the director of operations at the Canadian Opera Company (COC), John Leberg, developed a system for projecting a libretto translation above the stage. It debuted in a COC production of *Elektra* in 1983, and the rest of the opera world quickly followed suit.[59] Some companies, such as the Metropolitan Opera in New York, the Santa Fe Opera, and the Vienna Staatsoper, provide translated texts via individual viewfinders on the back of the seat ahead or on small adjustable screens that protrude from the stage-side wall in the boxes. The primary difference between the two media comes down to choice. The individual texts can be rendered in the language of the viewer's choice (within a range of standard options), and the texts are optional; they can be deactivated if an individual does not wish to see them, and they are often marketed as unobtrusive to others sitting in the vicinity. The far more prevalent phenomenon of supertitles projected above the proscenium, on the other hand, is restricted to a single language at a time and cannot be deactivated by the individual spectating audience member. (Whether the supertitles can be ignored is a matter of some debate.) Either way, the activity of the operagoer is now routinely compounded to include listening, spectating, *and* reading (if not smoking).[60]

Brecht's notion of complex seeing is not unfounded. The cognitive acts of reading and watching action on the stage amount to two kinds of pattern recognition, and the amount of attention required to note a particular type of pattern depends on whether one is a novice or an expert. While literate adults read almost automatically, there is a degree of attention competition at work if the spectating audience member is a novice. The projected text and the simultaneous action on the stage are in different locations, and they present different spatial and temporal patterns that require recognition and perception. A novice may find the attention competition between watching, reading, and listening to be a distraction, but the titles may also help her to notice things she would not otherwise have seen.[61] It is a tradeoff, and it is highly subjective. Naturally the quality of the titles affects perception; titlists must consider timing, congruence, accuracy of translation, and line length. Some titlists have expressed concern that the projected titles above the proscenium are an intrusion into the illusion of the stage, a by-product Brecht certainly would have applauded.[62]

Brecht's audience experienced multimedia stimuli almost exclusively within the context of live performance and cinema, and he could not have imagined the contemporary audience member who is conditioned to read, look, and listen at a very sophisticated, integrated level, thanks to near constant interaction with technology. My students have never experienced opera without some kind of text projected on to the visual field, mostly via subtitles on DVD and television. (The omission of titles from the worrisome lyrics of "Batti, batti" in an otherwise subtitled production of *Don Giovanni* on DVD elicited virulent negative commentary.) Cognitive scientists confirm that human beings are ever more experienced and therefore adept at integrating such stimuli, but for the nonexpert spectating audience member at a nonliteral staging of a canonical opera, the cognitive premise of complex seeing still stands.

Of course, neither could Brecht have anticipated that today's spectating audiences would be unaccustomed to engagement in any language other than their native tongue or in English, the lingua franca of technology. Paradoxically, under these conditions it would seem that to be truly estranged from the opera and to perceive it as defamiliarized one would have to experience it in an unknown language, as most North Americans did before the mid-1980s, and supertitles are actually designed to have the opposite effect. In 1997 Levin anticipated that projected translations of the libretto would result in "a forced redistribution of aesthetic wealth," meaning any spectating audience member would now have access to details previously known to only a select few (those fluent in the frequently foreign language of the opera or intimately familiar with its text).[63] Now spectating audience members can follow the recitative closely enough to get clever jokes and wordplay and to understand complex details of notoriously circuitous plots, assuming supertitles are done well. Levin has argued persuasively that supertitles can liberate the production from its tautological obligation to clarify and explain the literary text, thus facilitating the proliferation of nonliteral productions of canonical opera.[64]

Another distinction is that Brecht's use of projected titles and placards did not provide continuous translation of ongoing events. They were used intermittently and sparingly, as an addition to the visual field, but they did not translate one aspect of the production text into another medium (from aural-oral to visual). Written text onstage provided subtext, additional text, or commentary, not the literal text being uttered by the performers. But in a strange, perhaps even insidious way, this may be what happens with opera titles as well. A complete translation of the libretto is rarely what one reads above the stage. A libretto contains far too much text to be presented in either literal or poetic translation, so the titlist renders an interpretation in short lines that can be projected two at a time. Titles are a translated adaptation, cut and edited for this format. The often-anonymous titlist, then, is an additional authorial presence, one whose authority is frequently conflated with that of the librettist, but her effect on the operagoer's experience at any given performance today may well outweigh that of the librettist. One has only to think of the titles in Peter Sellars's Mozart-DaPonte trilogy to recognize their significance. Because he hewed closely to the score and libretto, the auditory stimuli (eighteenth-century music and Italian language) were utterly faithful to the traditional work concept, while the anachronistic visual stimuli (contemporary staging and titles in English slang) provided their counterpoint.

As Brecht himself recognized as early as 1931, however, "It is to be feared that titles and permission to smoke are not of themselves enough to lead the audience to a more fruitful use of the theatre."[65] We may never know, as one is not likely to have the experience of simultaneously watching and smoking, reading and listening in an indoor opera house today, and contemporary spectating audiences are considerably more adept at sensory integration than their predecessors. But the point is the efficacy of the method, not of the style. With that I turn to twenty-first-century means (productions) and moments (experiences) of estrangement in specific performances of nonliteral stagings of canonical opera.[66]

MEANS AND MOMENTS OF ESTRANGEMENT WITH OPERA

Late September 2005 was a moment of operatic excess in Berlin. Each of the three opera houses planned a premiere for the weekend of 23–25 September: The Deutsche Oper unveiled the German premiere of Nicholas Maw's *Sophie's Choice;* the Staatsoper presented a new production of Verdi's *La forza del destino* by Stefan Herheim; and the Komische Oper pinned its hopes on Calixto Bieito's new staging of Puccini's *Madame Butterfly.* The last two were often paired in the press, as they represented new treatments of beloved masterpieces by directors whose credentials carried more than a whiff of scandal. The Norwegian Herheim is a wunderkind whose controversial *Entführung aus dem Serail* opened the Salzburg Festival in 2003 and, thanks in part to the lucrative allure of notoriety, was revived the following year. Spanish theater director Bieito was better known, having burst on the opera scene with his much-ballyhooed *Un ballo in maschera* in Barcelona in 2001. In 2004 he forged a partnership with the Komische Oper in Berlin that has delivered two of its most profitable and, not coincidentally, controversial shows: an *Entführung* in 2004 and *Butterfly* in 2005. Indignant critics and patrons accused the intendants at both houses of scandal mongering and pandering. Yet the buzz surrounding the two productions generated revenue for their respective houses, elevated Herheim's profile considerably, and cemented Bieito's reputation as a lightning rod for publicity.

Of course, one person's revelatory exegesis is another person's clichéd Eurotrash. Personal taste and experience inevitably shape perception. Nor are shock tactics, and their attendant reception as scandal, necessarily synonymous with estrangement. Estrangement is not just experiencing the unexpected; its defining quality is that it yields perspicacity. Shock is one means of initiating estrangement but it is not the only means, and its overuse has precisely the opposite effect. Prudently administered, shock can evoke a delightful frisson; excessively deployed, it either becomes monotonous or scandalizes the audience to such a degree that communication ceases.[67] The public relations campaign preceding that weekend in September 2005 titillated potential audiences with the prospect of shock and scandal based on the directors' reputations, and comparisons were inevitable. Only a few days separated my attendance at Herheim's *La forza* from my attendance at Bieito's *Butterfly*. I had followed the media hype before the premieres and was aware that their respective openings had occasioned some controversy but deliberately eschewed reviews and conversations with eyewitnesses until I saw the productions in person. Nor did I read the program notes, lest I be persuaded to accept a directorial concept I might otherwise have found incomprehensible. I like both of these operas, but they are not personal favorites; I am neither a Verdi nor a Puccini specialist. I did not consider myself particularly invested in preconceived notions of their work concepts. I had a handful of prior live performances in my memory, each pleasant enough but none transcendent.

I approached the two performances with the intention of attending to the means and moments of estrangement in each context. The Komische Oper performs all operas in German and without supertitles, and I had anticipated some disorientation from hearing the quintessentially Italianate *Butterfly* sung in German, but that was not the case. The contemporary setting, in which Pinkerton takes a sex tour of the Orient, is already latent in the libretto in which U.S. Navy personnel stationed in Japan exploit exotic local women. Bieito endowed the ubiquitous and coveted blue American passport with symbolic significance that worked well throughout the production, but the perpetual graphic sex, misogyny, and garish colors, while initially quite provocative, became monochromatic. Certainly the finale, in which Butterfly killed Suzuki and the child instead of herself, was shocking, but the jolt was not followed by understanding. Perhaps Puccini's music has something to do with this. It is already so overripe with Romantic, chromatic longing and sorrow that Bieito's excessive staging can only be tautological. My experience with his production of Mozart's *Entführung*, on the other hand, featured many of the same visual tropes in counterpoint to Mozart's classical music and was rife with moments of estrangement.[68]

La forza del destino (The Force of Destiny) was far more susceptible to the estrangement of a nonliteral production, and the comparative restraint of Verdi's music facilitated that success. The discrete moments and means of estrangement I experienced while attending Herheim's production of *La forza* were hardly earth-shattering epiphanies. They were small flashes of surprise or disorientation followed by recognition, experienced psychologically and physically. Such moments are among the greatest pleasures of attending, and attending to, nonliteral productions of canonical opera in live performance. The accumulation of these moments defines the experience of such events, but their specificity is frequently omitted from analyses of performances. There are noteworthy exceptions, of course. In his work on the uses of rhythm in nonliteral productions of Mozart operas by Bieito and Thomas Bischoff, Clemens Risi isolates discrete moments of estrangement and analyzes their efficacy.[69] Similarly, Abbate's accounts of individual voices in specific performances frequently have the quality of estrangement, as she describes the unexpected awareness of a singer's physicality through extremes of virtuosity or vocal distress.[70] More often, however, the operagoing experience is summarized with the benefit of hindsight. Individual moments of estrangement and their attendant pleasures are flattened out in favor of a final, assimilated response that was possible only after one had witnessed the entire performance.

The problem, of course, is that live performance is not experienced "generally"; it is experienced specifically and temporally. Information is gathered over the course of an evening, from one discrete moment to the next. Taken in the aggregate these moments determine the totality of our experience, but they tend to be sublimated to an overall impression in retelling after the fact. The purpose is to illustrate the kinds of attention that may yield opportunities for the pleasures of estrangement in nonliteral productions of canonical opera. It is an admittedly subjective account because the experience of estrangement is itself highly individualistic. I anticipate that some of my responses may correspond to those of others who were in attendance that evening, but ultimately the capacity for estrangement and the decision to avail oneself of it are unique to each spectating audience member.

Estrangement with Stefan Herheim's 'La forza del destino'

I experienced my first moment of estrangement almost as soon as maestro Michael Gielen took up his baton.[71] I anticipated the much-beloved overture as a sonic and psychological transitional space in which to immerse myself in the opera. The brass and their insistent, resounding E will herald the arrival of the telltale "fate" motif in the strings, I thought, followed by a medley as harbinger of the many great tunes to come. Instead, the stage action began immediately. Sure enough, there was the E in the familiar rhythm—but it was *pianissimo* and played by flutes and clarinets. The next thing I knew the Marquis of Calatrava bid his daughter Leonora good night and we were off. Would there be no overture? Deprived of the standard transitional phase and the opportunity to relish a favorite piece, I was suddenly aware of expectations I had not known I had until they were thwarted. Unbeknownst to me and, apparently, to many of my fellow audience members, this was the 1862 version of Verdi's opera, which does not have an overture (it was added in 1869, when Verdi revised the work for La Scala). In this case, estrangement was not the result of directorial intervention but of an unexpected encounter with a perfectly legitimate if less familiar version of the opera.[72] Perhaps I was more invested in the work concept than I had realized.

The set was dominated by an enormous four-poster bed, a predictable if outsized fixture for a daughter's bedroom. There were two red-haired women onstage, one wearing a white dressing gown with black robe and the other a black dressing gown with white robe. Which one was Leonora? The inverse similarity of their appearances was too striking to be an accident, but in what interpretation, I wondered, would Curra, a servant and comprimario role, be equal to her mistress, the prima donna? I looked to the supertitles for clarification, and by the end of the act had decided that the actress singing the role of Curra was, more importantly, playing the role of Leonora's alter ego; to what end, I did not know. Leonora clutched a stuffed toy Pegasus, and a giant statue of the mythical creature appeared upstage. Perhaps it was a symbol of youthful innocence or an avatar that would rescue these ill-fated characters from themselves. When the act ended, I was sitting upright and forward in my seat and had been intently scanning the stage and supertitles for clues. I was in a state of rapt attention.

I discerned the significance of Curra's character as Leonora's alter ego in the second act, when Leonora sought refuge at a monastery. The role of Padre Guardiano was performed by the same bass who had sung the Marquis in the first act, and he wore a similar costume. The moment he appeared onstage I experienced another moment of estrangement: confusion. He looks and sounds like the Marquis, but isn't the father dead? This confusion was followed by a flash of illumination: The roles of the biological father and the Catholic father (whose name literally means "guard") were conflated to represent the ubiquitous power of the male authority figure in a patriarchal society. The symbolism of the combined father figure illuminated the doubled female lead. Suddenly I remembered a moment in act 1 that I had discarded as incomprehensible at the time: The Marquis having sex with Curra the alter ego on the bed while Leonora and Alvaro stood nearby. This cast considerable doubt on the protection the priest offered in the hermitage, as he appeared to be in collusion with the incestuous Marquis. Perhaps Curra would shadow Leonora throughout, alternately acting out Leonora's inappropriate fantasies and falling victim to those of the other characters. The singer playing Curra also sang the role of Preziosilla in the third act, which meant that character could also be interpreted as

Leonora's double. Both are mezzo-soprano roles and therefore easily combined from a vocal perspective. More important, the timbral contrast to Leonora's clarion soprano convinced me that the combined character was the embodiment of the heroine's darker side.

The finale of act 2 is a religious ceremony in which the priest-father instructs the assembled monks that Leonora is a hermit who is to be left undisturbed in a cave. In Herheim's staging this ritual included communion, and one by one the supplicants processed to partake of the elements of the Eucharist. The body that had been sacrificed, however, was that of the Pegasus, and it had not undergone the requisite transubstantiation. When its enormous, butchered body appeared on the altar it elicited expressions of dismay in the audience, as several sitting nearby whispered to their neighbors, squirmed in their seats, or clicked their tongues. As the chorus intoned the hymn that closes the act, each communicant in turn dipped his hands into the Pegasus's body and then withdrew them dripping with blood. My mind raced with possible interpretations: a commentary on organized religion as myth? a gloss on the destruction of innocence under patriarchal oppression? Then the chorus members stepped to the front of the stage and raised their bloodied hands at us, still singing the final chorus. The houselights came up before the end of the act, exposing the audience as the chorus confronted us with blood on their hands and, if their aggressive stance toward us was any indication, on ours as well.

Given the plot, the lush, four-part Romantic harmony and sacred text were to be expected, and staging religious ritual typically suggests rote predictability. Against those expectations Herheim's interpretation of the scene was first illuminating (the symbolism of the doubled father having elucidated the doubling of Leonora), then repulsive (the bloody body of the poor Pegasus as the host), and finally confrontational (the surprising elimination of the fourth wall). The scene that should have provided Leonora and, by extension, the audience with a safe haven of amnesty was instead revealed to be a site of judgment and accusation.

The third act continued to implicate the audience with an extraordinary staging of us for ourselves. We reentered the house to find the stage transformed into the facade of the Staatsoper on Unter den Linden, where patrons congregate at intermission in all but the most inclement of weather conditions—in fact, where we had just been standing. I was immediately put in mind of photographs I had seen of the famous Neuenfels production of *Aida*. My companions and I laughed when we identified the pretzel salesman from whom we had bought our snacks, a fixture of intermissions at houses in Berlin. Dressed in contemporary street clothes, the chorus (they?

we?) milled about at ground level, on the steps, and on the second level that functions rather like a balcony, glasses of *Sekt* and programs in hand. When the bell rang, they reentered the house and the doors closed behind them, just as they had closed behind us only moments before. We were amused and, it must be said, flattered to have been incorporated into the production. Perhaps the end of act 2 had been a bit heavy-handed, but now Herheim ingratiated himself to us with a delightful acknowledgment of our presence.

After the encounter between Alvaro and Carlo, which was also staged in front of the house, the chorus-audience poured back out of the Staatsoper onto the stage for intermission, singing the soldiers' battle song. Clearly the operagoing public was not going to war, but they sang lustily of its glory. Leonora's double sang from the upper level while the chorus-audience adored her as a diva. A ragtag band of new recruits entered, begging for food, and the chorus-audience chased them off to war. As Leonora's double led them in the merry "Rataplan" song, a series of giant banners unfurled on the upper level, replicas of those the Staatsoper flies to advertise the operas being performed. The first dropped to her left: "Schicksal" (destiny). Moments later the second descended to her right: "Macht" (power). Aha— the opera's title in German, just as it had been advertised outside. Then a third banner was unfurled in the center: "Frei" (free). There was an audible gasp in the house, as the allusion to "Arbeit macht frei," the slogan that marked the entrances of Nazi concentration camps, resonated throughout the house. The second word was not a noun at all; it was a verb.

I struggled with that concept as the chorus-audience grew ever more frenzied. Their fanatic adulation mutated into murderous rage; they descended upon Leonora's double, ripped her limb from limb, and ate her alive. I desperately attempted to impose meaning on the scene and came up with nothing more than the observation that this act of cannibalism paralleled the Pegasus Eucharist at the end of the previous act. A children's chorus made its way to the catwalk that separates the orchestra pit from the audience. Stripped to their underwear they revealed the words "Krieg" and "Kunst" (war, art) scrawled on their torsos in black paint. I stared uncomprehending at the chaos on the stage and read the words inscribed there over and over again: fate, power, free, war, art.

It was with a jolt that I realized that Herheim had implicated the spectating audience—me—in a host of sins and crimes against humanity: solipsism, warmongering, conspicuous consumption, exploitation. Despite the warning at the end of act 2, I had become an eager accomplice after the flattery of the opening scene in act 3.[73] The third act became opera about Opera—operagoing and operagoers. I immediately thought of *Mahagonny,* the opera which took "opera" as its subject, the culinary opera, in which the proof of the pudding is in the eating. Rapacious aficionados who devour the divas they worship were the same bloodthirsty spectators who sang the glories of conquering war heroes in "Rataplan."[74] Craving war for the vicarious thrill of absolute power, they eventually carried out their murderous fantasies themselves. The mise-en-scène was in stark contrast to the ringing C-major vivacity of the music itself, which treated war like child's play in its obsessive repetition of the nonsensical onomatopoeia "Rataplan," French for the tattoo of drums, gunfire, and galloping hooves of battle. Under Herheim's direction, the war moved from colorful background plot device to clear and present danger. They—we—were also the patrons, supporting cultural institutions yet turning a blind eye to the social ills around them—us—and consuming art in lieu of engaging with reality.

I was anxious for act 4 to begin so that I could replace the grisly image in my mind with something—anything—else. The stage remained dark, and the orchestra played on. Funny, I did not remember a lengthy prelude to the final act, yet the music was reassuringly familiar. It was the beloved 1869 overture we had not heard at the beginning of the evening! Inserted into the opera rather than introducing the work, its meaning was radically transformed. The fate motif was particularly ominous; the anticipation of Leonora's final duet with Alvaro was far more bittersweet now that the end was imminent rather than three hours away; the appearance of Leonora's second act aria was reminiscent rather than foreshadowing; the melody from her duet with the priest-father was an uncomfortable emblem of patriarchal betrayal.

The unforeseen emergence of the overture at this point was utterly disorienting. To follow such a powerful moment of defamiliarization with the most familiar music of the entire opera felt like comfort, but displaced. Listening to the overture before a darkened stage I also experienced a strange sense of déjà vu, as if we were once more at the very beginning of the work, although, of course, the overture was precisely how the opera had *not* begun. In the final act I relished the lyrical perfection of "Pace, pace, mio Dio" and the exquisite beauty of Norma Fantini's *pianissimo* high notes. The priest-father consummated his desire for Leonora's double, the three lead characters died, the resurrected and reconstituted Pegasus returned for the apotheosis, and the audience cheered and jeered in more or less equal proportions.[75] Afterward, my companions and I compared notes and impressions.[76] I should note that there were dozens of other memorable moments, and some of those may have been more significant to Herheim's concept, but these are the experiences that made the greatest impression at the time.

I read dramaturge Alex Meier-Dörzenbach's essay in the program and discovered the multivalent significance of the Pegasus. (Historically, the image of the flying horse has embodied two divergent qualities: powerful warrior strength and artistic creativity. In this production, and in keeping with the heterogeneous nature of Verdi's opera, Herheim exploited the various facets of the Pegasus as an all-purpose and thus unifying symbol of sexuality, dreams, power, and creativity.)[77]

The next day I read the reviews I had been avoiding and began assembling my overall impressions of the performance. Some critics complained that the production was overloaded and accused Herheim of using every gimmick ever associated with director's opera. (A legitimate point, but I reasoned that his choices reflected the hodgepodge nature of La forza itself.) Others compared it to previous interpretations I had not seen, such as the iconic Neuenfels production scheduled for revival at the Deutsche Oper just a few weeks later and a 1965 staging by Herheim's mentor Götz Friedrich. I read what I could about those stagings and went on to attend the Neunfels revival, savoring the rare opportunity to see the two in such close proximity. This provided an additional layer of vocal and visual intertextuality when Frank Porretta, the tenor who had sung Alvaro in the Herheim production at the Staatsoper, reprised the role in the Neuenfels production at the Deutsche Oper a month later.

All the information I gathered in the weeks following the first performance gradually became integrated into my assessment. When a student asked me to describe it some months later, I recounted the distinctive highlights: the doubled roles, the Pegasus, the staging of the audience, the displaced overture, Fantini's divine pianissimo. Only when she reframed her question to ask if I had enjoyed the performance—did I take pleasure in it—did I realize that, in an effort to demonstrate mastery of the opera's production, I had also revised and mastered my experience, effectively neutralizing the disconcerting and illuminating moments of estrangement that had defined the performance and been the source of pleasure in the moment. Her innocent query prompted me to recover the discrete moments of surprise and comprehension and proved to be a means of defamiliarization in its own right.

The fact that estrangement has become the predominant aesthetic of director's opera—and a preferred mode of experience for many spectating audience members in live performance—suggests that Brecht's relationship with opera has finally reached a state of symbiosis, albeit in the afterlife. In fact, the entire epic theater project—the audience contract, the theories of gestus and estrangement—comes full circle in these productions, back to its operatic roots. This reconciliation of the apparently incompatible, and the two dozen or so opera projects that form the nearly continuous backdrop to Brecht's creative activity, comprise the basis for my claim that his engagement with opera was not just influential but essential to his theoretical and dramatic oeuvres.

Notes

ABBREVIATIONS

Where two of the following sources are cited together in a single note, it indicates that the original German text is found in one source (*BFA* or *MumT*) and its English translation in the other (*BoT* or *Collected Plays*). A single reference, such as *Debatte*, indicates that primary documents are reprinted in that source.

BBA	Bertolt-Brecht-Archiv, Akademie der Künste, Berlin
BFA	Brecht, *Werke. Große kommentierte Berliner und Frankfurter Ausgabe,* 30 vols., ed. Werner Hecht, Jan Knopf, Werner Mittenzwei, and Klaus-Detlef Müller (Berlin: Aufbau Verlag; Frankfurt: Suhrkamp Verlag, 1988–2003)
BoT	Brecht, *Brecht on Theatre: The Development of an Aesthetic,* ed. and trans. John Willett (New York: Hill and Wang, 1992)
Collected Plays	Brecht, *Collected Plays,* edited and translated by John Willett, Ralph Manheim, and Tom Kuhn. 8 vols. (London: Methuen, 1994–2001; published by A&C Black as of 2006)
Debatte	Joachim Lucchesi, *Das Verhör in der Oper: Die Debatte um die Aufführung "Das Verhör des Lukullus" von Bertolt Brecht und Paul Dessau* (Berlin: Basisdruck, 1993)
Europe	Kim Kowalke, *Kurt Weill in Europe* (Ann Arbor, MI: UMI Research Press, 1979)
HEA	Hanns-Eisler-Archiv, Akademie der Künste, Berlin
HEGA	Hanns Eisler Gesamtausgabe [Hanns Eisler Collected Works], edited by the International Hanns Eisler Gesellschaft, in cooperation with Stephanie Eisler and the Hanns-Eisler-Archiv, Akademie der Künste, Berlin

Journals	Brecht, *Journals, 1934–1955*, ed. John Willett, trans. Hugh Rorrison (New York: Routledge, 1996)
MumT	Kurt Weill, *Musik und musikalisches Theater. Gesammelte Schriften*, ed. Stephen Hinton and Jürgen Schebera with Elmar Juchem (Mainz: Schott, 2000)
PDA	Paul-Dessau-Archiv, Akademie der Künste, Berlin
WLRC	Weill-Lenya Research Center, Kurt Weill Foundation, New York

INTRODUCTION

1. Joachim Lucchesi and Ronald K. Shull, *Musik bei Brecht* (Frankfurt am Main: Suhrkamp, 1988); Albrecht Dümling, *Laßt euch nicht verführen: Brecht und die Musik* (Munich: Kindler Verlag, 1985); more recently, Kurt Weill, *Musik und musikalisches Theater. Gesammelte Schriften*, ed. Stephen Hinton and Jürgen Schebera with Elmar Juchem (Mainz: Schott, 2000), hereafter *MumT*, and Albrecht Riethmüller, ed., *Brecht und seine Komponisten* (Laaber, Germany: Laaber Verlag, 2000). See also the long-awaited first volume in the new critical edition of Eisler's complete works: *Die Rundköpfe und die Spitzköpfe*, Hanns Eisler Gesamtausgabe series 5, vol. 3, ed. Thomas Ahrend and Albrecht Dümling (Leipzig: Breitkopf and Härtel, 2002).

2. The most comprehensive and successful of these studies is Christoph Nieder's; he argues persuasively in "Bertolt Brecht und die Oper: Zur Verwandtschaft von epischem Theater und Musiktheater," *Zeitschrift für Deutsche Philologie* 111, no. 3 (1992): 262–283, that epic opera is connected to both opera seria and music drama. He takes as points of departure Ulrich Weisstein's essay "Von reitenden Boten und singenden Holzfällern: Bertolt Brecht und die Oper," in *Brechts Dramen: Neue Interpretationen*, ed. Walter Hinderer (Stuttgart: Philipp Reclam, 1984), 266–299, and Reinhold Grimm, "Brecht und Nietzsche," in *Brecht und Nietzsche oder Geständnisse eines Dichters. Fünf Essays und ein Bruchstück* (Frankfurt am Main: Suhrkamp, 1979), 162 and 168–169. See also Jürgen Söring, "Wagner und Brecht: Zur Bestimmung des Musik-Theaters," in *Richard Wagner, 1883–1983: Die Rezeption im 19. und 20. Jahrhundert. Gesammelte Beiträge des Salzburger Symposions*, ed. Gerhard Croll (Stuttgart: H.-D. Heinz, 1984), 451–473. Racu Marina's essay "'Geist der Musik' oder 'Kulinarische Kunst'? (Nochmals zum Problem 'Brecht und die Oper')," *Communications* 23, no. 3 (November 1994): 67–76, posits that the influence between opera and Brecht was reciprocal, but the examination of Brecht's influence upon opera is limited to its most literal manifestations in the pieces of Soviet and GDR composers and does not take into account staging or production style. In "Die epische Oper als Erneuerung eines Genres," *Beiträge zur Theorie und Praxis des sozialistischen Theaters* (Berlin: Verband der Theaterschaffenden der Deutschen Demokratischen Republik, 1988), 28–45, Jürgen Schebera offers a brief history of Brecht's association with opera in the 1920s and then discusses

his collaborations with Weill and Dessau but does not consider music theater pieces with Eisler as related to opera.

3. Vera Stegmann, "Brecht contra Wagner: The Evolution of the Epic Music Theater," in *A Bertolt Brecht Reference Companion*, ed. Siegfried Mews (Westport, CT: Greenwood Press, 1997), 249. Regarding opera in Brecht's youth, see particularly Werner Frisch and K. W. Obermeier, eds., with Gerhard Schneider, *Brecht in Augsburg: Erinnerungen, Texte, Fotos* (Frankfurt am Main: Suhrkamp, 1976), 58–59, 111; Hanns Otto Münsterer, *The Young Brecht*, ed. and trans. Tom Kuhn and Karen J. Leeder (London: Libris, 1992), 123; Lucchesi and Shull, *Musik bei Brecht*, 91; Dümling, *Laßt euch nicht verführen*, 36, 38; Weisstein, "Von reitenden Boten und singenden Holzfällern," 266–299; and Josef Rufer, "Brechts Anmerkungen zur Oper," *Stimmen. Monatsblätter für Musik* 1, no. 7 (1948): 193–198.

Brecht's reconsideration of opera as genre and institution was already under way by 1920, when he complained about the mediocre company in Augsburg. "Perhaps the public does go for the bigger noise. . . . But it's not just a matter of people's preference for music, rather for lavishness—as well as sheer habit." Brecht, "A Reckoning," *Der Augsburger Volkswille*, 14 May 1920. Reprinted in *Brecht on Theatre: The Development of an Aesthetic*, ed. and trans. John Willett (New York: Hill and Wang, 1992), 5. Hereafter *BoT*. Original in Brecht, *Werke. Große kommentierte Berliner und Frankfurter Ausgabe*, 30 vols., ed. Werner Hecht, Jan Knopf, Werner Mittenzwei, and Klaus-Detlef Müller (Berlin: Aufbau Verlag; Frankfurt am Main: Suhrkamp Verlag, 1988–2003), 21:64. Hereafter *BFA*, volume and page number.

4. Friedrich Nietzsche, *Der Fall Wagner; Nietzsche contra Wagner* (Leipzig: Alfred Kröner, 1908). See also Thomas Steiert, ed., *"Der Fall Wagner": Ursprünge und Folgen von Nietzsches Wagner-Kritik* (Laaber, Germany: Laaber Verlag, 1991), and Reinhold Grimm, *Brecht und Nietzsche oder Geständnisse eines Dichters*. For a music-theoretical perspective, see Leslie David Blasius, "Nietzsche, Riemann, Wagner: When Music Lies," in *Music Theory and Natural Order from the Renaissance to the Early Twentieth Century*, ed. Suzannah Clark and Alexander Rehding (Cambridge: Cambridge University Press, 2001), 93–107.

5. See Martin Puchner, introduction and "Richard Wagner: The Theatocracy of the Mime," in *Stage Fright: Modernism, Anti-Theatricality, and Drama* (Baltimore: Johns Hopkins University Press, 2002), 1–28 and 31–55, respectively. Part of the anxiety about the fate of opera was related to the rise of technology, and film in particular. See Bryan Gilliam, "Stage and Screen: Kurt Weill and Operatic Reform in the 1920s," in *Music and Performance during the Weimar Republic*, ed. Gilliam (Cambridge: Cambridge University Press, 1994), 1–12.

6. Puchner, *Stage Fright*, 139–156; W. Anthony Sheppard, *Revealing Masks: Exotic Influences and Ritualized Performance in Modernist Music Theater* (Berkeley: University of California Press, 2001), 6–7; Ulrich Weisstein, "Cocteau, Stravinsky, Brecht, and the Birth of Epic Opera," *Modern Drama* 5

(1962): 142–153; Stegmann, "Brecht contra Wagner"; Stegmann, *Das epische Musiktheater bei Strawinsky und Brecht: Studien zur Geschichte und Theorie* (New York: Lang, 1991); Stephen Hinton, "The Concept of Epic Opera: Theoretical Anomalies in the Brecht-Weill Partnership," in *Das musikalische Kunstwerk: Festschrift Carl Dahlhaus,* ed. Hinton (Laaber, Germany: Laaber Verlag, 1988), 285–294.

7. Stegmann, "Brecht contra Wagner," 238–260; Mary A. Cicora, *Wagner's "Ring" and German Drama: Comparative Studies in Mythology and History in Drama* (Westport, CT: Greenwood Press, 1999), 131–168; Weisstein, "Cocteau, Stravinsky, Brecht"; Weisstein, "Von reitenden Boten und singenden Holzfällern," 275–276; Stegmann, *Das epische Musiktheater bei Strawinsky und Brecht;* Hinton, "Theoretical Anomalies," 285–294; Frisch and Obermeier, *Brecht in Augsburg;* Münsterer, *The Young Brecht.* When the *New York Times* critic John Rockwell reviewed Hans Jürgen Syberberg's film *Parsifal,* he described its crowning achievement as the virtually impossible unity of the two: "It's as if Wagner's hypnotic allure and Brecht's intellectualized alienation have been somehow mystically unified." John Rockwell, "Hans Syberg's *[sic]* adaptation of *Parsifal,*" *New York Times,* 23 January 1983. The mystery of Syberberg's cinematic transubstantiation aside, film can lay claim to perhaps the strangest convergence of the two iconic figures: The 1983 television miniseries *Wagner,* with Richard Burton in the title role, also featured Brecht's son-in-law Ekkehárd Schall as Liszt and Wagner's great-granddaughter Daphne Wagner as Princess Metternich.

8. See, for example, David Tompkins, "Review of Nora M. Alter and Lutz Kopenick, eds., *Sound Matters: Essays on the Acoustic of Modern German Culture,*" H-German, H-Net Reviews, April 2006. www.h-net.org/reviews/show rev/cgi?path=208271159992212, accessed 27 April 2006. Tompkins notes "the juxtaposition of Richard Wagner and Bertolt Brecht" as a kind of "recurring motif" throughout the book.

9. Cicora, *Wagner's "Ring" and German Drama,* 1.

10. Three letters attest to Brecht's objections to the title "librettist." The first, to Universal Edition, is dated 15 February 1930, and in it he insists on his right to be named the author of the opera, not just the author of the text. The second is also to Universal Edition, dated 19 December 1932, and in it he reasserts his rights as the author to the opera *Mahagonny,* not a "pure librettist." Both are omitted from the critical editions of Brecht correspondence and are housed in the Universal Edition collections of the Wiener Stadt- und Landesbibliothek, Musiksammlung. I am grateful to Esbjörn Nyström for calling these to my attention and providing copies. The third letter is to Weill, dated 23 June 1943, in which he objected to the terms of a contract for *Schweyk* in which he was reduced to "a pure librettist, without any author's rights" (*BFA* 29:270). Brecht, *Letters,* ed. John Willett, trans. Ralph Manheim (New York: Routledge, 1990), 356.

11. See Nieder, "Brecht und die Oper," 275–276; Ernst Schumacher, *Die dramatischen Versuche Bertolt Brechts, 1918–1933* (Berlin: Rütten and Loen-

ing, 1955), 216–217; Theodor W. Adorno, "Wagners Aktualität (1965)," in *Gesammelte Schriften*, ed. Rolf Tiedemann (Frankfurt am Main: Suhrkamp, 1997), 16:558; Marianne Kesting's report that the Soviet director Meyerhold perceived a connection between Wagner and Brecht in "Wagner/Meyerhold/Brecht oder Die Erfindung des 'epischen' Theaters," *Brecht Yearbook/Brecht-Jahrbuch* 7 (1977): 113; and Hilda Meldrum Brown, *Leitmotiv and Drama: Wagner, Brecht, and the Limits of "Epic" Theatre* (Oxford: Clarendon Press, 1991).

12. Theodor W. Adorno, "Wagner's Relevance for Today," in *Essays on Music*, ed. Richard Leppert, trans. Susan H. Gillespie (Berkeley: University of California Press, 2002), 596.

13. Kim Kowalke, *Kurt Weill in Europe* (Ann Arbor, MI: UMI Research Press, 1979), 115–116, hereafter *Europe*; Hinton, "Theoretical Anomalies," 290; Nieder, "Brecht und die Oper," 269–270; Frank Schneider, "Mozart und das epische Musiktheater," in *Mozart in der Musik des 20. Jahrhunderts. Formen ästhetischer und kompositionstechnischer Rezeption*, ed. Wolfgang Gratzer and Siegfried Mauser (Laaber, Germany: Laaber Verlag, 1992), 187–197; Mário Vieira de Carvalho, "From Opera to 'Soap Opera': On Civilizing Processes, the Dialectic of Enlightenment and Postmodernity," *Theory, Culture, and Society* 12, no. 2 (1995): 41–62; and Stegmann, "Brecht contra Wagner," 252.

14. Matthew Wilson Smith, *The Total Work of Art: From Bayreuth to Cyberspace* (New York: Routledge, 2007), 78 and 79.

15. Puchner, *Stage Fright*, especially 1–58 and 139–156; and Patrick Carnegy, *Wagner and the Art of the Theatre* (New Haven, CT: Yale University Press, 2006), especially 238–239. For another perspective on how this has manifested itself on the opera stage see Herbert Lindenberger, "Anti-theatricality in Twentieth-Century Opera," in *Against Theatre: Creative Destructions on the Modernist Stage*, ed. Alan Ackerman and Martin Puchner (New York: Palgrave Macmillan, 2006), 58–75. For a primer on "theatricality" as term and concept, see "Theatricality: An Introduction," in *Theatricality*, ed. Tracy C. Davis and Thomas Postlewait (Cambridge: Cambridge University Press, 2003), 1–39.

16. Hans-Thies Lehmann acknowledges the "overpowering authority" of Brecht's epic theater as the definitive form of modern theater and says its propagation has obstructed critical assessment of "newer theatre aesthetics." *Postdramatic Theatre*, trans. Karen Jürg-Munby (London: Routledge, 2006), 29. Because Brecht took "the fable (story) as the sine qua non" of the theater, Lehmann interprets his epic theater not as new but as "a renewal and completion of classical dramaturgy" and argues convincingly that "postdramatic theatre is a post-Brechtian theatre" (33).

17. Cited in ibid., 33.

18. Sometimes "what he understood opera to be" revealed a willful ignorance or misreading of Wagner for the sake of argument. Brecht intended to disparage Wagner's use of leitmotif as pointless tautology in "The Notes to the Opera *Mahagonny*," but what he proposed instead is actually a rather good summation of Wagner's own theory. Hinton quotes Dahlhaus's assessment: "It

is simply absurd to accuse a technique of being tautologous whose point and dramaturgic function consist, on the contrary, in constituting a 'second plot' alongside the events made manifest by verbal and scenic means—an imaginary drama, that is, compounded of references backwards and forwards and which outstretches the consciousness of the characters involved." Carl Dahlhaus, "'Am Text entlang komponiert.' Bemerkungen zu einem Schlagwort," in *Für und wider die Literaturoper,* ed. Sigrid Wiesmann (Laaber, Germany: Laaber, 1982), 194, cited in Hinton, "Theoretical Anomalies," 291. Scholars have noted that there are several ways in which music dramas are also epic, at least in theory if not in practice: They share a penchant for narrative, monologue, and common tropes of plot and character. Nieder, "Brecht und die Oper," 275–276; Schumacher, *Die dramatischen Versuche Bertolt Brechts,* 216–217; Adorno, "Wagners Aktualität (1965)," 558; and Kesting, "Wagner/Meyerhold/Brecht."

19. Lawrence Kramer, *Opera and Modern Culture: Wagner and Strauss* (Berkeley: University of California Press, 2004), 9.

20. Richard Wagner, *Opera and Drama,* trans. William Ashton Ellis (Lincoln: University of Nebraska Press, 1995), 46. It is quite tempting to take Ellis's translation of Wagner's "hübsche Melodien" as "delicious melodies" because it aligns so perfectly with Brecht's derision of culinary opera, but Ellis's artful rendering is not meant to be taken literally in this manner. Original German in Wagner, *Oper und Drama* (Dresden: L. Ehlermann, 1943), 25.

21. My three points are consistent with those W. Anthony Sheppard cited as the features modernists identified as being in need of revision in their definitions of opera: venue, function, and artistic mission (*Revealing Masks,* 6–7). I also follow Sheppard's designation of the traits associated with modernism: "[It] places a high premium on the generation of new genres of artistic production, on the exploration of extremes of expression, and on abstraction and formalization," and its "propensity for radical innovation" was motivated by "self-conscious rejection of nineteenth-century conventions and the desire to synthesize the arts" (Sheppard, *Revealing Masks,* 8).

22. Roger Parker confirms that it is no simple matter to answer the deceptively simple question "What exactly is opera?" *Remaking the Song: Operatic Visions and Revisions from Handel to Berio* (Berkeley: University of California Press, 2006).

23. See Paisley Livingston, *Art and Intention: A Philosophical Study* (Oxford: Clarendon Press, 2005), 55; and Sherri Irvin, "The Artist's Sanction in Contemporary Art," *Journal of Aesthetics and Art Criticism* 63, no. 4 (2005): 315–316.

24. Roswitha Mueller refers to *The Rise and Fall of Mahagonny* as antiopera because of Brecht's claims that it was not of the traditional, culinary kind, but the fact remains that *Mahagonny* is universally accepted as an opera because of its continuous music. Mueller, "Learning for a New Society: The *Lehrstück,*" in *The Cambridge Companion to Bertolt Brecht,* 2nd ed., ed. Peter Thomson and Glendyr Sacks (Cambridge: Cambridge University Press, 2006), 101. Wulf Konold's more recent work employs the same term but reserves it for

pieces composed after the 1960s. Konold, "Oper—Anti-Oper—Anti-Anti-Oper," in *Musiktheater heute: Internationales Symposion der Paul Sacher Stiftung Basel 2001,* ed. Hermann Danuser and Matthias Kassel (Mainz: Schott, 2003), 52–57.

25. Eric Bentley, "The Influence of Brecht," in *Re-interpreting Brecht: His Influence on Contemporary Drama and Film,* ed. Pia Kleber and Colin Visser (Cambridge: Cambridge University Press, 1990), 187.

26. There is also "Das Lehrspiel von Tristan und Isolde: Oper von Kurt Weill" with text by Richard Wagner, Bertolt Brecht, Caspar Neher, Eric Simon, and Hans Weigen. According to Weill-Lenya Research Center archivist Dave Stein, it was cobbled together by Eric Simon, the clarinetist and music educator who had directed the chorus for the Vienna performance of *Mahagonny* in 1931. It is dated "Berlin—Wien, 13.—15. März 1932. Kopiert: Sherman, Conn. 5. Juni 1967." Weill-Lenya Research Center series 30, box 1, folder 8. Hereafter WLRC.

27. I have used the English titles of Brecht's texts as rendered in the Methuen edition (published by A&C Black as of 2006) because it is the most current English translation of Brecht's plays, spearheaded by prominent scholars John Willett, Ralph Manheim, and Tom Kuhn, and it is rapidly becoming the standard English-language version of Brecht. Their translations may differ from previous translated titles, however. For example, *The Decision* is their translation for *Die Maßnahme,* which is elsewhere translated more literally as *The Measures Taken.*

28. Bertolt Brecht, "The Modern Theatre Is the Epic Theatre: Notes to the Opera *Aufstieg und Fall der Stadt Mahagonny,*" in *BoT:*33–42, *BFA* 24:78–86.

29. "The play is really the production of a new spectator, an actor who starts where the performance ends, who only starts so as to complete it, but in life." Louis Althusser, *For Marx,* trans. B. R. Brewster (New York: Verso, 1996), 152.

30. The term "spect-actor" is borrowed from the videogame industry. Brecht's theories of audience engagement have found some currency in videogame research, particularly in the work of Gonzago Frasca; see chapter 5 for references.

31. Susan Bennett, *Theatre Audiences: A Theory of Production and Reception,* 2nd ed. (London: Routledge, 1997). The other primary point of departure is reader response theory, although she acknowledges that it is not entirely adequate for the communal, temporal experience of live theater.

32. Neil Blackadder, *Performing Opposition: Modern Theater and the Scandalized Audience* (Westport, CT: Praeger, 2003), xiii–xiv. See also chapter 5 of the present volume.

33. Willmar Sauter, *The Theatrical Event: Dynamics of Performance and Perception* (Iowa City: University of Iowa Press, 2000), 2. Bennett, Blackadder, and Sauter follow Brecht in privileging the visual, using the word "spectator" interchangeably with "audience" and focusing on the perception of visual stimuli. See chapter 5 of the present volume.

34. Erika Fischer-Lichte and Jens Roselt, "Attraktion des Augenblicks—

Aufführung, Performance, performativ und Performativität als theaterwissenschaftliche Begriffe," *Paragrana. Internationale Zeitschrift für Historische Anthropologie* 10, no. 1 (2001): 239, cited in Christel Weiler, "Etwas ist dran: Vorurteile zum Lehrstück," in *Kunst der Aufführung—Aufführung der Kunst*, ed. Erika Fischer-Lichte, Clemens Risi, and Jens Roselt (Berlin: Theater der Zeit, 2004), 144.

35. Weiler, "Etwas ist dran," 144. See also Astrid Oesmann, who studies "the development of Brecht's concept of theatre as a 'counterpublic sphere,' a space in which participants (those acting and those watching) can learn to observe and understand the power relations that shape their lives," which is the space that fosters this new kind of audience. Oesmann, *Staging History: Brecht's Social Concepts of Ideology* (Albany: State University of New York Press, 2005), 3. She develops this concept in chapter 3, 89–128.

36. Dümling, *Laßt euch nicht verführen*, 667.

37. Andre Briner, *Paul Hindemith* (Mainz: Schott, 1971), 71–72.

38. Lucchesi and Shull, *Musik bei Brecht*, 584.

39. This was reported in the Danish newspaper *Berlingske Tidende* on 14 June 1935. Brecht and Ruth Berlau worked on a text in London in the summer of 1936, but it never progressed beyond a few sketches and there is no evidence that Eisler ever began the music. Lucchesi and Shull, *Musik bei Brecht*, 652–653.

40. Lucchesi and Shull, *Musik bei Brecht*, 663–665.

41. Only two theater pieces—the ballet *The Seven Deadly Sins*, his last project with Weill, and the "tale of horror" *Round Heads and Pointed Heads*, written with Eisler—were conceived with music in this period. The other dramatic texts (*The Horatians and the Curiatians, Mother Courage and Her Children,* the radio play *The Trial of Lucullus, Good Person of Szechwan, Senora Carrar's Rifles, The Life of Galileo, What Is the Price of Iron?, Mr. Puntila and His Man Matti,* and *The Resistible Rise of Arturo Ui*) included literary collaborators only, although most acquired musical settings after the fact.

42. Marc Silbermán, "Gestus," in *Historisch-kritisches Wörterbuch des Marxismus*, ed. Fritz Haug (Hamburg: Argument, 2001), 662. The recuperation of corporeality after late-nineteenth-century naturalism is a modernist feature that can be traced to aesthetics and stage practices of the first half of the nineteenth century. Daniel Albright, *Untwisting the Serpent: Modernism in Music, Literature, and Other Arts* (Chicago: University of Chicago Press, 2000), 102.

43. See Brecht's essays "On the Use of Music in an Epic Theater" (1935), "Criticism of the New York Production of *The Mother*" (1935), and "On Gestic Music" (1937) in *BoT* 84–90, 81–84, and 104–106, respectively. *BFA* 22:155–164, original in English, and 22:329–331.

Brecht's penchant for pre-Wagnerian operatic characteristics has been established, and yet mimesis was also one of Nietzsche's complaints about Wagner. Mary Ann Smart, *Mimomania: Music and Gesture in Nineteenth-Century Opera* (Berkeley: University of California Press, 2004), 4 and 167. Other crucial encounters in the development of gestus in sound include Weill, the Chinese opera singer Mei Lanfang, and the Russian critic Viktor Shklovsky's concept of *priyom ostraneniya* (device for making strange).

44. Kenneth Fowler's underutilized study of music and gestus boldly puts its finger on a nagging problem in Brechtian scholarship: Scholars "are not so much interested in examining the relationship between text and music in Brecht's work as they are in proving the adequacy of Brecht's theoretical statements or commentary to his pieces. Their real project, then, would . . . [be] the reproduction of Brecht." Fowler, *Received Truths: Bertolt Brecht and the Problem of Gestus and Musical Meaning* (New York: AMS Press, 1991), 14.

45. Carolyn Abbate, *Unsung Voices: Opera and Musical Narrative in the Nineteenth Century* (Princeton, NJ: Princeton University Press, 1991), 10.

46. Patrice Pavis, *Languages of the Stage: Essays in the Semiology of the Theatre* (New York: Performing Arts Journal Publications, 1982), 39–49; and Darko Suvin, "Haltung (Bearing) and Emotions: Brecht's Refunctioning of Conservative Metaphors for Agency," in *Zweifel—Fragen—Vorschläge. Bertolt Brecht anläßlich des Einhundertsten*, ed. Thomas Jung (Frankfurt am Main: Peter Lang, 1999), 43–58.

47. Brecht appears to have misunderstood the style of acting in Chinese opera, but that misinterpretation nevertheless informed his work on gestus in the period. To the best of my knowledge, no one has explored the significance of the fact that Mei Lanfang was a performer of Chinese *opera*. The Chinese-gestus connection has been subjected fruitfully to feminist interpretation by Carol J. Martin, "Brecht, Feminism, and Chinese Theatre," *Drama Review* 43, no. 4 (1999): 77–85. See also Min Tian, "'Alienation-Effect' for Whom? Brecht's (Mis)Interpretation of the Classical Chinese Theatre," *Asian Theatre Journal* 14, no. 2 (1997): 200–222.

48. Also in 1944 Brecht recommended to the conductor Otto Klemperer that he establish a trade union opera house in Berlin and wean audiences from Wagner, suggestions which indicate that he continued to both distrust the opera establishment and concern himself with the rehabilitation of the genre and the institution. Brecht, *Journals, 1934–1955*, ed. John Willett, trans. Hugh Rorrison (New York: Routledge, 1996), entry for July 1944. Hereafter *Journals*.

49. The American version of *The Tales of Hoffmann* was never realized, and efforts to revive the project for the East German film company DEFA in 1949, with musical assistance from Eisler, were also futile.

50. Hans Peter Neureuter, "Stückfragmente und Stückprojekte: Befund und Theorie," in *Brecht Handbuch in fünf Bänden*, ed. Jan Knopf (Stuttgart: J. B. Metzler, 2001), 1:52–54.

51. Brecht, *Der Untergang des Egoisten Johann Fatzer*, ed. Heiner Müller (Frankfurt am Main: Suhrkamp, 1994). Müller's use and interpretation of Brecht, particularly in *Mauser*, which reworks and critiques Brecht's Lehrstück *The Decision*, is not unrelated to the present discussion but is beyond its immediate scope.

52. *BFA* 10. The publication of these fragments en masse decontextualizes them from their larger textual networks, but this isolation also brings certain

creative trends to the fore, such as the prevalence of texts that Brecht identified at some point as representing a musical genre, and the fact that he anticipated the inclusion of music in virtually every unfinished piece. Neureuter, "Stückfragmente und Stückprojekte,"·54. Because Brecht's generic definitions and designations are slippery, Neureuter instead shapes his overview of the incomplete texts according to the scheme Brecht set out for Eric Bentley when he was planning an English-language edition of the complete works (it did not come to fruition). The categories were "the continuation of tradition (significant theme, rich narrative, great roles)" and "The NEW (Dialectical realism)." Bentley, *Bentley on Brecht*, 2nd ed. (New York: Applause, 1999), 294–295.

53. Neureuter, "Stückfragmente und Stückprojekte," 54. According to Tom Kuhn, there are no plans to publish English translations of the fragments in the Methuen series.

A significant exception is Oesmann's *Staging History*. Oesmann included the recently published fragments in the primary sources she consulted in support of her argument that Brecht's work was less indebted to Marxist theory than is generally assumed and that he remains relevant in the postcommunist world. In his assessment of the fragments Neureuter cites several now-canonical works on fragments and editing Brecht that have informed my summary: Gert Ueding, "Das Fragment als literarische Form der Utopie," *Etudes Germaniques* 41, no. 3 (1986): 351–362; Eberhard Ostermann, *Das Fragment. Geschichte einer ästhetischen Idee* (Munich: Wilhelm Fink Verlag, 1991); and Gerhard Seidel, *Bertolt Brecht. Arbeitsweise und Edition. Das literarische Werk als Prozeß* (Berlin: Akademie-Verlag, 1977). For a critique of the *BFA* in terms of both process and product see Brecht archivist Erdmut Wizisla and Marta Ulvaeus, "Editorial Principles in the Berlin and Frankfurt Edition of Bertolt Brecht's Works," *Drama Review* 43, no. 4 (1999): 31–39. Wizisla and Ulvaeus make clear that a Brecht edition initiated by scholars and publishers from both East and West Germany in the mid-1980s was symbolically significant for literature, much as the joint enterprise of the *Neue Bach-Ausgabe*, begun in 1954, had been for musicology. They are particularly critical of volume ten, however, in which the editors elected to disregard the signatures of the Bertolt-Brecht-Archiv. This means it is virtually "impossible to reconstruct versions," a frustration this author shares (Wizisla and Ulvaeus, "Editorial Principles," 32). For further critique of volume ten, see Neureuter, "Stückfragmente und Stückprojekte," 65.

54. Neureuter, "Stückfragmente und Stückprojekte," 54; and Jennifer R. Shaw, "Schoenberg's Choral Symphony, 'Die Jakobsleiter,' and Other Wartime Fragments" (PhD diss., State University of New York–Stony Brook, 2002), 44.

55. Aestheticians have recently conceded the utility of a limited type of actual intentionalism that is useful for this discussion. (It should be noted that the philosophers are dealing with nonperformance art, and therefore the distinction between text and work generally made by scholars of music and theater does not pertain in their analyses. Sometimes they use the term "work" to indicate what performance scholars would designate as "text.") Sherri Irvin argues

that the artist's intentions are relevant inasmuch as one can rely upon what the artist has *sanctioned,* and this can extend to the determination that a piece is finished or unfinished. Sherri Irvin, "The Artist's Sanction in Contemporary Art," *Journal of Aesthetics and Art Criticism* 63, no. 4 (2005): 326. Paisley Livingston identifies two markers of completion: genetic and aesthetic. Genetic completion acknowledges the creator's intentionality in determining whether something is finished: "A work is genetically complete only if its maker or makers decides it is so." Aesthetic completion means that "the item in question, when appreciated in light of the relevant artistic categories, manifests certain features that are positively valued within those categories, such as coherence, resolution, the right sort of denouement, the possession of all the essential or characteristic elements of the genre or form, and so on" (Livingston, *Art and Intention*, 55 and 54, respectively).

56. Shaw, "Schoenberg's Choral Symphony," 5, referring to Robert Morris, "Modes of Coherence and Continuity in Schoenberg's Piano Piece, Opus 23, No. 1," *Theory and Practice* 17 (1992): 5.

57. Neureuter, "Stückfragmente und Stückprojekte," 52. See also Herta Ramthun, who lists 156 such items under the heading "Stückfragmente, -entwürfe, -projekte," in *Bertolt-Brecht-Archiv: Bestandsverzeichnis des literarischen Nachlasses* (Berlin: Aufbau Verlag, 1969), 1:275–398.

58. Neureuter, "Stückfragmente und Stückprojekte," 52.

59. Here I do not refer to the Romantic fragments of Schlegel, Novalis, and Hölderlin, who composed fragments *as fragments,* intentionally producing incomplete, idealized symbols of unattainable wholeness. See Manfred Frank, *Einführung in die frühromantische Ästhetik* (Frankfurt am Main: Suhrkamp, 1989); and Philippe Lacoue-Labarthe and Jean-Luc Nancy, *The Literary Absolute: The Theory of Literature in German Romanticism,* trans. Philip Barnard and Cheryl Lester (Albany: State University of New York Press, 1988). With regard to musical fragments in the same period see Charles Rosen, *The Romantic Generation* (Cambridge: Harvard University Press, 1995), 41–115. For a related analysis that extends beyond the Romantics see Wolfgang Rathert, "Ende, Abschied und Fragment. Zu Ästhetik und Geschichte einer musikalischen Problemstellung," in *Abschied in die Gegenwart. Teleologie und Zuständlichkeit in der Musik,* ed. Otto Kolleritsch (Vienna: Universal Edition, 1998), 211–235. These exploratory texts are examples of Livingston's fourth kind of fragment (Livingston, *Art and Intention,* 60).

60. Michael Franz, "Die Krise des 'Werk'–Begriffs," in *Brecht 83. Brecht und Marxismus. Dokumentation,* ed. Brecht Zentrum der DDR (East Berlin: Henschelverlag, 1983), 212. Franz's interpretation of all challenges to the work concept as literal manifestations of Marxism is strained at times but insightful nevertheless.

61. Ibid., 213–215. Creation by collective rather than individual has long been perceived as a serious threat to conventional notions of "the work." Livingston cites Jack Stillinger: "At present, critical appreciation of a masterwork requires it to be the product of a single organizing mind." Stillinger, *Multiple*

Authorship and the Myth of Solitary Genius (Oxford: Oxford University Press, 1991), 138. Livingston, "Author, Individual, and Collective," in *Art and Intention*, 62–90.

62. Malik argued that Brecht's preferred generic designation "actually only belong[s] in specialized circles, like, for instance, technical experiments" and anticipated that any published text whose title boldly asserts its status as a test, an experiment, or an unproven theory would find neither a large nor understanding audience. Wieland Herzfelde, "Über Bertolt Brecht," in *Erinnerungen an Brecht*, ed. Hubert Witt (Leipzig: Reclam, 1964), 129–138, cited in Wizisla and Ulvaeus, "Editorial Principles," 34.

63. In the case of Brecht's published texts, the *BFA* may inadvertently contribute to the confusion. Wizisla and Ulvaeus note that the arrangement Brecht had with Suhrkamp in 1953 was according to the principle of *Fassung letzter Hand* (final edition), while the *BFA* editorial board opted for the principle of *früher Hand* (early edition) to emphasize genesis and provenance, but this choice may also obscure the fact that even Brecht's published oeuvre was subject to flux. Lion Feuchtwanger observed that "Brecht held everything he had created as provisional, in process. Books that he had allowed to be published long ago, plays he had produced countless times, were in no way finished for him, and even the *works* he loved most . . . he observed as fragments. He . . . attached less importance to the completion of the *work* than to the process of the *work*" (emphasis added; see proviso in n. 55 regarding "text" and "work"). Feuchtwanger, "Bertolt Brecht," in *Bertolt Brecht: Leben und Werk im Bild. Mit autobiographischen Texten, einer Zeittafel und einem Essay*, ed. Werner Hecht (Leipzig: Gustav Kiepenheuer Verlag, 1981), 271.

64. *BFA* 27:93. Some evidence contradicts the image of Brecht as a performance-centered author, however, particularly where musical genres were concerned. He was wont to publish texts in new versions that do not consider their relationship to a musical score, so that it is impossible to fit the playwright's revised lyrics to the original musical settings. Not only does this generate a host of practical problems for the performers, suggesting that musical realization in performance was conceived differently, but it effectively precludes any performance that might approximate aesthetic or genetic completion. This is discussed in chapter 1. The number of musical texts left in various states of completion and the nearly continual presence of a composer in his circle at any given time indicates that music was an important generative force for the conception of a text but not for its later states, which might involve mutation into other, nonmusical, even nonperforming genres.

For a comprehensive case study of the problems that arise with various text versions, see Esbjörn Nyström, *Libretto im Progress: Brechts und Weills "Aufstieg und Fall der Stadt Mahagonny" aus textgeschichtlicher Sicht* (Bern: Peter Lang, 2005).

65. There is a sizable, sophisticated body of scholarship in musicology, performance studies, and aesthetics devoted to the ontology of musical and theatrical pieces that distinguishes between the performance and the text as well as

the performance and the production. The Institute for Theater Studies at the Free University in Berlin has undertaken a long-term project to develop a theory of performance based on this premise. See Erika Fischer-Lichte, "Einleitende Thesen zum Aufführungsbegriff," in *Kunst der Aufführung,* 11–26. Abbate theorizes the performance as separate with regard to the physicality of opera performance, particularly of the voice, for both singer and audience in "Music—Drastic or Gnostic?" *Critical Inquiry* 30, no. 3 (2004): 505; and in "Opera; or, The Envoicing of Women," in *Musicology and Difference,* ed. Ruth A. Solie (Berkeley: University of California Press, 1993), 225–258; and *In Search of Opera* (Princeton, NJ: Princeton University Press, 2001). More recently see Philip Auslander's critique of Nicholas Cook's "Between Process and Product: Music and/as Performance," *Music Theory Online* 7, no. 2 (2001) in "Musical Personae," *Drama Review* 50, no. 1 (2006): 100–119. Auslander's model concerns performing musicians who cultivate stage personae in concert, but his argument that such personae are co-created with audiences has applications for dramatic performers as well.

66. *Grove Music Online,* ed. Laura Macy, http://www.grovemusic.com .proxy.library.vanderbilt.edu, s.v. "Editing," accessed 20 February 2006. His concept is indebted to the phenomenological philosophy of Roman Ingarden.

67. Perhaps it is more accurate to say that performance represented completion in the abstract, while in reality it was the closest possible approximation to it. It bears noting that this is not the equivalent of needing a performer to act as a conduit for the voice of the author or needing a performer so that she may be animated by the author's text.

68. Susanne Langer, *Feeling and Form: A Theory of Art* (New York: Scribner, 1953).

69. Abbate, "Drastic," 505, and her translation of Vladimir Jankélévitch, *Music and the Ineffable* (Princeton, NJ: Princeton University Press, 2003).

70. This is detailed in the correspondence between Brecht, his agent George Marton, Muse, Weill, and Paul Robeson's wife Eslanda. See documents reprinted in *Kurt Weill: A Life in Pictures and Documents,* by David Farneth, with Elmar Juchem and Dave Stein (Woodstock, NY: Overlook Press, 2000), 211–213. See also Michael M. Kater, "Weill und Brecht: Kontroversen einer Künstlerfreundschaft auf zwei Kontinenten," in *Brecht und seine Komponisten,* 63–67.

71. Lucchesi and Shull, *Musik bei Brecht,* 909, and Dümling, *Laßt euch nicht verführen,* 543.

72. Brecht also worked with Boris Blacher, a composer who had an opera ready for production but was very pessimistic about its prospects. Blacher maintained that because no new opera since Strauss's 1912 *Der Rosenkavalier* had caught on with the public, audiences must be content with older repertoire. Brecht recorded his response in his journal: "I argue that these fulfill the old function of opera better, and a new function has not been found. The revolutionary bourgeoisie's operas (*Don Giovanni, Magic Flute, Figaro, Fidelio*) were inflammatory; opera has made no efforts in that direction since 1912" (*Journals,* entry for 29 April 1950).

73. See Joy H. Calico, "'Für eine neue deutsche Nationaloper': Opera in the Discourses of National Identity and Legitimation in the German Democratic Republic," in *Music and German National Identity,* ed. Celia Applegate and Pamela Potter (Chicago: University of Chicago Press, 2002), 190–204; and Sigrid Neef and Hermann Neef, *Deutsche Oper im 20. Jahrhundert: DDR, 1949–1989* (Berlin: Peter Lang, 1992).

74. See Joachim Lucchesi, ed., *Das Verhör in der Oper: Die Debatte um die Aufführung "Das Verhör des Lukullus" von Bertolt Brecht und Paul Dessau* (Berlin: Basisdruck, 1993), for a collection of primary documents related to the opera and the controversy. Hereafter *Debatte.*

75. Hans Bunge, ed., *Die Debatte um Hanns Eislers "Johann Faustus": Eine Dokumentation* (Berlin: Basisdruck, 1991). For the libretto see Eisler, *Johann Faustus: Fassung letzter Hand,* ed. Bunge (Berlin: Henschelverlag, 1983); Eisler, *Johann Faustus: Oper* (Leipzig: Faber and Faber, 1996); and Peter Schweinhardt, ed. *Hanns Eislers Johann Faustus: 50 Jahre nach Erscheinen des Operntexts 1952. Symposion* (Wiesbaden: Breitkopf and Härtel, 2005).

76. Brecht drafted a text, but the libretto to Dessau's 1973 opera *Einstein* was ultimately written by Karl Mickel, and Dessau's operatic setting of Brecht's *Puntila* came after the playwright's death (1957–59). I am indebted to Ralf Bülow of the Landesmuseum für Technik und Arbeit for the information that the first opera about Einstein was the three-act *Der Chronoplan* (1930), libretto by Julia Kerr and score by Alfred Kerr, but there appears to be no connection.

77. Mary Fulbrook, *Anatomy of a Dictatorship: Inside the GDR, 1949–1989* (Oxford: Oxford University Press, 1995), 3–4.

78. Jonathan Kalb argues, "In an era saturated with information that spins an illusion of universal democratic zeal, Brecht's genre of explicitly didactic drama grounded in datedly disruptive montage structures has lost even the limited ability to achieve *Verfremdung* (alienation—the making available of alternative choices in interpretation and action) that it once had" (*The Theater of Heiner Müller* [Cambridge: Cambridge University Press, 1998], 19). Kalb's otherwise excellent book includes no consideration of music, either with regard to its role in Brecht's plays or in Müller's.

79. Fredric Jameson, *Brecht and Method* (London: Verso, 1998), 18. He refers to the ubiquity of Brecht and his work during the observance of his centennial in 1998. It is conceivable that a similar backlash may follow the commemoration of the fiftieth anniversary of his death in 2006.

80. Elizabeth Wright, *Postmodern Brecht: A Re-presentation* (London: Routledge, 1989).

81. Oesmann, *Staging History.*

82. Loren Kruger, *Post-Imperial Brecht: Politics and Performance, East and South* (Cambridge: Cambridge University Press, 2004), and *The Drama of South Africa: Plays, Pageants, and Publics since 1910* (New York: Routledge, 1999). Also Burton Bollag, "Dramatic Intervention," *Chronicle of Higher Education* 48, no. 41 (21 June 2002), A48; Nicholas Brown, "People's Theater in East

Africa: The *Lehrstücke* of Ngugi wa Thiong'o," *Communications* 27, no. 1 (1998): 23–27; Lorena B. Ellis, *Brecht's Reception in Brazil* (New York: Peter Lang, 1995); and *Brecht Yearbook/Brecht Jahrbuch* 14 (1989), which is dedicated to scholarship on Brecht in Asia and Africa.

83. Peter Monaghan, "For Brecht: An Ironic Encore," *Chronicle of Higher Education* 51, no. 34 (29 April 2005): A14. The coverage included two additional sidebars: "Playing Brecht," a report on several recent plays that take Brecht as their subject; and "Brecht in Context," an interview with Eric Bentley, in which he says he disagrees with Fuegi's portrayal of Brecht but appreciates the fact that Fuegi's work shook up the discipline. *Communications* 34 (2005) reprinted Monaghan's articles with twenty-two pages of responses from Brecht scholars who disagreed with the assessment put forth in the *Chronicle*. See also the recent collection of interviews in which artists and philosophers discuss the importance of Brecht's influence for their work. Frank-Michael Raddatz, *Brecht frißt Brecht: Neues episches Theater im 21. Jahrhundert* (Leipzig: Henschel, 2007).

84. In his analysis of *The Decision*, William Rasch challenges Brecht's political relevance in a different way, asking "whether the 'lesson' that the *Lehrstück* (teaching play) invites us to learn is a political lesson, or whether participation in the revolutionary process is meant to be training for life in a post-political state." William Rasch, *Sovereignty and Its Discontents: On the Primacy of Conflict and the Structure of the Political* (London: Birkbeck Law, 2004), 65.

85. Heiner Müller, "To Use Brecht without Criticizing Him Is to Betray Him," trans. Marc Silberman, *Theater* 17, no. 2 (Spring 1986): 31–33. David Bathrick and Andreas Huyssen, "Producing Revolution: Heiner Müller's *Mauser* as Learning Play," *New German Critique* 8 (Spring 1976): 110–121; Benton Jay Komins, "Rewriting, Violence, and Theater: Bertolt Brecht's *The Measures Taken* and Heiner Müller's *Mauser*," *Comparatist* 26 (May 2002): 99–119.

86. *The Contingent* was produced in 2000 at the Theater am Turm in Frankfurt and the Schaubühne in Berlin, and in 2001 at the United Nations Headquarters in New York. See Alexander Stephan, "Soeren Voima schreiben mit *Das Kontingent* Brechts *Maßnahme* weiter," *Brecht Yearbook/Brecht-Jahrbuch* 26 (2001): 61–79. Alan Sikes also argues for the relevance of the Lehrstück in the post–cold war era in "Restaging the Revolution: Aesthetics, Politics, and the Question of Collective Action," *Journal of Dramatic Theory and Criticism* 17, no. 2 (Spring 2003): 123–137.

87. Brecht, "The Major and Minor Pedagogy," in *Brecht on Art and Politics*, ed. Tom Kuhn and Steve Giles, trans. Laura Bradley, Steve Giles, and Tom Kuhn (London: Methuen, 2003), 88–89. German in BFA 21:396.

88. Kruger, *Post-Imperial Brecht*, 43–45.

89. Andrjez Wirth, "Vom Dialog zum Diskurs: Versuch einer Synthese der nachbrechtschen Theaterkonzepte," *Theater heute* 1 (January 1980): 16.

90. Cited in Hubert Witt, ed., *Brecht As They Knew Him*, trans. John Peet (New York: International Publishers, 1975), 227–228.

1. LEHRSTÜCK, OPERA, AND THE NEW AUDIENCE CONTRACT OF THE EPIC THEATER

1. In this chapter I use "Lehrstück" in the singular form in the same way in which I use "opera" in the singular form, which is to say as a reference to an individual text or as a generic designation. The exception to this rule is the text *Lehrstück*, in which the term denotes its proper title. The plural form, "Lehrstücke," is used in the same way in which I use "operas" in the plural, that is, as a reference to multiple pieces.

2. The concept of the audience contract was generated in Carolyn Abbate's National Endowment for the Humanities seminar "Opera: Interpretations, Stagings, Readings" in the summer of 2002. It emerged from discussion about the essay "*Don Giovanni;* or, the Art of Disappointing One's Admirers," by Ann Smock, in *Enigmas: Essays on Sarah Kofman*, ed. Penelope Deutscher and Kelly Oliver (Ithaca, NY: Cornell University Press, 1999), 49–66. Regarding the use of theater as an experimental microcosm of society, see Darko Suvin, *To Brecht and Beyond: Soundings in Modern Dramaturgy* (Brighton, England: Harvester Press, 1984), 83–111. I am indebted to Professor Suvin for his generous correspondence concerning the material in this chapter.

3. My argument that the Lehrstücke are integral to the trajectory of Brecht's epic theory follows Oesmann, Steinweg, Nägele, Bathrick, and Huyssen in rejecting simplistic political readings of them as propagandistic outliers unrelated to his mature writings. Astrid Oesmann, *Staging History: Brecht's Social Concepts of Ideology* (Albany: State University of New York Press, 2005); Reiner Steinweg, *Das Lehrstück: Brechts Theorie einer politisch-ästhetischen Erziehung* (Stuttgart: J. B. Metzler, 1972); Rainer Nägele, *Theater, Theory, Speculation: Walter Benjamin and Scenes of Modernity* (Baltimore: Johns Hopkins University Press, 1991); David Bathrick and Andreas Huyssen, "Producing Revolution: Heiner Müller's *Mauser* as Learning Play," *New German Critique* 8 (Spring 1976): 110–121.

4. Stephen Hinton observes the results of Weill's simultaneous engagement with Lehrstück and opera in *Die Bürgschaft*, which Weill described as an "epic opera." I am grateful to Hinton for sharing his unpublished manuscript "Weill's Musical Theater: Stages of Reform" (2007).

5. The title translations are taken from the most recent English edition of Brecht, *Collected Plays*, 8 volumes, ed. and trans. John Willett, Ralph Manheim, and Tom Kuhn (London: Methuen, 1994–2001; published by A&C Black as of 2006). Hereafter *Collected Plays*, volume and page number. *The Decision* is elsewhere commonly referred to as *The Measures Taken*. The standard German titles of these pieces are *Der Lindberghflug/Der Flug der Lindberghs* (later *Der Ozeanflug*), *Das Badener Lehrstück vom Einverständnis, Der Jasager/Der Neinsager, Die Maßnahme*, and *Die Ausnahme und die Regel;* the operas are *Die Dreigroschenoper* and *Aufstieg und Fall der Stadt Mahagonny*.

6. The classic study remains Steinweg, *Das Lehrstück*. See also Roswitha Mueller, "Learning for a New Society: The *Lehrstück*," in *The Cambridge Com-*

panion to Brecht, 2nd ed., ed. Peter Thomson and Glendyr Sacks (Cambridge: Cambridge University Press, 2006), 101–117; Karl-Heinz Schoeps, "Brecht's *Lehrstücke:* A Laboratory for Epic and Dialectic Theater," in *A Bertolt Brecht Reference Companion,* ed. Siegfried Mews (Westport, CT: Greenwood Press, 1997), 70–87; Fredric Jameson, *Brecht and Method* (London: Verso, 1998); and Taekwan Kim, *Das Lehrstück Bertolt Brechts: Untersuchungen zur Theorie und Praxis einer zweckbestimmten Musik am Beispiel von Paul Hindemith, Kurt Weill und Hanns Eisler* (Frankfurt am Main: Peter Lang, 2000). For a summary of the arguments that criticize Steinweg's analysis as ahistorical, see Rekha Kamath, *Brechts Lehrstück-Modell als Bruch mit den bürgerlichen Theatertraditionen* (Frankfurt am Main: Peter Lang, 1983), 52–53.

Wulf Konold also uses the term "anti-opera," but only with regard to music theater after 1960. Konold, "Oper—Anti-Oper—Anti-Anti-Oper," in *Musiktheater heute: Internationales Symposion der Paul Sacher Stiftung Basel 2001,* ed. Hermann Danuser and Matthias Kassel (Mainz: Schott, 2003), 47–60.

7. Gerhard Fischer, "The Lehrstück Experience on a Contemporary Stage: On Brecht and the GRIPS-Theater's *Voll auf der Rolle,*" *Modern Drama* 31, no. 3 (1988): 372.

8. Mueller, "Learning for a New Society," 118.

9. Cited in Steinweg, *Das Lehrstück,* 87. See also Brecht, "On the Theory of the Lehrstück," translated in Jonathan Kalb, *The Theater of Heiner Müller* (Cambridge: Cambridge University Press, 1998), 26. For a systematic critique of Steinweg's 1972 study see Klaus-Dieter Krabiel, *Brechts Lehrstücke: Entstehung und Entwicklung eines Spieltyps* (Stuttgart: Metzler Verlag, 1993). Steinweg and Ingrid D. Koudela summarize and revise previous responses in *Lehrstück und episches Theater: Brechts Theorie und die theaterpädagogische Praxis* (Frankfurt am Main: Brandes and Apsel, 1995), 110–117.

10. Jameson, *Brecht and Method,* 63. Werner Mittenzwei refers to it as "art without an audience." Mittenzwei, "Brecht und die Schicksale der Materialästhetik," in *Brechts Tui-Kritik. Aufsätze, Rezensionen, Geschichten,* ed. Wolfgang Fritz Haug (Karlsruhe: Argument Verlag, 1976), 199. See also two other volumes edited by Steinweg, *Brechts Modell der Lehrstücke, Zeugnisse, Diskussionen, Erfahrungen* (Frankfurt am Main: Suhrkamp, 1976); and *Auf Anregung Bertolt Brechts: Lehrstücke mit Schülern, Arbeitern, Theaterleuten* (Frankfurt: Suhrkamp, 1978).

11. The questionnaire and Eisler's program notes in which he states that this particular performance is more like an event are reproduced in facsimile in Brecht, *Die Maßnahme: Lehrstück. Das Exemplar eines Kritikers von der Uraufführung am 13.12.1930 gefunden, transkribiert, kommentiert und herausgegeben von Reinhard Krüger,* ed. Reinhard Krüger (Berlin: Weidler Buchverlag, 2001), 73–75. *Collected Plays* 3:232–234.

12. In a 1930 essay he distinguished between major pedagogy, as experienced in the participatory Lehrstück, and minor pedagogy, which "merely carries out a democratimion of theatre in the transitional era of the first revolution." Evidently minor pedagogy was better than none at all where these texts

were concerned. Brecht, *Brecht on Art and Politics,* ed. Tom Kuhn and Steve Giles, trans. Laura Bradley, Steve Giles, and Tom Kuhn (London: Methuen, 2003), 88. BFA 21:396. See also Kalb, "*The Horatian:* Building the Better Lehrstück," *New German Critique* 64 (Winter 1995): 173 n. 20; and David Barnett, "Heiner Müller As the End of Brechtian Dramaturgy," *Theatre Research International* 27, no. 1 (2002): 50.

13. Stephen Hinton refers to Brecht's "de-musicalization" of the genre in "Lehrstück: An Aesthetics of Performance," in *Music and Performance during the Weimar Republic,* ed. Bryan Gilliam (Cambridge: Cambridge University Press, 1994), 66.

14. Klaus-Dieter Krabiel, "Das Lehrstück: Ein mißverstandenes Genre," *Der Deutschunterricht: Beiträge zu seiner Praxis und wissenschaftlichen Grundlegung* 46, no. 6 (1994): 16. Krabiel attributes the significance of music to this genre's association with Gebrauchsmusik. Other important sources by Krabiel are his "Lehrstück" entry in *Die Musik in Geschichte und Gegenwart: Allgemeine Enzyklopädie der Musik,* 2nd ed.; "Das Lehrstück von Brecht und Hindemith: Von der Geburt eines Genres aus dem Geist der Gebrauchsmusik," *Hindemith Jahrbuch* 24 (1995): 146–179, and *Brechts Lehrstücke.* Krabiel's insistence upon the primacy of music is one of his main points of conflict with Steinweg. Krabiel is also dubious of interpretations of the genre as comedic; see "Rhetorik der Utopie—Rhetorik der Komödie? Bemerkungen zu einer Untersuchung der Lehrstücke Brechts und ihrer Rezeption in der Fachkritik," *Wirkendes Wort: Deutsche Sprache in Forschung und Lehre* 40, no. 2 (1990): 209–219.

15. "The Lehrstück is valued as a musical genre, as both musical expression and the driving force of a socially intense situation." Dorothea Kolland, "Musik und Lehrstück," in *Maßnehmen: Bertolt Brecht/Hanns Eislers Lehrstück Die Maßnahme. Kontroverse, Perspektive, Praxis,* ed. Inge Gellert, Gerd Koch, and Florian Vaßen (Berlin: Theater der Zeit, 1998), 175. For Andrzej Wirth, the primary advantage of a professional production such as that by the Berliner Ensemble was "their brilliant execution of the very difficult vocal and musical score, which doesn't leave out a single note of Eisler's music," although he regretted the use of professional actors in roles meant for amateurs (Wirth, "The Lehrstück as Performance," *Drama Review* 43, no. 4 [1999]: 119). The present author attended the final dress rehearsal on 14 September 1997. This event, which marked the centennials of both playwright and composer, was met with great fanfare. See *Kontroverse, Perspektive, Praxis;* Brecht, *Die Maßnahme: Zwei Fassungen: Anmerkungen,* ed. Judith Wilke (Frankfurt am Main: Suhrkamp, 1998); Susanne Winnacker, *Wer immer es ist, den ihr hier sucht, ich bin es nicht: Zur Dramaturgie der Abwesenheit in Bertolt Brechts Lehrstück Die Maßnahme* (Frankfurt am Main: Peter Lang, 1997); and Albrecht Dümling, "Eisler und Brecht: Bilanz einer produktiven Partnerschaft," *Neue Zeitschrift für Musik* 159, no. 6 (1998): 4–9, among others.

16. Mueller notes that *The Exception and the Rule* is also different in subject matter from the other pieces designated as Lehrstücke, as it is the only one

that "deals explicitly with the contradiction in bourgeois society." Mueller, "Learning for a New Society," 108. *The Exception* was set to music in 1938 by Nissim Nissimov and then by Paul Dessau in 1948.

17. Hinton summarizes relevant articles in "Lehrstück," 66–68. He begins with Karl Laux's report from the Baden-Baden Festival published in *Zeitschrift für Musik*, an abridged version of which appeared in the first issue of *Musik und Gesellschaft* in 1930. This was followed by two articles, "Lehrstück" by Hilmar Trede and Hans Boettcher and "Lehrstück und Theater" by Gerhart Scherler. These essays cite the pieces by composer and author, while the 1931 *Melos* essay "Lehrstück und Schuloper" by Siegfried Günther gives credit by composer's name only. The pieces identified are *Das Wasser* (cantata by Ernst Toch and Alfred Döblin), *Der neue Hiob* (Lehrstück by Hermann Reutter and Robert Seitz), *Wir bauen eine Stadt* (play for children by Hindemith and Seitz), *Das Eisenbahnspiel* (Lehrstück by Paul Dessau and Seitz), *Das schwarze Schaf* (Paul Höffer), *Cress ertrinkt* (school play by Wolfgang Fortner and A. Zeitler), *Jobsiade* (school opera by Wolfgang Jacobi and Seitz), and *Der Reisekamerad* (school opera by Hans Joachim Moser, after Hans Christian Andersen).To this list could also be added *Tadel der Unzuverlässigkeit* (Dessau and Seitz) and *Kinderkantate* (text and music by Dessau).

18. Brecht originally published *He Who Said Yes* and *He Who Said No* as school operas in *Versuche 11–12*, vol. 4 (Berlin: Gustav Kiepenheuer Verlag, 1931), although how one would perform the second text as an opera when it had no musical setting is unclear. He referred to the first text as a school opera in "On the Use of Music in an Epic Theatre" (*BoT* 90, *BFA* 22:164).

19. "Brecht never exactly had a doctrine to teach, not even 'Marxism' in the form of a system," but he did teach the method of dialectical thought. Jameson, *Brecht and Method*, 2 and 79–80. Furthermore, it is no accident, as Loren Kruger has noted, that "Brecht's conception of the participant audience emerges in negotiation with party discipline." Kruger, *Post-Imperial Brecht: Politics and Performance, East and South* (Cambridge: Cambridge University Press, 2004), 26.

20. Weill, "Über meine Schuloper *Der Jasager*," *Die Scene* 20 (August 1930): 232–233. *MumT* 119–120, *Europe* 530.

21. Krabiel discusses many of these issues in "Die Lehrstücke Brechts als editorisches Problem," in *Der Text im musikalischen Werk: Editionsprobleme aus musikwissenschaftlicher und literaturwissenschaftlicher Sicht*, ed. Walther Dürr (Berlin: Erich Schmidt, 1998), 331–345. Brecht's textual revisions to pieces he had written with Weill appear to have been calculated to exclude the composer from the finished product.

22. Regarding revisions to *The Decision* between its premiere and its publication, see Ludwig Hoffmann, "Verhalten im Klassenkampf: Von der 'Maßnahme' zur 'Mutter,'" in *Theater der Kollektive: Proletarisch-revolutionäres Berufstheater in Deutschland, 1928–1933. Stücke, Dokumente, Studien*, ed. Hoffmann and Klaus Pfützner (Berlin: Henschelverlag, 1980), 1:363–378. Hoffmann reads Brecht's changes as a response to complaints from Marxist critics that the play represented a separation of theory and praxis rather than the result

of post-performance public discussions. Revisions were made in conjunction with Eisler, who reworked music as necessary.

23. Patrick Primavesi notes that while the Baden-Baden Festival was primarily a musical event, its experimental theme was "Radiokunst für die Massen im technischen Zeitalter." Primavesi, "Apparat ohne Zuschauer? Zur Dekonstruktion des Mediums in Brechts *Ozeanflug,*" *Brecht Yearbook/Brecht-Jahrbuch* 24 (1999): 84.

24. See Oscar Thompson's eyewitness account of the festival in "The Baden-Baden Festival: Music for Wireless and Films," *Musical Times* 70, no. 1039 (1929): 800.

25. See Dümling regarding the hands-on pedagogical ground the collaborators shared and where they parted ways in " 'Agire e meglio che sentire': L'aspetto pedagogico in Brecht e Hindemith," in *Paul Hindemith nella cultura tedesca degli anni Venti,* ed. Carlo Piccardi (Milan: Unicopli, 1991), 220–242.

26. Mueller, "Learning for a New Society," 106. Perhaps "piano reduction" rather than "piano excerpt" was intended, and "instrumentation" instead of "musical form," but as it stands, the descriptions are misleading and inaccurate.

27. Hindemith, preface to *Lehrstück* (Mainz: Schott, 1929). Excerpts are cited in translation in Hinton, "Lehrstück," 65. Preface in *Collected Plays,* 3:214–216.

28. Mueller, "Learning for a New Society," 106. Hinton notes that the *BFA* uses *Das Lehrstück vom Einverständnis* rather than the earlier version, despite its policy to publish "as a matter of principle the authorized and established first editions." The editors refer to Brecht's *Versuche* editions, which he published independently of the composers, but those are not necessarily the earliest authorized versions. Thirteen productions of the original version took place during 1929–33, but there is no evidence that the revised version was ever performed (Hinton, "Lehrstück," 183 n. 37). For further related critique of the *BFA,* see the introduction. Willett and Manheim rectified this problem by printing in contrasting typeface any text Brecht added later that has no musical setting (*Collected Plays* 3:21–43). Dümling notes the general inadequacy of the *BFA* with regard to commentary on musical settings in " 'Im Stil der Lehrstücke': Zu Entstehung und Edition von Eislers Musik für Brechts Gorki-Bearbeitung 'Die Mutter,' " in *Der Text im musikalischen Werk,* 374.

29. John Willett, "*Die Maßnahme:* The Vanishing Lehrstück," in *Hanns Eisler: A Miscellany,* ed. David Blake (New York: Harwood Academic Publishers, 1995), 80.

30. As quoted in ibid. Willett reports that the pair was performed together during Brecht's lifetime "in a small New York production by the Living Theatre." How the music was handled is not specified.

31. Jameson, *Brecht and Method,* 61–62.

32. Heiner Müller, *Mauser* (Berlin: Rotbuch, 1978), 68. His trilogy of texts for this purpose includes *Philoktet* (1958–64), *The Horatian* (1968), and *Mauser* (1970). All three are concerned with the notion of "necessary" killing, particularly *Mauser* and its relationship to *The Decision.* See Benton Jay Komins,

"Rewriting, Violence, and Theater: Bertolt Brecht's *The Measures Taken* and Heiner Müller's *Mauser*," *Comparatist* 26 (May 2002): 99–119; and David Bathrick and Andreas Huyssen, "Producing Revolution: Heiner Müller's *Mauser* as Learning Play," *New German Critique* 8 (Spring 1976): 110–121. Francine Maier-Schaeffer discusses all three as Lehrstücke in *Heiner Müller et le "Lehrstück"* (Berne: Peter Lang, 1992). See also Kalb, "*The Horatian*," 161–173.

33. "Kurt Weill Has Secured a Niche of His Own at 35" (interview), *New York World Telegram*, 21 December 1935. *MumT* 469.

34. Wirth, "Lehrstück as Performance," 113. Lucchesi, music director for the 1997 Berliner Ensemble production of *The Decision*, writes about this also in "Das Stück wirkt mit der Musik ganz anders!" in *Kontroverse, Perspektive, Praxis*, 189–195.

35. The necessity of performance is the fundamental difference Hans-Thies Lehmann notes between Peter Szondi's landmark work, *Theory of the Modern Drama*, which treats plays as literature, and his own approach of "systematically paying attention to theater as performance" in his work on postdramatic theater (Lehmann, *Postdramatic Theatre*, trans. Karen Jürs-Munby [London: Routledge, 2006], 2–3).

36. "In my experience with Lehrstück projects students often want to perform their own music, which I consider to be pedagogically legitimate and perhaps an elegant approach: self-devised discipline in the performance." Wirth, "Lehrstück as Performance," 114.

37. See reports of workers' chorus rehearsals for *The Decision*. Friedrich Deutsch, "Probenerfahrung bei der Maßnahme," *Der Anbruch* 13, no. 1 (1931); and H. H. Stuckenschmidt, "Ein politisches Oratorium: Brecht-Eisler 'Die Maßnahme,'" *Berliner Zeitung*, 15 December 1930. These articles are reprinted in Brecht, *Die Maßnahme. Kritische Ausgabe mit einer Spielanleitung von Reiner Steinweg*, ed. Reiner Steinweg (Frankfurt am Main: Suhrkamp, 1972), 324–336. Wirth also noted that the music contradicts the text when lyrics are sung: "The sentences that come across as theses lose their dogmatic call and become performance material wanting to be sung—the musicalizing and singing invalidating ideology" ("Lehrstück as Performance," 115). Certainly the passage of time and the historical specificity of some texts must be taken into account when considering such a change of meaning in modern-day performance.

38. The New Music Festival in Berlin had commissioned *He Who Said Yes*, but when the program committee rejected *The Decision* on the basis of the quality of the text (no music had been composed yet), Weill and Brecht suspected that the reasons were rather more political than aesthetic; the artists withdrew *He Who Said Yes* in protest. Weill published his response to the situation as "Musikfest oder Musikstudio," *Melos* 9 (May–June 1930): 230–232. *MumT* 115–118, *Europe* 527–529. Eisler's open letter to the program committee was published in part in *Berliner Börsen-Courier*, 13 May 1930; it appears in its entirety in Eisler, *Musik und Politik: Schriften, 1924–1948*, ed. Günter Mayer (Leipzig: VEB Deutscher Verlag für Musik, 1985), 103–105; and in English in *Collected Plays* 3:343–344.

39. The original libretto and collaborative score of *Lindbergh Flight* are available in *Paul Hindemith: Szenische Versuche*, Sämtliche Werke, series 1, vol. 6, ed. Rudolf Stephan (Mainz: Schott, 1982), xix–xxiii and 105–207, respectively. For an English translation, in which Brecht's later additions are differentiated by contrasting typeface, see *Collected Plays* 3:1–20.

40. Matthew Wilson Smith reminds readers that "the legal context" from which *Lindbergh Flight* emerged "is important, as laws over the control of radio were still developing in 1929." The ban on listening to wireless transmissions was lifted in 1923, and only nine radio stations since 1925 had "been permitted to broadcast on a regional basis." See Smith's brilliant assessment of Brecht's connection to Wagner's Gesamtkunstwerk in *The Total Work of Art: From Bayreuth to Cyberspace* (New York: Routledge, 2007), 71–91; regarding *Lindbergh* in particular, see 84–91.

41. The only sections of *Lehrstück* not set to music are the film clip (or dance), a single line at the end of the first section, the unaccompanied readings at the beginning and end of section 5, and the dialogue for the infamous dismemberment in section 6. Brecht substantially revised this text, adding several completely new scenes, moving the clown dismemberment to scene 3, and turning the role of the Airman into a composite of three mechanics and a pilot. The *BFA* does not include this text; the closest is *BFA* 3:25–46, 410–419; *Collected Plays* 3:21–44. See Krabiel, "Das Lehrstück von Brecht und Hindemith," 146–179; and Hinton, *The Idea of Gebrauchsmusik: A Study of Musical Aesthetics in the Weimar Republic (1919–1933) with Particular Reference to the Works of Paul Hindemith* (New York: Garland Publishing, 1989).

42. The fact that the text of *He Who Said Yes* is attributed to Brecht when Hauptmann did the lion's share of the work is an instance in which Brecht's preferred working method (that of the collective) ultimately benefited his reputation more than those of his literary collaborators. See especially the controversial John Fuegi, *Brecht and Company: Sex, Politics, and the Making of the Modern Drama* (New York: Grove Press, 1994); and John Willett et al., "A Brechtbuster Goes Bust: Scholarly Mistakes, Misquotes, and Malpractices in John Fuegi's *Brecht and Company*," *Brecht Yearbook/Brecht-Jahrbuch* 20 (1995): 259–367.

43. Kurt Weill, *Der Jasager: Schuloper in zwei Akten* (Vienna: Universal Edition, 1930). *Collected Plays* 3:45–60 has emendations in contrasting typeface. *BFA* 3:47–72, 420–430.

44. Willett, "Vanishing Lehrstück," 80. For a fascinating account of the afterlife of the Lehrstücke, particularly *The Decision*, see Robert Adlington, "Louis Andriessen, Hanns Eisler and the Lehrstück," *Journal of Musicology* 21, no. 3 (2004): 381–417. See also Alan Sikes for an endorsement of the utility of the genre in the post–cold war era in "Restaging the Revolution: Aesthetics, Politics, and the Question of Collective Action," *Journal of Dramatic Theory and Criticism* 17, no. 2 (2003): 123–137.

45. An anonymous article in volume ten of *Melos* (1931) reported that *He Who Said Yes* also garnered criticism, from groups as disparate as the National-

ists, the Wagner Youth, and the orthodox branch of the church. For reviews and articles representative of the ideological debate over *The Decision,* see section G of Brecht, *Die Maßnahme. Kristische Ausgabe.* Eventually Brecht denied permission to perform the piece in an effort to prevent its misuse as anticommunist, cold war propaganda. This only succeeded in preventing performances by those who were sympathetic to or objective about its message but did not dissuade those who wanted to use the text to prove Stalinist brutality, and it was often staged without Eisler's music as anticommunist propaganda. Brecht's heirs continued to deny requests to perform the text until 1987, when it was performed legally and with Eisler's music at the Almeida Festival for perhaps the first time since the early 1930s. Willett, "Vanishing Lehrstück," 88–89.

46. Hanns Eisler, *Die Maßnahme. Lehrstück von Bert Brecht,* piano reduction by Erwin Ratz (Vienna: Universal Edition, 1931). I am grateful to Hilary Poriss for procuring this score. Text changes from the 1930 premiere are documented in *Collected Plays* 3:90–91, BFA 3:73–125, 431–448.

47. The anonymous author of "Die gefährliche Maßnahme" called it a "Chorwerk" (*Berlin am Morgen,* 24 January 1933), as did a police report (Institut für Marxismus-Leninismus beim ZK der SED). Reprinted in Brecht, *Die Maßnahme. Kritische Ausgabe,* 411–412.

48. Krüger, *Die Maßnahme,* 123. See also Robert Cohen: "The new art is a mass art, one imagines oneself as a participant in one of those huge worker choirs that filled the stage for the premiere of *The Decision.*" Cohen, "Brechts ästhetische Theorie in den ersten Jahren des Exils," in *Ästhetiken des Exils,* ed. Helga Schreckenberger (Amsterdam: Rodopi, 2003), 56.

49. The cast list from the original program is reproduced in *Paul Hindemith Szenische Versuche,* xi, and in *Collected Plays* 3:316. In a letter to his friend Hans Curjel, Klemperer's assistant at the Kroll, Weill reported the following: "Baden-Baden was very shitty. Hindemith's work on *Lindbergh Flight* was of a superficiality that will be hard to outbid. It has clearly been proven that his music is too simple for Brecht's texts. It is amazing that the press has discovered this as well, and they now present me as the shining example of how Brecht needs to be composed." WLRC series 40 correspondence with Hans Curjel 851002, dated 2 August 1929. This assessment was not universal, however; Oscar Thompson's review of the premiere praised Hindemith's music at the expense of Weill's.

50. The cast list from the original program is reproduced in *Paul Hindemith Szenische Versuche,* xiii, and in *Collected Plays* 3:326. Theo Lingen, one of the clowns, went on to enjoy a successful career as an actor in comic film.

51. See Gerd Rienäcker, "Musik als Agens. Beschreibungen und Thesen zur Musik des Lehrstückes *Die Maßnahme* von Hanns Eisler," in *Kontroverse, Perspektive, Praxis,* for specific choral analysis.

52. The choir at the premiere was known as "Arbeiterchor Groß-Berlin" from the DAS (Deutscher Arbeiter Sängerbund) and consisted of three groups: Schubertchor, Gemischte Chor Groß-Berlin, and Gemischte Chor Fichte, conducted by Karl Rankl. This information appeared in an advertisement for the

performance published in *Die Welt am Abend*, 13 December 1930. Brecht, *Die Maßnahme. Kritische Ausgabe*, 323.

53. In "Das Lehrstück von Brecht-Eisler: *Die Maßnahme*," *Berliner Börsencourier*, 15 December 1930, Heinrich Strobel writes that Eisler is the only young composer writing "Zweckmusik" (functional music). Regarding the significance of the mass choral movement and attendant reviews, see Hoffmann and Pfützner, *Theater der Kollektive*, 310–314.

54. These include "Solidarity Song," composed for the film *Kuhle Wampe* in 1930, and the thirteen songs of opuses 13, 14, 17, 19, and 21, composed 1928–30. The first song of opus 13 calls for speaker, side drum, and cymbals, and opus 15 includes side drum; otherwise the songs are all unaccompanied. Opuses 14 and 17 are for men's voices only. See Joy H. Calico, "Brecht and His Composer/Eisler and His Librettist," *Communications* 34 (June 2005): 68–69.

55. Hanns Eisler, *Tempo der Zeit. Kantata für Alt- und Bass-Solo, Sprecher, gemischten Chor und kleines Orchester Opus 16*, piano reduction by Erwin Ratz (Vienna: Universal Edition, 1930).

56. Stuckenschmidt, "Ein Politisches Oratorium." Reprinted in Brecht, *Die Maßnahme. Kritische Ausgabe*, 325–326.

57. Rienäcker also notes this in "Musik als Agens," 182–183.

58. These melodramas included Richard Strauss's *Enoch Arden*, 1890; Max von Schilling's *Das Hexenlied*, 1902; and Engelbert Humperdinck's melodrama opera *Königskinder*, 1897.

59. Kalb, *Theater of Heiner Müller*, 41–42. See Erika Fischer-Lichte, "Producing the *Volk* community—The *Thingspiel* Movement, 1935–36," in *Theatre, Sacrifice, Ritual: Exploring Forms of Political Theatre* (London: Routledge, 2005), 122–158. Note also the speaking choruses chanted by the Labor Corps in Leni Riefenstahl's iconic *Triumph of the Will*; Smith, *The Total Work of Art*, 95. Another powerful example of accompanied speech for choir is the whisper chorus in the "Sicherheit" movement of Eisler's *Deutsche Sinfonie*.

60. Regarding the description of *The Decision* as an oratorio, see for example H. H. Stuckenschmidt, "Ein politisches Oratorium"; an anonymous author described it as a "profane oratorio" in "Musik im Propagandakampf," *Vossische Zeitung*, 15 December 1930; and another titled his review "Das Oratorium von morgen: *Die Maßnahme*," *Berlin am Morgen*, 16 December 1930. These are reprinted in Brecht, *Die Maßnahme. Kritische Ausgabe*, 324–336, 333–334, and 338–340, respectively.

Dümling notes that Bach's St. Matthew Passion is a model for *The Decision* in "Bilanz einer produktiven Partnerschaft" and in "Eisler/Brecht oder Brecht/Eisler? Perspektiven, Formen und Grenzen ihrer Zusammenarbeit," in *Brecht und seine Komponisten*, ed. Albrecht Riethmüller (Laaber, Germany: Laaber, 2000), 96–97. See also Rienäcker, "Musik als Agens," 180–189, and Lucchesi, "Das Stück wirkt mit der Musik ganz anders!" in *Kontroverse, Perspektive, Praxis*, 195. Rudolf Würmser traces structural influences to oratorio and cantata in "*Der Lindberghflug* und das *Lehrstück*: Bertolt Brechts

Versuche zu einer neuen Form des Musiktheaters auf dem Baden-Badener Musikfest 1929," in *Alban Bergs "Wozzeck" und die Zwanziger Jahre. Vorträge und Materialien des Salzburger Symposions 1997*, ed. Peter Csobádi et al. (Anif/Salzburg, Austria: Muller-Speiser, 1999), 547–556; and Jonathan Eaton detects the influence of oratorio through the Lehrstück and beyond to Weill's next opera in *"Die Bürgschaft* in 1998: A Passion Play for the Twentieth Century," *Kurt Weill Newsletter* 16, no. 1 (1998): 4–5. Similarly, Christoph Khittl finds lingering influences of the Lehrstück in Hindemith's oratorio in "'Das Unaufhörliche—Großes Gesetz': Musikpädagogische Exkurse zu Hindemiths und Benns Oratorium," *Musik und Bildung: Praxis Musikerziehung* 27, no. 3 (1995): 50–54. For Eisler on his and Brecht's use of St. John Passion as a model, see *Fragen Sie mehr über Brecht: Gespräche mit Hans Bunge* (Leipzig: VEB Deutscher Verlag für Musik, 1975), 67.

61. Lutz Weltmann, "Anmerkung zu Brechts 'Versuchen,'" *Die Literatur: Monatsschrift für Literaturfreunde* 33 (October 1930–September 1931): 245–246.

62. Cited in Hinton, "Lehrstück," 64. Hinton notes that there have been many exhaustive studies on Brecht and religion. Primary among them are Hans Pabst, *Brecht und die Religion* (Graz: Verlag Styria, 1977), and G. Ronald Murphy, *Brecht and the Bible: A Study of Religious Nihilism and Human Weakness in Brecht's Drama of Mortality and the City* (Chapel Hill: University of North Carolina Press, 1980).

63. See Dümling, "Eisler und Brecht," 6; Hinton, "Lehrstück," 59–73; Schoeps, "Brecht's *Lehrstücke*," in *A Bertolt Brecht Reference Companion*, 70–87; and Klaus Lazarowicz, "Die Rote Messe: Liturgische Elemente in Brechts *Maßnahme*," *Literaturwissenschaftliches Jahrbuch* 17 (1977): 205–220. The musical connections to oratorio and cantata in form and function are discussed later in this chapter.

64. Hinton, "Lehrstück," 62. He refers to Eberhard Rohse's study, which examines Brecht's catechistic education in great detail. Rohse, *Der frühe Brecht und die Bibel: Studien zum Augsburger Religionsunterricht und zu den literarischen Versuchen des Gymnasiasten* (Göttingen, Germany: Vandenhoeck und Ruprecht, 1983).

65. Hinton, "Lehrstück," 64.

66. See Rienäcker, "Musik als Agens," for specific choral analysis.

67. Steinweg, *Das Lehrstück*, 188–190. Kalb cites Brecht and Eisler both as having described the choral music as too religious and emotional (*Theater of Heiner Müller*, 32).

68. The most comprehensive source for information on the opera's complicated genesis, reception history, and legal battles is Stephen Hinton, ed., *Kurt Weill: The Threepenny Opera* (Cambridge: Cambridge University Press, 1990). See also the critical edition and extensive commentary by Hinton, ed., in Weill, *Die Dreigroschenoper: Ein Stück mit Musik in einem Vorspiel und acht Bildern nach dem Englischen des John Gay übersetzt von Elisabeth Hauptmann* (New

York: Kurt Weill Foundation for Music, 2000). Regarding Brecht's text see Brecht, *Die Dreigroschenoper. Der Erstdruck 1928 mit einem Kommentar von Joachim Lucchesi* (Frankfurt am Main: Suhrkamp, 2004).

69. "Formally speaking, *The Threepenny Opera* represents the prototype of opera: it contains elements of opera and elements of spoken theatre." Brecht, from the Volksbühne program booklet as an introduction to the Schiffbauerdamm production, cited in Hinton, *Threepenny Opera*, 122. Weill in *MumT* 72–75, *Europe* 486–488; *MumT* 92–96, *Europe* 506–509. See also Hinton, "Zur Urform der Oper," in *Vom Kurfürstendamm zum Broadway Kurt Weill (1900–1950)*, ed. Bernd Kortländer, Winrich Meiszies, and David Farneth (Düsseldorf: Droste Verlag, 1990), 40–46.

70. Regarding the development of the libretto see Esbjörn Nyström's magisterial *Libretto im Progress: Brechts und Weills "Aufstieg und Fall der Stadt Mahagonny" aus textgeschichtlicher Sicht* (Bern: Peter Lang, 2005); regarding the consequences of editorial decisions in a text with such a complicated history, see Edward Harsh, "Excavating *Mahagonny*: Editorial Responses to Conflicting Visions," in *Der Text im Musikalischen Werk*, 346–360.

71. Hinton, "The Concept of Epic Opera: Theoretical Anomalies in the Brecht-Weill Partnership," in *Das musikalische Kunstwerk: Festschrift Carl Dahlhaus*, ed. Hinton (Laaber, Germany: Laaber Verlag, 1988), 286. See John White's analysis in *Bertolt Brecht's Dramatic Theory* (Rochester, NY: Camden House, 2004), 26–76. Weill's publications included "Vorwort zum Regiebuch der Oper *Aufstieg und Fall der Stadt Mahagonny*," *Anbruch* 12 (January 1930): 5–7; "Anmerkungen zu meiner Oper *Mahagonny*," *Die Musik* 22 (March 1930): 440–441; "Zur Uraufführung der Oper *Mahagonny*," *Leipziger Neueste Nachrichten*, 8 March 1930. Reprinted in *MumT* 102–108, *Europe* 514–519.

72. On Brecht's use of the term "apparatus" in this essay, see Smith, *The Total Work of Art*, 82.

73. BFA 24:76, BoT 35–36.

74. *MumT* 95, *Europe* 508–509.

75. Walter Benjamin, "What Is Epic Theatre?" in *Understanding Brecht*, trans. Anna Bostock (London: Verso, 2003), 22. *Gesammelte Schriften*, ed. Rolf Tiedemann and Hermann Schweppenhäuser (Frankfurt am Main: Suhrkamp, 1972–89), 2:538.

76. Brecht was not opposed to pleasure on principle. On the contrary, he derived great pleasure from work and learning, but this is not the kind of inebriated pleasure implied in his deliberate choice of the term "*Genuß*."

77. Smith's close reading of this famous passage is enlightening. He notes that the statements usually cited as the most damning are in fact introduced equivocally: "*so long as* the expression 'Gesamtkunstwerk' means that the integration is a muddle, *so long as* the arts are supposed to be 'fused' together" (emphasis added in Smith, *The Total Work of Art*, 75). Apparently Brecht still held out hope for the opera genre. Smith reads this as a rejection of this particular manifestation of the total work of art but not of the concept per se.

78. BFA 24:79, BoT 37–38.

79. *MumT* 95, *Europe* 508.

80. Hinton, "Theoretical Anomalies," 290; *Europe* 115–116; Nieder, "Bertolt Brecht und die Oper," 362–383; and Mário Vieira de Carvalho, "From Opera to 'Soap Opera': On Civilizing Processes, the Dialectic of Enlightenment and Postmodernity," *Theory, Culture, and Society* 12, no. 2 (May 1995): 41–62. Brecht was also quite knowledgeable about Mozart's operas and effusive in his praise of them; he described *Don Giovanni* as "the peak [that] has never again been scaled" (*Journals*, entry for 8 June 1943). Lucchesi sees Mozart as the model stage composer to which Brecht returned throughout his life. Lucchesi, "'. . . Denn die Zeit kennt keinen Aufenthalt': Busoni, Weill, und Brecht," in *Berliner Begegnungen: Ausländische Künstler in Berlin 1918 bis 1933*, ed. Klaus Kändler, Helga Karolowski, and Ilse Siebert (Berlin: Dietz, 1987), 46–52. The passage in *Don Giovanni* that elicited such high praise was the second act of the opera, the finale of which is as near to sophisticated continuous music as one is apt to find before Wagner. The precise manifestation of that modeling may be less a matter of form and more a matter of Mozart's gift for what Frank Schneider describes as a gestural conception of drama; Frank Schneider, "Mozart und das epische Musiktheater," in *Mozart in der Musik des 20. Jahrhunderts: Formen ästhetischer und kompositionstechnischer Rezeption*, ed. Wolfgang Gratzer and Siegfried Mauser (Laaber, Germany: Laaber Verlag, 1992), 187–197. Schneider treats Mozart's influence on the composers with whom Brecht collaborated in their willingness to mix high and low art in a single text, rather than the influence of Mozart upon the playwright directly.

81. Vieira de Carvalho, "From Opera to 'Soap Opera,'" 48.

82. *BFA* 24:80, *BoT* 38.

83. See for example Weill's statements in the foreword to the production book, in which he says of *Threepenny Opera:* "Therefore it is the ideal form of musical theater, for only such situations can be set to music in closed forms, and a sequence of situations arranged according to musical considerations resulted in the heightened form of musical theater: opera." And of *Mahagonny:* "The subject matter . . . made possible an organization of the text according to purely musical precepts." *MumT* 103, *Europe* 514. See chapter 2 for a detailed analyses of gestus in specific songs.

84. *Europe* 115.

85. *BFA* 24:66, *BoT* 45.

86. *BFA* 24:65, *BoT* 45.

87. *BFA* 24:59, *BoT* 44. See chapter 5 for discussion of "smoking-and-watching."

88. See chapter 2 on gestus, in which I argue that the singing voice posed a problem in this regard.

89. Kowalke, "Singing Brecht versus Brecht Singing: Performance in Theory and Practice," in *Music and Performance during the Weimar Republic*, 74–93.

90. *BFA* 24:66, *BoT* 45 (cited in Kowalke, "Singing Brecht," 90). Lotte Lenya's tireless promotion of Weill's music is largely responsible for preserving his legacy, but the many recordings she made after she was past her vocal prime

(and sounding nothing like she had sounded when she originated these roles) also contributed to this performance practice tradition.

91. Carl Dahlhaus, "Traditionelle Dramaturgie in der modernen Oper," in *Musiktheater heute: Sechs Kongreßbeiträge*, ed. Hellmut Kühn (Mainz: Schott, 1982), 25 (cited in Hinton, "Theoretical Anomalies," 290).

92. Vera Stegmann, "Brecht contra Wagner: The Evolution of the Epic Music Theater," in *A Bertolt Brecht Reference Companion*, 247; Ernst Schumacher, *Die dramatische Versuche Bertolt Brechts, 1918–1933* (Berlin: Rütten and Loening, 1955), 281.

93. Oesmann notes Adorno's similar misgivings about Brecht's didacticism. "*Lehre* (teaching) falls short in comparison with theory because it entails a commitment to obeying the rules of communication—meaning domination—and is thus unavoidably propagandistic" (Oesmann, *Staging History*, 9).

94. Nicola Chiaromonte, *The Worm of Consciousness and Other Essays* (New York: Harcourt Brace Jovanovich, 1976), 138 (cited in Kalb, *Theater of Heiner Müller*, 39).

95. See chapter 5, in which I argue that this liberation is precisely what occurs in nonliteral stagings of canonical operas.

2. THE OPERATIC ROOTS OF GESTUS IN 'THE MOTHER' AND 'ROUND HEADS AND POINTED HEADS'

1. See Marc Silberman, "Gestus" entry in *Historisch-kritisches Wörterbuch des Marxismus*, ed. Fritz Haug (Hamburg: Argument, 2001), 660–666; and Marc Silberman, "Brecht's Gestus; or, Staging Contradictions," *Brecht Yearbook/Brecht-Jahrbuch* 31 (2006): 318–335. See also Peter Brooker, "Key Words in Brecht's Theory and Practice of Theatre," in *The Cambridge Companion to Brecht*, 2nd ed., ed. Peter Thomson and Glendyr Sacks (Cambridge: Cambridge University Press, 2006), 219–222. The mid-1930s was also the period during which he encountered the Chinese opera performer Mei Lanfang in Moscow, whose acting made an enormous impression on Brecht; he referred to it in numerous essays and in his journal. There has been considerable research on this connection, but none to my knowledge has addressed the significance of the fact that Mei Lanfang was an opera singer, not just an actor. See Min Tian, "'Alienation Effect' for Whom? Brecht's (Mis)Interpretation of the Classical Chinese Theatre," *Asian Theatre Journal* 14, no. 2 (1997): 200–222, and Ronnie Bai, "Dances with Mei Lanfang: Brecht and the Alienation Effect," *Comparative Drama* 32, no. 3 (1998): 389–433. I am grateful to Fred and Lea Wakeman and Haun Saussy for assistance on this topic. Carol J. Martin's triangulation of Brecht, feminism, and Chinese theater is less successful but initiates an important line of inquiry. Martin, "Brecht, Feminism, and Chinese Theatre," *Drama Review* 43, no. 4 (1999): 77–85. See Silberman, "Brecht's Gestus; or Staging Contradictions," regarding Brecht in feminist theory, 329–331.

2. In 1935 Brecht wrote, "The concern of the epic theater is thus eminently

practical." "On the Use of Music in an Epic Theatre," in *BoT* 86, *BFA* 22:158. See also Siegfried Mews, "Anmerkungen zur Oper *Aufstieg und Fall der Stadt Mahagonny*," in *Brecht Handbuch in fünf Bänden,* ed. Jan Knopf (Stuttgart: J. B. Metzler, 2001–2003), 4:50–51.

3. Eric Salehi, "No Brecht-fest in America: Revisiting the Theatre Union's 1935 Production of *The Mother*," *On-stage Studies* 21 (1998): 75–97. See also the review of that production by Stanley Burnshaw, "The Theatre Union Produces *Mother*," *New Masses,* December 1935, 27–28. Burnshaw is quick to point out that they did not attempt to reproduce the show strictly according to "the Brecht-Eisler theory" but made some adjustments based on the Theatre Union's perception of American taste and audiences. Regarding the stage design for the Theatre Union's production, see Anne Fletcher, "The Gestus of Scene Design: Mordecai Gorelik and the Theatre Union's Production of Brecht's *The Mother." Theatre History Studies* 23 (June 2003): 95–108. See also Laura Bradley, *Brecht and Political Theatre:"The Mother" on Stage* (Oxford: Clarendon Press, 2006), particularly pages 142–154.

4. As previously noted, the English titles follow those in the Methuen editions of Brecht's plays. The original German titles are *Die Mutter* and *Die Rundköpfe und die Spitzköpfe.*

5. There are significant exceptions to the rule that gestus scholarship by nonmusicologists is essentially amusical, such as the work of John Willett, Vera Stegmann, and Peter Ferran, but most treatments fail to credit Kurt Weill with any influence, despite considerable evidence that he brought an idea of gestus to their collaboration and that it took shape for both of them during that period. See Patrice Pavis for a director's perspective: "On Brecht's Notion of Gestus," in *Languages of the Stage: Essays in the Semiology of the Theatre* (New York: Performing Arts Journal Publications, 1982), 39–49; Martin Esslin for a performer's perspective: "Some Reflections on Brecht and Acting," in *Re-interpreting Brecht: His Influence on Contemporary Drama and Film,* ed. Pia Kleber and Colin Visser (Cambridge: Cambridge University Press, 1990), 135–146; and Christine Kiebuzinska for a theoretical perspective: "Brecht and the Problem of Influence," in *A Bertolt Brecht Reference Companion,* ed. Siegfried Mews (Westport, CT: Greenwood Press, 1997), 47–69. Kiebuzinska cites numerous influences on the concept of gestus, including Charlie Chaplin, Russian constructivism, Eisenstein's montage, and Shklovsky's *ostranenie* (defamiliarization), but never mentions Weill.

6. Jan Knopf refutes the oft-repeated axiom that gestus was never properly defined by Brecht with a statement the playwright made in 1940: "Unter einem Gestus sei verstanden ein Komplex von Gesten, Mimik und (für gewöhnlich) Aussagen, welchen ein oder mehrere Menschen zu einem oder mehreren Menschen richten." ("By gestus is understood a complex of gestures, facial expressions, and usually ordinary statements which one or more persons direct toward one or more persons.") *BFA* 22:616, translation my own. He takes exception with Silberman's *Wörterbuch* article for limiting its treatment to the realm of

theater at the expense of poetry. Because the 1940 definition postdates the period examined in this chapter it is not used as the basis for this discussion. Knopf, "Gestus," in *Brecht Handbuch in fünf Bänden*, 4:226–231.

7. Silberman, *Wörterbuch*, 662.

8. See Rainer Nägele and Darko Suvin regarding the relationship between gestus and Haltung. Nägele, following Benjamin, writes that gestus constitutes the smallest element of Haltung, therefore condensing the dialectic of stasis and motion. Nägele, *Theater, Theory, Speculation: Walter Benjamin and the Scenes of Modernity* (Baltimore: Johns Hopkins University Press, 1991), 135–166. Suvin defines Haltung as "the union of a subject's body-orientation in spacetime of that body's insertion into major societal 'flow of things.'" Suvin, "Haltung (Bearing) and Emotions: Brecht's Refunctioning of Conservative Metaphors for Agency," in *Zweifel—Fragen—Vorschläge. Bertolt Brecht anläßlich des Einhundertsten,* ed. Thomas Jung (Frankfurt am Main: Peter Lang, 1999), 44–45. This is discussed in the final section of the present chapter.

9. Gotthold Ephraim Lessing, *Hamburgische Dramaturgie*, entry for 12 May 1767, ed. Otto Mann (Stuttgart: Alfred Kroner Verlag, 1958), 20. The translation by Victor Lange does not distinguish between gestus and gesture: *Hamburg Dramaturgy* (New York: Dover Publications, 1962), 17. See M. Flaherty, "Lessing and Opera: A Re-evaluation," *Germanic Review* 44, no. 2 (1969): 95–109. Flaherty argues that interpretations that treat Lessing as either an enemy of opera or a forerunner of Wagner are overly simplistic and fail to read his opera writings in the context of his entire oeuvre. When Lessing wrote the critique in question he had just begun a three-year stint as dramaturge to the German National Theater in Hamburg, the city in which the first public opera house outside Venice had opened almost a century earlier and to whose theatrical history opera had contributed considerably in the interim. See also Klaus Kleinschmidt, "Lessing und die Musik: Zur Erörterung musikalischer Themen in den Schriften des Kunstrichters," *Musik und Gesellschaft* 29, no. 3 (1979): 129–136.

10. Tom Kuhn, "Brecht and Willett: Getting the Gest," *Brecht Yearbook/Brecht-Jahrbuch* 28 (2003): 261.

11. Peter Ferran, "The *Threepenny* Songs: Cabaret and the Lyrical *Gestus*," *Theater* 30, no. 3 (2000): 7.

12. *Pastimes at Home and School: A Practical Manual of Delsarte Exercises and Elocution* (Chicago: W. B. Conkey Co., 1897).

13. Émile Jaques-Dalcroze, *Eurhythmics: Art and Education*, ed. Cynthia Cox, trans. Frederick Rothwell (London: Chatto and Windus, 1930).

14. W. R. Vollbach, "The Collaboration of Adolphe Appia and Émile Jaques-Dalcroze," in *Paul A. Pisk: Essays in His Honor*, ed. John Glowacki (Austin: University of Texas Press, 1966), 192–202.

15. See Katherine Bliss Eaton, *The Theater of Meyerhold and Brecht* (Westport, CT: Greenwood Press, 1985), and Christine Kiebuzinska, *Revolutionaries in the Theater: Meyerhold, Brecht, and Witkiewicz* (Ann Arbor, MI: UMI Research Press, 1985).

16. Daniel Albright, *Untwisting the Serpent: Modernism in Music, Literature, and Other Arts* (Chicago: University of Chicago Press, 2000), 102. The fourth chapter is entitled simply "Gestus," which he defines at the onset as follows: "A gestus is a bodily pose or gesture that speaks; a hieroglyph corporeally embodied in a human performer; a whole story (gest) contracted into a moment. The term gestus was popularized by Lessing and was taken up enthusiastically by Weill and Brecht."

17. Ibid., 102.

18. Ibid., 103.

19. Brecht's essay "Über gestische Musik" is undated but has been traced to 1937 and treats a wide variety of gests that are not musical and do not emanate from the actors' bodies onstage. In that expanded capacity, a gest is any particularized, stylized element of a production that shows the social relationship of humans to one another. Such elements included the "music (lyrics, performance, music proper), speech (choice of words, the manner in which they are spoken), the stage set (use of props, costumes, masks), and scenic design (lighting, scenery)" (Silberman, *Wörterbuch*, 665). As discussed later in the present chapter, Brecht's essay is uncharacteristically hypothetical and appears calculated to facilitate productions without his supervision.

20. Mary Ann Smart, *Mimomania: Music and Gesture in Nineteenth-Century Opera* (Berkeley: University of California Press, 2004), 171. Smart notes that Wagner's *Opera and Drama* has "acquired a perverse authority—respected, in essence, for its uselessness in understanding the music." I would not characterize Brecht's theory as useless for understanding his plays but find Smart's method of highlighting rather than ignoring the inconsistencies particularly useful. With regard to Wagner and mimesis see also Martin Puchner, "Richard Wagner: The Theatocracy of the Mime," in his book *Stage Fright: Modernism, Anti-Theatricality, and Drama* (Baltimore: Johns Hopkins University Press, 2002), 31–58.

21. See Kenneth Fowler's provocative study *Received Truths: Bertolt Brecht and the Problem of Gestus and Musical Meaning* (New York: AMS Press, 1991). Fowler derides the unreflective critical application of Brecht's theories to his projects, including scholarly willingness to accept on blind faith his assumption that music has meaning: "Though every remark that musical meaning remains unproven must eventually demand that the problem be thematized, it is mentioned in this study only to refer to the fact that the particular critic is going to great lengths to prove that adequacy of Brecht's prescriptions for music, when he or she can or does not lay a theoretical foundation for such an interpretation" (2–3).

22. Ibid., 5–14. Fowler compares readings of Eisler's song "In Praise of Communism" by Albrecht Dümling, Georg Knepler, and Karl Schönewolf. Fowler finds that each author presupposes that the music means something and then analyzes the text-music relationship in such a manner as to prove the validity of Brecht's assertions about that particular song. The analyses differ in the details, but all "prove" Brecht's theory.

23. Brecht applied the concept of gestus, if not the term, to the plays *Edward II* (1924) and the various iterations of *Mann ist Mann* (1926 and following). See Michael Morley, "Suiting the Action to the Word: Some Observations on *Gestus* and *gestische Musik*," in *A New Orpheus*, ed. Kim Kowalke (New Haven, CT: Yale University Press, 1986), 183–201. The *Keuner* fragment of 1929 used "Haltung to describe the dynamics of the body in the process of social change" (Silberman, *Wörterbuch*, 664).

24. *BoT* 36, *BFA* 4:77.

25. *BoT* 42.

26. Kuhn notes that Willett's choice of "gest" shares a common Latin root, "*gero*," meaning "I bear," with "jest." This etymology facilitates a slippage from bearing to story to joke that is quite appropriate for Brecht. Kuhn, "Brecht and Willett," 261.

27. *BoT* 42.

28. Brooker, "Key Words," 219.

29. *Webster's Dictionary*, 1913 edition.

30. Nevertheless, the authority granted Willett's commentary, and the fact that this conflation has evidently gone unnoted, leaves open the possibility that subsequent critiques predicated upon this passage may be more reflective of Weill's understanding of gestus in 1931 than of Brecht's at that time.

31. Kim Kowalke, "Singing Brecht vs. Brecht Singing: Performance in Theory and Practice," in *Music and Performance during the Weimar Republic*, ed. Bryan Gilliam (Cambridge: Cambridge University Press, 1994), 81. Joachim Lucchesi interprets Weill as the mediator between Brecht and Busoni. See "Versuch eines Vergleichs: Kurt Weill als Mittler zwischen Brecht und Busoni," *Musik und Gesellschaft* 40, no. 3 (1990): 132–134.

32. Ferruccio Busoni, *Sketch of a New Aesthetic in Music*, 1st ed., in *Three Classics in the Aesthetic of Music*, trans. Theodore Baker (New York: Dover Publications, 1962), 83.

33. Vera Stegmann, "Brecht contra Wagner: The Evolution of the Epic Music Theater," in *A Bertolt Brecht Reference Companion*, 252.

34. Fritz Hennenberg, "Brecht und Weill im Clinch?" *Berliner Beiträge zur Musikwissenschaft: Beihefte zur Neuen Berlinischen Musikzeitung* 9, no. 2 (1994): 3–24.

35. Kurt Weill, "Busonis *Faust* und die Erneuerung der Opernform," in *Jahrbuch Oper* (Vienna: Jahrbuch 1926 der Universal-Edition, 1926), 53–56. Reprinted in *MumT* 54–58, *Europe* 468–472.

36. Kurt Weill, "Ferruccio Busoni: Zu seinem 60. Geburtstag," *Der deutsche Rundfunk* 4 (28 March 1926): 872 (*MumT* 302–303, *Europe* 476–477).

37. Kurt Weill, "Der Musiker Weill," *Berliner Tageblatt*, 25 December 1928, p. 4 of the special insert. *MumT* 68–72. Translation with Schoenberg's marginalia appears in Alexander L. Ringer, *Arnold Schoenberg: The Composer as Jew* (Oxford: Clarendon Press, 1990), 83–102. See also Kowalke, "Singing Brecht."

38. Hennenberg, "Brecht und Weill im Clinch?" 11. He also sees precedent for estrangement in Busoni's work.

39. Ferruccio Busoni, "The Oneness of Music and the Possibilities of the Opera," in *The Essence of Music, and Other Papers,* trans. Rosamond Ley (New York: Dover Publications, 1957), 12–13. The essay first appeared in *Von der Einheit der Musik* (Berlin: M. Hesse, 1922). See also Busoni, "Über die Möglichkeiten der Oper," in *Von der Macht der Töne: Ausgewählte Schriften* (Leipzig: Verlag Philip Reclam, 1983), 121–135.

40. In his essay "On Rhymeless Verse with Irregular Rhythms," Brecht wrote extensively about the significance of rhythm for gestus in his play *Edward II* (1924), but the essay dates from 1938 and thus postdates the play by fourteen years. If his recollections are accurate, then he and Weill shared the opinion that rhythm was an essential means of establishing gestus in the 1920s, but the anachronistic nature of the essay prevents reliable use of it in this context. *BoT* 115–120, *BFA* 22:357–364.

41. Weill, "Über den gestischen Charakter der Musik," *Die Musik* 21, no. 6 (March 1929): 419–423 (*MumT* 83–88, *Europe* 491–496).

42. *MumT* 88, *Europe* 495.

43. *MumT* 86, *Europe* 493.

44. *MumT* 85, *Europe* 492.

45. *BoT* 45, *BFA* 24:66.

46. Kowalke has interpreted this as a power play to regain control of the *Threepenny* juggernaut by forging an alliance between the actor and the playwright's text at the expense of the music. Kowalke, "Brecht Singing."

47. Smart, *Mimomania,* 166. She notes that this shift is most eloquently argued in Carl Dahlhaus, *Die Bedeutung des Gestischen in Wagners Musikdramen* (Munich: R. Oldenbourg, 1970).

48. Smart, *Mimomania,* 28.

49. Friedrich Nietzsche, *Nietzsche Contra Wagner,* in *The Portable Nietzsche,* ed. and trans. Walter Kaufmann (New York: Penguin, 1968), 665 (cited in Smart, *Mimomania,* 4 and 167). See also Puchner, *Stage Fright,* 32–33.

50. Smart, *Mimomania,* 4.

51. Nietzsche, *Nietzsche Contra Wagner,* 665 (cited in Smart, *Mimomania,* 168). See also Puchner, *Stage Fright,* 35.

52. Smart, *Mimomania,* 168.

53. Ibid., 29. Ulrich Weisstein quotes Stravinsky on this subject, saying he "always had a horror of listening to music with [his] eyes shut" because "the sight of the gestures and movements of the various parts of the body producing the music" is "fundamentally necessary if it is to be grasped in all its fullness." Weisstein, "Brecht und das Musiktheater. Die epische Oper als Ausdruck des europäischen Avantgardismus," in *Kontroversen, alte und neue. Akten des VII. Internationalen Germanisten-Kongresses, Göttingen 1985,* ed. Albrecht Schöne (Tübingen, Germany: Niemeyer, 1986), 84. Igor Stravinsky, *An Autobiography* (New York: Norton, 1962), 72.

54. Smart, *Mimomania,* 168.

55. In the interest of preserving, or reviving, said relevance for contemporary audiences, directors may substitute music by other composers. Peter Ferran

has composed new music for productions of *The Exception and the Rule* and *The Good Person of Szechwan*. See Ferran, "Musical Composition for an American Stage: Brecht," *Brecht Yearbook/Brecht-Jahrbuch* 22 (1997): 253–281; and "Music and Gestus in *The Exception and the Rule*," *Brecht Yearbook/Brecht-Jahrbuch* 24 (1999): 227–245. The production of *Caucasian Chalk Circle* staged at Vanderbilt University in February 2004 used no music composed for that play by Dessau or Eisler. Director Jeffrey Ullom substituted newly composed music by a student, Jay Navarro, as well as excerpts from music by Prince, Public Enemy, Dead Can Dance, and Ballet Mechanique. Correspondence between the author and Ullom, 4 August 2004.

56. See Ania Kepia, "The Relationship of Brecht's *Die Mutter* to Its Sources: A Reassessment," *German Life and Letters* 38, no. 3 (1985): 233–248 (*BFA* 24:110–200, Brecht, *Collected Plays* 3:351–394). For reviews of the 1932 production, which received over thirty performances in various venues around Berlin that year, see those reprinted in Ludwig Hoffmann and Klaus Pfützner, ed., *Theater der Kollektive. Proletarisch-revolutionäres Berufstheater in Deutschland, 1928–1933. Stücke, Dokumente, Studien* (Berlin: Henschelverlag, 1980), 1:404–421. The 1935 production in New York generated additional songs and an orchestral reduction for two pianos; the 1936 version for concert performance there was similar but eliminated "In Praise of Communism." In the 1949 cantata version, Eisler reinstated "Communism," added an overture and two more songs, and substantially revised the extant "Like the crow" to incorporate an extensive quotation from the *Magnificat* by J. S. Bach. The 1951 version for the Berliner Ensemble featured an expanded orchestra; regarding that production see Werner Hecht, ed., *Materialien zu Bertolt Brechts "Die Mutter"* (Frankfurt am Main: Suhrkamp, 1969). Given its many incarnations it is important to note that the versions of the songs analyzed here are those to which Brecht and Eisler referred in the writings discussed below.

57. Fred Fischbach, "Pour une nouvelle lecture des pièces de Brecht a lumière de la musique de scène de Hanns Eisler," *Recherches Germaniques* 13 (1983): 137–166.

58. For an analysis of this song, see Jürgen Elsner, "'Lob des Kommunismus': Bemerkungen zu Hanns Eislers Musik zur *Mutter*," *Musik in der Schule* 29, no. 9 (1978): 291–294.

59. *Collected Plays* 3:116, *BFA* 3:285.

60. Dümling, "Eisler und Brecht: Bilanz einer produktiven Partnerschaft," *Neue Zeitschrift für Musik* 159, no. 6 (1998): 4–9; Frank Schneider, "Bach als Quelle im Strom der Moderne (Von Schönberg bis zur Gegenwart)," in *Jahrbuch des Staatlichen Instituts für Musikforschung Preussischer Kulturbesitz*, ed. Günther Wagner (Berlin: De Gruyter, 1994), 110–125; Peter Schleuning, *Warum wir von Beethoven erschüttert werden und andere Aufsätze über Musik* (Frankfurt am Main: Roter Stern, 1978), 75–94. Schleuning argues that the use of the quotation calls into question the date of the song, but since his book appeared it has been determined that the quotation *was* added in 1949. See n. 56 above.

61. *Collected Plays* 3:132, and *BFA* 3:302.

62. *Collected Plays* 3:138, and *BFA* 3:310.

63. See Salehi, "No Brecht-fest." He argues that previous studies of this production have relied upon anecdotal evidence gleaned from interviews with Theatre Union board members and other participants and that perspective has served to reduce the conflict to one of incompatible personalities (Brecht and Eisler versus the American director Victor Wolfson and the board) rather than incompatible ideologies. The inflammatory language Brecht used to criticize the production only exacerbates this viewpoint. Willett also notes that Brecht's rather uncharitable account downplays important points: the Theatre Union had been interested primarily in Gorky's play and were unfamiliar with Brecht's work or how he might have adapted the text; and only a few of those involved with the theater were in fact communists. *Collected Plays* 3:369. This final point in particular illustrates one of the complications inherent in the United Front policy; see chapter 3 regarding the United Front versus the Popular Front.

64. *BoT* 88, *BFA* 22:162.

65. Ibid.

66. *BoT* 81–84, *BFA* 24:169–173.

67. Eisler, "The Theatre Union's Production of *Mother*," in *Musik und Politik: Schriften, 1924–1948*, ed. Günter Mayer (Leipzig: VEB Deutscher Verlag für Musik, 1985), 360. The original was in English.

68. Ibid.

69. Weill to Lenya, in a letter dated 6 April 1934. Reprinted in *Speak Low (When You Speak Love): The Letters of Kurt Weill and Lotte Lenya*, ed. and trans. Lys Symonette and Kim Kowalke (Berkeley: University of California Press, 1996), 124.

70. Hanns-Eisler-Archiv 4007, p. 2. Hereafter HEA. Cited in the critical apparatus to Eisler, *Die Rundköpfe und die Spitzköpfe*, Hanns Eisler Gesamtausgabe series 5, vol. 3, ed. Thomas Ahrend and Albrecht Dümling (Leipzig: Breitkopf and Härtel, 2002), xiv and xxii.

71. Regarding its connection to the Shakespeare play see D. B. Douglas, "The Beginnings of *Die Rundköpfe und die Spitzköpfe*: Bertolt Brecht's Fragmentary Adaptation of Shakespeare's *Measure for Measure*," *Aumla-Journal of the Australasian Universities' Modern Language Association* 64 (November 1985): 198–219.

72. David Bathrick, "A One-Sided History: Brecht's Hitler Plays," in *Literature and History*, ed. Leonard Schulze and Walter Wetzels (Lanham, MD: University Press of America, 1983), 181–196.

73. The fact that the first volume of the new Eisler Complete Works project (hereafter HEGA—Hanns Eisler Gesamtausgabe) was the critical edition of *Round Heads* confirms that there is good reason to resurrect the piece from a musical perspective—indeed, it contains many of Eisler's best songs—but the plot remains an obstacle to contemporary stagings. A rare exception occurred in December 2007, when David Gordon directed a dance-theater work entitled *Uncivil Wars: Collaborating with Brecht and Eisler* at The Kitchen in New York.

The show combines *Round Heads and Pointed Heads* with other writings by Brecht and Eisler.

74. *Collected Plays* 4:22–23, BFA 4:168.

75. *Collected Plays* 4:91, BFA 4:239. Brecht's German lyrics feature a clever double entendre that defies translation. The "Marie" in "Wo ich Liebe sah und schwache Knie, war's beim Anblick von Marie" is Berliner slang for money. Leonard J. Lehrman, "Continental Clashes of Culture at Convention, Cabaret, and Concert," *Aufbau* 65, no. 2 (1999): 13.

76. I am indebted to Peter Burkholder's work on the borrowing habits of Charles Ives for establishing the significant distinctions between stylistic allusion, quotation, and various gradations in between. Burkholder, *All Made of Tunes: Charles Ives and the Uses of Musical Borrowing* (New Haven, CT: Yale University Press, 1995), 1–7.

77. For ease of reproduction these examples are based on the piano-vocal reduction reissued in 1998, which is musically consistent with the new HEGA critical edition in full score. Hanns Eisler, *Zehn Lieder aus "Die Rundköpfe und die Spitzköpfe"* (Leipzig: Deutscher Verlag für Musik, 1998).

78. Eisler to Brecht, 24 August 1936. Bertolt-Brecht-Archiv (hereafter BBA) 479/01. HEGA *Round Heads*, xxiii.

79. For a rare English-language analysis of this song, see Gerd Rienäcker, "The Invigorating Effect of Music? Making Music about Music in Brecht and Eisler's 'Song of the Invigorating Effect of Money,' " in *Hanns Eisler: A Miscellany*, ed. David Blake (New York: Harwood Academic Publishers, 1995), 91–102.

80. The recording by Dagmar Krause does not use the instrumentation specified in the score—the flute part is played instead by an electric guitar—but it does resist the temptation to pause before the final measure; instead, the song plows full steam ahead into the final bar, and the effect is entirely different than that heard on other recordings. Hanns Eisler, *Tank Battles: The Songs of Hanns Eisler*, sung by Dagmar Krause, Voiceprint CD 138. Gisela May's recording is exemplary except for the ritard at the end. *Brecht Songs*, sung by Gisela May, Berlin Classics 2165–2.

81. *Collected Plays* 4:86–87, BFA 4:234–235. See Reinhold Grimm, "Brechts Rad der Fortuna," on the recurring motif of the wheel of fortune in Brecht's texts. Grimm, *Brecht und Nietzsche oder Geständnisse eines Dichters: Fünf Essays und ein Bruchstück* (Frankfurt am Main: Suhrkamp, 1979), 138–155.

82. *Collected Plays* 4:23, BFA 4:168.

83. See for example the study by Daisy Bertrand and Carolyn Drake, "The Quest for Universals in Temporal Processing in Music," *Annals of the New York Academy of Sciences* 930 (June 2001): 17–27.

84. *BoT* 87, BFA 22:159.

85. Ferran, "The *Threepenny* Songs," 6.

86. The otherwise exemplary commentary appended to the new HEGA critical edition of *Die Rundköpfe und die Spitzköpfe* perpetuates the questionable

equivalence of Song with gestic music. The editors insert Brecht's definition of "gestic Song-Musik" into their discussion of the letter Eisler wrote about "Lied der Nanna" and "Kuppellied" as if they were synonymous. They then state that "Eisler's songs to *Rundköpfe und die Spitzköpfe* cannot all be subsumed under the category of 'gestic music,' although they clearly betray the influence of 'Song-Musik,'" as if only Songs could be gestic, when the essay they quote had already identified the music from *The Mother* as gestic. They acknowledge that Brecht did not use the term Song with regard to the music for *The Mother* but do not concede that gestic music can take another form. HEGA *Round Heads,* xxiii.

87. Eisler to Brecht, 14 October 1936. BBA 479/02–08. This is also evidence in the argument against nonsung performance practice. Eisler referred to these pieces as lieder rather than Songs but clearly considered them gestic (cited in HEGA *Round Heads,* xxiii).

88. *BoT* 104–105, *BFA* 22:329–331.

89. Carolyn Abbate, *Unsung Voices: Opera and Musical Narrative in the Nineteenth Century* (Princeton, NJ: Princeton University Press, 1991), 10. See also Michelle Duncan's critique of Abbate in "The Operatic Scandal of the Singing Body: Voice, Presence, Performativity," *Cambridge Opera Journal* 16, no. 3 (2004): 283–306.

90. Silberman, *Wörterbuch,* 666.

91. To the best of my knowledge, the only scholar currently pursuing a theory of gestus that pertains directly to music is Peter Ferran; see "The *Threepenny* Songs," "Musical Composition for an American Stage," and "Gestus in *The Exception and the Rule.*" He has rightly observed that music is the one element of a production that is so important as to be on a par with the text itself in determining the character of a text (unlike the actors, sets, costumes, lighting, and staging), and he composes replacement scores for musical settings by Brecht's original collaborators. He describes his own work as that of collaboration (albeit after the fact) and attempts to meet what he describes as Brecht's requirements for gestic music. His is a fascinating and important course of study, but its premise—that particular extant settings are not suitably gestic for contemporary audiences—is not immediately relevant to this chapter.

92. Suvin, "Haltung (Bearing) and Emotions," 45.

93. Nägele, *Theater, Theory, Speculation,* 152.

94. Peter Ferran to the author, undated correspondence. Ferran went on to note that one could also describe the situation in the inverse, as one in which speech interrupts song, as if the predominant texture were sung, and spoken drama disrupts that texture. This is tempting when one is demonstrating that epic theater is grounded in opera, but the preponderance of speech in *Round Heads* renders this problematic.

95. Nägele, *Theater, Theory, Speculation,* 152.

96. Pavis, "On Brecht's Notion of Gestus," 45.

97. *BoT* 44–45, *BFA* 24:66.

98. Kowalke, "Brecht Singing," 82.

99. Abbate, *Unsung Voices*, 11. See Abbate's account of attending a performance of *Meistersinger* in 2001 in which Ben Heppner was experiencing extreme vocal duress: "Heppner became a unique human being in a singular place and time, falling from the high wire again and again." Abbate, "Music—Drastic or Gnostic?" *Critical Inquiry* 30, no. 3 (2004): 535. Duncan has noted Abbate's tendency to categorize the voice in terms of extremes.

100. This is reminiscent of Abbate's and Vladimir Jankélévitch's notion of the singer as the ventriloquized automaton animated by the text, as opposed to the more traditional view of the singer literally breathing life into the text. Abbate, *In Search of Opera* (Princeton, NJ: Princeton University Press, 2001). She refers to Vladimir Jankélévitch, *La musique et l'ineffable* (Paris: Seuil, 1982), translated into English by Abbate, *Music and the Ineffable* (Princeton, NJ: Princeton University Press, 2003).

101. These theories include Marcel Mauss on techniques of the body, Pierre Bourdieu on habitus, and Elin Diamond on gestus and the gendered body. See especially Diamond's *Unmaking Mimesis: Essays on Feminism and Theatre* (London: Routledge, 1997), which includes an updated version of her essential essay "Brechtian Theory/Feminist Theory: Toward a Gestic Feminist Criticism," *Drama Review* 32, no. 1 (1988): 82–94. Diamond's pioneering work deals with the visual, showing, spectating body but does not treat the audible, sounding, listening body.

102. Pavis, "Brechtian Gestus and Its Avatars in Contemporary Theatre," trans. Hector Maclean, *Brecht Yearbook/Brecht-Jahrbuch* 24 (1999): 179.

103. Pavis, "On Brecht's Notion of Gestus," 46.

104. See chapter 5 regarding multisensory stimuli and integration for spectating audience members.

105. This seems an especially fruitful line of inquiry for work clearly descended from or related to gestus, such as performativity and presence. For the former see especially the work of Polish scholars Malgorzata Sugiera and Mateusz Borowski at Jagiellonian University, Kraków. Their planned cycle of three biennial conferences under the common heading "Aspects of Performativity in Contemporary Writing for the Stage" began in December 2007. With regard to presence, see Hans Ulrich Gumbrecht, "Production of Presence, Interspersed with Absence: A Modernist View of Music, Libretti, and Staging," in *Music and the Aesthetics of Modernity*, ed. Karol Berger and Anthony Newcomb (Cambridge: Harvard University Press, 2005): 343–356.

3. FRAGMENTS OF OPERA IN AMERICAN EXILE

1. The German titles of the three original plays are *Die Geschichte der Simone Machard*, *Schweyk im zweiten Weltkrieg*, and *Der kaukasische Kreidekreis;* Brecht did not include *The Duchess of Malfi* in his collected works; he revised *Leben des Galilei;* and *Furcht und Elend des dritten Reiches* became *The Private Life of the Master Race*.

2. In 1944 Brecht drafted a libretto based on his "Ballad of Marie Sanders,

the Jew's Whore," written in 1935 to mark the codification of Nazi anti-Semitism in the Nuremberg Laws. He and Dessau made notes about several musical numbers, but there is no evidence that the composer composed any music for "Ballad."

3. Ernst Bloch went so far as to suggest that Wagner's operas could be saved with an infusion of Karl May, whose kitschy novels set in the American Wild West were among Brecht's childhood favorites. Christina Ujma, " 'Der strenge und der schwärmende Ton': Notes on Bloch and Brecht in the Twenties and Thirties," trans. Jonathan Long, in *Bertolt Brecht Centenary Essays*, ed. Steve Giles and Rodney Livingstone (Amsterdam: Rodopi, 1998), 39. The peak of Brecht's obsession with Americana in general is the "travesty of American myths" in his sketches for *Revue* (1926), intended for Max Reinhardt. Stereotypes of The Girl, recordings, advertising, boxing, Tarzan, and Tahiti are all presented with great irony. See BFA 10:382–385 (cited in Hans Peter Neureuter, "Stückfragmente und Stückprojekte: Befund und Theorie," in *Brecht Handbuch in fünf Bänden*, ed. Jan Knopf [Stuttgart: J. B. Metzler, 2001], 1:57). See also Joy H. Calico, "Brecht on Opera and/in the Americas," *Opera Quarterly* 22, no. 3 (forthcoming). While revising this chapter I was privileged to respond to an address by Lydia Goehr at the Vanderbilt University Department of Philosophy's annual Politics, Criticism, and the Arts conference (April 2006), in which she discussed Adorno's Singspiel fragment "Der Schatz des Indianer-Joe." My immersion in her paper no doubt influenced this chapter for the better.

4. These texts include *In the Jungle of the Cities, Mahagonny* (both Songspiel and opera), *Happy End, St. Joan of the Stockyards, Lindbergh Flight,* and *The Bread Shop*. Other, incomplete projects include *Dan Drew, The Fall of the Paradise of the City of Miami,* and *Joe Fleischhacker. Dan Drew, The Breadshop,* and *Joe Fleischhacker* can be interpreted as earlier versions of *St. Joan of the Stockyards*. James K. Lyon, *Bertolt Brecht in America* (Princeton, NJ: Princeton University Press, 1980), 4. See Patrick Primavesi, "Joe Fleischhacker in Chikago," in *Brecht Handbuch*, 1:147. Lyon's book remains the definitive study and is complemented by another volume he edited entitled *Brecht in den USA* (Frankfurt am Main: Suhrkamp, 1994).

5. The influence of Norwegian Knut Hamsun's American adventures in German translation is apparent in *Prairie: Opera after Hamsun.* Roland Jost, "Prärie," *Brecht Handbuch*, 1:111. See Knut Hamsun, *Knut Hamsun Remembers America: Essays and Stories, 1885–1949,* ed. and trans. Richard Nelson Current (Columbia: University of Missouri Press, 2003). Hamsun's 1910 play *Livet i vold* (variously translated as *In the Grip of Life* and, on Broadway in 1923–24, as *In the Claws of Life*) features the character Negro Boy in a prominent role. See also Monika Žagar, "Knut Hamsun's 'White Negro' from *Ringen Sluttet* (1936)—or the Politics of Race," in *Legacies of Modernism: Art and Politics in Northern Europe, 1890–1950,* ed. Patrizia C. McBride, Richard W. McCormick, and Monika Žagar (New York: Palgrave Macmillan, 2007), 55–65. A review of German public libraries in 1930 revealed that Jack London was the most widely read author, Upton Sinclair (a Brecht favorite) was number ten, and

Hamsun ranked sixteenth. His works were favorably reviewed by Hermann Hesse, a powerful arbiter of German literary taste in this period. I am indebted to Christian Rogowski for this reference. Günther Goratowski, "Was der deutsche Bürger liest. Ein Rundgang durch deutsche Volksbibliotheken," *Uhu* 6, no. 8 (1930): 34–37.

The Man from Manhattan (1924) features a long narrative in which the character Anne Smith recounts the "discovery" of America from the perspective of Native Americans: the theft of land, the reckless plunder of resources, and the construction of cities.

6. Despite intensive sleuthing and assistance from dozens of people and institutions over the course of several years, I have been unable to locate any primary documents as evidence of the adaptation by Clarence Muse.

7. Notes include the statement that "the history of jazz is the history of the Negro," which is followed by a list of eight other "slight influences" ranging from sacred music of the fourteenth century to French musical impressionism. Cited in Joachim Lucchesi and Ronald K. Shull, *Musik bei Brecht* (Frankfurt am Main: Suhrkamp, 1988), 186. BBA 158/10. Lucchesi and Shull make the plausible suggestion that these notes arose from a discussion with William Dieterle about his film *Syncopation* (1942), which was a history of jazz.

8. See Errol G. Hill and James V. Hatch, *A History of African American Theatre* (Cambridge: Cambridge University Press, 2003); Rena Fraden, *Blueprints for a Black Federal Theatre, 1935–1939* (Cambridge: Cambridge University Press, 1994); and Laura Browder, *Rousing the Nation: Radical Culture in Depression America* (Amherst: University of Massachusetts Press, 1998).

9. Joachim Gerhard Ludovicus Anton Riesthuis, "African American and German Exile Writers, 1933–1952" (PhD diss., University of Chicago, 2004), 4. See Bill V. Mullen and James Edward Smethurst, eds., *Left of the Color Line: Race, Radicalism and Twentieth-Century Literature of the United States* (Chapel Hill: University of North Carolina Press, 2003).

10. Riesthuis notes that reception history reflects the cold war climate, as Robert A. Bone accused the radical authors of having been mouthpieces for the party in *The Negro Novel in America* (New Haven, CT: Yale University Press, 1965), and Cruse derided the influence of Jewish communists on the Black Nationalist agenda in *Crisis of the Negro Intellectual*. Riesthuis considers Henry Louis Gates Jr.'s subsequent rehabilitation of these authors through depoliticization in the 1980s and their current contextualization in revisionist studies ("African American and German Exile Writers," 7–9). By 1944, however, agendas began to diverge, and Wright and Ellison in particular distanced themselves from the party. The alliance with communism would come back to haunt other African Americans during the McCarthy era, none more so than Robeson, whose staunch support of the Soviet Union after the war cost him his performing career as well as a prominent role in the burgeoning civil rights movement.

11. That fall, Houseman launched plays by respected African American

playwrights: *Walk Together Chillun!* by Frank Wilson and *Conjur Man Dies* by Rudolph Fisher.

12. Martha Dreiblatt to Wilella Waldorf, cited in Lyon, *Bertolt Brecht in America*, 19. It should be noted that responses to all-black shows ran the gamut and reveal the complexity of race relations at the time. See particularly Ray Allen and George P. Cunningham, "Cultural Uplift and Double Consciousness: African American Responses to the 1935 Opera *Porgy and Bess*," *Musical Quarterly* 88, no. 3 (2005): 342–369. It is often asserted that Brecht saw a performance of *Green Pastures* at this time as well, but that cannot be corroborated. The revival was only on Broadway in 1935 between 26 February and 27 April, and he did not arrive until October.

13. Lyon, *Bertolt Brecht in America*, 17.

14. Brecht's 1919 play *Trommeln in der Nacht* (Drums in the Night) treated the return of the soldier Kragler to Germany after four years of internment in an African POW camp. He is presented as a "Negro" from "Africa," and as such his reappearance is doubly disruptive, but this in no way reflects an awareness of the specific racial context of the United States.

15. Hauptmann's English transcription is BBA 341/46–51.

16. There is an enormous body of literature on this community. Two recent studies are Ehrhard Bahr, *Weimar on the Pacific: German Exile Culture in Los Angeles and the Crisis of Modernism* (Berkeley: University of California Press, 2007), and, for general audiences, David Wallace's *Exiles in Hollywood* (Pompton Plains, NJ: Limelight Editions, 2006).

17. Many artists involved in the film industry were also active in the New York theater scene, but this cross-fertilization did not include blacks to the extent that it included nonblacks. There are conspicuous exceptions, such as Langston Hughes's screenplay for the musical *Way Down South*, written with Clarence Muse in 1939.

18. Transcript of podium discussion in *Hanns Eisler der Zeitgenosse: Positionen, Perspektiven: Materialien zu den Eisler-Festen, 1994–95*, ed. Günter Mayer (Leipzig: Deutscher Verlag für Musik, 1997), 87. In all fairness it should be noted that for part of that time Eisler's and Brecht's movements were restricted because of their status as enemy aliens, which required them to observe a curfew between 8:00 P.M. and 6:00 A.M. and, with the exception of commuting to work, to remain within a five-mile radius of their homes. See newspaper clipping in *Journals* 213. Several entries in the vicinity of this clipping (March 1942) refer to the curfew.

19. Regarding the portrayal of African Americans in mainstream Hollywood films see Donald Bogle, *Toms, Coons, Mulattoes, Mammies and Bucks: An Interpretive History of Blacks in American Films*, 4th ed. (New York: Continuum, 2001). Regarding black cinema in particular see Gladstone L. Yearwood, *Black Film as a Signifying Practice: Cinema, Narration and the African American Aesthetic Tradition* (Trenton, NJ: Africa World Press, 2000).

20. I am indebted to James K. Lyon for sharing a copy of his correspondence

with Muse, in which Lyon asked several specific questions about the production. Muse's response was friendly but evasive. Brecht's account is a convoluted saga involving several vaguely identified people—(the brother of "[Robert] Thören (now a film writer for MGM)," a "Mr. Gebert in Seattle," and an unnamed "man in California")—an "indescribably miserable translation" by Fritz Wreede, and a fund-raising campaign that outpaced the completion of the text and suddenly required urgent action from Weill (Brecht to Weill, dated early to mid-April 1942; *BFA* 30:226–7).

21. Crawford's tour played San Francisco 26 April—8 May and then Oakland 9–13 June 1942 but did not go to Los Angeles. By that time the Muse project had been shelved. It is unlikely that Brecht would have seen the production because of the curfew and travel restrictions imposed upon enemy aliens in March of that year.

22. Unsigned contract dated 24 February 1942. WLRC series 40, box 1, folder 15.

23. See Kim H. Kowalke, "*The Threepenny Opera* in America," in *Kurt Weill: "The Threepenny Opera*," ed. Stephen Hinton (Cambridge: Cambridge University Press, 1990), 90–95; Michael Kater, "Weill und Brecht: Kontroversen einer Künstlerfreundschaft auf zwei Kontinenten," in *Brecht und seine Komponisten*, ed. Albrecht Riethmüller (Laaber, Germany: Laaber Verlag, 2000), 63–72; and David Farneth, with Elmar Juchem and Dave Stein, *Kurt Weill: A Life in Pictures and Documents* (Woodstock, NY: Overlook Press, 2000), 211–213.

24. Brecht to Weill, March 1942. Translation in Kowalke, "*The Threepenny Opera* in America," 91. *BFA* 29:221–222.

25. A newly discovered letter from Weill to Louis Simon, dated 26 July 1939, confirms this report: "I am pleased to hear that Harold Smith has finished the third act of the colored Dreigroschenoper and I am looking forward to see what he has done." WLRC, simon390726. The letter indicates that the recipient had been involved in the Federal Theatre Project. Dave Stein, WLRC archivist, believes the recipient may be Louis M. Simon, who directed Allison Hughes's *The Trial of Dr. Beck* in 1937 under the auspices of the FTP. "Harold Smith" could be Harold Jacob Smith (1912–70), coauthor of the screenplay for *Inherit the Wind.*

26. Weill to Brecht, 13 March 1942. WLRC series 40, box 1, folder 18. See also the telegram from Weill to Eslanda Robeson in which he requests a meeting on the subject, dated 17 March 1942. WLRC Robeson correspondence file. A comparison of the cordial, businesslike tone of Weill's letters to Brecht and Marton with his more candid reports of these events in his letters to Lenya, who was on tour at the time, reveals that Weill wanted to help but was justifiably wary of Brecht's propensity for selfish, shady business dealings. See *Speak Low (When You Speak Love): The Letters of Kurt Weill and Lotte Lenya,* ed. and trans. Lys Symonette and Kim Kowalke (Berkeley: University of California Press, 1996).

27. Brecht to Weill dated early or mid-April 1942. It certainly precedes Weill's receipt of the contract from Marton. *BFA* 30:226–7.

28. Brecht to Weill, 28 March 1942. *BFA* 30:225–226. Marton was not, as the editorial comments indicate on p. 660, Weill's agent; he represented Brecht.

29. Adorno to Weill, 31 March 1942. Original letter held by Yale University Music Library, Papers of Kurt Weill and Lotte Lenya (MSS 30), box 47, folder 18. English translation in Elmar Juchem, "A Letter Surfaces: Kurt Weill's Reply to Theodor W. Adorno, April 1942," *Kurt Weill Newsletter* 21, no. 2 (2003): 4.

30. Weill to Adorno, 7 April 1942. This letter was long thought to be lost, but a copy was rediscovered in the Theodor W. Adorno Archiv, Frankfurt am Main. Published in "A Letter Surfaces."

31. Weill to Marton, 20 April 1942. WLRC Marton correspondence file.

32. Weill to Eslanda Robeson, 11 June 1942. WLRC Robeson correspondence file. Her response, dated 15 July 1942, indicates that she and her husband were taken aback by the situation: "Just so there will be no confusion: we feel the idea of a Negro Theater is a splendid idea, but I must say the actual workings of it at the moment are not so splendid!!"

33. Muse to Lyon, 20 November 1972. Lyon's private collection.

34. The extent of Brecht's involvement in *Duchess* is difficult to determine, and accounts are contradictory. The opportunity arose to write something for Elisabeth Bergner, a former member of the Brecht circle and the most successful of the German émigré actresses, and her husband Paul Czinner agreed to underwrite it. Brecht drove away his first collaborator (H. R. Hays) and completed the adaptation of Webster's play with W. H. Auden instead. Czinner hired George Rylands, a highly regarded but provincial director whose method bore no resemblance to Brecht's, and a power struggle ensued. Ultimately Brecht's name appeared in none of the publicity, and he did not include the play in the German edition of his collected works. Negative reviews of both *Duchess* and *The Private Life* complained about amateur or experimental characteristics, which could be indicators of misunderstood Brechtian theater practice, a poor production, or both.

35. Mixed-cast productions were far less common than either all-black or all-white shows in this period. Certainly the logistical difficulties of touring with such a cast, which would have required separate travel and hotel accommodations, would have been daunting. Other mixed-cast shows in the 1940s included *Harriet* (1943), *On the Town* (1944), *Bloomer Girl* (1944), *The Hasty Heart* (1945), *Show Boat* (1946 and 1948 revivals), *Jeb* (Ossie Davis's Broadway debut, 1945), *Set My People Free* (1948), *The Iceman Cometh* (1946), *Home of the Brave* (1946), and *The Respectful Prostitute* (1946). Hill and Hatch, *A History*, 532. Evidently none of the black actors in those shows performed in whiteface.

36. The subject of whiteface has generated little scholarship compared to blackface. Despite its examination of other aspects of its subject, whiteface is mentioned only briefly in Mary F. Brewer, *Staging Whiteness* (Middletown, CT: Wesleyan University Press, 2005), 167. The landmark publication in racechange research remains Susan Gubar, *Racechanges: White Skin, Black Face in American Culture* (New York: Oxford University Press, 1997), but it does not treat

whiteface. See also Helen Gilbert, "Black and White and Re[a]d All Over Again: Indigenous Minstrelsy in Contemporary Canadian and Australian Theatre," *Theatre Journal* 55, no. 4 (2003): 679–698.

37. Steven Watson, *Prepare for Saints: Gertrude Stein, Virgil Thomson, and the Mainstreaming of American Modernism* (Berkeley: University of California Press, 2000), 206–208, 212, and 261.

38. Both actors had performed leading roles in Welles's *Macbeth* (Ellis as Macduff and Lee as Banquo) and had enjoyed success on Broadway in a range of plays. In 1949 they would also share the screen in *Lost Boundaries*, a film about racism and passing.

39. Ann Hornemann, "Exiled German Playwright Happy in Developing Democratic Theatre," in *Brecht in den USA*, 104–107.

40. According to the program, the actors who played German soldiers were William Malten and Ludwig Roth. Roth was born in Munich, and William Malten appears to have been white as well, so the identity of the actor to whom she refers here is unknown. Program reproduced in Lyon, *Brecht in den USA*, 191–193.

41. Outside of the racially charged context of the United States, exaggerated white makeup and masks are frequently associated with Asian theatrical traditions, such as Japanese Noh and Chinese opera; see W. Anthony Sheppard, *Revealing Masks: Exotic Influences and Ritualized Performance in Modernist Music Theater* (Berkeley: University of California Press, 2001). Neither the depth of Brecht's knowledge of these art forms nor the extent of their influence should be overstated, however. His usage of masks for productions of *The Decision* and *The Good Person of Szechwan* "anticipates and enriches anthropologist Michael Taussig's famous conceptualization of 'the face' by using the face both as a cultural disguise and a as a tool for political education rather than as a marker of identity." Astrid Oesmann's *Staging History: Brecht's Social Concepts of Ideology* (Albany: State University of New York Press, 2005), 5, also 161–171. Regarding masks see also Gerda Baumbach, "Die Maske und die Bestie oder Die Primitivität der westlichen Schauspielkunst. Brechts Verwendung von Theatermasken," *Maske und Kothurn* 42, nos. 2–4 (2000): 209–240. Masks and whiteface are also tools of the clown, another character of which the playwright availed himself, perhaps most infamously in the third part of the *Baden-Baden Cantata* in 1929. Whiteface and masks, while related for theatrical purposes, do not elicit identical responses, particularly when race is involved in the context of the American theater. Under the influence of Karl Valentin, Brecht first used whiteface to show soldiers who were literally scared to death in his 1924 production of *Edward II* in Munich; he used the device again in conjunction with prosthetic facial features for comic effect in *Man Is Man* in 1931. Joel Schachter, "Brecht's Clowns: *Man Is Man* and after," in *The Cambridge Companion to Brecht*, 2nd ed., ed. Peter Thomson and Glendyr Sacks (Cambridge: Cambridge University Press, 2006), 90–100. Charlie Chaplin's Tramp, replete with whiteface, also remained a touchstone for Brecht as he developed his theory of epic performance practices.

42. Gubar, *Racechanges,* 5.

43. Gilbert, "Black and White," 680–681.

44. Burton Rascoe, *New York World Telegram,* 12 June 1945. Perhaps the most perceptive review was written by Kappo Phelan for *The Commonweal,* who praised the use (but not the content) of the placards and projections as well as the conspicuous placement of the projectionist. Phelan also provided a serviceable explanation of estrangement, which he called "distance." He concluded that Brecht's future lay in television rather than live theater because that mechanical and technological medium could better serve his theory. Phelan, "The Stage and Screen," *Commonweal,* 29 June 1945.

45. Gilbert has criticized Gubar's racechange theory as unrealistic in its presentation as "a utopian process that enhances cross-race dialogue and transcends racial differences" and invokes Dorinne Kondo's argument that racial impersonation is "systematically encoded and maintained in structures of white privilege that persist despite individual intentionality" ("Black and White," 681). The reference is to Dorinne Kondo, "(Re)Visions of Race: Contemporary Race Theory and the Cultural Politics of Racial Crossover in Documentary Theatre," *Theatre Journal* 52, no. 1 (2000): 100.

46. Mona Z. Smith, *Becoming Something: The Story of Canada Lee* (New York: Faber and Faber, 2004), 219. Smith discusses this incident in general (218–227) and also reproduces two relevant photographs in the unpaginated photo section. I am indebted to Joel Haney for research assistance on this topic.

47. Louis Calta, "*Duchess of Malfi* Due at Barrymore," *New York Times,* 15 October 1946, 39.

48. Bert McCord, "*Duchess of Malfi* Tonight," *New York Herald Tribune,* 15 October 1946, 19.

49. Howard Barnes, "The Theaters," *New York Herald Tribune,* 16 October 1946, 23.

50. Brooks Atkinson, "The Play," *New York Times,* 16 October 1946, 35.

51. One must also entertain the possibility that the use of whiteface was a publicity stunt, a strategy to which Brecht was not averse on principle. As such it would reveal a crass indifference to Lee's and Ellis's personal situations, however.

52. Cited in Smith, *Becoming Something,* 111.

53. Cited in ibid., 113. On the other hand, the irascible white critic Westbrook Pegler took umbrage that a black man portrayed a white villain, stating indignantly, "Our blackface white men always play comedy Negroes with no malice or disparagement of the colored people in anything they did." Cited in Smith, *Becoming Something,* 224–225. Pegler, "As Pegler Sees It," King Features Syndicate (Hearst), 7 May 1947. Lee's situation within the context of a Brecht production brings to mind Henry Louis Gates Jr.'s essay on the life of Anatole Broyard, the brilliant African American critic who passed for white his entire life. Gates sees a connection between passing and modernism that touches upon the significance of fragments for the modernist project: "The thematic elements of passing—fragmentation, alienation, liminality, self-fashioning—echo

the great themes of modernism." Gates, "The Passing of Anatole Broyard," in *Thirteen Ways of Looking at a Black Man* (New York: Random House, 1997), 200.

54. Interestingly enough, a different update of John Gay's classic soon enjoyed a brief Broadway stint in a mixed-cast production called *Beggar's Holiday*, a title that pays homage to its namesake if not to its generic parody. The music was by Duke Ellington, the orchestration by Billy Strayhorn, and the book and lyrics by John La Touche. Hill and Hatch report that the cast, crew, and orchestra were all integrated and that race was not a factor in the story itself (*A History*, 344). The show lasted just fourteen weeks on Broadway, but that was long enough to preclude any revival of *Threepenny Opera* in New York at this time. See also Hinton, *Kurt Weill's "The Threepenny Opera,"* 99. Weill later wrote to Arthur Lyons about *Beggar's Holiday* and his own plans for Americanizing *Threepenny Opera* as "an American period piece, taking place in the New York Bowery around 1890, with an election in the center of action" (29 September 1947). Original in the Weill-Lenya papers, Yale Music Library, box 47, file 10. Thanks to Dave Stein of the WLRC for this reference.

55. Jost Hermand, " 'Manchmal lagen Welten zwischen uns!' Brecht und Eislers *Deutsche Symphonie*," in *Brecht und seine Komponisten*, ed. Albrecht Riethmüller (Laaber, Germany: Laaber Verlag, 2000), 127.

56. Despite, and sometimes because of, the politically volatile situation, some composers took up dodecaphony for the first time in the 1930s. The Nazis' association of that method with the Jewish Schoenberg motivated Paul Dessau to use it as a means of antifascist resistance. Peter Petersen, "In Paris begonnen, in New York vollendet, in Berlin verlegt: 'Les Voix' von Paul Dessau," in *Musik im Exil: Folgen des Nazismus für die internationale Musikkultur*, ed. Hanns-Werner Heister, Claudia Maurer Zenck, and Peter Petersen (Frankfurt am Main: Fischer Taschenbuch Verlag, 1993), 438. See also Thomas Phleps, " '. . . Ich kann mir gar nicht vorstellen etwas Schöneres': Das Exilschaffen Hanns Eislers," 475–511, in the same volume; and *Entartete Musik: Dokumentation und Kommentar*, ed. Dümling and Peter Girth (Düsseldorf: Dkv. der kleine Verlag, 1993), 235 (cited in Kyung-Boon Lee, *Musik und Literatur im Exil: Hanns Eislers dodekaphone Exilkantate* [New York: Lang, 2000], 71–72). At the other end of the spectrum Winfried Zillig and Paul Klenau, a Schoenberg student and an acquaintance, respectively, enjoyed considerable success writing twelve-tone music under the Nazis by constructing rows that lent themselves to diatonicism and were suggestive of tonal centers. When paired with acceptable plots, Zillig found that this usage did not impede the success of his operas. Klenau's operas were also deemed acceptable, as he took pains to trace his twelve-tone roots to Wagner rather than to Schoenberg and vehemently declared his allegiance to the Third Reich. Thomas Phleps, "Zwölftöniges Theater: 'Wiener Schüler' und Anverwandte in NS-Deutschland," in *"Entartete Musik" 1938—Weimar und die Ambivalenz. Ein Projekt der Hochschule für Musik Franz Liszt Weimar zum Kulturstadtjahr 1999*, ed Hanns-Werner Heister (Saarbrücken: Pfau, 2001), 179–215. While Eisler's consonant dodecaphony may invite comparison

to the music of Zillig and Klenau, his combination of twelve-tone music with leftist political texts and agendas distinguishes his usage from theirs.

57. Conflict among members began in 1919, when Lenin declared the Third International to be the Communist International, or Comintern, thereby claiming communist leadership of the world socialist movement. At the Second Congress in 1920, the membership established twenty-one conditions to distinguish communists from socialists. The United Front came too late to help the Germans, but Comintern chapters in France and Czechoslovakia, alarmed by the swift demise of the powerful German Communist Party, seized upon the proposal with zeal. Regarding music and the Popular Front in France, see Leslie Sprout, "Music for a 'New Era': Composers and National Identity in France, 1938–1945" (PhD diss., University of California–Berkeley, 2000), especially 1–35.

58. The shift can be attributed to some combination of the "'triple interaction' of national factors, internal dynamics in the Comintern leadership and the shifting requirements of Soviet diplomacy." Julian Jackson, *The Popular Front in France: Defending Democracy, 1934–1938* (Cambridge: Cambridge University Press, 1988), 35 (cited in Kevin McDermott and Jeremy Agnew, *The Comintern: A History of International Communism from Lenin to Stalin* [New York: St. Martin's Press, 1997], 121–122). Bulgarian Georgi Dimitrov, head of the Comintern in Moscow, proposed a shift to the Popular Front in 1934; see the proposal and Stalin's annotations in Dimitrov and Joseph Stalin, *Dimitrov and Stalin, 1934–1943: Letters from the Soviet Archives*, ed. Alexander Dallin and F. I. Firsov, documents trans. Vadim A. Staklo (New Haven, CT: Yale University Press, 2000), 7–16. Stalin also had concerns to the east. The rise of Hitler in the west and the prospect of renewed conflict with Japan via its invasion of China could have meant fighting on both fronts. Furthermore, the Chinese Communist Party had "a greater degree of distance from Moscow, not only geographically but also in attitude and autonomy, than virtually any other section of the Comintern." Dallin and Dimitrov and Stalin, *Dimitrov and Stalin*, 83. I am indebted to Fred Wakeman Jr. for reminding me of the significance of China in this context. Despite Stalin's approval the new strategy met with substantial international opposition, so much so that the Comintern's Seventh International Congress was postponed from September 1934 to July 1935 to give the organization time to shore up support. This change of course was abruptly reversed in 1939 with the Nazi-Soviet Non-aggression Pact, and then resumed just as suddenly in 1941, after Germany violated that treaty and invaded the Soviet Union. Stalin terminated the Comintern in 1943 as a conciliatory gesture toward his new allies, Great Britain and the United States.

59. Excerpted from Georgi Dimitrov's address published in English in the *Daily Worker* on 24 August 1935 under the headline "Working Class Unity Is Bulwark against Fascism, says Dimitroff." I am indebted to Edgardo Salinas for research assistance with regard to the *Daily Worker*. The same uncredited translation, albeit with different subheadings, appears with the italics given here in Dimitrov, *The United Front against Fascism: Speeches Delivered at the Seventh*

World Congress of the Communist International, July 25–August 20, 1935 (New York: New Century Publishers, 1945), 5–94; quotation from 36–37. See a slightly different translation in Dimitrov, *Against Fascism and War* (New York: International Publishers, 1986), 1–94.

60. *Daily Worker,* 24 August 1935; Dimitroff, *United Front against Fascism,* 39.

61. "Translate Comintern Decisions into Everyday Work!" *Daily Worker,* 23 August 1935, 6. See also the speech delivered by Earl Browder, general secretary of the Communist Party USA, at the Seventh Congress. It was published under the headline "The Formation of a Workers' and Farmers' Labor Party as a Bulwark against the Growing Fascist Offensive," with secondary headlines "Need of Lasting Coalition of Workers and Farmers and Middle Class Stressed" and "Working Class Unity Essential as Driving Force in Winning Over the Mass Millions—Question Raises Problem of Organic Unity of All Fighters for Socialism" (*Daily Worker,* 28 August 1935, 3). I am indebted to Edgardo Salinas for research assistance in this matter.

62. Albrecht Dümling, "Zwölftonmusik als antifaschistisches Potential: Eislers Ideen zu einer neuen Verwendung der Dodekaphonie," in *Die Wiener Schule und das Hakenkreuz: Das Schicksal der Moderne im gesellschaftspolitischen Kontext des 20. Jahrhunderts,* ed. Otto Kolleritsch (Vienna: Universal Edition, 1990), 99 and 94.

63. "Avantgarde Kunst und Volksfront," *Die neue Weltbühne,* 9 December 1937. Reprinted in Eisler, *Musik und Politik: Schriften, 1924–1948,* ed. Günter Mayer (Leipzig: VEB Deutscher Verlag für Musik, 1985), 398.

64. As chairman he attempted to negotiate collaborations with the Internationale der Arbeitersänger and the Internationale Gesellschaft für Neue Musik, although these bodies were leery of working too closely with Moscow. In the same year Eisler toured the United States, giving concerts and lectures in roughly thirty-five cities; he worked on his magnum opus *Deutsche Sinfonie* and had the premiere of *Kleine Sinfonie* in London; he participated in Workers' Music festivals in Strasbourg, Reichenberg/Liberac, and Prague; he worked with Brecht in Denmark; and the pair went to the United States to oversee the Theatre Union's production of *The Mother.* Eisler's interpretation of the Popular Front aesthetic was compatible with cultural politics in the Soviet Union and with the Moscow-based Comintern leadership for only a brief period, however. By 1937, when Eisler and Ernst Bloch challenged György Lukács's claims that expressionism was an unacceptable medium for the Popular Front in "Avantgarde Kunst und Volksfront," the winds had shifted. Thus began his fall from grace in Moscow, and by 1939, when he expressed disgust with the Non-aggression Pact, he was persona non grata. His wife, Lou, recalled that they were ostracized by all who toed the party line at that time. Albrecht Betz, *Hanns Eisler: Musik einer Zeit, die sich eben bildet* (Munich: edition text + kritik, 1976), 152.

65. Whether Eisler was a member of the Communist Party has been the subject of long debate. In the absence of conclusive evidence to the contrary, and in agreement with Eisler's statements before the House Committee on Un-

American Activities, those scholars who are willing to take a position on the subject maintain that he was not. See Günter Mayer, "War der 'Karl Marx der Musik' Parteimitglied oder nicht?" in *Hanns Eisler der Zeitgenosse*, ed. Mayer (Leipzig: Deutscher Verlag für Musik, 1997), 67–76. It is also likely that his fate in the early years of the GDR would have been far worse had he been a member. This observation comes courtesy of Anson Rabinbach and Therese Hörnigk. It is worth remembering that his brother Gerhart Eisler was a Comintern official, and his sister Ruth Fischer was a rising star as well, until August 1936, when she was dismissed as a Trotskyite; after that she undertook a virulent anti-Stalinist campaign that included testifying against both brothers in the United States.

66. The *Kleine Sinfonie* had represented a similar synthesis in a purely instrumental work. The massive *Deutsche Sinfonie*, a choral orchestral work best described as a three-movement symphony in which political cantatas with texts by Brecht and Ignazio Silone are embedded, would be his most ambitious effort to embody this political and aesthetic view. See the masterly study by Thomas Phleps, *Hanns Eislers Deutsche Sinfonie. Ein Beitrag zur Ästhetik des Widerstands* (Kassel: Bärenreiter, 1988).

67. French literati issued a vaguely worded invitation to appeal to the widest possible swath of exiled writers—"antifascism" is conspicuously absent from the text, but many speeches featured procommunist themes nonetheless. There was also considerable support for pacifism, incompatible though it seemed to be with antifascism at that time. Roger Shattuck, "Writers for the Defense of Culture," *Partisan Review* 51, no. 3 (1984): 400–401. For complete primary documents of the conference see *Pour la défense de la culture. Les texts du Congrès international des écrivains Paris, juin 1935*, ed. Sandra Teroni and Wolfgang Klein (Dijon, France: Editions Universitaires de Dijon, 2005).

68. The first version of "Fünf Schwierigkeiten beim Schreiben der Wahrheit" was published in *Pariser Tageblatt*, 12 December 1934, and a revised version appeared in *Unsere Zeit* 8, nos. 2–3 (April 1935): 23–24. BFA 22:74–89. In translation see *Brecht on Art and Politics*, ed. Tom Kuhn and Steve Giles (London: Methuen, 2003), 141–156. The speech, entitled "Eine notwendige Feststellung zum Kampf gegen die Barbarei," was published in *Mitteilungen* 4 on 27 June 1935. A revised version appeared in issue 5, published at the end of July 1935. BFA 22:141–146 and *Brecht on Art and Politics*, 157–162. An unpublished English translation entitled "A Needed Inquiry Regarding the Struggle against Barbarism" by Eva Goldbeck is thought to have been supervised by Brecht. It is held in the Marc Blitzstein papers of the Wisconsin Historical Society. Albrecht Betz, *Exil und Engagement: Deutsche Schriftsteller im Frankreich der dreißiger Jahre* (Munich: edition text + kritik, 1986), 109.

69. Brecht to George Grosz, July 1935. BFA 22:931.

70. See also Robert Cohen, "Brechts ästhetische Theorie in den ersten Jahren des Exils," in *Ästhetiken des Exils*, ed. Helga Schreckenberger (Amsterdam: Rodopi, 2003), 55–70.

71. Lee notes that the tension between Brecht and Eisler may be attributed

to the fact that Brecht needed Eisler in order to work at that time, whereas Eisler had a lot of other opportunities. Lee, *Musik und Literatur*, 30. He cites Werner Mittenzwei, *Das Leben des Bertolt Brechts, oder, der Umgang mit den Welträtseln* (Frankfurt am Main: Suhrkamp, 1986), 561.

72. Eisler's oft-quoted account, in which he attributed his and Brecht's inability to complete *Goliath* to their geographical separation in exile, is found in Eisler, *Fragen Sie mehr über Brecht: Gespräche mit Hans Bunge* (Leipzig: VEB Deutscher Verlag für Musik, 1975), 81.

73. Primary sources consulted are BBA 519/1–142, 464/1–7, and 1768/53; and HEA 1.1.336, 3.1.4272, 3.1.1833, 3.1.457, 5.3.938, and 3.4.4267. BBA sources are reproduced in *BFA* 10:753–789, but unfortunately the editor does not use the siglia of the BBA, so it is virtually "impossible to reconstruct versions," a frustration this author shares. See Erdmut Wizisla and Marta Ulvaeus, "Editorial Principles in the Berlin and Frankfurt Edition of Bertolt Brecht's Works," *Drama Review* 43, no. 4 (1999): 32. Also Neureuter, "Stückfragmente," 65.

74. Albrecht Dümling, *Laßt euch nicht verführen: Brecht und die Musik* (Munich: Kindler Verlag, 1985), 442. Glaeser identifies "Gad" as a reference to one of the five capital cities of the Philistines and the hometown of Goliath (*BFA* 10:1213). In Luther's translation of 1 Samuel 17, Goliath is identified as a giant from "Gat" (spelled "Gath" in contemporary English translations). When Saul turned on David he took refuge in Gath, and the ark of the covenant was secreted there before it was returned to the Israelites. Brecht's spelling of the word with a final "d" instead of a "t" may also allude to another word with multiple, intriguing Old Testament associations. "Gad" means "luck" and was the name given to Jacob's seventh son; it was also the name of a pagan deity who already had a sizeable following in Canaan, which is described as the land of the Philistines at least three times in the Old Testament. Gad was also the name of a region in which the Gadites, a warlike tribe, settled on the south side of Israel. Finally, Gad was the name of a prophet who served King David; he advised the king to build an altar on the future site of the temple and assisted with sacred music. Such multivalent etymology and its resulting wordplay appealed to Brecht; given his knowledge of the Bible, the choice of "Gad" instead of "Gat" suggests layers of possible signification.

75. Christine Bühler, "Goliath," in *Brecht Handbuch in fünf Bände*, 1:338.

76. Dümling notes the allusion without identifying a specific model in *Laßt euch nicht verführen*, 442.

77. The reference to Lortzing may surprise non-Germans, as his popularity in his homeland has always far exceeded his reputation elsewhere. His operas were among the most performed on the German stage between 1850 and 1950 and enjoyed a particular resurgence between 1933 and 1943. John London attributes this to Lortzing's oft-repeated desire to write quintessential German music theater, his catchy melodies, and his uncomplicated plots. London, *Theatre under the Nazis* (Manchester, England: University of Manchester Press, 2000), 145. I am indebted to Hilary Poriss, who recognized that the quotation might be a reference to Lortzing. See Jürgen Lodemann, *Lortzing: Leben und Werk des*

dichtenden, komponierenden und singenden Publikumslieblings, Familien-vaters und komisch tragischen Spielopernweltmeisters aus Berlin (Göttingen, Germany: Steidl, 2000), 440–543; and Lodemann, *Oper—O reiner Unsinn. Albert Lortzing, Opernmacher* (Freiburg: Wuz, 2005). I am unable to ascertain whether Brecht or Eisler was familiar with *Regina*. It was performed for the first time in 1899 in an adaptation by L'Arronge but fell out of the repertoire until Wilhelm Neef revived it in Rostock in 1953. Lortzing, *Regina: Oper in drei Akten*, ed. Irmlind Capelle (Milan: Ricordi, 1998), xxix n. 122.

78. "Die armen Leute" may also allude to the German title of the Dostoyevsky novel *Arme Leute (Poor Folk)*. Dostoyevsky was enormously popular in Germany in the first third of the twentieth century and appealed to both ends of the political spectrum in the Weimar Republic. Some members of the Left "valued him for exposing the ills of capitalist society, seeing him as a fellow Marxist in Christian guise," while "Nazi critics lauded his mystical nationalism and animosity toward the West." Steven Gary Marks, *How Russia Shaped the Modern World: From Art to Anti-Semitism, Ballet to Bolshevism* (Princeton, NJ: Princeton University Press, 2003), 80. According to Walter Benjamin, Brecht once blamed Dostoyevsky for an illness Benjamin suffered; Benjamin, *Understanding Brecht*, trans. Anna Bostock (New York: Verso, 2003), 112. György Lukács's engagement with Dostoyevsky continued throughout his lifetime.

79. HEA 3.1.4272; 5.3.938 9v–10r, 11r, and 457, respectively. A few terms used in this section may warrant clarification. In manuscript studies "r" stands for recto (right), the front face of a manuscript leaf, and "v" stands for verso (left), the backside of a manuscript leaf. "Particell" is the term for a compressed short score frequently used by composers at the draft stage, and "partitur" refers to passages that are scored in parts.

80. BFA 10:1213.

81. A second row and its standard permutations are worked out on folio 2r of HEA 457: C–D –E♭–D–F♯–F–E–B♭–A♭–G–A–B. Two additional rows and their standard permutations (I, R, RI) are found on folio 11v of HEA 938 but do not recur elsewhere in the sketches: A♭–F–G–E♭–E–F♯–D–C–B–B♭–D♭– A, and B–E–F–A♭–E♭–D–D♭–B♭–C–A–G–G♭. Eisler did not use any versions of these last three rows in the drafts for *Goliath*, however, nor did he use transpositions of row 1.

82. There was also some discussion of casting David as a trouser role, to be sung by a soprano, but they eventually decided he would be a tenor. Lucchesi and Shull, *Musik bei Brecht*, 664. Since no music survives for David it is not known if he would have remained a tenor, particularly given the fact that Eisler's music for Goliath indicates that he would have been a tenor.

83. Tim Howell, "Eisler's Serialism: Concepts and Methods," in *Hanns Eisler: A Miscellany*, ed. David Blake (New York: Harwood Academic Publishers, 1995), 102–132. Howell's analysis of Eisler's twelve-tone methodology is based on the *String Quartet* (1938) and demonstrates that these features were already evident in *8 Klavierstücke* (1925).

84. Brecht to Eisler, early 1941. "Denn *goliath* bringe ich hanns mit. wenn

der stille ozean still genug ist, werde ich den zweiten akt vorbereiten" (HEA 3.4.4267).

85. Glaeser, note to 780, 26–782, 16, B 9 (BFA 10:1212).

86. Brecht to Eisler, July 1941: "Wie gesagt, den *goliath* habe ich mit, ich warte damit auf dein signal" (HEA 3.1.4272).

87. The Feuchtwanger Memorial Library, Specialized Libraries and Archival Collections, at the University of Southern California holds an undated letter from Brecht to Eisler written when he heard Eisler was moving to California. Contents suggest that it was written shortly after the curfew was imposed on 25 March 1942 and before Eisler's arrival on 15 April 1942.

88. *Journals* 21 April 1942.

89. "Eventuell als Einlage für 'Goliath' zu verwenden (In der 'Sänger-kriegsszene') (Dann für Streicher setzen!)" (HEA 1.1.336).

90. Dümling, "Zwölftonmusik als antifaschistisches Potential," and Phleps, ". . . Ich kann mir gar nicht vorstellen etwas Schöneres."

91. Dümling, *Friedrich Hölderlin: Vertont von Hanns Eisler, Paul Hindemith, Max Reger* (Munich: Kindler, 1981), 99–100; and Hanns-Werner Heister, "Hollywood and Home: Hanns Eisler's 'Hölderlin-Fragmente' for Voice and Piano," in *Hanns Eisler: A Miscellany*, 217–223.

92. In 1921 Thomas Mann had called for the unification of cultural heritage and socialism in a convergence of Hölderin with Marx; Lukács described Hölderin as a man without a home; and setting his poems was variously construed as an act of inner emigration (Paul Hindemith) or antifascist resistance (Gideon Klein). Dümling, *Hölderlin*, 12, 16, 85–91.

93. *Journals* 25 June 1943. Brecht had never shown any particular interest in Hölderlin, but his first project upon returning to Europe in 1947 would be a production of Hölderin's *Antigone* as a vehicle for his wife, Helene Weigel. Ulrich Weisstein attributes this sudden interest to Eisler's *Fragment* settings. Weisstein, "Imitation, Stylization and Adaptation: The Language of Brecht's *Antigone* and Its Relation to Hölderlin's version of *Sophocles*," *German Quarterly* 46, no. 4 (1973): 581–604.

94. Schlegel's definition is cited in Philippe Lacoue-Labarthe and Jean-Luc Nancy, *The Literary Absolute: The Theory of Literature in German Romanticism*, trans. Philip Barnard and Cheryl Lester (Albany: State University of New York Press, 1988), 43.

95. *Journals* 6 November 1944. The Feuchtwanger Memorial Library, Specialized Libraries and Archival Collections, at the University of Southern California, also holds a copy of Eisler's contract for the film score of *Jealousy* dated 18 October 1944. Their records indicate that it pertains to *Goliath*, but neither Feuchtwanger Librarian Marje Schuetze-Coburn nor I can determine the relevance.

96. Lee argues that the hostile response to Eisler's music in reviews of the Copenhagen production of *Round Heads and Pointed Heads* in 1936 may have already confirmed that "there was little hope of successfully bringing an epic opera to the stage." Eisler's score for *Round Heads and Pointed Heads* had been

diatonic, melodic, and cabaret inflected, however, while the music for *Goliath* represented a completely different approach (Lee, *Musik und Literatur*, 41, citing Monika Wyss, *Brecht in der Kritik* [Munich: Kindler, 1977], 464). The greatest significance of *Goliath* for Brecht's American exile actually may have been more personal: *Goliath* was the last link to Steffin, one of his most valued partners, and her handwritten notes are scattered throughout surviving drafts. Brecht did not initiate any new opera projects until some three and a half years after her death.

97. For a comparison of Eisler's text with earlier *Faust* legends see Joy H. Calico, "The Politics of Opera in the German Democratic Republic, 1945–1961" (PhD diss., Duke University, 1999), 222–248. For essays regarding various aspects of Eisler's project see Peter Schweinhardt, ed., *Hanns Eislers Johann Faustus: 50 Jahre Nach Erscheinen des Operntexts 1952. Symposion* (Wiesbaden: Breitkopf und Härtel, 2005). The 1952 edition was reissued in 1996 with an afterword by Jürgen Schebera; Hans Bunge's 1983 publication of the 1952 libretto based on Eisler's corrections to that text forms the basis for Peter Palmer's English translation in Blake, *Hanns Eisler: A Miscellany*, 259–357. Regarding the cultural political crisis that followed publication of the libretto see Bunge, *Die Debatte um Hanns Eislers "Johann Faustus": Eine Dokumentation* (Berlin: Basisdruck, 1991).

98. For standardization purposes I have used the English titles that correspond to the translations in the Methuen edition of Brecht's works throughout this book. Editors John Willett and Ralph Manheim translate the title of this fragment as *Journeys of the God of Luck* in Brecht's *Journals*, but native German speakers advise that "Happiness" is more accurate in this context than "Luck." After consulting with Tom Kuhn, who confirmed that Methuen has no plans to publish translations of Brecht's fragments, I decided to depart from their usage in this instance and translate the title as "Happiness."

99. Heiner Müller, "Fatzer ± Keuner," *Brecht Yearbook/Brecht-Jahrbuch* 10 (1981): 15–21. Regarding the predecessors to and influence of Müller's statement see Stefan Mahlke, "Brecht ± Müller: German-German Brecht Images before and after 1989," *Drama Review* 43, no. 4 (1999): 40–49.

100. Marc Silberman, "Brecht Today," *Logos* 5, no. 3 (2006), http://www .logosjournal.com/issue_5.3/silberman.htm#_edn12#_edn12, accessed 10 June 2007.

101. Cavalieri's *Rappresentatione di Anima, et di Corpo* (1600), the first known play set entirely to music, is a dialogue between the Soul and the Body; Monteverdi's *Orfeo* (1607) opens with a prologue sung by Music; and the prologue of his *L'incoronazione di Poppea* (1643) features Virtue, Piety, and Love.

102. "Twenty years after completing *Baal* I was preoccupied with an idea (for an opera) related to the same basic theme." Foreword to the first volume of Brecht's collected plays, published in 1953, "Bei Durchsicht meiner ersten Stücke," *BFA* 23:241, translation in *Collected Plays* 1:370.

103. Much has been made of the fact that Brecht did not refer to Dessau as a collaborator, a title he reserved for Weill and Eisler only; some have concluded

that Dessau contributed little to their projects and was merely the musically trained vessel through which Brecht's desires were channeled. Certainly Dessau was more deferential than the other two, but it seems unlikely that theirs was an entirely one-sided relationship. Kowalke, "Brecht and Music: Theory and Practice," in *The Cambridge Companion to Brecht*, 223; Thomas R. Nadar, "Brecht and His Musical Collaborators," in *A Bertolt Brecht Reference Companion*, ed. Siegfried Mews (Westport, CT: Greenwood Press, 1997), 270. The most thorough study of this relationship, albeit ideologically straitjacketed, is Fritz Hennenberg, *Dessau-Brecht: Musikalische Arbeiten* (Berlin: Henschel, 1963). At times Brecht's assessment of Dessau as a composer was certainly less than charitable—in 1944 he described him as "much less developed [than Eisler] and tied up in routine"—and Dessau's posthumous reputation lags far behind that of the other two composers; *Journals*, entry for 6 November 1944. Nevertheless, work with Dessau dominated the last decade of Brecht's life.

104. Dessau published these in his collection of Brecht settings shortly after the playwright's death, *Lieder und Gesänge* (Berlin: Henschelverlag, 1957), 12–19.

105. There is a tantalizing reference to Johnny Appleseed in the Papers of Kurt Weill and Lotte Lenya (Irving S. Gilmore Library, Yale University), but no evidence that Weill ever discussed the subject with Brecht. Subseries IX.B, folder 71/21, contains a clipping entitled "Johnny Appleseed: A Radio Script about a Great American Pioneer" by Bernard C. Schoenfeld, published in *Scholastic Journal*, 16 September 1940, as well as nine additional pages of notes about Appleseed culled from other sources. Even if Brecht had known the story of Johnny Appleseed, it is unlikely that he would have known the current account, although he would certainly have appreciated the revisionism. Apparently Appleseed did not plant apple trees across the nation so that people could eat fruit but rather so that they could make alcoholic cider. He is credited with bringing healthy fruit to the frontier only after apple trees were destroyed by radical Prohibitionists and farmers developed a propaganda campaign to counter the fanaticism. See chapter 1 in Michael Pollan, *The Botany of Desire: A Plant's-Eye View of the World* (New York: Random House, 2002).

106. I am indebted to Claudia Schlee for assistance with this translation.

107. Dessau, *Lieder und Gesänge*, 20. According to Glaeser, no evidence of that complete text has been found and only a short scrap can be definitively dated to this period (*BFA* 10:1258). See also *BFA* 23:241–42.

108. Heiner Müller, *Theater-Arbeit* (Berlin: Rotbuch, 1975), 7–18. For critical commentary see Müller, *Die Stücke*, ed. Frank Hörnigk (Frankfurt am Main: Suhrkamp, 2000), 1:543–544. He later published several of the poems from the end of the fragment separately as free-standing texts. *A Heiner Müller Reader*, ed. and trans. Carl Weber (Baltimore: Johns Hopkins University Press, 2001), 67–79.

109. Müller, *Heiner Müller Reader*, 69. Stefan Mahlke chronicles the fate of Brecht's parable plays and notes that their decline in East Germany was necessitated by "a rhetorical understanding of the parable, which recognizes the

poetic text to be a medium to convey political ideas. Since the 70s, and especially after the fall of socialism, this assumed communication of messages is considered obsolete." Beginning in the 1970s, Brecht's "parable plays were not considered fully valid plays because their abstractness supposedly stood in the way of a full individualization of the characters." Mahlke, "Brecht ± Müller," 48 and 45, respectively.

110. Francine Maier-Schaeffer, "Écriture de fragment *Glücksgott* de Heiner Müller à la lumière de se savant-textes inédits," *Etudes Germaniques* 56, no. 3 (2001): 343–368.

111. Documents pertaining to DWV 313, as the Müller's *G. G.* project is designated, are in Paul-Dessau-Archiv (hereafter PDA) 1.74.829. These documents consist of fifteen folios typescript with handwritten annotations. They are undated, but PDA archivists have tentatively dated it 1960.

112. The *G. G.* project with Hacks is designated DWV 334. Documents pertaining to Hacks's treatment are PDA 1.74.830, 1.74.1444.1–3, 1.74.832.1–2, and 1.74.831.1–2. Hacks is relatively little known today, particularly when compared to Müller. The inclusion of an interview with Hacks in the 1985 anthology *Essays on German Theater* (ed. Margaret Herzfeld-Sander [New York: Continuum, 1985], 304–10) suggests that he was well-regarded at that time, but his reputation has suffered post-Wende.

113. I am grateful to Katrin Völkner, Cary Nathenson, Marc Silberman, and Claudia Schlee for assistance with the question of the Elks and Peter Hacks.

4. 'LUCULLUS': OPERA AND NATIONAL IDENTITY

1. This is distinct from the argument put forth by Wolfgang Emmerich, widely repeated, and then cogently refuted by Loren Kruger, in which East German culture is nothing more than "an instrument of the paternalist state." Kruger rightly notes that this assessment is more indicative of "the triumphal tenor of Cold War melodrama than to the actual complexity of GDR life," as will be seen in this chapter (Kruger, *Post-Imperial Brecht: Politics and Performance, East and South* [Cambridge: Cambridge University Press, 2004], 58). Her critique is of Emmerich's "Gleichzeitigkeit, Vormoderne und Postmoderne in der Literatur der DDR," in *Bestandsaufnahme Gegenwartsliteratur*, ed. Hans Ludwig Arnold (Munich: edition text + kritik, 1988), especially 199–200.

2. Kruger, *Post-Imperial Brecht*, 62. She quotes Heiner Müller regarding Brecht as mascot from "Fatzer ± Keuner," *Brecht Yearbook/Brecht-Jahrbuch* 10 (1981): 14–21.

3. Meredith A. Heiser-Duron argues that Brecht became a master strategist, and that by 1953 he was both "committed and cynical" with regard to the GDR and to the socialist project, a perspective not unrelated to my model of pleasing two audiences simultaneously. "Brecht's Political and Cultural Dilemma in the Summer of 1953," *Communications* 30 (June 2001): 48.

4. Richard Dellamora and Daniel Fischlin, eds., *The Work of Opera: Genre, Nationhood, and Sexual Difference* (New York: Columbia University Press,

1997), 3. See also Peter Csobádi and Gernot Gruber, eds., *Politische Mythen und nationale Identitäten im (Musik-)Theater: Vorträge und Gespräche des Salzburger Symposions 2001* (Anif/Salzburg: Verlag Mueller-Speiser, 2003). Also relevant in this context is Marina Frolova-Walker's research on the significance of opera for the Soviet project in " 'National in Form, Socialist in Content': Musical Nation-Building in the Soviet Republics," *Journal of the American Musicological Society* 51, no. 2 (1998): 339–352 in particular.

5. David Bathrick, *The Powers of Speech: The Politics of Culture in the GDR* (Lincoln: University of Nebraska Press, 1995), 42.

6. The Central Committee published "Für eine neue deutsche Nationaloper," *Neues Deutschland*, 1 November 1952.

7. See Emmerich, "Gleichzeitigkeit," 199–200, and Kruger's critique of this argument generally, *Post-Imperial Brecht*, 56–61. Marina Frolova-Walker argues that socialist realism, and its occasional music in particular, should be judged by different criteria because it was essentially the liturgical music for the ritual of an atheistic state religion. "Stalin and the Art of Boredom," *Twentieth-Century Music* 1, no. 1 (2004): 101–124.

8. For studies of socialist realism as a strict code too difficult to follow, see Régine Robin, *Socialist Realism: An Impossible Aesthetic*, trans. Catherine Porter (Stanford, CA: Stanford University Press, 1992); and Boris Grois, *The Total Art of Stalinism: Avant-Garde, Aesthetic Dictatorship, and Beyond*, trans. Charles Rougle (Princeton, NJ: Princeton University Press, 1992). For research on the destabilizing nature of socialist realism see Thomas Lahusen and Eugeny Dobrenko, eds., *Socialist Realism without Shores* (Durham, NC: Duke University Press, 1997).

9. Andrei Zhdanov, *Essays on Literature, Philosophy, and Music* (New York: International Publishers, 1950), 81.

10. The quotation is from a volume published by Soviet composers and musicologists in 1950 and published in German as *Die sowjetische Musik im Aufstieg: Eine Sammlung von Aufsätzen*, by Soiuz Kompozitorov SSSR, trans. Nathan Notowicz (Halle: Mitteldeutscher Verlag, 1952), 23. The longest chapter is entitled "The Primary Task of Soviet Composers: On Soviet Opera."

11. See especially Peter Davies and Stephen Parker, "Brecht, SED Cultural Policy and the Issue of Authority in the Arts: The Struggle for Control of the German Academy of the Arts," in *Bertolt Brecht: Centenary Essays*, ed. Steve Giles and Rodney Livingston (Amsterdam: Rodopi, 1998), 193.

12. See Norman Naimark, *The Russians in Germany: A History of the Soviet Zone of Occupation, 1945–1949* (Cambridge: Harvard University Press, 1995), 459–464. See also David Pike, *The Politics of Culture in Soviet-Occupied Germany, 1945–1949* (Stanford, CA: Stanford University Press, 1992), 582–612. Intellectuals were well aware of the situation, as is evident in a letter Eisler sent to Brecht from Prague: "They are waiting for you in Berlin, and you could really have everything there: theater, flat, car and chauffeur." Eisler to Brecht, 5 June 1948. BBA, Viktor S. Cohen Collection, VI.55.

13. Catherine Epstein, *The Last Revolutionaries: German Communists and Their Century* (Cambridge: Harvard University Press, 2003), 137.

14. Citizenship was not a simple matter. Many returning to eastern Germany had taken citizenship elsewhere in wartime and needed to have their German citizenship reinstated. Because the GDR was not officially recognized as a state in the West, its citizens could also have documented status from West Germany, or the federal Republic of Germany (FRG). I am grateful to Daniela Reinhold for clarifying Dessau's status in this context.

15. For a study of Jewish Communists in the GDR see Karin Hartewig, *Zurückgekehrt. Die Geschichte der jüdischen Kommunisten in der DDR* (Cologne: Böhlau, 2000). For a comprehensive pan-German approach, see Jay Howard Geller, *Jews in Post-Holocaust Germany, 1945–1953* (Cambridge: Cambridge University Press, 2005); and for a synopsis see Jeffrey Herf, *Divided Memory: The Nazi Past in the Two Germanys* (Cambridge: Harvard University Press, 1997), 69–161.

16. Herf, *Divided Memory*, 112.

17. Ibid., 108.

18. Epstein, *Last Revolutionaries,* 139.

19. The Mexico City enclave came under particular scrutiny for its pro-Jewish efforts during the war. It included prominent former SED member Paul Merker, who was not Jewish, and several others who were (Alexander Abusch, Erich Jungmann, and Leo Zuckermann). Regarding their pro-Jewish activities in Mexico City and their fate in the purges see Herf, *Divided Memory*, 40–68 and 106–161, respectively.

20. See Hans Bunge, ed., *Die Debatte um Hanns Eislers "Johann Faustus":
Eine Dokumentation* (Berlin: Basisdruck, 1991); and Peter Schweinhardt, ed., *Hanns Eislers "Johann Faustus": 50 Jahre nach Erscheinen des Operntexts 1952. Symposion* (Wiesbaden: Breitkopf and Härtel, 2005). See also Joy H. Calico, "'Für eine neue deutsche Nationaloper': Opera in the Discourses of Unification and Legitimation in the German Democratic Republic," in *Music and German National Identity,* ed. Celia Applegate and Pamela Potter (Chicago: University of Chicago Press, 2002), 190–204.

21. Gerhard Müller, "Zeitgeschichtliche Aspekte der *Lukullus*-Debatte," in *Paul Dessau: Von Geschichte gezeichnet,* ed. Klaus Angermann (Hofheim, Germany: Wolke, 1995), 148.

22. Roger Sessions, *The Trial of Lucullus* (New York: E. B. Marks Company, 1981).

23. Brecht revised the radio play further in 1949–50. Regarding the differences between these primary versions of the play see Brecht, *Collected Plays,* 4:373–391. The editors do not consider changes made to the libretto during the course of composing the opera, nor do they distinguish between the libretto entitled *Das Verhör des Lukullus* and the 1949–50 play of the same name, but they do note major differences between play versions and the final libretto. See also *BFA* 6:410–431.

24. These five settings are housed in the PDA, Akademie der Künste, Berlin.

The holdings of the PDA are cataloged in Daniela Reinhold, ed., *Paul Dessau, 1894–1979: Dokumente zu Leben und Werk* (Berlin: Henschel, 1995). For the texts to the 1940 radio play, the libretto for the March 1951 production, and the final libretto see *BFA* 6:87–173. Versions of the libretto in print are not always identical to intermediary versions of the text as set by Dessau.

25. Brecht was not the first twentieth-century German dramatist to put Lucullus on the stage, although earlier versions tended to play his reputation as comic parody. See Erik Meyer-Helmund, *Lucullus: Burleske Oper in 3 Akten frei nach A. von Kotzebue* (1908); and Dessau's cousin, operetta composer Max Winterfeld, known as Jean Gilbert, *Die Braut des Lucullus. Operette in 3 Akten von Rudolph Schanzer und Ernst Welisch* (1921). A cookbook by Friedrich J. Hampel, *Lucullus: Ein Handbuch der Wiener Kochkunst* (Vienna: R. Lechner, 1915), also took a lighthearted view of his reputation.

26. Joachim Lucchesi has collected valuable primary documents in *Debatte*. The introduction to that volume is published in an English translation by David W. Robinson in Joachim Lucchesi, "From Trial to Condemnation: The Debate over Brecht/Dessau's 1951 Opera *Lucullus*," *Contemporary Theatre Review* 4, no. 2 (1995): 13–21.

27. Kurt Bork to Stefan Heymann, 25 May 1950 (*Debatte* 31–33).

28. *Journals*, entry for 15 January 1951.

29. Brecht, "Zur Lukullus Oper," 1951 (*Debatte* 83).

30. "Ernst Hermann Meyer über *Das Verhör des Lukullus*," 12 March 1951 (*Debatte* 80). This language is remarkably similar to that which had been used in typical Nazi critiques of Jewish music, which highlights how quickly the tide turned against Jewish party members in the immediate postwar period.

31. *Debatte* 82.

32. Nina Freund's minutes (*Debatte* 83–101); Käthe Rülicke's minutes (*Debatte* 101–122).

33. Journalist Dieter Borkowski witnessed Honecker's instructions: "You have been called here because we are planning an action today that should teach a lesson to certain formalists and parasites among our artists. . . . I am speaking of Bertolt Brecht and Paul Dessau, who still have not broken with the alien tendencies of formalism and cosmopolitanism. . . . You will go to the opera tonight with free tickets, and at the intermission, you will give these decadent artists a proper chorus of whistles." Dieter Borkowski, *Für jeden kommt der Tag: Stationen einer Jugend in der DDR* (Frankfurt am Main: Suhrkamp, 1981), 329; translation by David W. Robinson in Lucchesi, "From Trial to Condemnation," 19.

34. Reprinted in *Debatte* 157. An emended version appeared in *Einheit* under the title "Der Kampf gegen den Formalismus in Kunst und Literatur, für eine fortschrittliche deutsche Kultur," *Einheit* 8–9 (1951). See also Elimar Schubbe, ed., *Dokumente zur Künste- Literatur- und Kulturpolitik der SED, 1946–1970* (Stuttgart: Seewald Verlag, 1972), 178–186. Excerpts of the speech were also published in *Neues Deutschland* on 23 March 1951 and are reprinted in *Debatte* 192–193.

35. Draft of Lauter's speech included with Protocol 37 of the Politbüro of the

SED Central Committee 6 March 1951 (*Debatte* 74). Tompkins notes that the speech Lauter delivered was written in consultation with Walter Ulbricht, the Politburo, and a Soviet political officer, Vladimir Semjonow. David Tompkins, "Composing the Party Line: Music and Politics in Poland and East Germany, 1948–1957" (PhD diss., Columbia University, 2004), 62 n. 148.

36. The quotation is from published excerpts in *Neues Deutschland*, 23 March 1951. "Auszüge aus dem Referat des Genossen Hans Lauter auf der 5. Tagung des ZK" (*Debatte* 192–193).

37. Werner Oehlmann, "Hinter verschlossenen Türen," *Der Tagesspiegel*, 20 March 1951 (*Debatte* 325–326).

38. H. H. Stuckenschmidt, "Dessau-Brecht: Das Verhör des Lukullus Uraufführung im Admiralspalast," *Die Neue Zeitung*, 21 March 1951 (*Debatte* 327–329).

39. Heinz Lüdecke, " 'Das Verhör des Lukullus': Ein mißlungenes Experiment in der Deutschen Staatsoper," *Neues Deutschland*, 22 March 1951 (*Debatte* 329–331).

40. Walter Lennig, "Brecht am Scheidewege: Der Dichter in dem Dilemma der 'fortschrittlichen Freiheit,' " *Die Welt*, 21 May 1951 (*Debatte* 333–334).

41. Reinhold, *Paul Dessau*, 97.

42. Rülicke notes in *Debatte* 226–227.

43. Ibid.

44. The PDA manuscript sources cited here are as follows: version 3 = 1.74.403.1–2 and 1.74.393–396; version 4 = 1.74.401.1–2 and 1.74.404–409; and version 5 = 1.74.411.1–2. The source of examples 2 and 3 can best be described as versions 2–4 = 1.74.1265.1. The source for examples 4, 5, and 6 = 1.74.411.2–3. Source of text for "Once upon a Time" is 1.74.407.2–3. I also consulted a conductor's score of version 4 (1.74.1266) and the prompter's score for that version (1.74.401.2). For a graphic representation of text changes, omissions, and additions among these versions see Reinhold, *Paul Dessau*, 199–208. The versions of the libretto that Dessau set as 1–4 do not correspond directly to published versions of the text. The most widely available score in print is a conflation of 4 and 5. It is cataloged as *Das Verhör des Lukullus* (Zurich: Ars Viva Verlag, 1965), but the title page bears the revised title.

45. *Debatte* 206, 211. Letters indicate that the revised text was enclosed, but those enclosures do not survive. Gerhard Müller has written that the change of title was the only revision party members demanded, but that position is contradicted by Reinhold's careful assembly of Dessau's various settings and the letters above (151 n. 6). His point that so much controversy resulted in such minimal alteration is well taken, however.

46. Text changes noted in *BFA* 6:416–417. The accompanying chart is a bit misleading because it reflects only changes in scene distribution and not changes in text content and conflates versions that are discrete in Dessau's settings identified above.

47. *Debatte* 88, 90–91. The purely literary changes are tracked in *BFA* 6:416–419, beginning with the radio play, which had no music.

48. See the editorial notes in *Collected Plays* 3:333–342.

49. Gerhard Müller, 147–148.

50. *BFA* 16:721–723.

51. This taped recording is occasionally broadcast on German radio, as on 1 May 2004 by Deutschlandfunk with discussion by Lucchesi and Friedrich Dieckmann.

52. Brecht referred to the role as that of a "buffo tenor, reminiscent of Julius Liban [sic]" (*BFA* 6:415). The singer was probably Julius Lieban (1857–1940), a member of the Berlin Court Opera Ensemble at the end of the nineteenth century. He began his career as a baritone and later became a tenor famous for his interpretation of Mime. He is best described as a character tenor and a popular teacher of heroic tenors in the 1920s and 1930s. I thank David Hamilton for this information.

53. Gerd Rienäcker, "Zu einigen Gestaltungsproblemen im Opernschaffen von Paul Dessau," in *Sammelbände zur Musikgeschichte der DDR*, ed. Hans Alfred Brockhaus and Konrad Niemann (Berlin: Verlag Neue Musik, 1971), 2:112. Also Rienäcker, "Brechts Einfluß auf die Oper. Gestaltungsmethoden im Bühnenwerk Paul Dessaus," *Musik und Gesellschaft* 26, no. 2 (1976): 71–76.

54. Rienäcker, "Gestaltungsprobleme," 115.

55. PDA 1.74.404.1 grouped with 1.74.404.2 and dated 27 February 1951. In one draft, Dessau reduced the Queen's aria to a simple strophic song with two verses and syllabic text setting in a low range. An additional sketch indicates that he considered omitting her aria entirely, and yet another features a simplified melodic line with ornate melismas on the syllable "ah" inserted between phrases of text. In version 3 he cut the third verse but returned to a more elaborate setting, and in versions 4 and 5 he eliminated the second verse.

56. For a representative collection of these responses see *Debatte* 339–370.

57. See correspondence between Rentzsch and a General Münzer in the summer of 1952, in which Rentzsch instructs him to prevent the planned production of *The Judgment* from taking place in Dresden (*Debatte* 281–283).

5. BRECHT'S LEGACY FOR OPERA

1. Susan Bennett, *Theatre Audiences: A Theory of Production and Reception*, 2nd ed. (London: Routledge, 1997).

2. Loren Kruger, *Post-Imperial Brecht: Politics and Performance, East and South* (Cambridge: Cambridge University Press, 2004), 43. She cites *BFA* 22:211–212, 401–402. References to English equivalents are to *BoT*, unless otherwise specified.

3. Of course, the defamiliarization of a canonical opera presupposes a certain universal opera-going experience with which a spectating audience member is already familiar. Those who bring that experience to a nonliteral staging of a canonical text such as Herheim's 2005 production of *La forza del destino* at the Staatsoper will engage with that event much differently than operagoers who have never seen that opera before or who have minimal exposure to opera in

general. This is not to say that the seasoned operagoer will necessarily *like* Herheim's production—in fact, quite the contrary is often the case—but it does mean that the experience is qualitatively different.

4. Opera with a capital "O" is borrowed from Lawrence Kramer, *Opera and Modern Culture: Wagner and Strauss* (Berkeley: University of California Press, 2004), 2–3.

5. Willmar Sauter, *The Theatrical Event: Dynamics of Performance and Perception* (Iowa City: University of Iowa Press, 2000), 2.

6. With regard to implicating and including the audience in an opera production, see Clemens Risi, "Shedding Light on the Audience: Hans Neuenfels and Peter Konwitschny Stage Verdi (and Verdians)," *Cambridge Opera Journal* 14 (2002): 201–210.

7. Directors in German opera houses showed an early proclivity for nonliteral stagings of canonical works that continues to this day, but now the phenomenon can be experienced on stages throughout Europe and North America as well. It has only recently begun to attract serious scholarly attention in addition to the usual media furor. The standard-bearer in such research will surely turn out to be David Levin, *Unsettling Opera: Staging Mozart, Verdi, Wagner, and Zemlinsky* (Chicago: University of Chicago Press, 2007). Manuel Brug's sweeping *Opernregisseure heute* (Leipzig: Henschel, 2006) surveys the work of 138 opera directors and provides a useful reference guide. See also the collection of interviews with fifteen (in)famous opera directors in *Warum Oper? Gespräche mit Opernregisseuren*, 2nd ed., ed. Barbara Beyer (Berlin: Alexander Verlag, 2007).

8. Gundula Kreuzer, "Voices from Beyond: *Don Carlos* and the Modern Stage," *Cambridge Opera Journal* 18, no. 2 (2006): 151.

9. In a lively discussion about Christoph Schlingensief's controversial production of *Parsifal* at Bayreuth in 2007, Steven Reale described the experience as that of watching two films simultaneously; one film was a traditional staging stored in his memory, and the other was the live performance unfolding before him. Schlingensief's liberal use of film in this production may have contributed to this formulation, but the analogy is apt nonetheless. I am aware that nonliteral stagings of canonical operas and the phenomenon of director's opera in general do not serve the needs of all operagoers. James Hepokoski speculates, "What most spectators hope for, I suspect, is simply another encounter with a work they love—a rich encounter with conventionalized spectacle, sumptuously and brilliantly performed." My argument pertains to those who are stimulated by the estrangement experience of a nonliteral staging. Hepokoski, "Operating Stagings: Positions and Paradoxes. A Reply to David J. Levin," in *Verdi 2001: Atti del Convegno Internazionale—Proceedings of the International Conference. Parma–New York–New Haven*, ed. Fabrizio Della Seta, Roberta Montemorra Marvin, and Marco Marica (Florence: Olschki, 2003), 482.

10. Louis Althusser, *For Marx*, trans. B. R. Brewster (New York: Verso, 1996), 129–152.

11. The term "spect-actor" is borrowed from the videogame industry and

gaming theory. The Microsoft system that allows people to join online games as spectators for Xbox 360 titles is advertised as "generat[ing] a spectactor experience in real time from a game or event, such as highlights, instant replays, and unique views of action within the game" (http://news.punchjump.com/article .php?id=2113). Brecht's theories of audience engagement have found some currency in videogame research. See Gonzalo Frasca, "Videogames of the Oppressed: Critical Thinking, Education, Tolerance, and Other Trivial Issues," in *First Person: New Media as Story, Performance, and Game*, ed. Pat Harrington and Noah Wardrip-Fruin (Cambridge: MIT Press, 2004), 85–94; and "Rethinking Agency and Immersion: Playing with Videogame Characters," in *Proceedings of SIGGRAPH 2001*, Art Gallery, Art and Culture Papers, 12–17 August 2001, Los Angeles. See www.siggraph.org/artdesign/gallery/S01/essays/0378 .pdf (accessed 22 May 2006).

12. Erika Fischer-Lichte, "Einleitende Thesen zum Aufführungsbegriff," in *Kunst der Aufführung—Aufführung der Kunst*, ed. Erika Fischer-Lichte, Clemens Risi, and Jens Roselt (Berlin: Theater der Zeit, 2004), 11–26.

13. Many scholars have noted that John Willett's unfortunate mistranslation of the word *"Verfremdung"* as "alienation" has drastically and negatively affected the reception of Brecht's work in the English-speaking world. Some have proposed the rather awkward "distanciation" as a more accurate substitute. Based on the first English translation of Brecht's first usage of the term, Loren Kruger suggests "disillusion." While acknowledging the legitimacy of that word in its most literal sense, its connotations of disappointment are counterproductive in much the same way as the negative implications of alienation. Therefore I use the more standard alternative "estrangement" and hope to demonstrate distanciation and disillusion in my analysis. Kruger, "Making Sense of Sensation: Enlightenment, Embodiment, and the End(s) of Modern Drama," *Modern Drama* 43, no. 4 (2000): 562 n. 5.

14. Regarding agency for the opera audience, see Kevin Amidon, " 'Oh show us . . .': Opera and/as Spectatorship in *Aufstieg und Fall der Stadt Mahagonny*," *Brecht Yearbook/Brecht-Jahrbuch* 29 (2004): 223–236.

15. Regarding Brecht's use of *Genuß*, see BoT 36, BFA 22:77, and regarding *Vergnügen*, see BoT 73, BFA 22:112. In the original German he also uses "lustvoll" and "fröhlich," neither of which carry the negative connotations of "Genuß." Fredric Jameson argues persuasively in favor of the utility of Brecht's method for pleasure in *Brecht and Method* (London: Verso, 1998). In this context see especially "Estrangements of the Estrangement-Effect," 35–42.

16. Clemens Risi describes something similar in his theory of audience experience, but not specifically as it pertains to estrangement: "Perception as it happens in performance (especially in opera) is always an oscillation or alternation between the intellectual/semiotic and the sensorial/performative dimension" (Risi, personal email, 22 May 2006).

17. Michael Patterson, "Brecht's Legacy," in *The Cambridge Companion to Brecht*, ed. Peter Thomson and Glendyr Sacks (Cambridge: Cambridge University Press, 1994), 276.

18. *Jacobellis v. Ohio,* 378 U.S. 184, 197 (1964).

19. Patterson, "Brecht's Legacy," 273 and 282, respectively.

20. Eric Bentley, "The Influence of Brecht," in *Re-interpreting Brecht: His Influence on Contemporary Drama and Film,* ed. Pia Kleber and Colin Visser (Cambridge: Cambridge University Press, 1990), 186.

21. Marc Silberman, "A Postmodernized Brecht?" *Theatre Journal* 45, no. 1 (1993): 2.

22. Andrzej Wirth, "Vom Dialog zum Diskurs: Versuch einer Synthese der nachbrechtschen Theaterkonzepte," *Theater heute* 1 (January 1980): 16.

23. Maarten van Dijk, "Blocking Brecht," in *Re-interpreting Brecht,* 121 and 204 n. 14, quoted in Patterson, "Brecht's Legacy," 285.

24. Patterson, "Brecht's Legacy," 280.

25. Hans-Thies Lehmann, *Postdramatic Theatre,* trans. Karen Jürs-Munby (London: Routledge, 2006), 29. Lehmann readily acknowledges the significance of Brecht's work but argues against the standard interpretation advanced by Peter Szondi, which maintained that epic theater was a new dramatic form that broke with tradition. Lehmann argues that "the theory of epic theatre constituted a *renewal and completion of classical dramaturgy*" because Brecht was still committed to "a highly traditionalist thesis: the *fable (story)* remained the *sine qua non* for him." In fact, Lehmann asserts, "Postdramatic theatre is a *post-Brechtian theatre*" (emphases in original, 33). The Peter Szondi reference is to his *Theory of Modern Drama,* ed. and trans. M. Hays (Minneapolis: University of Minnesota Press, 1987).

26. David Levin, "'Va, pensiero'? Verdi and Theatrical Provocation," in *Verdi 2001,* 470. Levin's paper and responses to it by Hepokoski, Pierluigi Petrobelli, and Risi are published in the same volume and comprise a valuable complex of ideas about opera production, performance, perception, and reception. A revised version of Levin's essay appears as chapter 5 in Levin, *Unsettling Opera.*

27. For example, reviews of John Doyle's 2005 Broadway revival of *Sweeney Todd* invoked the adjective "Brechtian" to describe the stark, sparsely appointed stage and the experience of attending a performance in which the actors also carried around and played instruments throughout. It is perhaps no surprise, then, to find that Doyle and two of the actors from that show (Patti LuPone and Audra McDonald) were engaged by Los Angeles Opera for a new production of *The Rise and Fall of the City of Mahagonny* in 2007.

28. "Performances are in dialogue with each other along a changing continuum, rather than just consenting to or denying one particular style"; and "The audience's prior experience is a crucial element in what Nattiez would call the 'esthetic' sphere of the 'total musical fact.'" James Treadwell, "Reading and Staging Again," *Cambridge Opera Journal* 10, no. 2 (1998): 218 and 219, respectively. Treadwell's essay is a response to David Levin's "Reading a Staging/ Staging a Reading," *Cambridge Opera Journal* 9, no. 1 (1997): 47–71. A revised version of this essay appears as chapter 2 in Levin, *Unsettling Opera.* In this important early exchange on the subject, the distinction between production and performance has not yet been established, but it is clear from context that Tread-

well's first reference pertains to a production rather than to a performance. Levin's observation that literal productions of canonical opera tended to dominate in the United States while nonliteral productions were primarily the purview of European opera houses is still true, if to a lesser degree than it was in the mid-1990s. A change may be at hand, however. The Metropolitan Opera in New York is under new leadership in the form of general manager Peter Gelb, and Gérard Mortier will take the helm at the neighboring New York City Opera when his contract expires with the Paris National Opera in 2009. Gelb has implemented an ambitious plan to engage theater directors in a series of new stagings, and Mortier brings a reputation for iconoclasm and daring stagecraft. If they succeed in reinventing their respective companies, it will represent a major sea change in the opera culture of the United States.

29. Levin, " 'Va, pensiero'?" 470, and *Unsettling Opera,* 165–167.

30. Levin discusses the fact that Wagner's operas have been vehicles for the most vociferous proponents of both schools of thought on directorial interpretation, one literal and one critical, in "Reading a Staging," 47–61, and *Unsettling Opera,* 37–58. For more on that history see Patrick Carnegy, *Wagner and the Art of the Theatre* (New Haven, CT: Yale University Press, 2006).

31. "If instead one sweeps away all the costuming and has the participants, copying the practices of contemporary dance, dressed in sweat suits or even timeless outfits, one cannot avoid asking, what's the point? Why even bother doing it on stage? One wants to spare Mozart from this." Theodor W. Adorno, "Opera and the Long-Playing Record," in *Essays on Music,* ed. Richard Leppert, trans. Susan H. Gillespie (Berkeley: University of California Press, 2002), 284. The essay first appeared in *Der Spiegel* in 1969.

32. See for example James Hepokoski, "Operating Stagings," 480.

33. Treadwell, "Reading and Staging Again," 208.

34. I am overstating the case for the sake of argument. Obviously the scores of canonical operas do not indicate, for example, how long the conductor should wait for applause to subside after a favorite aria, nor do they dictate the precise duration of the silence that often follows significant cadences, fermatas, and so forth. These unscripted interruptions and silences are part of the aural ephemera essential to the experience of live performance but are absent from the inherited texts that form the basis of that performance.

35. I am indebted to John A. McCarthy, Roger Bechtel, and Marvin Carlson for guidance with regard to the tradition of *Regiebücher* in nonoperatic German theater and to David Rosen and Evan Baker for counsel regarding the tradition of the production book that is specific to opera.

36. Peter Brooker, "Key Words in Brecht's Theory and Practice of Theater," in *The Cambridge Companion to Brecht,* 2nd ed., ed. Peter Thomson and Glendyr Sacks (Cambridge: Cambridge University Press, 2006), 211.

37. For example, see Marna King, "The Model and Its Mutations in FRG Brecht Productions," *Gestus—the Electronic Journal of Brechtian Studies* 2, no. 3 (1986): 187–197.

38. David Rosen, "The Staging of Verdi's Operas: An Introduction to the Ricordi Disposizioni Sceniche," in *Report of the Twelfth Congress of the International Musicological Society 1977,* ed. Daniel Heartz and Bonnie Wade (Kassel: Bärenreiter, 1981), 446–447.

39. Roger Parker, *Remaking the Song: Operatic Visions and Revisions from Handel to Berio* (Berkeley: University of California Press, 2006).

40. In his assessment of Susan Bennett's *Theatre Audiences,* Neil Blackadder describes her work as "one of the most thorough examinations of the spectators' role . . . drawing on reception theory and other studies of reading and viewing." His primary point is that her work assumes a "passive, well-disposed audience" but does not account for "spectators who fail, or decline to play the role assigned to them in Bennett's model," as he does. Note the emphasis on audience members as *spectators* and not as listeners. Blackadder, *Performing Opposition: Modern Theater and the Scandalized Audience* (Westport, CT: Praeger, 2003), xiii–xiv. Another important aspect of spectatorship that I do not address in this chapter is gender; see Viv Gardner, "The Invisible Spectactrice: Gender, Geography, and Theatrical Space," in *Women, Theatre, and Performance: New Histories, New Historiographies,* ed. Maggie B. Gale and Gardner (Manchester, England: Manchester University Press, 2000), 25–45.

41. Recuperating the sonic component in theoretical discussions of opera is central to Abbate's entire project and can be traced as a thread running throughout her work. Most recently see "Music—Drastic or Gnostic?" *Critical Inquiry* 30 (2004): 505–536. For critiques of Abbate see Karol Berger, "Musicology According to Don Giovanni; or, Should We Get Drastic?" *Journal of Musicology* 22, no. 3 (2005): 490–501; and Michelle Duncan, "The Operatic Scandal of the Singing Body: Voice, Presence, Performativity," *Cambridge Opera Journal* 16, no. 3 (2004): 283–306. Duncan notes that other disciplines are generating models for this that address "the discrepancy between the 'metaphorisation of the voice' and 'its material articulation and audibility,' especially as media theory has granted agency to forms of media other than the scriptural and the technological" (284).

42. Sauter, *Theatrical Event,* 3.

43. Brecht recognized this, too. As discussed in chapter 1, he declared the continuous music of Wagner's music drama to be the source of its irrationality because the music could overpower an audience. When he eventually ceded the location of gestus to music he was confronted with the fact that sung music gives rise to the voice-object (chapter 2), and it is capable of displacing the primacy of the literary text in performance. And despite his repeated advocacy of music in the theater, Brecht's theoretical writings about the optimal audience experience privilege the visual to an extraordinary extent; consider the term *Zuschaukunst* (art of spectating), which he coined for the project of the audience. In fact, he wrote very little about the desired audience response to sound or music. (He also wrote remarkably little about hostile audience response,

despite his considerable experience with it as audience member, director, and playwright.) Blackadder, *Performing Opposition*, 175.

44. Durk Talsma, Tracy J. Doty, and Mary G. Woldorff, "Selective Attention and Audiovisual Integration: Is Attending to Both Modalities a Prerequisite for Early Integration?" *Cerebral Cortex* 17, no. 3 (2007): 679.

45. Ibid.

46. In his review of *Making Sense of Aristotle: Essays in Poetics* (London: Duckworth, 2001), edited by Oivind Andersen and Jon Haarberg, Andrew Ford observes the following about M. S. Silk's contribution to that volume: "[Silk] then turns to Brecht, appropriately seeing in his diametrically anti-Aristotelian views a conspicuous bearer of the *Poetics* into the twentieth century. Brecht's 'estrangement' was antithetical to neo-classical and romantic notions of catharsis." Silk, "Aristotle, Rapin, Brecht," 173–196. Ford, review of *Making Sense of Aristotle: Essays in Poetics, Bryn Mawr Classical Review* 20, 12 December 2002, http://ccat.sas.upenn.edu/bmcr/2002/2002–12–20.html (accessed 1 April 2006).

47. *BoT* 44, *BFA* 24:59.

48. *BoT* 8, *BFA* 21:134.

49. *BoT* 39, *BFA* 24:81.

50. *BoT* 9, *BFA* 21:135.

51. *BoT* 44, *BFA* 24:59.

52. Carolin Duttlinger has written that "various cultural anxieties first crystallized in what was perceived to be a widespread crisis of attention" during the Weimar Republic. She traces the themes of distraction *(Zerstreuung)* and attention *(Aufmerksamkeit)* in Benjamin's work and situates them within this larger context of anxiety. Duttlinger, "Between Contemplation and Distraction: Configurations of Attention in Walter Benjamin," *German Studies Review* 30, no. 1 (2007): 33.

53. Kruger, "Making Sense," 549.

54. Thomas J. Csórdas, "Somatic Modes of Attention," *Cultural Anthropology* 8, no. 2 (1993): 135–156 (cited in Fischer-Lichte, "Einleitende," 23).

55. Csórdas, "Somatic Modes," 138.

56. Cognitive psychologist Durk Talsma of the Vrije Universiteit in Amsterdam sees this theory as loosely related to the premotor theory of attention. Attention theories have focused on the moment in time at which selection takes place, some advocating early selection and others late selection. Both forms are probably involved. One theory explaining how and why we choose what we will attend to is the premotor theory of attention, which states that attention shifts to those objects to which we want it to shift. Personal correspondence with author, 28 May 2006.

57. Talsma, Doty, and Woldorff, "Selective Attention," 689.

58. Csórdas, "Somatic Modes," 138.

59. Robert Jordan, "Visual Aids," *Opera Canada* 42, no. 2 (2001): 20–22.

60. The *Cambridge Opera Journal* exchange between Levin and Treadwell regarding whether an operagoer "reads" an opera staging remains a fascinating

one. The rapprochement between semiotics and phenomenology suggests that one can do both—that is, read the signs analytically and watch the production for aesthetic purposes. Neither Levin nor Treadwell considers the act of *literally* reading (at) the opera, as is the case with supertitles.

61. Personal correspondence with Joe Lappin, emeritus professor of psychology, Vanderbilt Vision Research Center, 25 May 2006.

62. This insight is from Nancy Goldsmith, who generously shared information about her work as a titlist.

63. Levin, "Reading a Staging," 58, and *Unsettling Opera*, 52.

64. Ibid.

65. *BoT* 44, *BFA* 24:59.

66. David Levin's most valuable contribution to research on nonliteral productions of canonical opera lies in the area of dramaturgical analysis. His project includes the development of a "variegated vocabulary with which to assess [opera] productions, be they of familiar works or unknown ones . . . be they experimental . . . or conventional" (*Unsettling Opera*, xvii). It is hoped that my theory about the work of individual spectating audience members engaged with opera can act as a complement to Levin's analysis.

67. As a last resort, a sufficiently scandalized audience will exercise its agency by refusing to participate in the performance according to any of the culturally defined "available behaviors." James H. Johnson, *Listening in Paris* (cited in Blackadder, *Performing Opposition*, xvi). "A vituperative reaction to a radical staging is then at least always in part an attempt by the spectator to reassert his domination over the things of the world" (Duncan, "Operatic Scandal," 301).

68. See Levin's account of Bieito's *Entführung* in *Unsettling Opera*, xii–xiv. Mary Hunter has noted Mozart's susceptibility to alienation in an essay she wrote with Wye Jamison Allanbrook and Gretchen A. Wheelock entitled "Staging Mozart's Women," in *Siren Songs: Representations of Gender and Sexuality in Opera*, ed. Mary Ann Smart (Princeton, NJ: Princeton University Press, 2000), 59.

69. Clemens Risi, "Rhythm, Sense, and Sensibility: Performance Rhythms" (paper presented to the Music Theater Working Group of the International Federation for Theater Research, Saint Petersburg, July 2004). Published in German as "Am Puls der Sinne. Der Rhythmus einer Opernaufführung zwischen Repräsentation und Präsenz—zu Mozart-Inszenierungen von Calixto Bieito und Thomas Bischoff," in *TheorieTheaterPraxis*, ed. Hajo Kurzenberger and Annemarie Matzke (Berlin: Theater der Zeit, 2004), 117–127.

70. See for example Abbate's response to Ben Heppner's struggles in a particular performance of *Meistersinger* in "Drastic or Gnostic?" 535. Duncan cites Ruth Berghaus's *Pelléas et Mélisande* in her sophisticated theorization of performativity, but that account is generalized rather than specific (Duncan, "Operatic Scandal," 305–306).

71. A brief synopsis of the notoriously convoluted 1862 plot of *La forza del destino* may be of use. Leonora and her Peruvian lover Alvaro are poised to elope when they are discovered by her father. In the ensuing mayhem Alvaro

accidentally kills the father, and the lovers go on the lam. Eighteen months pass, during which time they get separated in flight; Leonora's brother Carlo pursues them in search of revenge. Leonora finds shelter with a community of monks and lives as an ascetic. Meanwhile Alvaro saves Carlo from would-be assassins and, unaware of one another's true identity, they pledge eternal brotherhood. Once they learn the truth, Carlo renews his oath for revenge. Alvaro, loath to kill yet another member of Leonora's family, takes refuge in the monastery. Eventually the two men duel. Carlo is mortally wounded and when Leonora approaches, he stabs his sister. She dies in Alvaro's arms, and then he kills himself.

72. This case, in which the later, revised version of the opera has become the standard, is rather the opposite of the crisis occasioned by Cecilia Bartoli's decision to substitute arias in *Le nozze di Figaro* at the Met. Parker, *Remaking the Song*, 42–66.

73. My sense that the staging of the audience for itself is a provocative if not outright aggressive maneuver was confirmed in August 2007, when I attended a performance of Katharina Wagner's production of *Der Meistersinger* at Bayreuth. Numerous reviewers criticized her staging for the ways in which it drew attention to the particularly problematic connection between the festival, *Meistersinger*, and the Third Reich, but I wondered if the ferocity of the resistance was exacerbated by her unflattering staging of the Bayreuth audience for itself in the finale.

74. Regarding the blood sport of diva worship in which singers are alternately adored and destroyed by the public see Ethan Mordden's *Demented: The World of the Opera Diva* (New York: Franklin Watts, 1984). Susan McClary refers to this in her foreword to Catherine Clément's *Opera; or, The Undoing of Women*, trans. Betsy Wing (Minneapolis: University of Minnesota Press, 1988), xvi.

75. Naturally, such nonliteral stagings of canonical operas are not universally admired. Detractors decry the hubris of directors who pursue their own ideas to the detriment of the score, libretto, or both, and even the most ardent admirer will concede that some nonliteral productions are ill considered.

76. Because I was inclined to reinterpret some of those moments after I gathered additional information in the weeks that followed, the descriptions above are based on notes I took that evening. Those initial responses are far less cogent than the layers of interpretation that followed, but they are as close to the performance experience as ekphrasis can be.

77. Alex Meier-Dörzenbach was extremely generous in his willingness to respond to e-mail queries about the production. He also facilitated contact with Jörn Weisbrodt, head of Artistic Production Special Projects at the Staatsoper, who kindly provided me with the *La forza Premierenspiegel* packet from their press office.

Bibliography

Abbate, Carolyn. *In Search of Opera.* Princeton, NJ: Princeton University Press, 2001.

———. "Music—Drastic or Gnostic?" *Critical Inquiry* 30, no. 3 (2004): 505–537.

———. "Opera; or, The Envoicing of Women." In *Musicology and Difference*, edited by Ruth A. Solie, 225–258. Berkeley: University of California Press, 1993.

———. *Unsung Voices: Opera and Musical Narrative in the Nineteenth Century.* Princeton, NJ: Princeton University Press, 1991.

Ackerman, Alan, and Martin Puchner, eds. *Against Theatre: Creative Destructions on the Modernist Stage.* New York: Palgrave Macmillan, 2006.

Adlington, Robert. "Louis Andriessen, Hanns Eisler and the Lehrstück." *Journal of Musicology* 21, no. 3 (2004): 381–417.

Adorno, Theodor W. *Essays on Music.* Edited by Richard Leppert. Translated by Susan H. Gillespie. Berkeley: University of California Press, 2002.

———. *Gesammelte Schriften.* Edited by Rolf Tiedemann. Frankfurt am Main: Suhrkamp, 1997.

Albright, Daniel. *Untwisting the Serpent: Modernism in Music, Literature, and Other Arts.* Chicago: University of Chicago Press, 2000.

Allanbrook, Wye Jamison, Mary Hunter, and Gretchen A. Wheelock. "Staging Mozart's Women." In *Siren Songs: Representations of Gender and Sexuality in Opera*, edited by Mary Ann Smart, 47–66. Princeton, NJ: Princeton University Press, 2000.

Allen, Ray, and George P. Cunningham. "Cultural Uplift and Double Consciousness: African American Responses to the 1935 Opera *Porgy and Bess.*" *Musical Quarterly* 88, no. 3 (2005): 342–369

Alter, Nora M., and Lutz Koepnick, eds. *Sound Matters. Essays on the Acoustics of Modern German Culture.* New York: Berghahn Books, 2004.

Althusser, Louis. *For Marx.* Translated by B. R. Brewster. New York: Verso, 1996.

Amidon, Kevin. " 'Oh show us . . .': Opera and/as Spectatorship in *Aufstieg und*

Fall der Stadt Mahagonny." *Brecht Yearbook/Brecht-Jahrbuch* 29 (2004): 223–236.

Auslander, Philip. "Musical Personae." *Drama Review* 50, no. 1 (2006): 100–119.

Bahr, Ehrhard. *Weimar on the Pacific: German Exile Culture in Los Angeles and the Crisis of Modernism.* Berkeley: University of California Press, 2007.

Bahr, Gisela E. "*Roundheads and Peakheads:* The Truth about Evil Times." In *Essays on Brecht,* edited by Gisela E.Bahr, 141–155. Chapel Hill: University of North Carolina Press, 1974.

———, ed. *Die Rundköpfe und die Spitzköpfe. Bühnenfassung, Einzelszenen, Varianten.* Frankfurt am Main: Suhrkamp, 1979.

Bai, Ronnie. "Dances with Mei Lanfang: Brecht and the Alienation Effect." *Comparative Drama* 32, no. 3 (1998): 389–433.

Balme, Christopher. "Editorial." *Theatre Research International* 29, no. 1 (2004): 1–3.

Barnett, David. "Heiner Müller As the End of Brechtian Dramaturgy." *Theatre Research International* 27, no. 1 (2002): 49–57.

Barranger, M. S. "The Shape of Brecht's *Duchess of Malfi.*" *Comparative Drama* 12, no. 1 (1978): 61–74.

Barthes, Roland. *Image/Music/Text.* Translated by Stephen Heath. New York: Hill and Wang, 1977.

Bathrick, David. "Agitproptheater in der DDR: Auseinandersetzung mit der Tradition." In *DDR-Dramatik,* edited by Ulrich Profitlich, 128–149. Frankfurt am Main: Suhrkamp, 1987.

———. "A One-Sided History: Brecht's Hitler Plays." In *Literature and History,* edited by Leonard Schulze and Walter Wetzels, 181–196. Lanham, MD: University Press of America, 1983.

———. *The Powers of Speech: The Politics of Culture in the GDR.* Lincoln: University of Nebraska Press, 1995.

———, and Andreas Huyssen. "Producing Revolution: Heiner Müller's *Mauser* as Learning Play." *New German Critique* 8 (Spring 1976): 110–121.

Bauer, Oswald Georg. "Das Sichtbare in der Oper." In *Oper von innen: Produktionsbedingungen des Musiktheaters,* edited by Udo Bermbach and Wulf Konold, 135–182. Berlin: Dietrich Reimer Verlag, 1993.

Baum, Ute. *Bertolt Brechts Verhältnis zu Shakespeare.* Berlin: Brecht-Zentrum der DDR, 1998.

Bauman, Mordecai, and Irma Commanday. "In Praise of Learning: Encounters with Hanns Eisler." *Brecht Yearbook/Brecht-Jahrbuch* 26 (2001): 14–33.

Baumbach, Gerda. "Die Maske und die Bestie oder Die Primitivität der westlichen Schauspielkunst. Brechts Verwendung von Theatermasken." *Maske und Kothurn* 42, nos. 2–4 (2000): 209–240.

Benjamin, Walter. *Gesammelte Schriften.* Edited by Rolf Tiedemann and Hermann Schweppenhäuser. 7 vols. Frankfurt am Main: Suhrkamp, 1972–89.

———. *Understanding Brecht.* Translated by Anna Bostock. New York: Verso, 2003.

Bennett, Susan. *Theatre Audiences: A Theory of Production and Reception*. 2nd ed. London: Routledge, 1997.

Bentley, Eric. *Bentley on Brecht*. Rev. 2nd ed. New York: Applause, 1999.

———. *The Brecht Commentaries*. New York: Grove Press, 1981.

———. "The Influence of Brecht." In *Re-interpreting Brecht: His Influence on Contemporary Drama and Film*, edited by Pia Kleber and Colin Visser, 186–195. Cambridge: Cambridge University Press, 1990.

Berg-Pan, Renate. *Bertolt Brecht und China*. Bonn: Bouvier, 1979.

Berger, Karol. "Musicology According to Don Giovanni; or, Should We Get Drastic?" *Journal of Musicology* 22, no. 3 (2005): 490–501.

Bertrand, Daisy, and Carolyn Drake. "The Quest for Universals in Temporal Processing in Music." *Annals of the New York Academy of Sciences* 930 (June 2001): 17–27.

Betz, Albrecht. *Exil und Engagement: Deutsche Schriftsteller im Frankreich der dreißiger Jahre*. Munich: edition text + kritik, 1986.

———. *Hanns Eisler: Musik einer Zeit, die sich eben bildet*. Munich: edition text + kritik, 1976.

———. *Hanns Eisler, Political Musician*. Translated by Bill Hopkins. Cambridge: Cambridge University Press, 1982.

Beyer, Barbara, ed. *Warum Oper? Gespräche mit Opernregisseuren*. 2nd ed. Berlin: Alexander Verlag, 2007.

Bienert, Martin. *Mit Brecht durch Berlin: Ein literarischer Reiseführer*. Frankfurt am Main: Insel, 1998.

Blackadder, Neil. *Performing Opposition: Modern Theater and the Scandalized Audience*. Westport, CT: Praeger, 2003.

Blake, David, ed. *Hanns Eisler: A Miscellany*. New York: Harwood Academic Publishers, 1995.

Blasius, Leslie David. "Nietzsche, Riemann, Wagner: When Music Lies." In *Music Theory and Natural Order from the Renaissance to the Early Twentieth Century*, edited by Suzannah Clark and Alexander Rehding, 93–107. Cambridge: Cambridge University Press, 2001.

Boal, Augusto. *Legislative Theatre: Using Performance to Make Politics*. Routledge: London, 1998.

———. *Theatre of the Oppressed*. Translated by Charles McBride and Maria-Odilia Leal McBride. New York: Urizen, 1979.

Bodek, Richard. *Proletarian Performance in Weimar Berlin: Agitprop, Chorus and Brecht*. Columbia, SC: Camden, 1997.

Bogle, Donald. *Toms, Coons, Mulattoes, Mammies and Bucks: An Interpretive History of Blacks in American Films*. 4th edition. New York: Continuum, 2001.

Bollag, Burton. "Dramatic Intervention." *Chronicle of Higher Education* 48, no. 41 (21 June 2002): A48.

Bone, Robert A. *The Negro Novel in America*. New Haven, CT: Yale University Press, 1965.

Borkowski, Dieter. *Für jeden kommt der Tag: Stationen einer Jugend in der DDR*. Frankfurt am Main: Suhrkamp, 1981.

Borwick, Susan. "Weill's and Brecht's Theories on Music in Drama." *Journal of Musicological Research* 4, nos. 1–2 (1982): 39–67.

Bradley, Laura. *Brecht and Political Theatre:"The Mother" on Stage*. Oxford: Clarendon Press, 2006.

Brecht, Bertolt. *Arbeitsjournal*. Vols. 1 and 2. Edited by Werner Hecht. Frankfurt am Main: Suhrkamp Verlag, 1973.

———. *Brecht on Art and Politics*. Edited by Tom Kuhn and Steve Giles. Translated by Laura Bradley, Steve Giles, and Tom Kuhn. London: Methuen, 2003.

———. *Brecht on Theatre: The Development of an Aesthetic*. Edited and translated by John Willett. New York: Hill and Wang, 1992.

———. *Collected Plays*. Edited and translated by John Willett, Ralph Manheim, and Tom Kuhn. 8 vols. London: Methuen, 1994–2004.

———. *Diaries, 1920–1922*. Edited by Herta Ramthun. Translated by John Willett. New York: St. Martin's Press, 1979.

———. *Die Dreigroschenoper. Der Erstdruck 1928 mit einem Kommentar von Joachim Lucchesi*. Frankfurt am Main: Suhrkamp, 2004.

———. *Journals, 1934–1955*. Edited by John Willett. Translated by Hugh Rorrison. New York: Routledge, 1996.

———. *Letters*. Edited by John Willett. Translated by Ralph Manheim. New York: Routledge, 1990.

———. *Die Maßnahme: Das Exemplar eines Kritikers von der Uraufführung am 13.12.1930*. Transcribed and edited with commentary by Reinhard Krüger. Berlin: Weidler Buchverlag, 2001.

———. *Die Maßnahme: Kritische Ausgabe mit einer Spielanleitung von Reiner Steinweg*. Edited by Reiner Steinweg. Frankfurt am Main: Suhrkamp, 1972.

———. *Die Maßnahme: Zwei Fassungen: Anmerkungen*. Edited by Judith Wilke. Frankfurt am Main: Suhrkamp, 1998.

———. *Der Untergang des Egoisten Johann Fatzer*. Edited by Heiner Müller. Frankfurt am Main: Suhrkamp, 1994.

———. *Werke. Große kommentierte Berliner und Frankfurter Ausgabe*. Edited by Werner Hecht, Jan Knopf, Werner Mittenzwei, and Klaus-Detlef Müller. 30 vols. Berlin: Aufbau Verlag; Frankfurt am Main: Suhrkamp Verlag, 1988–2003.

———, and Lion Feuchtwanger. *Bertolt Brecht: Leben und Werk im Bild. Mit autobiographischen Texten, ein Zeittafel und einem Essay*. Edited by Werner Hecht. Leipzig: Gustav Kiepenheuer Verlag, 1981.

———, and Hanns Eisler. *The Brecht-Eisler Song Book*. Edited and translated by Eric Bentley. New York: Oak Publications, 1967.

Breithaupt, Fritz. "Inversion der Tautologie: Die Waage und die Gerechtigkeit in *Die Rundköpfe und die Spitzköpfe*." *Brecht Yearbook/Brecht-Jahrbuch* 18 (1993): 85–103.

Brewer, Mary F. *Staging Whiteness*. Middlebury, CT: Wesleyan University Press, 2005.

Briner, Andre. *Paul Hindemith*. Mainz: Schott, 1971.

Brock, Hella. "Brechts Bedeutung für die Musikerziehung." *Musik und Gesellschaft* 28, no. 2 (1978): 72–78.

Brooker, Peter. "Key Words in Brecht's Theory and Practice of Theatre." In *The Cambridge Companion to Brecht*, 2nd ed., edited by Peter Thomson and Glendyr Sacks, 209–224. Cambridge: Cambridge University Press, 2006.

Browder, Laura. *Rousing the Nation: Radical Culture in Depression America*. Amherst: University of Massachusetts Press, 1998.

Brown, Hilda Meldrum. *Leitmotiv and Drama: Wagner, Brecht, and the Limits of "Epic" Theatre*. Oxford: Clarendon Press, 1991.

Brown, Nicholas. "People's Theater in East Africa: The Lehrstücke of Ngugi wa Thiongio." *Communications* 27, no. 1 (1998): 23–27.

Brug, Manuel. *Opernregisseure heute*. Leipzig: Henschel, 2006.

Bryant-Bertail, Sarah. *Space and Time in Epic Theater: The Brechtian Legacy*. Rochester, NY: Camden House, 2000.

Buck, Theo. *Brecht und Diderot oder über Schwierigkeiten der Rationalität in Deutschland*. Tübingen, Germany: Niemeyer, 1971.

Bunge, Hans, ed. *Die Debatte um Hanns Eislers "Johann Faustus": Eine Dokumentation*. Berlin: Basisdruck, 1991.

Burkholder, Peter. *All Made of Tunes: Charles Ives and the Uses of Musical Borrowing*. New Haven, CT: Yale University Press, 1995.

Busoni, Ferruccio. *Entwurf einer neuen Ästhetik der Tonkunst*. 2nd ed. Edited by Martina Weindel. Wilhelmshaven, Germany: Verlag der Heinrichshofen-Bücher, 2001.

———. *The Essence of Music, and Other Papers*. Translated by Rosamond Ley. New York: Dover Publications, 1957.

———. "Sketch of a New Esthetic of Music." In *Three Classics in the Aesthetic of Music*, translated Theodore Baker, 73–102. New York: Dover Publications, 1962.

———. *Von der Macht der Töne: Ausgewählte Schriften*. Leipzig: Verlag Philip Reclam, 1983.

Byford, Andy. "The Figure of the 'Spectator' in the Theoretical Writings of Brecht, Diderot, and Rousseau." *Symposium: A Quarterly Journal in Modern Literatures* 56, no. 1 (2002): 25–42.

Cahn, Geoffrey S. "Weimar Music in America: Its Reception and Impact." *Centennial Review* 29, no. 2 (Spring 1985): 186–204.

Calico, Joy H. "Brecht and His Composer/Eisler and His Librettist." *Communications* 34 (June 2005): 67–72.

———. "Brecht on Opera and/in the Americas." *Opera Quarterly* 22, no. 3 (forthcoming).

———. "'Für eine neue deutsche Nationaloper': Opera in the Discourses of Unification and Legitimation in the German Democratic Republic." In *Music and German National Identity*, edited by Celia Applegate and Pamela Potter, 190–204. Chicago: University of Chicago Press, 2002.

———. "The Politics of Opera in the German Democratic Republic, 1945–1961." PhD diss., Duke University, 1999.

Carnegy, Patrick. *Wagner and the Art of the Theatre*. New Haven, CT: Yale University Press, 2006.

Chen, Huimin. *Inversion of Revolutionary Ideals: A Study of the Tragic Essence of Georg Büchner's "Dantons Tod," Ernst Toller's "Masse Mensch," and Bertolt Brecht's "Die Maßnahme."* New York: Peter Lang, 1998.

Chiaromonte, Nicola. *The Worm of Consciousness and Other Essays*. New York: Harcourt Brace Jovanovich, 1976.

Cicora, Mary A. *Wagner's "Ring" and German Drama: Comparative Studies in Mythology and History in Drama*. Westport, CT: Greenwood Press, 1999.

Clément, Catherine. *Opera; or, The Undoing of Women*. Translated by Betsy Wing. Minneapolis: University of Minnesota Press, 1988.

Cohen, Robert. "Brechts ästhetische Theorie in den ersten Jahren des Exils." In *Ästhetiken des Exils*, edited by Helga Schreckenberger, 55–70. Amsterdam: Rodopi, 2003.

Cook, Bruce. *Brecht in Exile*. New York: Holt, Rinehart, and Winston, 1983.

Cotterill, Rowland. "In Defence of *Mahagonny*." In *Culture and Society in the Weimar Republic*, edited by Keith Bullivant, 190–200. Manchester, England: Manchester University Press, 1977.

Cruse, Harold. *The Crisis of the Negro Intellectual*. New York: Morrow, 1967.

Csobádi, Peter, and Gernot Gruber, eds. *Das Fragment im (Musik-) Theater, Zufall und/oder Notwendigkeit? Vorträge und Gespräche des Salzburger Symposions 2002*. Anif/Salzburg, Austria: Mueller-Speiser, 2005.

———, eds. *Politische Mythen und nationale Identitäten im (Musik-)Theater: Vorträge und Gespräche des Salzburger Symposions 2001*. Anif/Salzburg, Austria: Mueller-Speiser, 2003.

Csórdas, Thomas J. "Somatic Modes of Attention." *Cultural Anthropology* 8, no. 2 (1993): 135–156.

Dahlhaus, Carl. "'Am Text entlang komponiert.' Bemerkungen zu einem Schlagwort." In *Für und wider die Literaturoper*, edited by Sigrid Wiesmann, 185–195. Laaber, Germany: Laaber Verlag, 1982.

———. *Die Bedeutung des Gestischen in Wagners Musikdramen*. Munich: R. Oldenbourg, 1970.

———. "Traditionelle Dramaturgie in der modernen Oper." In *Musiktheater heute: Sechs Kongreßbeiträge*, edited by Hellmut Kühn, 20–33. Mainz: Schott, 1982.

Davies, David. *Art as Performance*. Malden, MA: Blackwell Publishing, 2004.

Davies, Peter, and Stephen Parker. "Brecht, SED Cultural Policy and the Issue of Authority in the Arts: The Struggle for Control of the German Academy of the Arts." In *Bertolt Brecht: Centenary Essays*, edited by Steve Giles and Rodney Livingston, 181–195. Amsterdam: Rodopi, 1998.

Davies, Stephen. *Musical Works and Performances: A Philosophical Exploration*. Oxford: Clarendon Press, 2001.

Davis, Tracy C., and Thomas Postlewait, eds. *Theatricality*. Cambridge: Cambridge University Press, 2003.

Dellamora, Richard, and Daniel Fischlin, eds. *The Work of Opera: Genre, Nationhood, and Sexual Difference.* New York: Columbia University Press, 1997.

Dessau, Paul. *Lieder und Gesänge.* Berlin: Henschelverlag, 1957.

———. *Das Verhör des Lukullus.* Zurich: Ars Viva Verlag, 1965.

Diamond, Elin. "Brechtian Theory/Feminist Theory: Toward a Gestic Feminist Criticism." *Drama Review* 32, no. 1 (1988): 82–94.

———. *Unmaking Mimesis: Essays on Feminism and Theater.* London: Routledge, 1997.

Diaz, Victor Rego, Kamil Uludag, and Gunter Willing, eds. *Brecht, Eisler, Marcuse 100: Fragen kritischer Theorie heute.* Hamburg: Argument, 1999.

Dibelius, Ulrich, and Frank Schneider, eds. *Neue Musik im geteilten Deutschland: Dokumente aus den fünfziger Jahren.* Berlin: Henschel, 1993.

Dimitrov, Georgi. *Against Fascism and War.* New York: International Publishers, 1986.

———. *The United Front against Fascism: Speeches Delivered at the Seventh World Congress of the Communist International, July 25–August 20, 1935.* New York: New Century Publishers, 1945.

———, and Joseph Stalin. *Dimitrov and Stalin, 1934–1943: Letters from the Soviet Archives.* Edited by Alexander Dallin and F. I. Firsov. Documents translated by Vadim A. Stoklo. New Haven, CT: Yale University Press, 2000.

Douglas, D. B. "The Beginnings of *Die Rundköpfe und die Spitzköpfe:* Bertolt Brecht's Fragmentary Adaptation of Shakespeare's *Measure for Measure.*" *Aumla-Journal of the Australasian Universities' Language and Literature Association* 64 (November 1985): 198–219.

———. "Bertolt Brecht's Development of a Minor Shakespearian Motif in *Die Rundköpfe und die Spitzköpfe.*" *Aumla-Journal of the Australasian Universities Language and Literature Association* 57 (May 1982): 40–50.

Dümling, Albrecht. " 'Agire e meglio che sentire': L'aspetto pedagogico in Brecht e Hindemith." In *Paul Hindemith nella cultura tedesca degli anni Venti,* edited by Carlo Piccardi, 220–242. Milan: Unicopli, 1991.

———. "Eisler/Brecht oder Brecht/Eisler? Perspektiven, Formen und Grenzen ihrer Zusammenarbeit." In *Brecht und seine Komponisten,* edited by Albrecht Riethmüller, 93–110. Laaber, Germany: Laaber Verlag, 2000.

———. "Eisler und Brecht: Bilanz einer produktiven Partnerschaft." *Neue Zeitschrift für Musik* 159, no. 6 (1998): 4–9.

———. *Friedrich Hölderlin: Vertont von Hanns Eisler, Paul Hindemith, Max Reger.* Munich: Kindler, 1981.

———. "Hearing, Speaking, Singing, Writing: The Meaning of Oral Tradition for Bert Brecht." In *Music and German Literature: Their Relationship since the Middle Ages,* edited by James M. McGlathery, 316–326. Columbia, SC: Camden, 1992.

———. " 'Im Stil der Lehrstücke': Zu Entstehung und Edition von Eislers Musik für Brechts Gorki-Bearbeitung *Die Mutter.*" In *Der Text im musikalischen Werk. Editionsprobleme aus musikwissenschaftlicher und literatur-*

wissenschaftlicher Sicht, edited by Walther Dürr, 361–381. Berlin: Erich Schmidt, 1998.

———. *Laßt euch nicht verführen: Brecht und die Musik.* Munich: Kindler Verlag, 1985.

———. "Zur Funktion der Reihentechnik in Eislers Deutscher Sinfonie." In *Bericht über den Internationalen Musikwissenschaftlichen Kongress Bayreuth,* edited by Christoph-Hellmut Mahling and Sigrid Wiesmann, 475–481. Kassel: Bärenreiter: 1981.

———. "Zwölftonmusik als antifaschistisches Potential: Eislers Ideen zu einer neuen Verwendung der Dodekaphonie." In *Die Wiener Schule und das Hakenkreuz: Das Schicksal der Moderne im gesellschaftspolitischen Kontext des 20. Jahrhunderts,* edited by Otto Kolleritsch, 92–106. Vienna: Universal Edition, 1990.

———, and Peter Girths, eds. *Entartete Musik: Dokumentation und Kommentar.* Düsseldorf: Dkv. der kleine Verlag, 1993.

Duncan, Michelle. "The Operatic Scandal of the Singing Body: Voice, Presence, Performativity." *Cambridge Opera Journal* 16, no. 3 (2004): 283–306.

Duttlinger, Carolin. "Between Contemplation and Distraction: Configurations of Attention in Walter Benjamin." *German Studies Review* 30, no. 1 (2007): 33–54.

Eaton, Jonathan. "*Die Bürgschaft* in 1998: A Passion Play for the Twentieth Century." *Kurt Weill Newsletter* 16, no. 1 (1998): 4–5.

Eaton, Katherine Bliss. *The Theater of Meyerhold and Brecht.* Westport, CT: Greenwood Press, 1985.

Eckhard, John. "Vexierbild 'Politische Musik': Stationen ihrer Entscheidung." In *Musik und Politik: Dimensionen einer undefinierten Beziehung,* edited by Bernhard Frevel, 13–21. Regensburg, Germany: Conbrio, 1997.

Eisler, Hanns. *Ernste Gesänge für Bariton und Streichorchester.* Leipzig: VEB Deutscher Verlag für Musik, 1975.

———. *Fragen Sie mehr über Brecht: Gespräche mit Hans Bunge.* Leipzig: VEB Deutscher Verlag für Musik, 1975.

———. *Johann Faustus: Fassung letzter Hand.* Edited by Hans Bunge. Berlin: Henschelverlag, 1983.

———. *Johann Faustus: Oper.* Commentary by Jürgen Schebera. Leipzig: Faber and Faber, 1996.

———. *Die Maßnahme. Lehrstück von Bert Brecht.* Piano reduction by Erwin Ratz. Vienna: Universal Edition, 1931.

———. *Materialien zu einer Dialektik der Musik.* Edited by Manfred Grabs. Leipzig: Verlag Philipp Reclam jun., 1973.

———. *Musik und Politik: Schriften, 1924–1948.* Edited by Günter Mayer. Leipzig: VEB Deutscher Verlag für Musik, 1985.

———. *Musik und Politik: Schriften, 1948–1962.* Edited by Günter Mayer. Leipzig: VEB Deutscher Verlag für Musik, 1982.

———. *Neuen Balladen aus dem Lehrstück "Die Mutter."* Leipzig: VEB Deutscher Verlag für Musik, 1977.

————. *A Rebel in Music: Selected Writings.* Edited by Manfred Grabs. Translated by Marjorie Meyer. New York: International Publishers, 1978.

————. *Die Rundköpfe und die Spitzköpfe.* Hanns Eisler Gesamtausgabe series 5, vol. 3. Edited by Thomas Ahrend and Albrecht Dümling. Leipzig: Breitkopf and Härtel, 2002.

————. *Tank Battles: The Songs of Hanns Eisler.* Sung by Dagmar Krause. Voiceprint CD138.

————. *Tempo der Zeit. Kantata für Alt- und Bass-Solo, Sprecher, gemischten Chor und kleines Orchester opus 16.* Piano reduction by Erwin Ratz. Vienna: Universal Edition, 1930.

————. *Zehn Lieder aus "Die Rundköpfe und die Spitzköpfe."* Leipzig: Deutscher Verlag für Musik, 1998.

Ellis, Lorena B. *Brecht's Reception in Brazil.* New York: Peter Lang, 1995.

Elsner, Jürgen. "'Lob des Kommunismus': Bemerkungen zu Hanns Eislers Musik zur *Mutter.*" *Musik in der Schule* 29, no. 9 (1978): 291–294.

Emmerich, Wolfgang. "Gleichzeitigkeit, Vormoderne, und Postmoderne in der Literatur der DDR." In *Bestandsaufnahme Gegenwartsliteratur,* edited by Hans Ludwig Arnold, 193–211. Munich: edition text + kritik, 1988.

Epstein, Catherine. *The Last Revolutionaries: German Communists and Their Century.* Cambridge: Harvard University Press, 2003.

Esslin, Martin. *Brecht: The Man and His Work.* New York: Doubleday, 1961.

————. "Some Reflections on Brecht and Acting." In *Re-interpreting Brecht: His Influence on Contemporary Drama and Film,* edited by Pia Kleber and Colin Visser, 135–146. Cambridge: Cambridge University Press, 1990.

Farneth, David, with Elmar Juchem and Dave Stein. *Kurt Weill: A Life in Pictures and Documents.* Woodstock, NY: Overlook Press, 2000.

Ferran, Peter W. "The Gestus in the 'Ballad of Mac the Knife.'" *Communications* 26, no. 1 (1997): 58–61.

————. "Music and Gestus in *The Exception and the Rule.*" *Brecht Yearbook/ Brecht-Jahrbuch* 24 (1999): 227–245.

————. "Musical Composition for an American Stage: Brecht." *Brecht Yearbook/ Brecht-Jahrbuch* 22 (1997): 253–281.

————. "New Measures for Brecht in America." *Theater* 25, no. 2 (1994): 9–23.

————. "The *Threepenny* Songs: Cabaret and the Lyrical Gestus." *Theater* 30, no. 3 (2000): 5–21.

Fischbach, Fred. "Pour une nouvelle lecture des pièces de Brecht à la lumière de la musique de scène de Hanns Eisler." *Recherches Germaniques* 13 (1983): 137–166.

Fischer, Gerhard. "The Lehrstück Experience on a Contemporary Stage: On Brecht and the GRIPS-Theater's *Voll auf der Rolle.*" *Modern Drama* 31, no. 3 (1988): 371–379.

Fischer-Lichte, Erika. *Ästhetik des Performativen.* Frankfurt am Main: Suhrkamp, 2004.

————. *Ästhetik Erfahrung. Das Semiotische und das Performative.* Tübingen, Germany: Francke, 2001.

———. *The Show and the Gaze of Theatre: A European Perspective.* Edited and translated by Jo Riley. Iowa City: University of Iowa Press, 1997.

———. *Theatre, Sacrifice, Ritual: Exploring Forms of Political Theatre.* London: Routledge, 2005.

———, Clemens Risi, and Jens Roselt, eds. *Kunst der Aufführung— Aufführung der Kunst.* Berlin: Theater der Zeit, 2004.

———, and Jens Roselt. "Attraktion des Augenblicks—Aufführung, Performance, performativ und Performativität als theaterwissenschaftliche Begriffe." *Paragrana. Internationale Zeitschrift für Historische Anthropologie* 10, no. 1 (2001): 237–253.

Flaherty, M. "Lessing and Opera: A Re-evaluation." *Germanic Review* 44, no. 2 (1969): 95–109.

Fletcher, Anne. "The Gestus of Scene Design: Mordecai Gorelik and the Theatre Union's Production of Brecht's *The Mother.*" *Theatre History Studies* 23 (June 2003): 95–108.

Ford, Andrew. Review of *Making Sense of Aristotle: Essays in Poetics,* edited by Oivind Andersen and Jon Haarberg. *Bryn Mawr Classical Review* 20, 12 December 2002. Http://ccat.sas.upenn.edu/bmcr/2002/2002–12–20.html, accessed 1 April 2006.

Fowler, Kenneth. *Received Truths: Bertolt Brecht and the Problem of Gestus and Musical Meaning.* New York: AMS Press, 1991.

Fraden, Rena. *Blueprints for a Black Federal Theatre, 1935–1939.* Cambridge: Cambridge University Press, 1994.

Frank, Manfred. *Einführung in die frühromantische Ästhetik.* Frankfurt am Main: Suhrkamp, 1989.

Franz, Michael. "Die Krise des 'Werk'–Begriffs." In *Brecht 83. Brecht und Marxismus: Dokumentation,* edited by Werner Hecht, 212–221. Berlin: Henschelverlag, 1983.

Frasca, Gonzalo. "Rethinking Agency and Immersion: Playing with Videogame Characters." In *Proceedings of SIGGRAPH 2001,* Art Gallery, Art and Culture Papers, 12–17 August 2001, Los Angeles. Www.siggraph.org/artdesign/ gallery/S01/essays/ 0378.pdf, accessed 22 May 2006.

———. "Videogames of the Oppressed: Critical Thinking, Education, Tolerance, and Other Trivial Issues." In *First Person: New Media as Story, Performance, and Game,* edited by Pat Harrington and Noah Wardrip-Fruin, 85–94. Cambridge: MIT Press, 2004.

Freeman, Sara. Review of "German Brecht, European Readings." *Brecht Yearbook/Brecht-Jahrbuch* 26 (2001): 334–338.

Freire, Paolo. *Pedagogy of the Oppressed.* Translated by M. B. Ramos. New York: Continuum, 1993.

Frisch, Werner, and K. W. Obermeier, eds., with Gerhard Schneider. *Brecht in Augsburg: Erinnerungen, Texte, Fotos.* Frankfurt am Main: Suhrkamp, 1976.

Frolova-Walker, Marina. "'National in Form, Socialist in Content': Musical Nation-Building in the Soviet Republics." *Journal of the American Musicological Society* 51, no. 2 (1998): 331–371.

―――. "Stalin and the Art of Boredom." *Twentieth-Century Music* 1, no. 1 (2004): 101–124.

Fuegi, John. *Brecht and Company: Sex, Politics, and the Making of the Modern Drama.* New York: Grove Press, 1994.

Fulbrook, Mary. *Anatomy of a Dictatorship: Inside the GDR, 1949–1989.* Oxford: Oxford University Press, 1995.

Gardner, Viv. "The Invisible Spectactrice: Gender, Geography, and Theatrical Space." In *Women, Theatre, and Performance: New Histories, New Historiographies,* edited by Maggie B. Gale and Viv Gardner, 25–45. Manchester, England: Manchester University Press, 2000.

Gates, Henry Louis, Jr. *Thirteen Ways of Looking at a Black Man.* New York: Random House, 1997.

Geller, Jay Howard. *Jews in Post-Holocaust Germany, 1945–1953.* Cambridge: Cambridge University Press, 2005.

Gellert, Inge, Gerd Koch, Florian Vaßen, eds. *Maßnehmen: Bertolt Brecht/ Hanns Eislers Lehrstück Die Maßnahme. Kontroverse, Perspektive, Praxis.* Berlin: Theater der Zeit, 1998.

Gilbert, Helen. "Black and White and Re(a)d All Over Again: Indigenous Minstrelsy in Contemporary Canadian and Australian Theatre." *Theatre Journal* 55, no. 4 (2003): 679–698.

Gilbert, Michael John T. *Bertolt Brecht's Striving for Reason, Even in Music: A Critical Assessment.* New York: Peter Lang, 1988.

Gill, Glenda. "Canada Lee: Black Actor in Non-traditional Roles." *Journal of Popular Culture* 25, no. 3 (Winter 1991): 79–89.

―――. *White Grease Paint on Black Performers: A Study of the Federal Theatre, 1935–1939.* New York: Lang, 1988.

Gilliam, Bryan. "From Hollywood to Berlin: The Influence of American Film on Weimar Music Theater." In *Amerikanismus, Americanism, Weill: Die Suche nach kultureller Identität in der Moderne,* edited by Hermann Danuser and Hermann Gottschewski, 147–159. Schliengen, Germany: Edition Argus, 2003.

―――. "Stage and Screen: Kurt Weill and Operatic Reform in the 1920s." In *Music and Performance during the Weimar Republic,* edited by Bryan Gilliam, 1–12. Cambridge: Cambridge University Press, 1994.

Gleber, Klaus. *Theater und Öffentlichkeit. Produktions- und Rezeptionsbedingungen politischen Theaters am Beispiel Piscator, 1920–1966.* Frankfurt am Main: Peter Lang, 1979.

Godlovitch, Stan. *Musical Performance: A Philosophical Study.* London: Routledge, 1998.

Goehr, Lydia. *The Imaginary Museum of Musical Works: An Essay in the Philosophy of Music.* Oxford: Clarendon Press, 1992.

Goratowski, Günther. "Was der deutsche Bürger liest. Ein Rundgang durch deutsche Volksbibliotheken." *Uhu* 6, no. 8 (1930): 34–37.

Grabs, Manfred, ed. *Hanns Eisler: Kompositionen, Schriften, Literatur. Ein Handbuch.* Leipzig: VEB Deutscher Verlag für Musik, 1984.

———. "Hanns Eislers Versuche um die Oper." *Sinn und Form* 33 (1981): 621–636.

———, ed. *Wer war Hanns Eisler? Auffassungen aus sechs Jahrzehnten.* Berlin: Verlag das europäische Buch, 1983.

Grier, James. *The Critical Editing of Music: History, Method, and Practice.* Cambridge: Cambridge University Press, 1996.

Grimm, Reinhold. *Brecht und Nietzsche oder Geständnisse eines Dichters. Fünf Essays und ein Bruchstück.* Frankfurt am Main: Suhrkamp, 1979.

Grois, Boris. *The Total Art of Stalinism: Avant-Garde, Aesthetic Dictatorship, and Beyond.* Translated by Charles Rougle. Princeton, NJ: Princeton University Press, 1992.

Gubar, Susan. *Racechanges: White Skin, Black Face in American Culture.* New York: Oxford University Press, 1997.

Gumbrecht, Hans Ulrich. "Production of Presence, Interspersed with Absence: A Modernist View of Music, Libretti, and Staging." In *Music and the Aesthetics of Modernity,* edited by Karol Berger and Anthony Newcomb, 343–356. Cambridge: Harvard University Press, 2005.

———. *Production of Presence: What Meaning Cannot Convey.* Stanford, CA: Stanford University Press, 2004.

Hake, Sabine. "Charlie Chaplin Reception in Weimar Germany." *New German Critique* 50 (Autumn 1990): 87–111.

Hampel, Friedrich J. *Lucullus: Ein Handbuch der Wiener Kochkunst.* Vienna: R. Lechner, 1915.

Hamsun, Knut. *Knut Hamsun Remembers America: Essays and Stories, 1885–1949.* Edited and translated by Richard Nelson Current. Columbia: University of Missouri Press, 2003.

Harsh, Edward. "Excavating *Mahagonny*: Editorial Responses to Conflicting Visions." In *Der Text im musikalischen Werk. Editionsprobleme aus musikwissenschaftlicher und literaturwissenschaftlicher Sicht,* edited by Walther Dürr et al., 346–360. Berlin: Erich Schmidt, 1998.

Hartewig, Karin. *Zurückgekehrt. Die Geschichte der jüdischen Kommunisten in der DDR.* Cologne: Böhlau, 2000.

Haug, Fritz, ed. *Historisch-kritisches Wörterbuch des Marxismus.* Hamburg: Argument, 2001.

Hecht, Werner. *Alles was Brecht ist: Fakten, Kommentare, Meinungen, Bilder.* Frankfurt am Main: Suhrkamp, 1998.

———. *Brecht im Gespräch. Diskussionen, Dialoge, Interviews.* Berlin: Henschelverlag, 1979.

———, ed. *Materialien zu Bertolt Brechts "Die Mutter."* Frankfurt am Main: Suhrkamp, 1969.

Heile, Björn. "Recent Approaches to Experimental Music Theatre and Contemporary Opera." *Music & Letters* 87, no. 1 (2006): 72–81.

Heinze, Helmut. *Brechts Ästhetik des Gestischen: Versuch einer Rekonstruktion.* Heidelberg, Germany: C. Winter, 1992.

Heiser-Duron, Meredith A. "Brecht's Political and Cultural Dilemma in the Summer of 1953." *Communications* 30 (June 2001): 47–56.

Heister, Hanns-Werner. "Hollywood and Home: Hanns Eisler's 'Hölderlin-Fragmente' for Voice and Piano." In *Hanns Eisler: A Miscellany*, edited by David Blake, 203–249. New York: Harwood Academic Publishers, 1995.

Hell, Julia, Loren Kruger, and Katie Trumpener. "Dossier: Socialist Realism and East German Modernism—Another Historians' Debate." *Rethinking Marxism* 7, no. 3 (1994): 37–44.

Hennenberg, Fritz. "Brecht und Weill im Clinch?" *Berliner Beiträge zur Musikwissenschaft: Beihefte zur Neuen Berlinischen Musikzeitung* 9, no. 2 (1994): 3–24.

———. *Dessau-Brecht: Musikalische Arbeiten*. Berlin: Henschel, 1963.

Hepokoski, James. "Operatic Stagings: Positions and Paradoxes. A Response to David J. Levin." In *Verdi 2001: Atti del Convegno Internazionale—Proceedings of the International Conference. Parma—New York—New Haven*, edited by Fabrizio Della Seta, Roberta Montemorra Marvin, and Marco Marica, 477–483. Florence: Olschki, 2003.

Herf, Jeffrey. *Divided Memory: The Nazi Past in the Two Germanys*. Cambridge: Harvard University Press, 1997.

Hermand, Jost, ed. *Brecht Liederbuch*. Frankfurt am Main: Suhrkamp, 1984.

———. "'Manchmal lagen Welten zwischen uns!' Brecht und Eislers 'Deutsche Symphonie.'" In *Brecht und seine Komponisten*, edited by Albrecht Riethmüller, 111–132. Laaber, Germany: Laaber Verlag, 2000.

Herzfeld-Sander, Margaret, ed. *Essays on German Theater*. New York: Continuum, 1985.

Herzfelde, Wieland. "Über Bertolt Brecht." In *Erinnerungen an Brecht*, edited by Hubert Witt, 129–138. Leipzig: Reclam, 1964.

Hill, Errol G., and James V. Hatch. *A History of African American Theatre*. Cambridge: Cambridge University Press, 2003.

Hilliker, Rebecca. "Brecht's Gestic Vision for Opera: Why the Shock of Recognition Is More Powerful in *The Rise and Fall of Mahagonny* than in the *Threepenny Opera*." In *Text and Presentation*, edited by Karelisa Hartigan, 77–92. Lanham, MD: University Press of America, 1988.

Hindemith, Paul. *Lehrstück*. Mainz: Schott, 1929.

———. *Paul Hindemith: Szenische Versuche*. Sämtliche Werke series 1, vol. 6. Edited by Rudolf Stephan. Mainz: Schott, 1982.

Hinton, Stephen. "The Concept of Epic Opera: Theoretical Anomalies in the Brecht-Weill Partnership." In *Das musikalische Kunstwerk: Festschrift Carl Dahlhaus*, edited by Stephen Hinton, 285–294. Laaber, Germany: Laaber Verlag, 1988.

———. *The Idea of Gebrauchsmusik: A Study of Musical Aesthetics in the Weimar Republic (1919–1933) with Particular Reference to the Works of Paul Hindemith*. New York: Garland Publishing, 1989.

———, ed. *Kurt Weill: The Threepenny Opera*. Cambridge: Cambridge University Press, 1990.

———. "Lehrstück: An Aesthetics of Performance." In *Music and Performance during the Weimar Republic,* edited by Bryan Gilliam, 59–73. Cambridge: Cambridge University Press, 1994.

———. Review of *Leitmotiv and Drama: Wagner, Brecht and the Limits of "Epic" Theatre,* by Hilda Meldrum Brown. *Music & Letters* 73, no. 2 (1992): 466–468.

———. "Zur Urform der Oper." In *Vom Kurfürstendamm zum Broadway: Kurt Weill (1900–1950),* edited by Bernd Kortländer, Winrich Meiszies, and David Farneth, 40–46. Düsseldorf: Droste Verlag, 1990.

Hoffmann, Ludwig, and Klaus Pfützner, eds. *Theater der Kollektive: Proletarisch-revolutionäres Berufstheater in Deutschland, 1928–1933. Stücke, Dokumente, Studien.* Vol. 1. Berlin: Henschelverlag, 1980.

Howell, Tim. "Eisler's Serialism: Concepts and Methods." In *Hanns Eisler: A Miscellany,* edited by David Blake, 102–132. New York: Harwood Academic Publishers, 1995.

Ihering, Herbert. *Von Reinhardt bis Brecht: Vier Jahrzehnte Theater und Film.* Berlin: Aufbau Verlag, 1959.

Ingarden, Roman. *The Ontology of the Work of Art.* Translated by Raymond Meyer and John T. Goldthwait. Athens: Ohio University Press, 1989.

———. *The Work of Music and the Problem of Its Identity.* Edited by Jean G. Harrell. Translated by Adam Czerniawski. Berkeley: University of California Press, 1986.

Innes, C. D. *Erwin Piscator's Political Theatre: The Development of Modern German Drama.* Cambridge: Cambridge University Press, 1972.

Irvin, Sherri. "The Artist's Sanction in Contemporary Art." *Journal of Aesthetics and Art Criticism* 63, no. 4 (Fall 2005): 315–326.

Jackson, Julian. *The Popular Front in France: Defending Democracy, 1934–1938.* Cambridge: Cambridge University Press, 1988.

Jameson, Fredric. *Brecht and Method.* London: Verso, 1998.

———. *Lust und Schrecken der unaufhörlichen Verwandlung aller Dinge. Brecht und die Zukunft.* Berlin: Argument, 1999.

Jankélévitch, Vladimir. *Music and the Ineffable.* Translated by Carolyn Abbate. Princeton, NJ: Princeton University Press, 2003.

Jaques-Dalcroze, Emile. *Eurhythmics: Art and Education.* Edited by Cynthia Cox. Translated by Frederick Rothwell. London: Chatto and Windus, 1930.

Jesse, Horst. *Brecht im Exil.* Munich: Verlag Das Freie Buch, 1997.

Jordan, Robert. "Visual Aids." *Opera Canada* 42, no. 2 (2001): 20–22.

Juchem, Elmar. "A Letter Surfaces: Kurt Weill's Reply to Theodor W. Adorno, April 1942." *Kurt Weill Newsletter* 21, no. 2 (2003): 4–5.

Jung, Thomas. "Die 'entgipsten' Lieder: Hanns Eislers Adaption Brechtscher Lieder für die *Deutsche Sinfonie.*" In *Zweifel—Fragen—Vorschläge. Bertolt Brecht anläßlich des Einhundertsten,* edited by Thomas Jung, 161–187. Frankfurt am Main: Peter Lang, 1999.

Kahnt, Hartmut. "Die Opernversuche Weills und Brechts mit *Mahagonny.*" In

Musiktheater heute. Sechs Kongreßbeiträge, edited by Hellmut Kühn, 63–93. Mainz: Schott, 1982.

Kalb, Jonathan. "The Horatian: Building the Better Lehrstück." *New German Critique* 64 (Winter 1995): 161–173.

————. *The Theatre of Heiner Müller.* Cambridge: Cambridge University Press, 1998.

Kamath, Rekha. *Brechts Lehrstück-Modell als Bruch mit den bürgerlichen Theatertraditionen.* Frankfurt am Main: Peter Lang, 1983.

Kater, Michael M. "Weill und Brecht: Kontroversen einer Künstlerfreundschaft auf zwei Kontinenten." In *Brecht und seine Komponisten,* edited by Albrecht Riethmüller, 51–74. Laaber, Germany: Laaber Verlag, 2000.

Kepia, Ania. "The Relationship of Brecht's *Die Mutter* to Its Sources: A Reassessment." *German Life and Letters* 38, no. 3 (1985): 233–248.

Kesting, Marianne. "Wagner/Meyerhold/Brecht oder Die Erfindung des 'epischen' Theaters." *Brecht Yearbook/Brecht-Jahrbuch* 7 (1977): 111–130.

Khittl, Christoph. "'Das Unaufhörliche—Großes Gesetz': Musikpädagogische Exkurse zu Hindemiths und Benns Oratorium." *Musik und Bildung: Praxis Musikerziehung* 27, no. 3 (1995): 50–54.

Kiebuzinska, Christine. "Brecht and the Problem of Influence." In *A Bertolt Brecht Reference Companion,* edited by Siegfried Mews, 47–69. Westport, CT: Greenwood Press, 1997.

————. *Revolutionaries in the Theater: Meyerhold, Brecht, and Witkiewicz.* Ann Arbor, MI: UMI Research Press, 1985.

Kim, Taekwan. *Das Lehrstück Bertolt Brechts. Untersuchungen zur Theorie und Praxis einer zweckbestimmten Musik am Beispiel von Paul Hindemith, Kurt Weill und Hanns Eisler.* Frankfurt am Main: Peter Lang, 2000.

King, Marna. "The Model and Its Mutations in FRG Brecht Productions." *Gestus—the Electronic Journal of Brechtian Studies* 2, no. 3 (1986): 187–197.

Kivy, Peter. *Authenticities: Philosophical Reflections on Musical Performance.* Ithaca, NY: Cornell University Press, 1995.

Klassen, Julie, and Ruth Weiner. "Reviving Brecht: Transformations, or the Reciprocity of Outward Signs and Inward States." In *Essays on Twentieth-Century German Drama and Theater: An American Reception, 1977–1999,* edited by Hellmut Hal Rennert, 212–218. New York: Peter Lang, 2004.

Kleber, Pia, and Colin Visser, eds. *Re-interpreting Brecht: His Influence on Contemporary Drama and Film.* Cambridge: Cambridge University Press, 1990.

Kleinig, Karl. "Hanns Eislers Lieder und Chöre zu Brechts *Die Mutter.*" *Volksmusik* 13, no. 8 (1968): 11–15; and 13, no. 9 (1968): 13–15.

Kleinschmidt, Klaus. "Lessing und die Musik: Zur Erörterung musikalischer Themen in den Schriften des Kunstrichters." *Musik und Gesellschaft* 29, no. 3 (1979): 129–136.

Knopf, Jan, ed. *Brecht Handbuch in fünf Bänden.* Stuttgart: J. B. Metzler, 2001–2003.

Knust, Herbert. "Piscator and Brecht: Affinity and Alienation." In *Essays on*

Brecht: Theater and Politics, edited by Siegfried Mews and Herbert Knust, 44–70. Chapel Hill: University of North Carolina Press, 1974.

Koebner, Thomas. "Die Zeitoper in den Zwanziger Jahren. Gedanken zu ihrer Geschichte und Theorie." In *Erprobungen und Erfahrungen: Zu Paul Hindemiths Schaffen in den zwanziger Jahren,* edited by Dieter Rexroth, 60–115. Mainz: Schott, 1978.

Kolland, Dorothea. "Musik und Lehrstück." In *Maßnehmen: Bertolt Brecht/ Hanns Eislers Lehrstück Die Maßnahme. Kontroverse, Perspektive, Praxis,* edited by Inge Gellert, Gerd Koch, and Florian Vaßen, 174–179. Berlin: Theater der Zeit, 1998.

Komins, Benton Jay. "Rewriting, Violence, and Theater: Bertolt Brecht's *The Measures Taken* and Heiner Müller's *Mauser.*" *Comparatist* 26 (May 2002): 99–119.

Kondo, Dorinne. "(Re)Visions of Race: Contemporary Race Theory and the Cultural Politics of Racial Crossover in Documentary Theatre." *Theatre Journal* 52, no. 1 (2000): 81–107.

Konold, Wulf. "Oper—Anti-Oper—Anti-Anti-Oper." In *Musiktheater heute: Internationales Symposion der Paul Sacher Stiftung Basel 2001,* edited by Hermann Danuser and Matthias Kassel, 47–60. Mainz: Schott, 2003.

Kowalke, Kim. "Accounting for Success: Misunderstanding *Die Dreigroschenoper.*" *Opera Quarterly* 6, no. 3 (1989): 18–38.

———. "Brecht and Music: Theory and Practice." In *The Cambridge Companion to Brecht,* 2nd ed., edited by Peter Thomson and Glendyr Sacks, 242–258. Cambridge: Cambridge University Press, 2006.

———. *Kurt Weill in Europe.* Ann Arbor, MI: UMI Research Press, 1979.

———. "Singing Brecht versus Brecht Singing: Performance in Theory and Practice." In *Music and Performance during the Weimar Republic,* edited by Bryan Gilliam, 74–93. Cambridge: Cambridge University Press, 1994.

———. "*The Threepenny Opera* in America." In *Kurt Weill: "The Threepenny Opera,"* edited by Stephen Hinton, 78–119. Cambridge: Cambridge University Press, 1990.

Krabiel, Klaus-Dieter. *Brechts Lehrstücke. Entstehung und Entwicklung eines Spieltyps.* Stuttgart: Metzler Verlag, 1993.

———. "Das Lehrstück: Ein mißverstandenes Genre." *Der Deutschunterricht: Beiträge zu seiner Praxis und wissenschaftlichen Grundlegung* 46, no. 6 (1994): 8–16.

———. "Das Lehrstück von Brecht und Hindemith: Von der Geburt eines Genres aus dem Geist der Gebrauchsmusik." *Hindemith Jahrbuch* 24 (1995): 146–179.

———. "Die Lehrstücke Brechts als editorisches Problem." In *Der Text im musikalischen Werk. Editionsprobleme aus musikwissenschaftlicher und literaturwissenschaftlicher Sicht,* edited by Walther Dürr, 331–345. Berlin: Erich Schmidt, 1998.

———. "Rhetorik der Utopie—Rhetorik der Komödie? Bemerkungen zu einer Untersuchung der Lehrstücke Brechts und ihrer Rezeption in der Fachkritik." *Wirkendes Wort: Deutsche Sprache in Forschung und Lehre* 40, no. 2 (1990): 209–219.

Kramer, Lawrence. *Opera and Modern Culture: Wagner and Strauss*. Berkeley: University of California Press, 2004.

Kreuzer, Gundula. "Voices from Beyond: *Don Carlos* and the Modern Stage." *Cambridge Opera Journal* 18, no. 2 (2006): 151–179.

Kruger, Loren. *The Drama of South Africa: Plays, Pageants, and Publics since 1910*. New York: Routledge, 1999.

———. "Making Sense of Sensation: Enlightenment, Embodiment, and the End(s) of Modern Drama." *Modern Drama* 43, no. 4 (2000): 543–563.

———. *Post-Imperial Brecht: Politics and Performance, East and South*. Cambridge: Cambridge University Press, 2004.

———. "'Wir treten aus unseren Rollen heraus': Theatre Intellectuals and Public Spheres." In *The Power of Intellectuals in Contemporary Germany*, edited by Michael Geyer, 183–211. Chicago: University of Chicago Press, 2001.

Kuhn, Tom. "Brecht and Willett: Getting the Gest." *Brecht Yearbook/Brecht-Jahrbuch* 28 (2003): 261–274.

Kuhnert, Heinz. "Zur Rolle der Songs im Werk von Bertolt Brecht." *Neue Deutsche Literatur* 11, no. 3 (1963): 77–100.

Lacoue-Labarthe, Philippe, and Jean-Luc Nancy. *The Literary Absolute: The Theory of Literature in German Romanticism*. Translated by Philip Barnard and Cheryl Lester. Albany: State University of New York Press, 1988.

Lahusen, Thomas, and Eugeny Dobrenko, eds. *Socialist Realism without Shores*. Durham, NC: Duke University Press, 1997.

Langer, Susanne. *Feeling and Form: A Theory of Art*. New York: Scribner, 1953.

Lanz, Doris. "Hanns Eisler als Vorbild für Wladimir Vogels erste Zwölftonkomposition? Überlegungen zu Vogels Violinkonzert von 1936/37." *Archiv für Musikwissenschaft* 62, no. 2 (2005): 137–150.

Lazarowicz, Klaus. "Die Rote Messe: Liturgische Elemente in Brechts *Maßnahme*." *Literaturwissenschaftliches Jahrbuch* 17 (1977): 205–220.

Lee, Kyung-Boon. *Musik und Literatur im Exil: Hanns Eislers dodekaphone Exilkantate*. New York: Lang, 2000.

Lehmann, Hans-Thies. *Postdramatic Theatre*. Translated by Karen Jürs-Munby. London: Routledge, 2006.

———, and Helmut Lethen. "Ein Vorschlag zur Güte. Zur doppelten Polarität des Lehrstücks." In *Auf Anregung Brechts. Lehrstücke mit Schülern, Arbeitern, Theaterleuten*, edited by Reiner Steinweg, 302–307. Frankfurt am Main: Suhrkamp Verlag, 1978.

Lehrman, Leonard J. "Continental Clashes of Culture at Convention, Cabaret, and Concert." *Aufbau* 65, no. 2 (1999): 13.

Lessing, Gotthold Ephraim. *Hamburg Dramaturgy*. Translated by Victor Lange. New York: Dover Publications, 1962.

———. *Hamburgische Dramaturgie*. Edited by Otto Mann. Stuttgart: Alfred Kroner Verlag, 1958.

Levin, David J., ed. *Opera through Other Eyes*. Stanford, CA: Stanford University Press, 1993.

———. "Reading a Staging/Staging a Reading." *Cambridge Opera Journal* 9, no. 1 (1997): 47–71.

———. "Response to James Treadwell." *Cambridge Opera Journal* 10, no. 3 (1998): 307–311.

———. *Unsettling Opera: Staging Mozart, Verdi, Wagner, and Zemlinsky*. Chicago: University of Chicago Press, 2007.

———. "'Va, pensiero'? Verdi and Theatrical Provocation." In *Verdi 2001: Atti del Convegno internationale—Proceedings of the International Conference. Parma—New York—New Haven*, edited by Fabrizio Della Seta, Roberta Montemorra Marvin, and Marco Marica, 463–475. Florence: Olschki, 2003.

Lindner, Burkhardt. "Das Messer und die Schrift: Für eine Revision der 'Lehrstückperiode.'" *Brecht Yearbook/Brecht-Jahrbuch* 18 (1993): 43–58.

Linn, Michael von der. "'Jonny,' 'Mahagonny,' and the Songs of Tin Pan Alley." In *Amerikanismus, Americanism, Weill: Die Suche nach kultureller Identität in der Moderne*, edited by Hermann Danuser and Hermann Gottschewski, 160–170. Schliengen, Germany: Edition Argus, 2003.

Livingston, Paisley. *Art and Intention: A Philosophical Study*. Oxford: Clarendon Press, 2005.

Lodemann, Jürgen. *Lortzing: Leben und Werk des dichtenden, komponierenden und singenden Publikumslieblings, Familienvaters und komisch tragischen Spielopernweltmeisters aus Berlin*. Göttingen, Germany: Steidl, 2000.

———. *Oper—O reiner Unsinn. Albert Lortzing, Opernmacher*. Freiburg: Wuz, 2005.

London, John. *Theatre under the Nazis*. Manchester, England: Manchester University Press, 2000.

Lortzing, Albert. *Regina: Oper in drei Akten*. Edited by Irmlind Capelle. Milan: Ricordi, 1998.

Lucchesi, Joachim. "'. . . Denn die Zeit kennt keinen Aufenthalt': Busoni, Weill, und Brecht." In *Berliner Begegnungen: Ausländische Künstler in Berlin, 1918 bis 1933*, edited by Klaus Kändler, Helga Karolowski, and Ilse Siebert, 46–52. Berlin: Dietz, 1987.

———. "From Trial to Condemnation: The Debate over Brecht/Dessau's 1951 Opera *Lucullus*." Translated by David W. Robinson. *Contemporary Theatre Review* 4, no. 2 (1995): 13–21.

———. "'Oh, Ihr Zeiten meiner Jugend!' Zu Brechts frühen Musikerfahrungen." In *Beiträge zur Theorie und Praxis des sozialistischen Theaters*, 46–64. Berlin: Verband der Theaterschaffenden der Deutschen Demokratischen Republik, 1984.

———. "Das Stück wirkt mit der Musik ganz anders!" In *Maßnehmen: Bertolt Brecht/Hanns Eislers Lehrstück Die Maßnahme. Kontroverse, Perspektive, Praxis*, edited by Inge Gellert, Gerd Koch, and Florian Vaßen, 189–195. Berlin: Theater der Zeit, 1998.

———, ed. *Das Verhör in der Oper: Die Debatte um die Aufführung "Das Ver-*

hör des Lukullus" von Bertolt Brecht und Paul Dessau. Berlin: Basisdruck, 1993.

―――. "Versuch eines Vergleichs: Kurt Weill als Mittler zwischen Brecht und Busoni." *Music und Gesellschaft* 40, no. 3 (1990): 132–134.

―――, and Ronald K. Shull. *Musik bei Brecht*. Frankfurt am Main: Suhrkamp, 1988.

Lyon, James K. *Bertolt Brecht in America*. Princeton, NJ: Princeton University Press, 1980.

―――, ed. *Brecht in den USA*. Frankfurt am Main: Suhrkamp, 1994.

Maclean, Hector. "Gestus in Performance: Brecht and Heiner Müller." *Brecht Yearbook/Brecht-Jahrbuch* 26 (2001): 81–96.

Mahlke, Stefan. "Brecht ± Müller: German-German Brecht Images before and after 1989." *Drama Review* 43, no. 4 (1999): 40–49.

Maier-Schaeffer, Francine. "Écriture de fragment *Glücksgott* de Heiner Müller à la lumière de se savant-textes inédits." *Etudes Germaniques* 56, no. 3 (2001): 343–368.

―――. *Heiner Müller et le "Lehrstück."* Berne: Peter Lang, 1992.

Mainka, Jürgen. "Musikalische Betroffenheit. Zum Begriff des Gestischen." *Beiträge zur Musikwissenschaft* 15, nos. 1–2 (1973): 61–80.

Marina, Racu. " 'Geist der Musik' oder 'Kulinarische Kunst'? (Nochmals zum Problem 'Brecht und die Oper')." *Communications* 23, no. 3 (1994): 67–76.

Marks, Steven Gary. *How Russia Shaped the Modern World: From Art to Anti-Semitism, Ballet to Bolshevism*. Princeton, NJ: Princeton University Press, 2003.

Martin, Carol J. "Brecht, Feminism, and Chinese Theatre." *Drama Review* 43, no. 4 (1999): 77–85.

―――, and Henry Bial, eds. *Brecht Sourcebook*. London: Routledge, 2000.

Martini, Fritz. *Deutsche Literatur im bürgerlichen Realismus, 1848–1898*. Stuttgart: J. B. Metzler, 1962.

May, Gisela. *Brecht Songs*. Berlin Classics CD 2165–2.

Mayer, Günter. "Hanns Eislers Beitrag zur Herausbildung einer kritischen Musikpraxis und –theorie." In *Brecht, Eisler, Marcuse 100: Fragen kritischer Theorie heute*, edited by Victor Rego Diaz, Kamil Uludag, and Gunter Willing, 33–41. Berlin: Argument Verlag, 1999.

―――, ed. *Hanns Eisler der Zeitgenosse: Positionen, Perspektiven: Materialien zu den Eisler-Festen, 1994–95*. Leipzig: Deutscher Verlag für Musik, 1997.

―――. "War der 'Karl Marx der Musik' Parteimitglied oder nicht?" In *Hanns Eisler der Zeitgenosse*, edited by Günter Mayer, 67–76. Leipzig: Deutscher Verlag für Musik, 1997.

Mayer, Hans. *Versuche über die Oper*. Frankfurt am Main: Suhrkamp, 1981.

McDermott, Kevin, and Jeremy Agnew, eds. *The Comintern: A History of International Communism from Lenin to Stalin*. New York: St. Martin's Press, 1997.

Mews, Siegfried, ed. *A Bertolt Brecht Reference Companion*. Westport, CT: Greenwood Press, 1997.

Mittenzwei, Johannes. *Das Musikalische in der Literatur: Ein Überblick von Gottfried von Strassburg bis Brecht.* Halle: Verlag Sprache und Literatur, 1962.

Mittenzwei, Werner. "Brecht und die Schicksale der Materialästhetik." In *Brechts Tui-Kritik. Aufsätze, Rezensionen, Geschichten,* edited by Wolfgang Fritz Haug, 175–212. Karlsruhe: Argument Verlag, 1976.

———. *Das Leben des Bertolt Brechts, oder, der Umgang mit den Welträtseln.* Frankfurt am Main: Suhrkamp, 1986.

Molkow, Wolfgang. "Paul Hindemith—Hanns Eisler. Zweckbestimmung und gesellschaftliche Funktion." In *Erprobungen und Erfahrungen. Zu Paul Hindemiths Schaffen in den Zwanziger Jahren,* edited by Dieter Rexroth, 35–46. Mainz: Schott, 1978.

Monaghan, Peter. "For Brecht: An Ironic Encore." *Chronicle of Higher Education* 51, no. 34 (29 April 2005).

Mordden, Ethan. *Demented: The World of the Opera Diva.* New York: Franklin Watts, 1984.

Morley, Michael. "Suiting the Action to the Word: Some Observations on *Gestus* and *gestische Musik.*" In *A New Orpheus,* edited by Kim Kowalke, 183–201. New Haven, CT: Yale University Press, 1986.

Morris, Robert. "Modes of Coherence and Continuity in Schoenberg's Piano Piece, Opus 23, No 1." *Theory and Practice* 17 (1992): 5–34.

Mueller, Roswitha. "Learning for a New Society: The *Lehrstück.*" In *The Cambridge Companion to Brecht,* 2nd ed., edited by Peter Thomson and Glendyr Sacks, 101–117. Cambridge: Cambridge University Press, 2006.

Mullen, Bill V., and James Edward Smethurst, eds. *Left of the Color Line: Race, Radicalism, and Twentieth-Century Literature of the United States.* Chapel Hill: University of North Carolina Press, 2003.

Müller, Gerhard. "Zeitgeschichtliche Aspekte der *Lukullus*-Debatte." In *Paul Dessau: Von Geschichte gezeichnet,* edited by Klaus Angermann, 144–151. Hofheim, Germany: Wolke, 1995.

Müller, Heiner. "Fatzer ± Keuner." *Brecht Yearbook/Brecht-Jahrbuch* 10 (1981): 14–21.

———. *A Heiner Müller Reader.* Edited and translated by Carl Weber. Baltimore: Johns Hopkins University Press, 2001.

———. *Mauser.* Berlin: Rotbuch, 1978.

———. *Die Stücke.* Vol 1. Edited by Frank Hörnigk. Frankfurt am Main: Suhrkamp, 2000.

———. *Theater-Arbeit.* Berlin: Rotbuch, 1975.

———. "To Use Brecht without Criticizing Him Is to Betray Him." Translated by Marc Silberman. *Theater* 17, no. 2 (1986): 31–33.

Münsterer, Hanns Otto. *The Young Brecht.* Edited and translated by Tom Kuhn and Karen J. Leeder. London: Libris, 1992.

Murphy, G. Ronald. *Brecht and the Bible: A Study of Religious Nihilism and Human Weakness in Brecht's Drama of Mortality and the City.* Chapel Hill: University of North Carolina Press, 1980.

Nadar, Thomas R. "Brecht and His Musical Collaborators." In *A Bertolt Brecht Reference Companion*, edited by Siegfried Mews, 261–278. Westport, CT: Greenwood Press, 1997.

Nägele, Rainer. *Theater, Theory, Speculation: Walter Benjamin and Scenes of Modernity.* Baltimore: Johns Hopkins University Press, 1991.

Naimark, Norman. *The Russians in Germany: A History of the Soviet Zone of Occupation, 1945–1949.* Cambridge: Harvard University Press, 1995.

Neef, Sigrid, and Hermann Neef. *Deutsche Oper im 20. Jahrhundert: DDR, 1949–1989.* Berlin: Peter Lang, 1992.

Neis, Edgar. *Erläuterungen zu Bertolt Brechts Lehrstücken.* Hollfeld, Germany: C. Bange Verlag, 1976.

Nichols, John G. "Saving the Fallen City of Mahagonny: The Musical Elaboration of Brecht's Epic Theatre." In *Text and Presentation* 14 (1993): 71–74.

Nieder, Christoph. "Bertolt Brecht und die Oper: Zur Verwandtschaft von epischem Theater und Musiktheater." *Zeitschrift für Deutsche Philologie* 111, no. 3 (1992): 262–283.

Nietzsche, Friedrich. *Der Fall Wagner; Nietzsche contra Wagner.* Leipzig: Alfred Kröner, 1908.

———. *The Portable Nietzsche.* Editied and translated by Walter Kaufmann. New York: Penguin, 1968.

Notowicz, Nathan. *Wir reden hier nicht von Napoleon. Wir reden von Ihnen! Gespräche mit Hanns Eisler und Gerhart Eisler.* Edited by Jürgen Elsner. Berlin: Verlag Neue Musik, 1971.

Nyström, Esbjörn. *Libretto im Progress. Brechts und Weills "Aufstieg und Fall der Stadt Mahagonny" aus textgeschichtlicher Sicht.* Bern: Peter Lang, 2005.

Oba, Masaharu. *Bertolt Brecht und das Nô-Theater im Kontext der Lehrstücke Brechts.* Frankfurt am Main: Peter Lang, 1984.

Oesmann, Astrid. *Staging History: Brecht's Social Concepts of Ideology.* Albany: State University of New York Press, 2005.

Ostermann, Eberhard. *Das Fragment. Geschichte einer ästhetischen Idee.* Munich: Wilhelm Fink Verlag, 1991.

Pabst, Hans. *Brecht und die Religion.* Graz: Verlag Styria, 1977.

Panofsky, Walter. *Protest in der Oper. Das provokative Musiktheater der zwanziger Jahre.* Munich: Laokoon, 1966.

Parker, Roger. *Remaking the Song: Operatic Visions and Revisions from Handel to Berio.* Berkeley: University of California Press, 2006.

Parmalee, Patty Lee. *Brecht's America.* Columbus: Published for Miami University by Ohio State University Press, 1981.

Pastimes at Home and School: A Practical Manual of Delsarte Exercises and Elocution. Chicago: W. B. Conkey Co., 1897.

Patterson, Michael. "Brecht's Legacy." In *The Cambridge Companion to Brecht*, edited by Peter Thomson and Glendyr Sacks, 273–287. Cambridge: Cambridge University Press, 1994.

———. *The Revolution in German Theatre, 1900–1933.* Boston: Routledge and Kegan Paul, 1981.

Pavis, Patrice. "Brechtian Gestus and Its Avatars in Contemporary Theatre." Translated by Hector Maclean. *Brecht Yearbook/Brecht-Jahrbuch* 24 (1999): 177–190.

———. "Der Gestus bei Brecht." *Brecht Yearbook/Brecht Jahrbuch* 23 (1998): 42–45.

———. *Languages of the Stage: Essays in the Semiology of the Theatre.* New York: Performing Arts Journal Publications, 1982.

Pestalozza, Luigi. "Busoni und Brecht?" In *Studien zur Berliner Musikgeschichte: Vom 18. Jahrhundert bis zur Gegenwart,* edited by Traude Ebert-Obermeier, 332–342. Berlin: Henschelverlag, 1989.

Petersen, Peter. "In Paris begonnen, in New York vollendet, in Berlin verlegt: 'Les Voix' von Paul Dessau." In *Musik im Exil: Folgen des Nazismus für die internationale Musikkultur,* edited by Hanns-Werner Heister, Claudia Maurer Zenck, and Peter Petersen, 438–459. Frankfurt am Main: Fischer Taschenbuch Verlag, 1993.

Phleps, Thomas. *Hanns Eislers Deutsche Sinfonie. Ein Beitrag zur Ästhetik des Widerstands.* Kassel: Bärenreiter, 1988.

———. "'. . . Ich kann mir gar nicht vorstellen etwas Schöneres.' Das Exilschaffen Hanns Eislers." In *Musik im Exil. Folgen des Nazismus für die internationale Musikkultur,* edited by Hanns-Werner Heister, Claudia Maurer-Zenck, and Peter Petersen. 475–511. Frankfurt am Main: Fischer, 1993.

———. "Zwölftöniges Theater—'Wiener Schüler' und Anverwandte in NS-Deutschland." In *"Entartete Musik" 1938—Weimar und die Ambivalenz. Ein Projekt der Hochschule für Musik Franz Liszt Weimar zum Kulturstadtjahr 1999,* edited by Hanns-Werner Heister, 179–215. Saarbrücken: Pfau, 2001.

Pike, David. *The Politics of Culture in Soviet-Occupied Germany, 1945–1949.* Stanford, CA: Stanford University Press, 1992.

Piscator, Erwin. *The Political Theatre: A History, 1914–1929.* Translated by Hugh Rorrison. New York: Avon, 1978.

———. *Das Politische Theater.* Berlin: Albert Schultz Verlag, 1929.

Poizat, Michel. *The Angel's Cry: Beyond the Pleasure Principle in Opera.* Translated by Arthur Denner. Ithaca, NY: Cornell University Press, 1992.

Pollan, Michael. *The Botany of Desire: A Plant's-Eye View of the World.* New York: Random House, 2002.

Primavesi, Patrick. "Apparat ohne Zuschauer? Zur Dekonstruktion des Mediums in Brechts *Ozeanflug.*" *Brecht Yearbook/Brecht-Jahrbuch* 24 (1999): 80–195.

Puchner, Martin. *Stage Fright: Modernism, Anti-Theatricality, and Drama.* Baltimore: Johns Hopkins University Press, 2002.

Raddatz, Frank-Michael. *Brecht frißt Brecht: Neues Episches Theater im 21. Jahrhundert.* Leipzig: Henschel, 2007.

Ramthun, Herta. *Bertolt-Brecht-Archiv: Bestandsverzeichnis des literarischen Nachlasses.* Vol. 1. Berlin: Aufbau Verlag, 1969.

Rasch, William. *Sovereignty and Its Discontents: On the Primacy of Conflict and the Structure of the Political.* London: Birkbeck Law, 2004.

Rathert, Wolfgang. "Ende, Abschied und Fragment. Zu Ästhetik und Geschichte einer musikalischen Problemstellung." In *Abschied in die Gegenwart. Teleologie und Zuständlichkeit in der Musik,* edited by Otto Kolleritsch, 211–235. Vienna: Universal Edition, 1998.

Rees, Tim, and Andrew Thorpe, eds. *International Communism and the Communist International, 1919–1943.* Manchester, England: Manchester University Press, 1998.

Reinhold, Daniela, ed. *Paul Dessau, 1894–1979: Dokumente zu Leben und Werk.* Berlin: Henschel, 1995.

Reiss, Erwin, and Thomas Radewagen. "'An alle!' Zum Kampf der Arbeiterbewegung um den Rundfunk in Deutschland, 1918–1933." In *Wem gehört die Welt—Kunst und Gesellschaft in der Weimarer Republik. Ausstellungsort, Staatliche Kunsthalle Berlin 21 August—23 October 1977,* edited by Neue Gesellschaft für bildende Kunst, 566–590. 2nd ed. Berlin: Die Gesellschaft, 1977.

Rienäcker, Gerd. "Brechts Einfluß auf die Oper. Gestaltungsmethoden im Bühnenwerk Paul Dessaus." *Musik und Gesellschaft* 26, no. 2 (1976): 71–76.

———. "Hanns Eisler über die Dummheit in der Musik." In *Brecht, Eisler, Marcuse 100: Fragen kritischer Theorie heute,* edited by Victor Rego Diaz, Kamil Uludag, and Gunter Willing, 42–52. Berlin: Argument Verlag, 1999.

———. "The Invigorating Effect of Music? Making Music about Music in Brecht and Eisler's 'Song of the Invigorating Effect of Money.'" In *Hanns Eisler: A Miscellany,* edited by David Blake, 91–102. New York: Harwood Academic Publishers, 1995.

———. "Musik als Agens. Beschreibungen und Thesen zur Musik des Lehrstückes *Die Maßnahme* von Hanns Eisler." In *Maßnehmen: Bertolt Brecht/Hanns Eislers Lehrstück Die Maßnahme. Kontroverse, Perspektive, Praxis,* edited by Inge Gellert, Gerd Koch, and Florian Vassen, 180–189. Berlin: Theater der Zeit, 1998.

———. "Musizieren mit und über Brecht: Brecht als Herausforderung." *Beiträge zur Theorie und Praxis des sozialistischen Theaters,* 5–27. Berlin: Verband der Theaterschaffenden der Deutschen Demokratischen Republik, 1984.

———. "Zu einigen Gestaltungsproblemen im Opernschaffen von Paul Dessau." In *Sammelbände zur Musikgeschichte der DDR,* edited by Hans Alfred Brockhaus and Konrad Niemann, 2:100–44. Berlin: Verlag Neue Musik, 1971.

Riesthuis, Joachim Gerhard Ludovicus Anton. "African American and German Exile Writers, 1933–1952." PhD diss., University of Chicago, 2004.

Riethmüller, Albrecht, ed. *Brecht und seine Komponisten.* Laaber, Germany: Laaber Verlag, 2000.

Ringer, Alexander. *Arnold Schoenberg: The Composer as Jew.* Oxford: Clarendon Press, 1990.

Risi, Clemens. "Am Puls der Sinne. Der Rhythmus einer Opernaufführung zwischen Repräsentation und Präsenz—zu Mozart-Inszenierungen von

Calixto Bieito und Thomas Bischoff." In *TheorieTheaterPraxis*, edited by Hajo Kurzenberger and Annemarie Matzke, 117–127. Berlin: Theater der Zeit, 2004.

———. "The Performativity of Operatic Performances as Academic Provocation." In *Verdi 2001: Atti del Convegno internationale—Proceedings of the International Conference. Parma—New York—New Haven*, edited by Fabrizio Della Seta, Roberta Montemorra Marvin, and Marco Marica, 489–498. Florence: Olschki, 2003.

———. "Rhythm, Sense and Sensibility: Performance Rhythms." Paper presented to the Music Theater Working Group meeting of the International Federation for Theater Research, Saint Petersburg, July 2004.

———. "Shedding Light on the Audience: Hans Neuenfels and Peter Konwitschny Stage Verdi (and Verdians)." *Cambridge Opera Journal* 14 (2002): 201–210.

———. "Swinging Signs, Representation and Presence in Operatic Performances: Remarks on Hans Neuenfels, Jossi Wieler, and a New Analytical Approach." *Arcadia* 36 (2001): 363–373.

Ritterhoff, Teresa. "Ver/Ratlosigkeit: Benjamin, Brecht, and *Die Mutter*." *Brecht Yearbook/Brecht-Jahrbuch* 24 (1999): 246–262.

Robin, Régine. *Socialist Realism: An Impossible Aesthetic*. Translated by Catherine Porter. Stanford, CA: Stanford University Press, 1992.

Rohse, Eberhard. *Der frühe Brecht und die Bibel: Studien zum Augsburger Religionsunterricht und zu den literarischen Versuchen des Gymnasiasten*. Göttingen, Germany: Vandenhoeck und Ruprecht, 1983.

Rosen, Charles. *The Romantic Generation*. Cambridge: Harvard University Press, 1995.

Rosen, David. "The Staging of Verdi's Operas: An Introduction to the Ricordi Disposizioni Sceniche." In *Report of the Twelfth Congress of the International Musicological Society 1977*, edited by Daniel Heartz and Bonnie Wade, 444–453. Kassel: Bärenreiter, 1981.

Rufer, Josef. "Brechts Anmerkungen zur Oper." *Stimmen. Monatsblätter für Musik* 1, no. 7 (1948): 193–198.

Salehi, Eric. "No Brecht-fest in America: Revisiting the Theatre Union's 1935 Production of *The Mother*." *On-stage Studies* 21 (1998): 75–97.

Sauter, Willmar. *The Theatrical Event: Dynamics of Performance and Perception*. Iowa City: University of Iowa Press, 2000.

Schachter, Joel. "Brecht's Clowns: *Man Is Man* and after." In *The Cambridge Companion to Brecht*, 2nd ed., edited by Peter Thomson and Glendyr Sacks, 90–100. Cambridge: Cambridge University Press, 2006.

Schanze, Helmut. *Drama im Bürgerlichen Realismus (1850–1890): Theorie und Praxis*. Frankfurt am Main: V. Klostermann, 1973.

Schebera, Jürgen. "Die epische Oper als Erneuerung eines Genres." In *Beiträge zur Theorie und Praxis des sozialistischen Theaters*, 28–45. Berlin: Verband der Theaterschaffenden der Deutschen Demokratischen Republik, 1988.

———. *Hanns Eisler. Eine Bildbiografie*. Berlin: Henschel Verlag, 1981.

———. *Hanns Eisler: Eine Biographie in Texten, Bildern, und Dokumenten.* Mainz: Schott, 1998.

———. *Hanns Eisler im USA-Exil: Zu den politischen, ästhetischen und kompositorischen Positionen des Komponisten, 1938 bis 1948.* Berlin: Akademie Verlag, 1978.

Schivelbusch, Wolfgang. "Optimistic Tragedies: The Plays of Heiner Müller." *New German Critique* 2 (Spring 1974): 104–113.

Schleuning, Peter. *Warum wir von Beethoven erschüttert werden und andere Aufsätze über Musik.* Frankfurt am Main: Roter Stern, 1978.

Schneider, Frank. "Bach als Quelle im Strom der Moderne (Von Schönberg bis zur Gegenwart)." In *Jahrbuch des Staatlichen Instituts für Musikforschung Preussischer Kulturbesitz,* edited by Günther Wagner, 110–125. Berlin: De Gruyter, 1994.

———. "Mozart und das episches Musiktheater." In *Mozart in der Musik der 20. Jahrhunderts: Formen ästhetischer und kompositionstechnischer Rezeption,* edited by Wolfgang Gratzer and Siegfried Mauser, 187–197. Laaber, Germany: Laaber Verlag, 1992.

Schoeps, Karl-Heinz. *Bertolt Brecht und Bernard Shaw.* Bonn: Bouvier, 1974.

———. "Brecht's *Lehrstücke:* A Laboratory for Epic and Dialectic Theater." In *A Bertolt Brecht Reference Companion,* edited by Siegfried Mews, 70–87. Westport, CT: Greenwood Press, 1997.

Schubbe, Elimar, ed. *Dokumente zur Künste- Literatur- und Kulturpolitik der SED, 1946–1970.* Stuttgart: Seewald Verlag, 1972.

Schumacher, Ernst. *Die dramatischen Versuche Bertolt Brechts, 1918–1933.* Berlin: Rütten and Loening, 1955.

Schwaen, Kurt. *Die Horatier und die Kuriatier. Ein Lehrstück von Bertolt Brecht für Chor und kleines Orchester.* Berlin: Verlag Neue Musik, 1958.

Schwanitz, Dietrich. "Intertextualität und Äquivalenzfunktionalismus: Vorschläge zu einer vergleichenden Analytik von Geschichten." *Wiener Slawistischer Almanach* suppl. 11 (1983): 27–51.

Schweinhardt, Peter, ed. *Hanns Eislers "Johann Faustus": 50 Jahre nach Erscheinen des Operntexts 1952. Symposion.* Wiesbaden: Breitkopf and Härtel, 2005.

Seidel, Gerhard. *Bertolt Brecht: Arbeitsweise und Edition. Das literarische Werk als Prozeß.* Berlin: Akademie-Verlag, 1977.

Sessions, Roger. *The Trial of Lucullus.* New York: E. B. Marks Company, 1981.

Shattuck, Roger. "Writers for the Defense of Culture." *Partisan Review* 51, no. 3 (1984): 393–416.

Shaw, Jennifer R. "Schoenberg's Choral Symphony, 'Die Jakobsleiter,' and Other Wartime Fragments." PhD diss., State University of New York–Stony Brook, 2002.

Sheppard, W. Anthony. *Revealing Masks: Exotic Influences and Ritualized Performance in Modernist Music Theater.* Berkeley: University of California Press, 2001.

Sikes, Alan. "Restaging the Revolution: Aesthetics, Politics, and the Question of

Collective Action." *Journal of Dramatic Theory and Criticism* 17, no. 2 (2003): 123–137.

Silberman, Marc, ed. and trans. *Bertolt Brecht on Film and Radio.* London: Methuen, 2000.

———. "Brecht Today." *Logos* 5, no. 3 (2006). Http://www.logosjournal.com/ issue_5.3/silberman.htm#_edn12#_edn1, accessed 10 June 2007.

———. "Brecht's Gestus; or, Staging Contradictions." *Brecht Yearbook/Brecht-Jahrbuch* 31 (2006): 318–335.

———. "Gestus." *Historisch-kritisches Wörterbuch des Marxismus,* edited by Fritz Haug, 660. Hamburg: Argument, 2001.

———. "A Postmodernized Brecht?" *Theatre Journal* 45, no. 1 (1993): 1–19.

Smart, Mary Ann. *Mimomania: Music and Gesture in Nineteenth-Century Opera.* Berkeley: University of California Press, 2004.

Smith, Matthew Wilson. *The Total Work of Art: From Bayreuth to Cyberspace.* New York: Routledge, 2007.

Smith, Mona Z. *Becoming Something: The Story of Canada Lee.* New York: Faber and Faber, 2004.

Smock, Ann. "*Don Giovanni;* or, the Art of Disappointing One's Admirers." In *Enigmas: Essays on Sarah Kofman,* edited by Penelope Deutscher and Kelly Oliver, 49–66. Ithaca, NY: Cornell University Press, 1999.

Soiuz Kompozitorov SSSR. *Die sowjetische Musik im Aufstieg: Eine Sammlung von Aufsätzen.* Translated by Nathan Notowicz. Halle: Mitteldeutscher Verlag, 1952.

Söring, Jürgen. "Wagner und Brecht: Zur Bestimmung des Musik-Theaters." In *Richard Wagner, 1883–1983: Die Rezeption im 19. und 20. Jahrhundert. Gesammelte Beiträge des Salzburger Symposions,* edited by Gerhard Croll, 451–473. Stuttgart: H.-D. Heinz, 1984.

Sprout, Leslie. "Music for a 'New Era': Composers and National Identity in France, 1938–1945." PhD diss., University of California–Berkeley, 2000.

Stegmann, Vera. "Brecht contra Wagner: The Evolution of the Epic Music Theater." In *A Bertolt Brecht Reference Companion,* edited by Siegfried Mews, 238–260. Westport, CT: Greenwood Press, 1997.

———. *Das epische Musiktheater bei Strawinsky und Brecht: Studien zur Geschichte und Theorie.* New York: Lang, 1991.

———. "*Frauenschicksale:* A DEFA Film Viewed in Light of Brecht's Critique of the Opera and Eisler/Adorno's Theory of Film Music." *German Studies Review* 28, no. 3 (2005): 481–500.

Steiert, Thomas, ed. "*Der Fall Wagner": Ursprünge und Folgen von Nietzsches Wagner-Kritik.* Laaber, Germany: Laaber Verlag, 1991.

Steinweg, Reiner. *Auf Anregung Bertolt Brechts: Lehrstücke mit Schülern, Arbeitern, Theaterleuten.* Frankfurt am Main: Suhrkamp, 1978.

———, ed. *Brechts Modell der Lehrstücke, Zeugnisse, Diskussionen, Erfahrungen.* Frankfurt am Main: Suhrkamp, 1976.

———. *Das Lehrstück: Brechts Theorie einer politisch-ästhetischen Erziehung.* Stuttgart: J. B. Metzler, 1972.

————, and Ingrid D. Koudela. *Lehrstück und episches Theater: Brechts Theorie und die theaterpädagogische Praxis.* Frankfurt am Main: Brandes and Apsel, 1995.

Stephan, Alexander. "Soeren Voima schreiben mit *Das Kontingent* Brechts *Maßnahme* weiter." *Brecht Yearbook/Brecht-Jahrbuch* 26 (2001): 61–79.

Stillinger, Jack. *Multiple Authorship and the Myth of Solitary Genius.* Oxford: Oxford University Press, 1991.

Stravinsky, Igor. *An Autobiography.* New York: Norton, 1962.

Sutcliffe, Tom. *Believing in Opera.* Princeton, NJ: Princeton University Press, 1996.

Suvin, Darko. "Haltung (Bearing) and Emotions: Brecht's Refunctioning of Conservative Metaphors for Agency." In *Zweifel—Fragen—Vorschläge. Bertolt Brecht anläßlich des Einhundertsten,* edited by Thomas Jung, 43–58. Frankfurt am Main: Peter Lang, 1999.

————. *To Brecht and Beyond: Soundings in Modern Dramaturgy.* Brighton, England: Harvester Press, 1984.

Szondi, Peter. *Theory of Modern Drama.* Edited and translated by M. Hays. Minneapolis: University of Minnesota Press, 1987.

Talsma, Durk, Tracy J. Doty, and Mary G. Woldorff. "Selective Attention and Audiovisual Integration: Is Attending to Both Modalities a Prerequisite for Early Integration?" *Cerebral Cortex* 17, no. 3 (2007): 679–690.

Taylor, Ronald. "Opera in Berlin in the 1920s: *Wozzeck* and the *Threepenny Opera.*" In *Culture and Society in the Weimar Republic,* edited by Keith Bullivant, 183–189. Manchester, England: Manchester University Press, 1977.

Teroni, Sandra, and Wolfgang Klein, eds. *Pour la défense de la culture. Les texts du Congrès international des écrivains, Paris, juin 1935.* Dijon, France: Editions Universitaires de Dijon, 2005.

Teschke, Holger. Review of *The Theatre of Heiner Müller,* by Jonathan Kalb. *Theater* 29, no. 2 (1999): 154–157.

Thompson, Oscar. "The Baden-Baden Festival: Music for Wireless and Films." *Musical Times* 70, no. 1039 (1929): 799–802.

Thomson, Peter, and Glendyr Sacks, eds. *The Cambridge Companion to Brecht.* 2nd. ed. Cambridge: Cambridge University Press, 2006.

Tian, Min. " 'Alienation-Effect' for Whom? Brecht's (Mis)Interpretation of the Classical Chinese Theatre." *Asian Theatre Journal* 14, no. 2 (1997): 200–222.

Tompkins, David. "Composing the Party Line: Music and Politics in Poland and East Germany, 1948–1957." PhD diss., Columbia University, 2004.

————. Review of *Sound Matters: Essays on the Acoustic of Modern German Culture,* edited by Nora M. Alter and Lutz Kopenick. H-German, H-Net Reviews, April 2006. Http://www.h-net.org/reviews/showrev/cgi?path=208271159992212, accessed 27 April 2006.

Treadwell, James. "Reading and Staging Again." *Cambridge Opera Journal* 10, no. 2 (1998): 205–220.

Tzara, Tristan. *Seven Dada Manifestos and Lampisteries.* Translated by Barbara Wright. London: Calder, 1977.

Ueding, Gert. "Das Fragment als literarische Form der Utopie." *Etudes Germaniques* 41, no. 3 (1986): 351–362.

Ujma, Christina. " 'Der strenge und der schwärmende Ton': Notes on Bloch and Brecht in the Twenties and Thirties." Translated by Jonathan Long. In *Bertolt Brecht Centenary Essays*, edited by Steve Giles and Rodney Livingstone, 33–48. Amsterdam: Rodopi, 1998.

Van Dijk, Maarten. "Blocking Brecht." In *Re-interpreting Brecht: His Influence on Contemporary Drama and Film*, edited by Pia Kleber and Colin Visser, 117–134. Cambridge: Cambridge University Press, 1990.

Vassen, Florian. "Bertolt Brechts 'Learning-Play': Genesis und Geltung des Lehrstücks." *Brecht Yearbook/Brecht-Jahrbuch* 20 (1995): 201–215.

Verband der Theaterschaffenden der Deutschen Demokratischen Republik. *Brecht und die Musik: Beiträge von den Brecht-Tagen 1984.* East Berlin: Druckkombinat Berlin, 1984.

Vieira de Carvalho, Mário. "From Opera to 'Soap Opera': On Civilizing Processes, the Dialectic of Enlightenment and Postmodernity." *Theory, Culture, and Society* 12, no. 2 (1995): 41–62.

Vollbach, W. R. "The Collaboration of Adolphe Appia and Emile Jaques-Dalcroze." In *Paul A. Pisk: Essays in His Honor*, edited by John Glowacki, 192–202. Austin: University of Texas Press, 1966.

Wächter, Hans-Christof. *Theater im Exil: Sozialgeschichte des deutschen Exiltheaters, 1933–1945.* Munich: C. Hanser, 1973.

Wagner, Richard. *Opera and Drama.* Translated by William Ashton Ellis. Lincoln: University of Nebraska Press, 1995.

Wallace, David. *Exiles in Hollywood.* Pompton Plains, NJ: Limelight Editions, 2006.

Watson, Steven. *Prepare for Saints: Gertrude Stein, Virgil Thomson, and the Mainstreaming of American Modernism.* Berkeley: University of California Press, 2000.

Weiler, Christel. "Etwas ist dran: Vorurteile zum Lehrstück." In *Kunst der Aufführung—Aufführung der Kunst*, edited by Erika Fischer-Lichte, Clemens Risi, and Jens Roselt, 144–163. Berlin: Theater der Zeit, 2004.

Weill, Kurt. *Aufstieg und Fall der Stadt Mahagonny.* Edited by David Drew. Vienna: Universal Edition, 1969.

———. *Die Dreigroschenoper: Ein Stück mit Musik in einem Vorspiel und acht Bildern nach dem Englischen des John Gay übersetzt von Elisabeth Hauptmann.* Edited by Stephen Hinton. New York: Kurt Weill Foundation for Music, 2000.

———. *Der Jasager. Schuloper in zwei Akten.* Vienna: Universal Edition, 1930.

———. *Der Lindberghflug.* Vienna: Universal Edition, 1930.

———. *Mahagonny Songspiel.* Edited by David Drew. Vienna: Universal Edition, 1963.

———. *Musik und musikalisches Theater. Gesammelte Schriften.* Edited by Stephen Hinton and Jürgen Schebera with Elmar Juchem. Mainz: Schott, 2000.

————, and Karoline Wilhelmine Blamauer (Lotte Lenya). *Speak Low (When You Speak Love): The Letters of Kurt Weill and Lotte Lenya*. Edited and translated by Lys Symonette and Kim Kowalke. Berkeley: University of California Press, 1996.

Weisstein, Ulrich. "Brecht und das Musiktheater. Die epische Oper als Ausdruck des europäischen Avantgardismus." In *Kontroversen, alte und neue. Akten des VII. Internationalen Germanisten-Kongresses, Göttingen 1985*, edited by Albrecht Schöne, 72–85. Tübingen, Germany: Niemeyer, 1986.

————. "Cocteau, Stravinsky, Brecht, and the Birth of Epic Opera." *Modern Drama* 5 (1962): 142–153.

————. "Imitation, Stylization, and Adaptation: The Language of Brecht's *Antigone* and Its Relation to Hölderlin's Version of *Sophocles*." *German Quarterly* 46, no. 4 (1973): 581–604.

————. "Von reitenden Boten und singenden Holzfällern: Bertolt Brecht und die Oper." In *Brechts Dramen: Neue Interpretationen*, edited by Walter Hinderer, 266–299. Stuttgart: Philipp Reclam, 1984.

Weltmann, Lutz. "Anmerkung zu Brechts 'Versuchen.'" *Die Literatur: Monatsschrift für Literaturfreunde* 33 (October 1930–September 1931): 245–246.

White, John. *Bertolt Brecht's Dramatic Theory*. Rochester, NY: Camden House, 2004.

Willett, John. *Caspar Neher: Brecht's Designer*. London: Methuen, 1986.

————. "*Die Maßnahme*: The Vanishing Lehrstück." In *Hanns Eisler: A Miscellany*, edited by David Blake, 79–89. New York: Harwood Academic Publishers, 1995.

————. *The Theatre of Bertolt Brecht. A Study from Eight Aspects*. London: Methuen, 1967.

————. *The Theatre of Erwin Piscator*. New York: Holmes and Meier Publishers, 1979.

————, et al. "A Brechtbuster Goes Bust: Scholarly Mistakes, Misquotes, and Malpractices in John Fuegi's *Brecht and Company*." *Brecht Yearbook/ Brecht-Jahrbuch* 20 (1995): 259–367.

Wimsatt, W. K., Jr. *The Verbal Icon: Studies in the Meaning of Poetry*. Lexington: University of Kentucky Press, 1954.

Winnacker, Susanne. *Wer immer es ist, den ihr hier sucht, ich bin es nicht: Zur Dramaturgie der Abwesenheit in Bertolt Brechts Lehrstück Die Maßnahme*. Frankfurt am Main: Peter Lang, 1997.

Wirth, Andrzej. "The Lehrstück as Performance." *Drama Review* 43, no. 4 (1999): 113–121.

————. "Vom Dialog zum Diskurs: Versuch einer Synthese der nachbrechtschen Theaterkonzepte." *Theater heute* 1 (January 1980): 16–19.

Witt, Hubert, ed. *Brecht as They Knew Him*. Translated by John Peet. New York: International Publishers, 1975.

————, ed. *Erinnerungen an Brecht*. Leipzig: Reclam, 1964.

Wittig, Peter. "Der Abtrünnige Schönberg-Schüler: Anmerkungen zu Hanns Eisler." In *Alban Bergs "Wozzeck" und die Zwanziger Jahre. Vorträge und*

Materialien des Salzburger Symposions 1997, edited by Peter Csobádi et al., 557–569. Anif/Salzburg, Austria: Müller-Speiser, 1999.

Wizisla, Erdmut, and Marta Ulvaeus. "Editorial Principles in the Berlin and Frankfurt Edition of Bertolt Brecht's Works." *Drama Review* 43, no. 4 (1999): 31–39.

Wright, Elizabeth. *Postmodern Brecht: A Re-presentation*. London: Routledge, 1989.

Wu, Zuguang, et al. *Peking Opera and Mei Lanfang. A Guide to China's Traditional Theatre and the Art of Its Great Master*. Beijing: New World Press, 1981.

Würmser, Rudolf. "*Der Lindberghflug* und *das Lehrstück:* Bertolt Brechts Versuche zu einer neuen Form des Musiktheaters auf dem Baden-Badener Musikfest 1929." In *Alban Bergs "Wozzeck" und die Zwanziger Jahre. Vorträge und Materialien des Salzburger Symposions 1997*, edited by Peter Csobádi et al., 547–556. Anif/Salzburg, Austria: Müller-Speiser, 1999.

Wyss, Monika. *Brecht in der Kritik*. Munich: Kindler, 1977.

Yearwood, Gladstone L. *Black Film as a Signifying Practice: Cinema, Narration and the African American Aesthetic Tradition*. Trenton, NJ: Africa World Press, 2000.

Žagar, Monika. "Knut Hamsun's 'White Negro' from *Ringen Sluttet* (1936)—or the Politics of Race." In *Legacies of Modernism: Art and Politics in Northern Europe, 1890–1950*, edited by Patrizia C. McBride, Richard W. McCormick, and Monika Žagar, 55–65. New York: Palgrave Macmillan, 2007.

Zhdanov, Andrei. *Essays on Literature, Philosophy, and Music*. New York: International Publishers, 1950.

Žižek, Slajov. "Why Is Wagner Worth Saving?" *Journal of Philosophy and Scripture* 2, no. 1 (2004): 18–30.

———, and Mladen Dolar. *Opera's Second Death*. New York: Routledge, 2002.

Index

Abbate, Carolyn, 201n89, 202n99; on materiality and sonic perception, 148, 229n41; on singers' physicality, 157, 231n70; on voice-object, 8, 70, 73

Academy of the Arts, German, 122; Brecht in, 112

Actors, African American: Brecht on, 84–85; on Broadway, 79; white audiences and, 85; in whiteface, 83–87, 207nn35–36. *See also* Theater, African American

Adorno, Theodor: and black *Three-penny Opera* project, 82–83; on Brecht's didacticism, 192n93; and correspondence with Weill, 207nn29–30; on director's opera, 145, 228n31; on jazz, 83; "Wagner's Relevance for Today," 3

African Americans: actors, 83–87, 207nn35–36; in CPUSA, 79, 204n10; in film, 205n19; on political left, 79, 80–81. *See also* Race relations, American

Against War (Brecht/Eisler), 90

Agitprop, 28; speaking choruses in, 31–32

Aida (Verdi), nonliteral productions of, 141, 159

"Alabama Song" (Weill), gestus in, 50

Albright, Daniel, 45, 172n42, 195n16

Alienation: Brecht's use of, 15, 178n78; estrangement and, 140, 226n13; in Mozart's operas, 231n68. *See also* Estrangement

Allegory: of exile, 98; in *Voyages of the God of Happiness*, 12, 98, 103, 105, 107

Althusser, Louis, 7, 141

Antifascism: and the GDR, 110, 112, 127, 129, 134; of Popular Front, 88, 90; in *Round Heads and Pointed Heads*, 62–63, 92; of United Front, 88, 90; and Writers for the Defense of Culture, 213n67

Antigone (Brecht), model book of, 146

Anti-opera, 5; Lehrstücke as, 17, 18, 23, 27, 29, 31, 32, 35, 37; *Mahagonny* as, 170n24; music theater since the 1960s as, 181n6

Anti-Semitism: concerning returning German exiles, 114; Nazi, 203n2, 222n30; in Soviet bloc, 113–14, 138, 139

Appia, Adolphe, 45, 145

Appleseed, Johnny, 100, 218n105

Aristotle: *Poetics*, 230n46; unities of, 40

Attention: Benjamin on, 230n52; competition for, 153; crisis of, 230n52; premotor theory of, 230n56; somatic modes of, 142, 149–52

Attitude, establishment of, 54. *See also* Gests

Text: 10/13 Aldus
Display: Aldus
Compositor: BookMatters, Berkeley
Indexer: Roberta Engleman
Printer and binder: Maple-Vail Manufacturing Group